ALL-AMERICAN

LAWNS

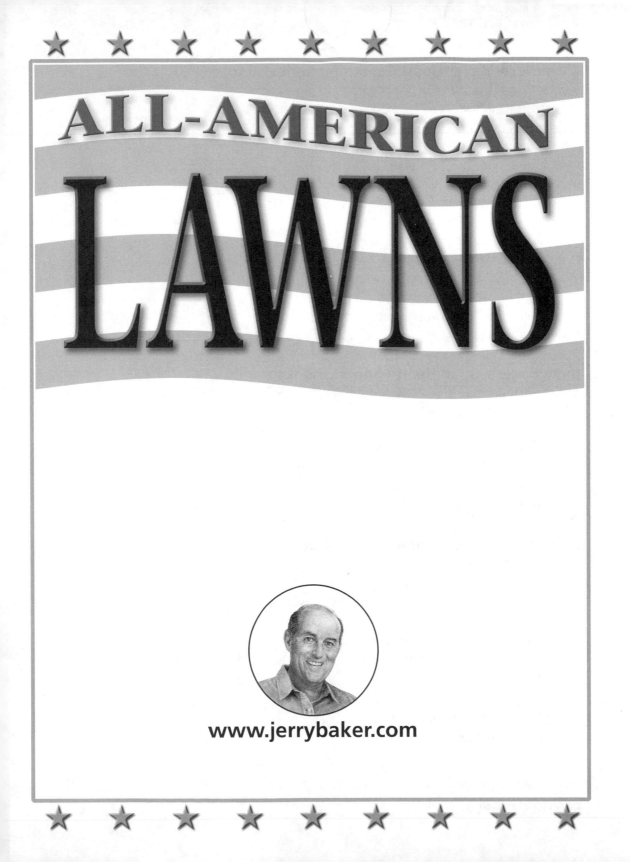

www.jerrybaker.com

ALL-AMERICAN LAWNS

1,776 Super Solutions to Grow, Repair, and Maintain the Best Lawn in the Land!

by Jerry Baker, America's Master Gardener®

Published by American Master Products, Inc.

Copyright © 2005 by Jerry Baker

Published by American Master Products, Inc. / Jerry Baker
Executive Editor: Kim Adam Gasior
Managing Editor: Cheryl Winters-Tetreau
Writer: Vicki Webster
Copy Editor: Nanette Bendyna
Interior Design and Layout: Nancy Biltcliff
Cover Design: Kitty Pierce Mace
Indexer: Nan Badgett

Publisher's Cataloging-in-Publication
(Provided by Quality Books, Inc.)

Baker, Jerry.
    Jerry Baker's all-American lawns : 1,776 super
solutions to grow, repair, and maintain the best lawn in
the land! / by Jerry Baker.
    p. cm. — (Jerry Baker's good gardening series)
    Includes index.
    ISBN 0-922433-61-5

    1. Lawns.   I. Title.

SB433.B113 2005   635.9'647
                               QBI04-200486

Printed in the United States of America
4 6 8 10 9 7 5 3   hardcover

Contents

Introduction

CHAPTER 12
When Mother Nature Frowns

CHAPTER 13
Oops, I Did It Again!

CHAPTER 14
Games People Play

CHAPTER 15
A Lawn? Who Needs It?!

Jerry's Blue Plate Specials

Index

Introduction

WHAT'S MORE AMERICAN than apple pie? A lush, green, toe-ticklin' lawn—that's what! Well, friends, whether you're starting a brand-new lawn, reviving one that's seen better days, or simply wanting to put a little more pep into your home ground, you've come to the right place. In this book, I'll show you how to turn any old yard into a regular field of dreams.

And, speaking of dreams, that's exactly where we'll start off: planning your perfect green scene. Now, don't panic—I know that a lot of home-landscaping books make the process sound so complicated that only Thomas Jefferson himself could do the job. But I'm here to tell you it just ain't so! In Chapter 1, you'll find tons of terrific tips to help you decide just how much lawn you really want, and how to lay it out in a way that'll give you and your family the most enjoyment with the least possible hassle.

Chapter 2 is about grass in all its great green glory. I'll give you a fast, fun lesson in turf grass anatomy, and we'll have a look-see at the whole roster of types and varieties, from enduring Hall of Famers to today's superstars. You'll learn which ones will perform like champs in your yard, no matter where you live in this gorgeous land of ours.

Then, in Chapters 3 and 4, you'll find everything you need to know to get a new lawn growing on the right root, or put a tattered, battered one on the road to recovery. I'll share my secrets for getting rid of old grass and weeds, leveling and grading your site, improving drainage, and turning ordinary dirt into rich, root-pleasing soil. I'll even hand you some helpful hints on hiring landscaping professionals (just in case you'd rather let someone else do the heavy lifting).

The next three chapters are chock-full of my tips, tricks, and tonics to help you deliver the best TLC a lawn could ever ask for. I'll lay out my super-simple routine for feeding, watering, and mowing at the right times, in the right way, and with the right equipment. And, because the seasons come and go at different times in our vast and varied country, I've made Chapter 8 your All-American Lawn-Care Calendar. Just by glancing at its pages, you'll know when to perform any chore, from sowing the first seeds of spring to putting your landscape to bed for the winter.

It's a sad fact of lawn life that, no matter how careful you are, trouble can gallop in like a gang of ornery outlaws gunnin' for John Wayne. Well, fear not, pardner! Whether you're facing a showdown with pesky pests, dastardly diseases, wicked weeds, or Mother Nature herself, Chapters 9 through 12 will give you a whole arsenal of ammo for your six-shooter. But what happens when the unintentional "villain" is you (or maybe the local road crew)? No problem! Just turn to Chapter 13 for my surefire strategy for battling accidental mishaps ranging from oil spills and fertilizer overdoses to herbicide and road-salt damage.

But enough about the serious stuff! Everybody knows that the all-American lawn is more than just a pretty piece of turf—it's also a playground. So, in Chapter 14, we'll look at a whole bunch of favorite Yankee pastimes. Whether your idea of first-class fun is a cutthroat croquet tournament, a lazy game of badminton, or a putting session on your own private green, you'll learn how to set the stage for action—and keep your grass looking great at the same time.

Finally, as strange as it may seem in a book about lawns, we'll turn our attention away from turf grass and consider some dandy alternatives. How come? Well, if you're like most of the folks I hear from, you've got some places in your yard where, no matter what you do, grass simply refuses to thrive. Or you're hankerin' to add a little pizzazz to your smooth, green carpet. Then again, maybe you'd simply prefer to spend less time and money on your lawn, and more on life's other pleasures—like loadin' up the old jalopy and headin' out to explore the U.S.A. That's why I've crammed a galaxy of great ideas into Chapter 15, including no-mow ornamental grasses and groundcovers, unthirsty native plants, and all-but-no-care decks, patios, and water features.

So what are we waiting for? Let's hoist the flag and start the green grass parade for our all-American lawns!

CHAPTER 1

The Lay of the Land

Whether the lawn of your dreams is groomed and striped like the outfield of your favorite all-American ballpark, or more casual and studded with spring bulbs and patches of clover, its perfection is in the eye of the beholder. And *you* are the beholder. What I mean is that there is no one kind of perfect lawn, any more than there's only one kind of perfect house that everyone in this country should live in. Your perfect lawn is what's perfect for you (and your family), and nobody else can decide that for you.

What we're going to do in the following pages is help you figure out what you need to achieve lawn perfection—whatever that means to you—while declaring your independence from doing too many landscaping chores.

☆ We Love Our Lawns!

Drive almost anywhere in this great country of ours on a sunny Saturday and you'll hear the hum of mowers and smell the fragrance of fresh-cut grass. Yep, a skirt of grassy green is practically a uniform around homes across the U.S.A.—we Americans have got ourselves a serious case of lawn-love, and it shows in the tender tending we lavish on our turf.

E PLURIBUS LAWNUM!

Early on in our nation's history (way back even before I was around), lawns were only for rich folks who had enough dough to pay other people to groom their grass. Everybody else in our mostly rural population was cultivating the packed-earth look around their front doors. It took a whole lot of invention and ingenuity—stuff like lawn mowers and garden hoses and suitable kinds of grass seed—to make having a lawn as much a part of the American dream as having the house to go along with it.

GOOD GRACIOUS, GRASS IS GREAT!

Now I expect if you're reading this book, that you're already aimin' for a grassy green lawn as at least part of your home landscape. But I've just gotta tell you a few of the many reasons why lawns are just so gosh-darn dandy!

★ **Lawns look good.** I'm not talking about art here, folks—the truth is that we humans are hardwired some-how to respond to nice, outdoorsy views. Looking out over a nice patch of green makes us feel calm and happy. There's even some evidence that hospital patients heal more quickly when they have a room with a landscape view.

★ **Grass gives our eyes a rest.** Some-times we need a visual break from the jumble of things we look at all day long. A lawn is a soothing alternative for our eyes to rest upon. It's also the perfect color (just as Mother Nature planned it, I suspect) to go with almost any color flower. A stretch of grassy green helps soothe potential clashes between incompatible posies, such as bright orange-red zinnias and hot pink impatiens.

★ **Turf is cool!** On a hot summer day, the surface temperature of your lawn is 30 to 40 degrees cooler than that of bare soil, and as much as 70 degrees cooler than paved surfaces. So don't bother trying to fry an egg on the lawn!

★ **Lawns protect the soil and prevent erosion.** All those little grassy roots (329,000 miles per square foot of turf!) keep the soil from washing away every time it rains.

★ **A nice crop of sod protects the water, too.** All those roots and the healthy crop of microorganisms that live with them help to filter water that passes through, keeping many nasty things from reaching the groundwater.

★ **Grass even makes air.** Like all green, growing plants, grass uses carbon dioxide and produces oxygen. A 2,500-square-foot area of grass produces enough oxygen for a family of four. I know I breathe easier just thinking about all the oxygen my healthy lawn produces!

Star-Spangled *Lawn* Lore

Guys like George Washington and Thomas Jefferson were so busy leading our young country that they didn't have time to mow the grand lawns at Mount Vernon and Monticello. (They didn't have lawn mowers, either!) Instead of scything over too-tall turf, both of these founding fathers grazed sheep on their lawns to keep the grass tidy. This ewes-full method also took care of fertilizing the grass and served as a handy source of lamb chops for dinner!

WHO'S ON FIRST?

Is your lawn going to be the site of neighborhood games of baseball? Or is hammock-swinging likely to be the most vigorous sport played in your yard? Think about how each member of your family (pets included) will use your lawn, and then decide how much turf you want, and how much you really need.

As you embark on your journey to enjoy the green, green grass of home, there are four major considerations:

Time. Even the most easy-care yard needs some routine maintenance. Before you turn your landscape into a full-scale replica of your favorite natural-turf football stadium (that's 48,000 square feet of grass, friends), think about how much time you have to spend caring for your lawn. Unless you're willing to spend every available free minute grooming the turf, you should also consider how many hours per week you *want* to spend on lawn maintenance. If your own time is in short supply, you may need to consider paying others to tend your lawn for you.

Money. I'm not telling you anything new when I say that stuff costs money. Whether you're starting a new lawn or refurbishing an existing one, you'll need to invest in seed, sod, sprigs, or plugs, as well as the tools it takes to care for all those tender grass plants. If you're launching a lawn on a strict budget, you can save your cash by choosing less costly (but more labor-intensive) options, such as seed instead of sod, or an hour behind the mower each week instead of a lawn-care service.

Climate. This is the factor that doesn't really change. There are turf-type grasses that are suitable for nearly every climate condition found across the United States. What you need to do—with some advice from ol' Jerry, of course—is pick out the ones that are best for your region. This isn't nearly as hard as it sounds, and in Chapter 2, I'll give you all kinds of guidance on tip-top turf selection. Bottom line on climate: You can work with Mother Nature, or you can work against her—and I know which way I'd choose!

Terrain. Take a look at your property and ponder how it will stack up against tasks like mowing and raking. Dig into the soil to see if you'll need to improve it before you plant grass, and to get an idea of the ratio of soil to rocks (Hint: you'll want more of the first, and less of the second). Check out the drainage, too, to identify potential wet spots, and look for bumps and slopes that can turn the simple task of mowing into a trip through an obstacle course. There are ways to adjust your landscape's terrain to make lawn care easier, but you want to make those adjustments *before* you start growing grass.

NORTH VS. SOUTH

Many climate factors have to be taken into account when you're selecting just the right grass for your yard. But let's start simply: There are cool-season grasses that grow better in places that have cold winters, and there are

---

Super★Secret

Time Is Money!

Once you've figured out how much lawn you want, and what kind(s) of grass you want in it, you may be faced with yet another decision: seed vs. sod vs. plugs vs. sprigs. Some kinds of grass, such as St. Augustine grass and hybrid Bermuda grass, are pretty much only sold as plugs, so that decision's already made for you if you're going with one of these warm-season grasses. But everyone else has to choose, and the decision's not always as straightforward as price would make it seem. For example, the cost of most grass seed per square foot is only a couple of pennies, while sod will run you as much as 75 cents per square foot. Seed's clearly the way to go, right? Well, maybe. But neither price includes labor— a mostly one-shot add-on for sod, but an ongoing cost (of your time) to keep a newly seeded lawn going.

warm-season grasses that thrive in our country's hot spots. Take a look at the list below that represents your region, and you'll get a quick introduction to the varieties that you can choose from:

Cool-season grasses. Bent grass, blue grama grass, fescues, Kentucky bluegrass, ryegrasses

Warm-season grasses. Bahia grass, Bermuda grass, centipede grass, St. Augustine grass, zoysia grass

ARE YOU AN ATHLETE, OR AN ATHLETIC SUPPORTER?

If you were the captain of your college badminton team, you might have a legitimate need for a lawn that includes a regulation badminton court. Likewise, if you think Junior's going to be the next Tiger Woods, you might want to install

a PGA-quality green where he can practice his putting. If you're considering these kinds of special lawn installations, don't miss Chapter 14, "Games People Play," where you'll find all sorts of great tips for turning your boring backyard into a field of dreams. (I suppose you could do that with a hammock, too.)

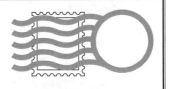

Here's some egg-citing news for any weekend warrior who tends a thick, healthy lawn—you can drop a raw egg on it from a height of 12 inches without so much as cracking the shell! That might not matter much to you (unless you're unusually clumsy with your groceries while crossing the yard), but it's good news for backyard athletes. Well-tended turf provides a nice cushion for falling objects and people, meaning fewer injuries from the traditional Turkey Day touch football game.

from the **MAIL BAG**

Dear Jerry,

My wife recently found out she's allergic to pollen. Should I pave over our lawn to give her some relief?

A. *You'll do your wife a bigger favor if you keep that lawn lush and healthy, and mow it regularly. Grass that's mowed on a regular schedule rarely gets a chance to bloom and send its pollen wafting into the air. And a thick, healthy lawn will actually catch other kinds of pollen (from trees and weeds), plus dust and dirt, and keep it all from adding to your wife's woes.*

THREE CHEERS FOR THE CHAISE LOUNGE!

Some of us are more concerned about falling out of our lawn chairs than leaping over the goal line, and there are plenty of landscape choices for those more sedate outdoor pleasures, too. Instead of cutting the grass, maybe you'd rather cut *out* the grass—out of your yard plan, that is. Our great nation has room for all kinds of viewpoints, and there's no law that says you have to have a patch of turf on your property. Here are some lawn alternatives that can help you turn mowing time into hammock time:

★ Decks and patios

★ Groundcovers

★ Ornamental grasses (see the list at right)

★ Outdoor play areas

★ Rock gardens

★ Wildflower meadows (that include meadow grasses)

I've gathered up loads of great grassless options in Chapter 15, in case you're thinking about reducing your total grass-covered yard space, or getting rid of it altogether.

10 TERRIFIC NONTURF GRASSES

I happen to think that all grasses are ornamental—except for weedy pests such as crabgrass and the like—but there are some grasses that go by the title "ornamental" because they're used more like perennials than like the kind of grass you'd grow and mow. Here's a list of my top 10 favorites:

Big bluestem
   (*Andropogon gerardii*)

Blue lyme grass (*Leymus arenarius*)

Bulbous oat grass (*Arrhenatherum elatius subsp. bulbosum 'Variegatum'*)

Fountain grass
   (*Pennisetum alopecuroides*)

Indian grass
   (*Sorghastrum nutans*)

Japanese silver grass
   (*Miscanthus sinensis*)

Job's tears
   (*Coix lacryma-jobi*)

Quaking grass (*Briza media*)

Side oats grama grass
   (*Bouteloua curtipendula*)

Switch grass
   (*Panicum virgatum*)

☆ Take Time to Plan, Man!

Now here's a piece of advice that most people find almost impossible to follow, and yet it's *so* important. If you're in the enviable position of starting with a clean slate—that is, a bare plot of land with no grass or other significant plantings—take your time! Because no one really enjoys living in the middle of a mud hole (or a dust bowl), folks often sacrifice the chance to do things right for the promise of quick coverage from a bag of cheap grass seed or a "deal" on hydroseeding (a professionally applied spray-on combination of grass seed, water, fertilizer, and mulch). Trust me, the satisfaction you get from this fast fix will wear out quicker than a pair of $2 flip-flops, leaving you with nothing but a lumpy, struggling, weedy lawn.

IT'S NOT A LAWN, IT'S A GRASS GARDEN!

Instead of thinking of your lawn as a single thing, consider it for a moment as hundreds of thousands, or even millions, of individual grass plants, each requiring the same stuff any plant needs: light, water, air, and food. If you were planting a million perennials in your yard, you'd do some preparing first so you could meet their needs and keep them alive and thriving. A lawn is just the same— you gotta prepare before you plant.

So, before you start throwing around handfuls of seed (or handfuls of money for sod), follow these steps:

STEP 1. Decide how much lawn you want and where it will be. Measure carefully, and dust off your geometry skills to figure out the area of your future "grass garden."

Dear Jerry,

Do I really need to *plan* a lawn? Can't I just buy some grass seed and toss it around where I want my yard to be?

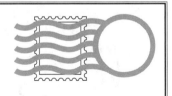

A. *No, you don't have to plan—if you're willing to risk creating a high-maintenance monster. But my Grandma Putt taught me that anything worth doing is worth doing right. By planning your lawn before you start tossing around the grass seed, you can head off problems like weeds, poor soil, and hard-to-mow spots before they have a chance to cause you even a minute's misery.*

STEP 2. Figure out what kind(s) of grass will grow best on your site, considering both climate conditions and the intended uses for your lawn. See Chapter 2 for the lowdown on choosing the right grass for your lawn. For example, you'll want to look at varieties of perennial ryegrass if your yard plays host to neighborhood sporting events or other high-traffic activities. If your lawn's down South and your goal is limited maintenance, take a look at slow-growing centipede grass for a yard that needs mowing only every couple of weeks.

STEP 3. Decide how you're going to apply the grass to the area. If you're planning to sow seed, you need to have a way to get that seed watered. If you're planning to use sod, you have to decide if you'll install it yourself (sod is heavy), or have a landscaper do it for you. Check out Chapter 3 for the full story on starting a lawn from scratch.

STEP 4. Prepare the soil! This is the step that gets skipped most often when people rush to get going. But skip this step, and you'll pay for it for the life of your lawn. Going for the quick grass fix will cost you in terms of weeds, watering, low spots, bumps, and other preventable lawn woes. See Chapter 3 to learn just how important site preparation is to the long-term health of your lawn.

STEP 5. Gather the tools you'll need. The end of a long day of lifting and laying sod is no time to discover that you don't have a way to water it—and the store's closed for the long holiday weekend. See "Tools of the Trade" below for a list of must-haves.

TOOLS OF THE TRADE

When you're planning out a new lawn, make sure your plan includes *everything* you'll need to get your grass growing:

★ A rake for roughing up the soil surface before you lay sod or sow, and for covering the seed once it's sown

★ Straw (or other lightweight organic material) for mulching newly sown seed

★ A board for distributing your weight as you work laying sod, so you don't compact the soil

★ A heavy-duty knife for cutting sod

★ A light roller for gently pressing the sod into contact with the soil

★ Enough hose to get water to every part of the yard

★ A good-quality sprinkler that distributes the water evenly

Bird-scare devices to discourage hungry birds from eating seeds, or a timer to turn your sprinkler on and off, can be worth the added investment.

GIVE YOUR LAWN WHAT IT NEEDS TO SUCCEED

The old saying, "A place for everything and everything in its place," works as well for lawns as it does for dirty socks: You can try to grow grass in a less-than-suitable site, and you can leave your laundry in the middle of the kitchen floor. But in both cases, you'll have a fight on your hands, whether it's keeping the grass growing in difficult conditions, or keeping your spouse

from tossing you out on your ear! It's better to toss the socks in the hamper, of course, and better to do your grass growing in a spot that offers just the ticket for tip-top turf:

• Plenty of good ol' sunshine

• Ample water (including access to a water source when Ma Nature fails to provide)

• Fertile soil

Sure, that sounds like a great spot for almost any kind of plant, and that's what you're looking for to ensure yourself a great-looking, easy-care kind of lawn.

DON'T BE A FOOL FOR TOOLS

Some major pieces of equipment can come in real handy when you're preparing to install a new lawn or renovate an old one. You'll see all the cool tools—tillers, vertical aerators, dethatchers, and more—you might need in Chapters 3 and 4. Do not—I repeat, DO NOT—go out and buy all of these things. You'll only need most of them once.

Sure, you're going to want a mower, and I've included lots of guidance in Chapter 7 to help you buy the one that's best suited to your yard. But most of the

Super ★ Secret

Don't Play Gary Cooper

If you really care about the health and well-being of your lawn, don't even approach your mower at high noon—or any time between the hours of 10 A.M. and 2 P.M. That's generally when the sun is at its fiercest, and grass that's clipped then is wide open to ol' Sol's burning power. Instead, schedule your mowing chores for early morning or early evening, when the sun isn't so intense. (You'll enjoy it more then, too!)

big machines are once-in-a-lawn's-life kind of deals, and there's no reason for the average homeowner to buy them. Even if it's something that you'll need as often as once every growing season, renting is the way to go. Call your local equipment rental company, and get its list of turf-care equipment. I'm betting they'll have everything you need. To save even more, offer to split the rental with your neighbor—you'll cut your costs, and your neighbor will finally do some work on his sorry-looking patch of grass!

BE PREPARED!

You can spend all the money you want on high-quality grass seed, the best sod, or top-notch plugs. And you can drop even more dough on the finest equipment for maintaining your lawn. But soil preparation is still the best investment you can make, and the best way to ensure good-looking grass. Here's what good soil prep promises— and delivers:

• Dense, uniform turf

• Grass that recovers more quickly from wear and stress

• Reduced need for water and fertilizer

• Reduced overall lawn maintenance

Star-Spangled *Lawn* Lore

Not so long ago, clover was a common ingredient in most grass-seed mixtures. In fact, it was considered the "summer savior" of green lawns when the Kentucky bluegrass fell prey to nastiness like crabgrass, mildew, or drought. Over time, though, as folks got fussier, they came to dislike clover because it stains clothing and it's very slippery when wet. But for my money, there are still some mighty fine reasons to grow a little clover in your lawn. Among its many pluses, clover:

★ *Fights off chinch-bug invasions naturally and safely*

★ *Draws rabbits away from munching on your flowers and vegetables*

★ *Attracts beautiful butterflies to your yard*

★ *Makes a dandy and very resilient groundcover*

★ *Adds valuable nitrogen to the soil—that is, if you dig it under in the fall*

★ *Might just have a lucky four-leafer for you to find!*

★ Make It Easy on Yourself

Now, I'm not joking when I tell you that planning is the key to avoiding loads of yard work down the line. Make smart choices at the beginning of the process, and your grass will do a lot for you and ask only a little in return. See, I love my lawn, but I'd much rather spend my time sitting in a chair on it than pushing a mower (or spreader) all over it! And I'll bet you feel the same way. So plan your turf (and the rest of your landscape) so you can enjoy it to the max while keeping work to a minimum.

SEEK SUCCESS, NOT PERFECTION

The first thing you can do to achieve maximum lawn pleasure without spending every spare moment working on it is to modify your view of how it should look. It should look good, sure, and green, definitely. Beyond that, it's up to you to decide whether your turf needs to be as mani-cured as the fairways at

Pebble Beach, or whether it can be a little—or a lot—more relaxed. Adjust your tolerance level accordingly, and you'll find your stress levels falling, and your lawn satisfaction flying high. Here's how to stop stressing:

Welcome weeds. The folks who study such things say that most people can look at a lawn that's got as much as 10 to 20 percent broadleaf weeds and think it looks just fine. After all, dandelions are cheery looking—especially when there's not much else in bloom—and their young greens make a tasty salad to liven up meals in the early spring.

Cozy up to clover. A few patches of clover help feed bees that pollinate fruit trees, vegetables, and flowers.

Mix it up. The hardest kind of lawn to maintain is one that's made up of only one kind of grass. Mother Nature doesn't grow things that way, and neither should you—at least not if you want a lawn that's easy to live with. When you start shopping for grass seed, you'll see that most of it comes in mixes. By combining different kinds of seed, you're protected from total lawn annihilation if one kind suffers from a pesky pest or damaging disease. For example, a cool-season lawn might include Kentucky bluegrass, perennial ryegrass, and creeping red fescue, while a warm-season yard could have a mixture of Bermuda, carpet, and Bahia grasses.

★ Make It Manageable

Remember how I said that having a lawn was really grass gardening? Well, the bigger the garden, the more care it needs. Only plant as much grass as you are willing and able to take care of (or willing and able to pay someone else to take care of). And while you're choosing a site that offers sunlight, water, and fertile soil, also look for the features in the tips below to make your grass easier to maintain.

LAWN LOGIC

There are lawns worth having, and then there are lawns that present such a challenge to maintain that you'd be better off getting rid of the lawn altogether. Here's a rundown of features that will make grass care a snap:

★ Slight to moderate slope for drainage. Ideally, the ground should slope just enough to prevent water from pooling anyplace in your yard, but not so much that you're thinking of hiring Spiderman to do your mowing.

★ Access for mowers and other equipment. Make sure your lawn mower fits through the gates in the fence without dismantling either the fence or the mower. Look out for strips of grass that are narrower than the cutting width of your mower—they may require extensive trimmer work if they're between non-mower-friendly surfaces. Prune tree branches to keep them from whacking you in the face as you mow, or replace grass under trees with no-mow groundcovers, mulch, or decking.

★ Limited interruptions (this means few things to work around). Create garden beds around trees, shrubs, perennials, and garden objects (everything from lawn art to bird feeders). Put picnic tables and benches on pavers or other nongrass surfaces.

KEEP IT ON THE LEVEL

Steep slopes make it hard to establish a lawn, and even harder to take care of one. Rain can come along and wash away your seed, sod, or sprigs, and the effort it took to put them there. Mowing on a steep slope is hard work, and it's dangerous. In places where the ground slopes more than 1 foot for every 6 feet of distance, you'll want to cover the area with something besides grass—preferably a nice groundcover that won't need mowing. Short, steep banks might call for terracing with timbers, stones, or landscape blocks to create beds where you can garden without fear of sliding down the slope.

BUT HOLD THE PANCAKES

I'm not saying you should waffle about the lay of your lawn, but you don't want it to be as flat as a pancake either. You want your turf to make the grade (by which I mean slope), but you don't want it to slope too much. If you're grading your yard before starting a new lawn, you can work toward the ideal: about 6 inches of rise over every 25 feet of distance. That's just enough of a slope to keep water from puddling up in any one area. You'll want to make sure that the slope in your lawn goes away from your house, too, to keep any water your landscape can't use from winding up in your basement.

HOLD THAT SLOPE!

Got a steep slope that you'd like to color green? Groundcovers other than grass can do the job in spots where the ground slopes as much as 1 foot for every 2 to 3 feet of distance. These great ground-grabbers will keep the soil in place and save you from the hazards of mountaineer mowing! (To learn more about nongrass groundcovers for all sorts of situations, check out Chapter 15.)

Super★Secret

What to Do Where It's Wet

If your lawn has a significant standing-water problem or if poor drainage is causing problems in your basement or around the foundation of your house, you'll want to look into permanent methods for redirecting the water. But if your yard simply has a low and frequently soggy spot that makes mowing difficult, giving in to Ma Nature's plan may be the way to go. Instead of filling and draining and going to a lot of trouble to dry out a damp place, turn it into a garden of plants that thrive in soggy sites. Willows and red- and yellow-twig dogwoods (*Cornus stolonifera* cultivars) like to sink their roots into damp soil. Perennials, such as irises and primroses, also favor moist locations, and you can add seasonal color with moisture-loving, shade-tolerant impatiens.

Ajuga (*Ajuga reptans*)

Common periwinkle (*Vinca minor*)

Creeping juniper (*Juniperus horizontalis*)

Daylilies (*Hemerocallis*)

English ivy (*Hedera helix* cultivars)

Japanese pachysandra (*Pachysandra terminalis*)

St. John's wort (*Hypericum calycinum*)

Virginia creeper (*Parthenocissus quinquefolia*)

Wintercreeper (*Euonymus fortunei*)

Woolly yarrow (*Achillea tomentosa*)

Shape Up!

Want to spend more time lifting a tall, cool glass of lemonade, and less time pushing a mower? Get your lawn—and your landscape—in shape, and that's exactly what you'll be doing. As you plan the area for your lawn, think about all the features that will be in that area: trees, birdbaths and feeders, flower beds, benches, paths, etc. How many of those things will you have to mow around? How close to each one will the grass be? Keep this in mind: Most mowers are not designed for making tight turns. The more stuff you've gotta go around when you mow, the longer it will take.

PUT YOUR LANDSCAPE INTO BED(S)!

Instead of scattering trees, shrubs, and other stuff all over your yard, create nice beds and borders that will look terrific and save you tons of headaches when it's time to cut the grass. You'll be doing the trees and shrubs a favor, too, by reducing the odds that you'll ding 'em with the mower while trying to cut the grass too near them. If you have existing trees that you're tired of trimming around, bring out the mulch and create beds around them. You'll be pleased as punch at how great these new beds look, and by how easy it is to mow around them instead of over bumpy tree roots.

LOOK AT THE BIG PICTURE

Wanna know how something's going to look in your yard—before you go to the expense and effort of buying and installing it? Try this simple visualization exercise: Take photos of your yard and make some enlarged copies of them. Then draw in features like benches, paths, trellises, and trees to see how they'll look. If you're shy about your artistic abilities, cut pictures out of catalogs and magazines, and glue them onto your landscape photos. Either way, you'll have a clearer picture of how things would look around the yard before you make a major purchase or dig a single hole.

LASSO A LANDSCAPE PLAN

Here's help for practical people who have a tough time imagining how a garden bed will look in their yard. Before you lift a shovel, let me tell you that dreaming's a whole lot easier than digging! Use this nifty rope trick to try out different shapes and sizes for your garden beds, and you won't have to put any muscle into it until you've got exactly what you want. Just grab a good long length of rope (or garden hose) and lay it out on the ground in the spot where you'd like your new bed to be. Play around with the shape until you get it where you want it—and then leave it in place for at least a day or two to see if you continue to like it. For an extra-realistic landscape simulation, stick a stake or a shovel into the bed in places where you're thinking of including trees or shrubs.

DON'T CUT CORNERS

Straight lines and soft curves are the way to go when you're creating those beds for your trees, shrubs, and perennials. Plan for corners that are greater than 90 degrees and long, gentle curves for easy mower maneuvering. Sharp corners, tight circles, and other fiddly shapes will make mowing a nightmare of twists and turns, instead of the smooth sailing it should be.

FULL SPEED AHEAD!

Here's a smart way to trim your turf-care time: Plan your lawn for straightforward mowing, and skip the time you'd spend tugging your machine backward (or shifting into reverse). Tight corners and finicky trimming can make mowing a real drag—don't include 'em in a lawn design, and get rid of 'em in an existing lawn. To locate places in your landscape where you need to make adjustments to the shape of your lawn, try mowing the whole thing without backing up. Anyplace that you can't trim while going forward should be a candidate for conversion to a garden bed, or a planting of no-mow groundcovers.

GET EDGY

You can make lawn maintenance even easier by installing edging and mowing strips around beds and borders. These handy bits of hardscaping let you run

---

Super ★ Secret

Much Ado About Mulch

Mulching around trees is a smart solution to the problem of mower vs. tree (Hint: the trees almost always lose this battle). But putting too much mulch too close to the trunk can be just as fatal as repeated mower abuse. Piling it up against the base of a tree promotes problems with rot, encourages the growth of undesirable sprouts, and invites voles and other rodents to nest in the mounds of mulch where they can dine on tender bark all winter long. To get the benefits of mulch without these hazards, apply it in a doughnut configuration, leaving a healthy 4 inches of space between the trunk and the surrounding material.

your mower's wheels right along the side of plantings to trim the grass without dinging the daisies or hacking the hydrangeas. (You'll learn all of the finer points of hardscape selection and installation in Chapter 15.)

☆ Get on the Right Track

People may tiptoe through the tulips, but they tend to gallop over grass. Think about traffic patterns in and around your lawn and plan suitable pathways for the most frequently traveled routes. Even the most resilient grasses (see "Top Turfs for Treadability" on page 46) will eventually succumb to the steady back-and-forth of a dog on a lead or kids following the most direct path to their favorite hangout.

SPRING FOR COLOR IN YOUR LAWN

Here's a tip that'll put some zing in your turf long before the grass begins to green up in the spring. Naturalize (that means plant 'em randomly, like they'd grow in nature) small flowering bulbs throughout your lawn (or even just in one section) and experience the real thrill of seeing flowers pop up a good month before you need to think about firing up the mower. Here's a list of

pretty little things that get along great with lawn grasses and arrive reliably each spring to treat winter-weary eyes:

Common snowdrop (*Galanthus nivalis*)

Crocuses (*Crocus*)

Daffodils (*Narcissus* hybrids)

Grape hyacinth (*Muscari armeniacum*)

Grecian windflower (*Anemone blanda*)

Siberian squill (*Scilla siberica*)

Summer snowflake (*Leucojum aestivum*)

Speaking of firing up the mower, you'll want to wait until these beauties are done blooming, and their foliage has died back, before you give your turf its first trim. If that poses a shaggy lawn problem, use these same bulbs to dress up a bed of groundcovers that you can mow around with ease.

TURF TRAFFIC

In spots where traffic causes turf troubles, you have three options:

1 Redirect the flow by installing a fence, hedge, or other barrier. Make

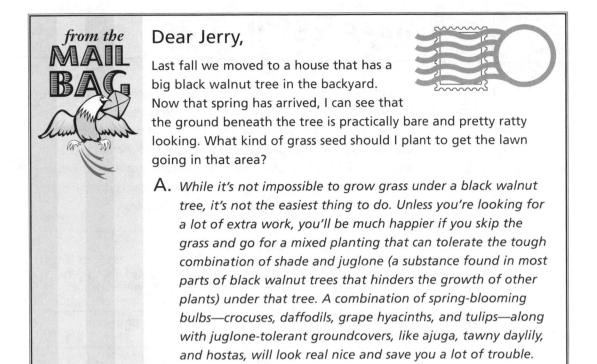

from the
MAIL BAG

Dear Jerry,

Last fall we moved to a house that has a big black walnut tree in the backyard. Now that spring has arrived, I can see that the ground beneath the tree is practically bare and pretty ratty looking. What kind of grass seed should I plant to get the lawn going in that area?

A. *While it's not impossible to grow grass under a black walnut tree, it's not the easiest thing to do. Unless you're looking for a lot of extra work, you'll be much happier if you skip the grass and go for a mixed planting that can tolerate the tough combination of shade and juglone (a substance found in most parts of black walnut trees that hinders the growth of other plants) under that tree. A combination of spring-blooming bulbs—crocuses, daffodils, grape hyacinths, and tulips—along with juglone-tolerant groundcovers, like ajuga, tawny daylily, and hostas, will look real nice and save you a lot of trouble.*

sure it's solid enough to keep kids, pets, or other scofflaws from cutting through, instead of going around.

2 Plant a super-resilient grass, like one of the perennial ryegrass varieties developed for use on playing fields. You'll need to keep traffic off the area until the new turf is well-established.

3 In places where no grass could hack it, lay down stepping stones, install a walkway of gravel or mulch, or go whole hog and pave with bricks or concrete. (For more on pathways, see "Perfect Paths for Every Plan" on page 18.)

Beyond Your Lawn

It's pretty likely—and downright desirable—that the landscape around your house will consist of more than just all that well-tended turf we've been talking about. Grass is great—no doubt about that. But trees are terrific, bushes are beautiful, perennials are pretty, and… you get the idea. And you'll probably want to include some features that enhance your enjoyment of the lawn, too: things like birdbaths and feeders, patios and pathways, flower beds, trees for shade, benches for sitting in that

Yankee Doodle Data

Perfect Paths for Every Plan

Pathways are there to help us get to where we want to go. Before you choose a paving material, consider who's going to be traveling the path and how quickly they'll need to go. Kids, for example, can hop happily from paver to paver and are also able to scamper over a path of coarse wood chips (although chips can be rough on bare feet). But Great Aunt Edna needs more secure footing for her daily constitutional around the rose garden and will appreciate a well-laid brick path that's wide enough to let her stroll on her favorite nephew's arm.

PATH MATERIAL	COMMENTS AND CONSIDERATIONS
Bricks	Classic look for garden paths; if not carefully installed, prone to heaving in areas where ground freezes in winter; can become slippery with moss in moist, shady locations.
Gravel or crushed stone	Provides firm footing; use a border of timbers or bricks to keep stones in the path and out of the lawn.
Log slices	Slices 1 to 2 inches thick, cut from logs at least 1 foot in diameter, make a nifty-looking rustic path.
Poured concrete	Most secure surface for frequently traveled paths and most accessible for less-than-nimble pedestrians; requires level surface; large areas may require professional installation.
Preformed pavers	Come in many colors, shapes, and styles; may be "strewn" in single file for casual, pond-hopping paths, or interlocked and laid like bricks for more formal effects.
Wood chips	Inexpensive and easily refreshed from year to year; use a border of landscape timbers or bricks to keep errant chips from escaping into your grass and running afoul of your mower.

shade, maybe even a bubbling fountain or a water garden. If this sounds like the yard of your dreams, take a look at Chapter 15. There, you'll find more lawn alternatives than you can shake a rake at, along with great ideas for water features and hardscaping to set off your lawn to perfection.

PICK LAWN PARTNERS WITH PRECISION

Part of enjoying your lawn is keeping it manageable, and there are loads of other landscape features that you can use to decorate your home environment, without adding to your lawn maintenance chores. When you're choosing nonlawn features, keep these factors in mind:

★ **Look for low-maintenance.** Landscape plants require care, too. Avoid excessive pruning chores by choosing trees and shrubs that will mature to the right size for your landscape.

★ **Get the biggest bang for your buck.** Select features that will add interest to your landscape all year long: evergreen trees, for example, or bushes with berries that will remain colorful through the winter.

★ **Plan your views.** Look at your landscape from inside your house. What do you see? Is there something interesting to look at every month of the year? Is there anything you'd like to screen from your view? Choose plants and structures that you enjoy looking at, and put these where you can see them from your favorite window.

Star-Spangled *Lawn* Lore

On average, American gardeners spend as much on lawn-related purchases as they do on purchases for their fruit and vegetable gardens. Yet almost none of 'em ever eats so much as one bite of grass!

★ **Check your "street scene."** As much as the view from inside your house should please you, you'll also want to create a pleasing perspective for people approaching your home. This is often referred to as "curb appeal," and it's very valuable if you are thinking of selling your home. How valuable? A swell-looking landscape can add as much as $30,000 to the value of a home appraised at $200,000 before the landscaping was taken into consideration. That's a whole lot of grass seed!

TERRIFIC TREE TENDING

If you've gone to the trouble of going out and spending your hard-earned money on a new tree or shrub for your landscape, it only makes sense to protect your investment with a first-rate planting hole. Yet the most common mistake people make when installing new landscape plants is digging a hole that's too deep and too narrow. And that very often spells doom for the plant. Here's how to do it right:

STEP 1. Dig a hole that will keep the plant at the same depth it was growing at in the nursery.

STEP 2. Make the hole at least three times the width of the plant's root ball or the container it was growing in.

STEP 3. Rough up the sides and bottom of the hole with a digging fork to keep water from pooling in the hole and drowning the roots.

STEP 4. Make a small mound of raised soil in the bottom of the hole to let water run away from the crown of the plant.

STEP 5. Don't amend the soil when you refill the hole.

STEP 6. Do press the soil firmly down around the roots, making sure that there are no air pockets that will let the roots dry out.

STEP 7. Water thoroughly after planting, and as needed in the following weeks.

SCRAP THE WRAP

Used to be, when you were planting a tree that came balled-and-burlapped, you could simply loosen the burlap around the top of the root ball, and leave it in the planting hole to decompose. Doing that with today's nursery plants is a recipe for failure, since the "burlap" around most modern root balls is usually synthetic, and destined to hang around for a long time. Get it outta there and you'll give your tree a better shot at success.

BLUE PLATE SPECIAL

TREE-PLANTING BOOSTER MIX

Serve up a hearty helping of this potent powder at planting time to give trees a surefire start. This mix helps the soil drain well *and* hold moisture—just what a newly planted tree needs.

4 lb. of compost
2 lb. of gypsum
1 lb. of Epsom salts
1 lb. of dry dog food
1 lb. of dry oatmeal

Mix the ingredients together in a bucket. Then work a handful or two into the bottom of the planting hole, and sprinkle another handful over the soil after planting.

TREES VS. TURF

Shallow-rooted trees can give grass a real run for its root space, and can cause you a whole lot of headaches if you're trying to grow a lawn around them. Save yourself a lot of frustration by skirting these types of trees with mulch, instead of grass. If you're considering any of these trees for your landscape plan, and you just gotta have them, then plan on installing them outside of your lawn area:

Beeches (*Fagus*)

Birches (*Betula*)

Elms (*Ulmus*)

Norway maple (*Acer platanoides*)

Silver maple (*Acer saccharinum*)

The Right Stuff

Once you have a plan in mind for your own personal patch of heaven, your next step is to choose the best grass—or combination of grasses—to plant there. Don't make the all-too-common mistake of running to the store and buying the first bag of grass seed you find. (That is, unless you want to spend a lot of time tending turf that's not suited to your site. In that case, go right ahead.) But I *guarantee* you'll be happier if you learn just enough about grasses to be able to figure out which ones will grow best in your yard. C'mon, it's worth it, and I've included everything you need to know right here in this chapter.

Grass Anatomy

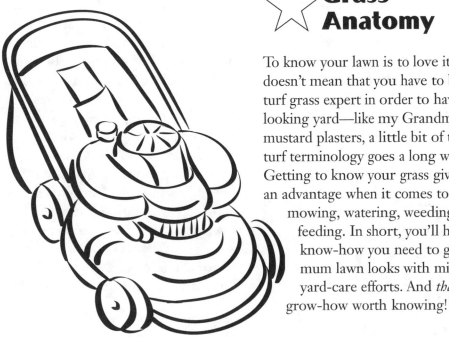

To know your lawn is to love it. But that doesn't mean that you have to become a turf grass expert in order to have a great-looking yard—like my Grandma Putt's mustard plasters, a little bit of technical turf terminology goes a long way! Getting to know your grass gives you an advantage when it comes to sowing, mowing, watering, weeding, and feeding. In short, you'll have the know-how you need to get maximum lawn looks with minimal yard-care efforts. And *that* is some grow-how worth knowing!

GROUNDCOVER NO. 1

So just how did grass become America's groundcover of choice? That's simple! Grass is tops because it:

★ Tolerates traffic (That means you can walk on it!)

★ Can be mowed to a uniform height

★ Spreads rapidly and covers the ground effectively

★ Looks good, too!

That's a combination of qualities that few other plants can match! And, what's especially important is the location of the plant's crown, the growing point that sends shoots up and roots down. The crown of a turf grass plant is right at soil level, well below the sharp mower blades that pass above it. This lets us lop off the leaves on a regular basis without damaging the part of the plant that keeps everything growing. And that's good news for lawn lovers everywhere!

Star-Spangled *Lawn* Lore

According to estimates, there are more than 31 million acres of grass growing across this great country of ours. That's an area the size of New England!

And here's another hard-to-believe fact: Of the thousands of species of grass in the world, only about 50 are suitable for growing as a lawn.

TURF TERMINOLOGY

Grasses may all look the same to you, but, of course, each kind has distinctive features that make it different from the other kinds. Turf grass scientists can look at the parts of a grass plant and tell you what species it is (and often what variety, too). Now, for regular ol' guys and gals like you and me, that level of detail is unnecessary. But all the same, it's helpful to know the parts of a grass plant so you can understand what happens when you mow, and learn how you can make your lawn grow thicker and greener.

Shoots. These can be either primary (the main stem growing up from the

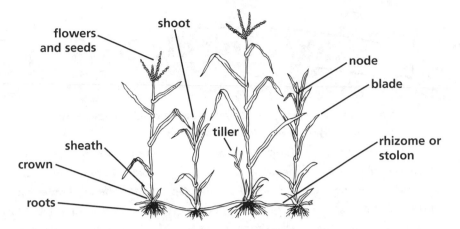

crown to produce flowers and seeds) or secondary (the leaf shoots that grow up around the primary shoot).

Sheath. The part of the grass leaf that encases the stem at its base.

Flowers and seeds. If you don't mow your lawn for a while, you'll see the feathery flowers rising up over the leaves. Grass flowers are usually pale tan to light green and not especially pretty. In short order, they'll become seeds that'll blow around until they land in a suitable spot and grow up into new grass plants.

Blade. Your mower's main target—the blade—is the upper part of the leaf that grows up and away from the stem.

Crown. Right at soil level you can see the spot where each grass plant is anchored in the soil. The base of each plant—where shoots and leaves grow

upward, and roots sink into the ground— is its crown.

Roots. These slender, pale grass roots might not look like much, but boy can they grow! Their hairlike fibers grow downward from the crown to spread out in search of water and nutrients in the soil.

Tiller. A common feature of bunch grasses, tillers are secondary shoots that grow up from the crown.

Node. Not the thing in the middle of your face! A node is a joint on a stem where sheaths and blades grow from.

Rhizome. These rootlike branches grow horizontally from the crown just below the soil surface, and produce shoots and roots that become new grass plants.

Stolon. Creeping horizontally over the soil surface, stolons grow outward from the crown to form new grass plants.

Yankee Doodle Data

Turf Textures

A grass's texture makes a difference in the overall appearance of your lawn, and it's something you'll want to consider when you're choosing the type(s) of turf you want to grow. Coarse-textured grasses, such as Bahia grass, may be more durable when it comes to high-traffic spots, but some folks find them too weedy looking. On the other hand, slender-leaved grasses, such as colonial bent grass, may do a better job of creating a classic lawn appearance, but they're not as rugged as some of their sturdier counterparts.

GRASS	TOLERANCE	TEXTURE
Annual ryegrass	Cool season	Coarse
Bahia grass	Warm season	Coarse
Bermuda grass	Warm season	Fine to medium
Blue grama grass	Warm season	Fine
Buffalo grass	Warm season	Fine
Carpet grass	Warm season	Coarse
Centipede grass	Warm season	Coarse
Colonial bent grass	Cool season	Fine
Fine fescue (chewings, creeping, and hard)	Cool season	Fine
Kentucky bluegrass	Cool season	Fine
Perennial ryegrass	Cool season	Fine to medium
St. Augustine grass	Warm season	Coarse
Tall fescue	Cool season	Medium to coarse
Zoysia grass	Warm season	Fine

TAKE A BIT OFF THE TOP

While roots undoubtedly make up the biggest percentage of a grass plant, almost all of what we see in our yards is grass leaves. Like all green plants, grass uses its leaves for photosynthesis, the process by which sunlight is converted into carbohydrates that feed the plant. And yet, unlike most other green plants, our home turf lets us trim off a bit of its leaves on a regular basis without complaint—as long as we don't cut off too much at a time. That's what makes grass so darn dandy as a lovely living carpet for our yards. And, it's also what separates it from other kinds of groundcovers, such as pachysandra, English ivy, and liriope, none of which would take kindly to a weekly haircut.

LEAVES OF GRASS

Among the types of turf we use in our yards, there are distinct variations in the size, shape, color, and growth rate of the leaves. That northern favorite, Kentucky bluegrass, for example, has upright, emerald green leaves that grow vigorously when temperatures range from 60° to 75°F. By comparison, warm-season centipede grass leaves are a light olive drab color, and they stay close to the ground. When

Star-Spangled *Lawn* Lore

Thomas Jefferson put a lawn at the heart of his design for the University of Virginia campus in Charlottesville. Known simply as "The Lawn," it includes three turf-topped terraces that stretch over 255 feet in length.

the mercury lingers in the 80° to 95°F range, centipede grass spreads rapidly via stolons, but it rarely grows taller than 4 inches. Clearly, a bluegrass lawn will need more mowing than a yard covered with centipede grass, but it may also be more likely to satisfy your idea of what a lawn should look like.

GRASSES ON THE GROW

One of the totally terrific things about turf is how it stretches out its roots (and other parts) to cover the soil in your yard. Grass plants have four different ways to spread themselves around your lawn:

Tillers. Bunch-type grasses, such as tall fescue, ryegrasses, and blue grama grass, produce these new shoots around their crowns, growing into dense, soil-hugging clumps.

Rhizomes. Underground stems stretch out parallel to the soil surface, forming new plants at nodes along the way.

Stolons. Horizontal stems that grow over the soil surface, stolons also make new shoots and roots at their nodes.

Seeds. Uncut grass is bloomin' grass! While a lawn in bloom is generally shaggy looking and in need of mowing, it's also growing its own reinforcements. Those feathery flowers quickly turn into seeds that make their way to the soil where they grow up into more of that great green groundcover.

Some kinds of grass rely on a single mode of motion more than others. Buffalo grass, for example, reaches out

with stolons only, while Bermuda grass and zoysia grass spread by both stolons and rhizomes. To avoid that shaggy lawn look, and to cut down on the production of pesky pollen that makes susceptible folks sneeze, many improved turf varieties have been bred for a reduced tendency to bloom. Of course, this also reduces their tendency to toss their seeds around.

Star-Spangled *Lawn* Lore

You've probably heard of the Mason-Dixon line, but in turfgrass terms, it's the "bluegrass line," an imaginary line that marks the southernmost places where Kentucky bluegrass grows well. It might just as easily be called the "Bermuda grass line," since it's also the point where that warm-season turf takes over for its cool-season counterpart.

★ Lawn Climates of America

Gardeners know that certain plants grow better in certain climate conditions, and they've created special zones that stretch across the country to help them keep track of winter lows and summer highs. Of course, those standards apply to lawn grasses, but the zones aren't quite the same. Read on for my tips on how to make sure the grass you grow matches the climate you're growing in.

GRANDMA PUTT'S SOOTHING SUNBURN TONIC

If lawn care in the sunny South leaves you in the painful pink, cool your overheated hide with this aromatic "tea."

2 fresh garlic cloves, chopped
2 cups of water

Combine the garlic and water in a pan, and simmer for 5 minutes. Turn off the heat, cover the pan, and let the mixture steep for 45 minutes. Cool, strain, and store covered in the refrigerator. To soothe sunburned spots, soak a washcloth or hand towel in the cool garlic tea, wring out the excess liquid, and put the damp cloth on the painful area. Leave it on for about 20 minutes. Replace it with a freshly moistened cloth until you feel relief from the discomfort.

THE TRICKY TRANSITION ZONE

Because lawn grasses are divided into cool-season and warm-season groups, you might think that it would be simpler to separate the map into two large areas, one northern and one southern. And you'd be right—that's a pretty darned reasonable way to think about turf. Except there's a part, right in the middle, known as the transition zone.

The transition zone represents parts of the country where the climate teeters back and forth between what's good for warm-season grasses and what's good for cool-season ones. Often in these areas, cool-season turf languishes in the heat of summer, while warm-season grasses are prone to winter injury. Sometimes it's just a matter of watering through the summer to help a heat-tolerant bluegrass make it in the "zone," or you may need to find a particularly cold-hardy selection of Bermuda grass. This is where it makes a whole lot of sense to look around you and see what other folks in your area are growing successfully, instead of puzzling over maps and the labels on bags of grass seed.

Here are the states that fall in the transition zone:

★ Arkansas

★ Kentucky

★ Most of Kansas

★ North Carolina

★ Northern Texas

★ Oklahoma

★ South Carolina

★ Southern Illinois

★ Southern Indiana

★ Southern Missouri

★ Tennessee

★ Virginia

★ GET IN THE ZONE ★

TO help you figure out what kinds of turf will deliver top performance in your region, I've divided the country into six lawn zones, based on rainfall, summer heat, and winter cold. Check out the maps below to see where you fit in. I've also included a list of some of the kinds of grass that do best in that area.

You'll notice that I don't always list all the turf types that will grow in a particular zone. Grasses are pretty versatile plants, and most can grow—at least some of the time—outside the recommended boundaries. I just want to point you in the direction of the few kinds that are most likely to thrive in your zone.

Zone 1

Covers: northeastern Atlantic coast from southern Maine to the middle Atlantic states; Pacific Northwest coast from Washington to northern California

Zone 1 Best Bets ★ annual and perennial ryegrasses ★ bluegrass ★ colonial bent grass ★ tall and creeping fescues

Zone 2

Covers: southeastern Atlantic states and west through the Deep South and Gulf states

Zone 2 Best Bets ★ Bahia grass ★ Bermuda grass ★ centipede grass ★ turf-type tall fescue (northern part of zone) ★ zoysia grass

Zone 3

Covers: New England and Appalachian states, west through the Ohio Valley and Great Lakes

Zone 3 Best Bets ★ annual and perennial ryegrasses ★ bluegrass ★ tall and creeping fescues

Zone 4

Covers: Great Plains from central and west Texas north to the Canadian border

Zone 4 Best Bets ★ blue grama grass ★ bluegrass ★ buffalo grass ★ tall and creeping fescues ★ zoysia grass (southern plains)

Zone 5

Covers: California coast through southwestern desert

Zone 5 Best Bets ★ Bermuda grass ★ blue grama grass ★ buffalo grass ★ zoysia grass

Zone 6

Covers: Sierras, Great Basin, and Rocky Mountains

Zone 6 Best Bets ★ annual and perennial ryegrasses ★ blue grama grass ★ bluegrass ★ buffalo grass ★ tall and creeping fescues

Star-Spangled *Lawn* Lore

I don't know if any grasses came over on the Mayflower, or if any passed through the gates at Ellis Island, but our American lawns are descended from turf types from around the world. We got our idea for lawns mainly from England, but many grasses from that country couldn't handle the harsher climate we have here. So the U.S. Department of Agriculture got together with the U.S. Golf Association (because golfers are people who are really hooked on grass!) to try to find turfs that could take the heat and the cold (and falling golf balls). They tested European bluegrass (bet you thought it actually was from Kentucky!), Bermuda grass from Africa, fescues from Europe, and zoysia grass from Asia to develop mixtures of grasses that would survive and thrive in our all-American yards. And it looks like they did a pretty good job of coming up with something for everyone!

Great Grasses to Know and Grow

Good news, grass gardeners! Whether you're an active lawn lover or more of a laid-back lawn loafer, there are plenty of top-notch turf types for you to choose from. But where do you begin? Right here—read on to learn all about grass types and which are best for your location.

WARM UP, COOL DOWN

Let's start with a fundamental fact: There are basically two kinds of turf grass—cool-season and warm-season. Yes, there are literally hundreds of varieties of bluegrass and dozens of selections of Bermuda grass, but the bottom line remains the same: Kentucky bluegrass is a cool-season sod and Bermuda grass is on the warm-season side of the turf table. So, figuring out which kinds of grasses will thrive in your location starts with a few simple big-picture climate questions:

1 Does it routinely snow during the winter where you live?

2 Do winter temperatures consistently fall below 40°F?

A "yes" to these questions means you have a cool-season lawn. You need hardy turf that chooses dormancy over death when the snow flies and the temperatures plummet. Fill your yard with fescues, bluegrasses, and ryegrasses that will suit your site's specific needs, and enjoy the good-looking lawn that results.

If you answered "no" to questions 1 and 2, try these climate queries on for size:

3 Is Jack Frost an infrequent visitor where you live (and snow a real rarity)?

4 Do summer temperatures consistently climb into the 80° to 95°F range (and does summer last from April to October)?

Affirmatives here mean you live in a place where warm-season grasses are likely to thrive. Satisfy your lawn longings with hybrid Bermuda grass, St. Augustine grass, zoysia, or other charming southern sods.

If your answers to all of these questions are less than certain, you probably live in one of the dozen states in the transition zone. In some ways, that makes you lucky, because you'll have more grass choices for your lawn than folks living in places that are unquestionably meant for either cool-season or warm-season turf. But you may also have a harder time narrowing down your options to create a lawn that looks great through hot, humid summers *and* winters that are sometimes cold and snowy. Take a look at my 'Tweener Premium Mix on page 48—it's custom-made for good looks in tricky transition-zone landscapes.

TEMPERATURE'S RISIN'

The most popular cool-season grasses for lawns in the North are:

★ Annual ryegrass

★ Bent grass

★ Bluegrass

★ Chewings fescue

★ Creeping red fescue

★ Perennial ryegrass

★ Turf-type tall fescue

In the transition zone between North and South, two heat-tolerant cool-season grasses and one cold-tolerant warm-season turf perform well:

★ Bluegrass

★ Turf-type tall fescues

★ Zoysia grass

These warm-season grasses are popular in the South and Southwest:

★ Bahia grass

★ Bermuda grass

★ Blue grama grass

★ Buffalo grass

★ Carpet grass

★ Centipede grass

★ St. Augustine grass

★ Zoysia grass

★ COOL-SEASON GRASSES ★

WHAT'S cool about the cool-season grasses is the temperature range in which they do their best growing. Bluegrass, bent grass, fescues, ryegrass, and company are at the peak of their game on days when the mercury stays between 60° and 75°F. That means they thrive in cool (and moist) conditions—spring and fall across much of the country—and can be just as dormant in the middle of a hot, dry summer as they are in the dead of winter. Here's a rundown.

Annual Ryegrass (Lolium multiflorum)

The Scoop: Annual ryegrass is great for quick coverage on bare soil, and for overseeding southern lawns to keep them green through the winter months. But watch out for seed mixes that contain more than 20 percent annual ryegrass, or you'll find yourself reseeding the bare patches it leaves behind the following season. This grass needs water during extended dry periods, but is fairly resistant to problems. Annual ryegrass grows quickly and needs frequent mowing. If you use it to cover the ground while other more desirable grasses get started, be sure to water throughout the summer to help the other grasses get growing, and to give them an edge in their competition with the ryegrass.

>   **How It Looks:** Light green and coarse textured
>
>   **Grows in Lawn Zones:** 1 to 6
>
>   **Site and Soil:** Full sun to light shade; almost any soil type
>
>   **Mowing Height:** 1 to 2 inches
>
>   **Name to Know:** 'Gulf'

Colonial Bent Grass (Agrostis tenuis)

The Scoop: Popular for golf greens because of its low mowing height, colonial bent grass needs almost constant pampering to keep it looking good, and it's not fond of heavy traffic. Unless you want to spend lots of time watering and feeding your lawn, and then more time mowing it and battling disease problems, look for other fine-textured turfs that need less care. The story's a little different in the Pacific Northwest, however, where colonial bent grass seems particularly well adapted to the climate, and is gaining popularity as a low-maintenance turf.

How It Looks: Pale green with a very fine texture

Grows in Lawn Zones: 1 to 6

Site and Soil: Full sun; neutral to slightly acidic soil

Mowing Height: ½ to 1 inch

Names to Know: 'Alister', 'Allure', 'Egmont', 'Exeter', and 'Glory'

All in the Family: Handsome velvet bent grass *(A. canina)* has very fine texture and a spreading habit, but is intolerant of drought and extreme temperatures. Fine-textured creeping bent grass *(A. palustris)* spreads vigorously by stolons and stays low to the ground. Varieties include 'Penncross' and 'Evansville'.

Fine Fescues *(Festuca)*

The Scoop: Fine fescues include creeping red fescue *(F. rubra)*, chewings fescue *(F. rubra* var. *commutata)*, and hard fescue *(F. longifolia)*. For all their delicate good looks, the fine fescues are a sturdy group of grasses that tolerate cold temperatures, shade, and dry conditions better than other cool-season types. Don't do too much for these three—high fertility and excess moisture make fine fescues prone to disease problems, and none of them perform very well in the humid South's high temperatures. Creeping red fescue (it's only red at its base) spreads slowly by rhizomes; chewings and hard fescue are bunching grasses. Fine fescues are not good for high-traffic areas, but make an excellent easy-care lawn for difficult sites.

How They Look: Dark green and fine textured

Grow in Lawn Zones: 1, 3 to 6

Site and Soil: Sun to moderate shade; average to sandy, acidic soil

Mowing Height: 1½ to 3 inches

Names to Know: Creeping red fescue: 'Flyer', 'Rose', and 'Shademaster II'; chewings fescue: 'Capitol', 'Cascade', 'Jamestown II', 'Shadow', 'Tiffany', 'Treasure', and 'Wrigley'; hard fescue: 'Biljart', 'Brigade', 'Discovery', and 'Oxford'

(continued)

Cool-Season Grasses—continued

Kentucky Bluegrass (Poa pratensis)

The Scoop: Best-loved and best-known of all the lawn grasses, Kentucky bluegrass is a top-notch turf for cool, humid regions. Bluegrass tends to be shallow-rooted and needs watering during summer dry spells to keep it from going dormant; it may also need occasional dethatching. With more than 200 improved varieties available, you're almost sure to find one that meets your needs. Often sold in seed mixes with perennial ryegrass and fescues.

How It Looks: Dark green with fine to medium texture

Grows in Lawn Zones: 1, 3 to 6

Site and Soil: Full sun to light shade; fertile soil

Mowing Height: 2 to 2½ inches

Names to Know: 'Banff', 'Baron', 'Caliber', 'Challenger', 'Eclipse', 'Kenblue', 'Midnight', 'Monopoly', 'Monte Carlo', 'Preakness', 'Ram 1', and 'Unique'

All in the Family: Rough bluegrass (*P. trivialis*) resembles Kentucky bluegrass, but is more shade-tolerant and sometimes joins it in seed mixtures. Varieties include 'Sabre II', 'Lazer II', and 'Winterplay'. As you might suspect, Canada bluegrass (*P. compressa*) likes it in the coldest parts of the country; this grass is a bit less refined than its southern cousin, but grows well in poor conditions. 'Reubens' is an improved variety. Annual bluegrass (*P. annua*) is a coarse and pesky weed that you don't want in your lawn—watch out for it in cheap seed mixes.

Perennial Ryegrass (*Lolium perenne*)

The Scoop: Perennial ryegrass is an attractive and durable grass that's dandy for play areas and other busy lawn locations. Versatile enough to stand on its own in a lawn, it gets along well with other grasses and is often included in cool-season seed mixes. Perennial rye sprouts quickly and resists problems; it's used to overseed southern lawns for winter color, and to hold the soil in places where erosion is a concern. Tough leaves can mean tough mowing—a dull mower blade will tear perennial ryegrass and leave it brown and damaged at the tips.

How It Looks: Light green with a medium to coarse texture

Grows in Lawn Zones: 1, 3 to 6

Site and Soil: Full sun to light shade; wide range of soil types

Mowing Height: 2 to 3 inches

Names to Know: 'Blazer III', 'Caddieshack', 'Citation', 'Esquire', 'Jet', 'Manhattan', 'Pennant', 'Roadrunner', 'Saturn', and 'Wizard'

Tall Fescue (*Festuca arundinacea*)

The Scoop: Originally used in pastures, tall fescue has been polished up by plant breeders to become a popular choice for drought-tolerant, low-maintenance, high-traffic lawns. Less shade-tolerant than the fine fescues, tall fescue grows vigorously enough to crowd out weeds as well as other turf grasses. Improved selections are durable, disease-resistant, and attractive, and make good groundcovers for play areas. Tall fescue becomes stressed if mowed too short, and its coarser blades may look weedy amid fine-textured turf.

How It Looks: Medium green with a medium to coarse texture

Grows in Lawn Zones: 1, 3 to 6

Site and Soil: Full sun to light shade; most types of soil

Mowing Height: 2 to 3 inches

Names to Know: 'Alamo', 'Duster', 'Houndog V', 'Kentucky 31', 'Lancer', 'Olympic', 'Plantation', 'Rebel', 'Rembrandt', and 'Virtue'

THE "GRASS" THAT'S NOT

In the warmest parts of the country, where temperatures rarely dip too far below freezing, there's a mowable groundcover called dichondra that is used like a grass, but isn't one at all. Actually a member of the morning glory family, dichondra has kidney-shaped leaves that grow low to the ground, and it can be mowed to ½ to 1 inch high. Bright green and cushiony looking, it makes a pretty groundcover, but doesn't tolerate traffic, and needs regular watering and well-drained soil to grow at its best.

WHAT'S IN A NAME?

Shopping for grass is sort of like shopping for a car. When we talk about Kentucky bluegrass, fescues, or zoysia grass, it's like talking about sedans, minivans, or station wagons. You might first decide what *type* of vehicle you want, but then you'll get more specific and choose the brand with the *features* you want. It's like that with grass, too. Turf scientists have done lots of plant breeding to create named varieties that have significant improvements over their unrefined ancestors (which were probably meant for pastures

rather than home landscapes). Kentucky bluegrass, for example, is not very tolerant of shade. But bluegrass selections such as 'Eclipse' and 'Glade' grow pretty well in shady spots. Of course, that's just the tip of this grass blade—hundreds of turf varieties out there have been specially selected to solve all kinds of tricky conditions. So don't settle for just any ol' grass—look for the designer label, and get a lawn that matches your site (and maybe even your eyes!).

SCOTCH, COFFEE, AND MILK SHAKES

Grass seed is typically sold three different ways: straight, blends, or mixtures. "Straight" grass seed is a single species or variety of grass, unmixed with anything else. Your favorite coffee is probably a blend of different kinds of coffee beans and, likewise, grass seed blends are combinations of two or more varieties of a single species of grass, such as 'Aurora Gold' and 'Shademaster II' fine fescue. Like a milk shake (ice cream, syrup, and milk), seed mixtures combine varieties of two or more different species of grass, such as turf-type tall fescue, perennial ryegrass, and Kentucky bluegrass. Of course, the milk shake will taste better, but the grass seed will definitely look better on your lawn.

MAKE SOME LOCAL CALLS

As I've already mentioned, although there are only a handful of kinds of cool-season grasses and another handful of warm-season types, there are *hundreds* of improved turf varieties derived from them. Some of those named selections have been developed to satisfy very specific kinds of growing conditions, too—maybe even the exact climate that's right in your own backyard. So let me start by steering you in the right direction in terms of cool- vs. warm-season, and even within those categories. Then you should check in with a few local experts who can give you the lowdown on the very best grasses for your neighborhood.

For starters, look up your local Cooperative Extension office—these folks are connected with your state's land-grant university, and can get you the latest recommendations from their turf scientists. Then get even more local, and check in with your neighbors, especially if you're new to the scene and they're not. Growing conditions can vary greatly across a state, or even within a county, and finding out what works for the folks next door can be the fastest path to lawn success.

Super ★ Secret

A New Star for Shade

Long maligned as a pesky weed, supina bluegrass (*Poa supina*) is now stepping into the spotlight as a super-star for shade. Turf scientists in Germany and at several U.S. universities have been developing this lesser known bluegrass into a superior turf grass for shady, high-traffic landscapes. If you have shade, this one's worth looking for: Supina bluegrass is fine textured and disease-resistant with good, dark green color and the ability to withstand foot traffic. Two named varieties are currently available: 'Supra' and 'Supranova'.

SOME LIKE IT COOL

Unlike their companions on the list of warm-season grasses, both buffalo grass and blue grama grass can stand up to some pretty low temperatures (as low as -30° to -40°F). In fact, these hardy North American natives are good choices for dry landscapes across much of the United States, and are sometimes grown together in low-maintenance lawns. Both grow slowly, so they don't have to be mowed very often, and they're tolerant of droughty conditions, too. Neither one delivers what you'd call a classic-looking lawn, but they're down-right handsome in sites where better-known turf grasses would quickly give way to weeds and bare ground.

★ WARM-SEASON GRASSES ★

WARM-SEASON grasses are those terrific turfs that survive and thrive in our country's hot spots. These ground-grippers can really grow, grow, grow when temperatures climb into the 80° to 95°F range. A couple of them, (namely buffalo grass and blue grama grass) will also grow where the mercury sinks low. But most of these will give up the ghost when anything more than a light frost threatens. In general, warm-season lawn grasses tolerate dry conditions better than their northern counterparts; they're also better adapted to the steamy humid weather that invites all kinds of disease woes for bluegrasses, fescues, and ryegrasses.

Bahia Grass (*Paspalum notatum*)

The Scoop: This sturdy southern survivor won't satisfy your idea of a lawn if you've been raised on Kentucky bluegrass. But if your yard's located in the southern coastal regions, this is a great low-maintenance option. Bahia grass spreads slowly, but steadily, by sturdy rhizomes and forms a durable, weed-resistant lawn that's reasonably drought-tolerant and able to stand up to foot traffic. Bahia takes shade better than other warm-season grasses, too. Sharpen your mower blades if Bahia grass is your choice—its broad leaves are tough and need regular mowing.

How It Looks: Glossy light green and coarse textured

Grows in Lawn Zone: 2

Site and Soil: Sun to moderate shade in most soils; grows in sandy and infertile sites

Mowing Height: 2 to 2½ inches

Names to Know: 'Argentine' for the Florida peninsula and southern Texas; 'Pensacola' for the rest of Zone 2

Bermuda Grass (*Cynodon dactylon*)

The Scoop: In the sunny, humid South, Bermuda grass is as popular as Kentucky bluegrass is in the North. It earns its place as the No. 1 choice for southern lawns by being vigorous, fast-spreading, and deep-rooted to tolerate drought and heat. Bermuda grass is durable enough to withstand traffic, making it a favorite for playing fields in the South. It's also disease-resistant and salt-tolerant. In fact, its vigor is the main rap against Bermuda grass—it'll use its rapid-growing rhizomes and stolons to creep right out of your yard and into flower beds, and even over paved areas. If you're growing this turf, you'll want a lawn edger and the time to use it regularly! Bermuda grass is a true southerner, and turns brown at the first touch of frost, staying that way until spring. Overseeding it with ryegrass or fescue will give you a green lawn through the cooler winter months.

How It Looks: Medium to dark green with fine to medium texture

Grows in Lawn Zones: 2 and 5

Site and Soil: Full sun; well-drained, fertile soil

Mowing Height: 1 to 2 inches

Names to Know: 'Mirage', 'Mohawk', 'Princess', 'Pyramid', 'Riviera', 'Sahara', 'Savannah', 'Sundevil', 'Tifway', 'Tifway II', 'Yukon', and 'Yuma'

Blue Grama Grass (*Bouteloua gracilis*)

The Scoop: A nice-looking native grass that's gaining interest for use in lawns, blue grama grass gets along with little care. It's drought-tolerant, can take foot traffic, and resists most pests and diseases. Slow-growing with a tendency to form clumps, blue grama grass doesn't produce a classic-looking lawn, but it's a sure winner for low-maintenance lawns and meadow plantings, where it will grow up to 2 feet tall if it's not mowed. Blue grama grass is sometimes mixed with buffalo grass to create an unconventional, but not unattractive, easy-care turf.

How It Looks: Blue-green with fine texture

Grows in Lawn Zones: 3, 4, and 6

Site and Soil: Full sun to light shade; dry soil

Mowing Height: 1½ to 3 inches

Name to Know: 'Hachita'

All in the Family: Side oats grama grass (*B. curtipendula*) is a beautiful, clump-forming ornamental grass that grows to 2 feet tall.

(continued)

Warm-Season Grasses—continued

Buffalo Grass *(Buchloe dactyloides)*

The Scoop: Buffalo grass is a Great Plains native that's gaining favor as a low-maintenance turf for dry-summer regions. Slow-growing, it needs little fertilizing or watering, and grows only to heights of 4 to 6 inches when it's not mowed at all. Once established, buffalo grass handles foot traffic well, and is very drought-tolerant, although it will turn brown during extended dry periods in midsummer, as well as during the winter months. Its fine, blue-green blades can appear matted and don't fulfill everyone's idea of how a lawn should look, but this native is right at home in the dry prairie regions from Texas clear up to the Canadian border.

> **How It Looks:** Blue- to gray-green and fine textured
>
> **Grows in Lawn Zones:** 3, 4, and 6
>
> **Site and Soil:** Full sun and nearly any soil; best on heavy, alkaline soils
>
> **Mowing Height:** 2 to 3 inches
>
> **Names to Know:** 'Bison', 'Bowie', 'Cody', 'Prairie', 'Tatanka', and 'Texoka'

Carpet Grass *(Axonopus affinis)*

The Scoop: The rapidly spreading stolons of carpet grass allow it to form dense, compact turf that stands up to traffic and requires fairly little care. But carpet grass is not lovely to look at, and it doesn't fare well during dry spells without watering. It's also very cold sensitive and turns brown for the winter at the slightest hint of cold weather. Carpet grass needs frequent mowing to keep it looking good in a lawn, and is recommended only for those southern lawns where no other turf grasses will grow.

> **How It Looks:** Light green and coarse textured
>
> **Grows in Lawn Zone:** 2
>
> **Site and Soil:** Full sun to moderate shade; poor, acidic, wet soils
>
> **Mowing Height:** 1½ inches
>
> **Names to Know:** Flat grass and Louisiana grass are other names for carpet grass; breeding programs have largely ignored this Gulf Coast native

Centipede Grass (*Eremochloa ophiuroides*)

The Scoop: Sometimes called the "lazy man's grass," centipede grass grows low and slow, so you'll only have to get the mower out every couple of weeks. It's a light feeder, too, and tends to form thatch when it's overfertilized. A good choice for easy-care lawns across the South, centipede grass is shallow rooted and needs regular watering during dry periods. It spreads rapidly via creeping stolons to crowd out weeds in its way. In spite of its hundred-legged name, centipede grass doesn't appreciate heavy foot traffic, so it's not a good choice for play areas. In soils with high pH, this turf can turn yellow and may need applications of iron fertilizer to help it regain its greenish color.

How It Looks: Yellow-green and medium to coarse textured

Grows in Lawn Zone: 2

Site and Soil: Full sun to light shade in most soil types; best in acidic soils

Mowing Height: 1½ to 2 inches

Names to Know: 'Centennial', 'Oaklawn', and 'Tennessee Hardy'

St. Augustine Grass (*Stenotaphrum secundatum*)

The Scoop: In tough conditions, where few other grasses will grow, you might think this turf is saintly indeed—it's fairly shade-tolerant once established, thrives in southern heat, and also puts up with salt spray and wind in coastal areas. But St. Augustine grass needs frequent watering, and is a bit touchy on some other counts, too. Spreading vigorously by stolons, this grass tends to form thatch and needs regular raking and high mowing to limit buildup. You'll need to keep your mower blade well sharpened, too, to avoid browning the tips of the broad leaves. Not particularly cold-tolerant, it stays green later in the fall than Bermuda grass, but St. Augustine's dense sod limits the advantages of overseeding with cool-season grasses for winter color. Pests such as chinch bugs can also be a problem, as can diseases. Seed is not commonly available; most St. Augustine grass lawns are started from sprigs or plugs.

How It Looks: Light green with coarse, thick leaf blades

Grows in Lawn Zone: 2

Site and Soil: Full sun to light shade; most moist soil conditions

Mowing Height: 2 to 3 inches

Names to Know: 'Floratam', 'Palmetto', and 'Raleigh'

(continued)

Warm-Season Grasses—continued

Zoysia Grass *(Zoysia japonica)*

The Scoop: In the battle for southern lawn supremacy, zoysia grass has qualities that make it a contender against the reigning champ, Bermuda grass. Drought-tolerant and salt-tolerant, zoysia withstands moderate foot traffic and resists most pest problems. It spreads by stolons and rhizomes to form a dense turf that fends off weeds well. Although it survives cool temperatures well enough to grow farther north than most warm-season grasses, zoysia grass turns brown with the first hint of frost and remains that way until late spring. Its dense growth habit keeps overseeding with cool-season grass from being an option to solve this lengthy dormancy. Wiry leaf blades can be tough to mow (keep the blade sharpened), and also tough on bare feet walking through them. Slow growth habit helps reduce the amount of mowing that's needed.

> **How It Looks:** Deep green and fine textured
>
> **Grows in Lawn Zones:** 1 and 2
>
> **Site and Soil:** Full sun to light shade in well-drained, average soil; best in acidic soils
>
> **Mowing Height:** 1 to 2 inches
>
> **Names to Know:** 'Companion', 'Emerald', 'Meyer', and 'Zenith'

GRASS VS. WEEDS

If your lawn-care style tends to be laissez-faire, you'll want to choose turf that can take care of itself when weeds try to get a root-hold in your yard. Grasses that spread rapidly to form dense, healthy sod are better able to crowd out, shade out, and otherwise beat out bothersome weeds. For a lawn that'll whip weeds so you don't have to, choose Bermuda grass or Bahia grass for a warm-season yard, and turf-type tall fescue in cool-season sites.

Up Close and Personal

You've probably figured out by now that you can choose from all kinds of turf grasses to make a fantastic-looking lawn. That's what's so great about gardening—

even grass gardening—you can customize everything you do to suit your site, your tastes, and your needs. I'll bet there's at least one part of your yard—maybe even the whole darned thing—that's different from the general characteristics of the lawn zone you live in. Maybe you have a microclimate, a special spot where the temperature varies significantly from the rest of your landscape. Or perhaps there's a boggy area where the bluegrass grows lush and lank, and your mower gets stuck in the mud at least once each summer. Whatever you determine about the overall turf needs of your site, you need to think about these special spots separately and select grasses (or grass alternatives) that make sense for the unique conditions that exist in each place.

MICRO-WHAT?!

Just because it's called a microclimate, that doesn't mean you need a magnifier or a microscope to look at it. A microclimate is simply a little climate—a place where landscape features, including structures and topography, combine to alter growing conditions from what's normal in an area. A stone wall, for example, can create a microclimate on its southern side that's routinely a few degrees warmer than the surrounding yard. Slopes can cause microclimates, too, by allowing cool air to sink into low-lying "frost pockets" where tender

Star-Spangled Lawn Lore

You've probably heard about a tree growing in Brooklyn, but did you know they've got grass in Manhattan? Not only that, but copies (botanical clones, in fact) of the perennial ryegrass growing in New York City's Central Park have been planted across the country. That's right—the 'Manhattan' varieties (there are now improvements upon the original named variety) of perennial ryegrass all got their start in the 15-acre Great Lawn in the heart of the Big Apple!

plants may get nipped a week or two after the usual all-clear date. It's helpful to be aware of microclimates in your landscape and to know in advance how they might help or hinder your lawn, particularly if you're thinking about trying turf grasses that push the climate envelope where you live.

MADE IN THE SHADE

For most of us, the benefits of having shade trees in our yards outweigh the disadvantages of trying to grow grass

Yankee Doodle Data

Grass Feed Needs

Most types of turf do better with a bit of fertilizing during the growing season. (See Chapter 5 for my surefire mixes for feeding your lawn.) For some grasses, that nourishment—mainly in the form of nitrogen—can't come often enough, while other types can thrive with little or no fertilizer. Since applying fertilizer takes time and costs money, a yard that needs fewer meals each year is easier to care for. Here's a rundown of turf grass nitrogen needs from high to low.

COOL-SEASON GRASS	NITROGEN NEEDS	WARM-SEASON GRASS	NITROGEN NEEDS
Bent grass	High	Bermuda grass	High
Kentucky bluegrass	Moderate to high	St. Augustine grass	Moderate to high
Perennial ryegrass	Low to moderate	Zoysia grass	Low to moderate
Tall fescue	Low	Centipede grass	Low
Fine fescue	Low	Bahia grass	Low

beneath those trees. Still, most types of turf tend to be less than fond of shade, meaning more work for you to keep the grass growing in those under-sunny sites. To make the most of shady lawn areas, start by adjusting the environmental factors that are within your control:

1 Choose a shade-tolerant grass. You'll find a list of them in "A Few Shady Customers" on page 45.

2 Trim tree limbs to let in more light. You don't have to reduce your trees to telephone poles, just remove a few of the lower limbs to give the lawn below a fighting chance.

3 In heavy shade, consider growing other plants, such as English ivy or pachysandra, that are more tolerant of shade. You'll find plenty of great shady groundcovers in Chapter 15.

Then, adopt good care habits that will help your grass stay healthy in the shade:

4 Set your mower blade about ⅓ higher in shady areas to give your grass more leaves to grab the limited sunshine with.

5 Water deeply, but not too often. Wet, shady grass is more prone to diseases, but root competition from trees means

the turf growing around them needs more water to stay in the game.

6 Remove fallen tree leaves and grass clippings—these will shade the lawn even more.

A FEW SHADY CUSTOMERS

As a general rule, seed mixes for shady yards should contain more fescue than bluegrass. Some cool-season grasses that tolerate shade well include:

★ Chewings fescue

★ Creeping bent grass

★ Creeping red fescue

★ Hard fescue

★ Rough bluegrass

If you live where warm-season grasses grow best, check out this pair of shade-tolerant grasses:

★ St. Augustine grass

★ Zoysia grass

SMART SLOPE SOLUTIONS

Slopes are for skis, not for mowers, spreaders, and other lawn equipment. If tending your yard means hitting the slopes, plant those difficult-to-maintain spots with easy-care grasses that need less mowing, watering, and fertilizing:

On cool-season slopes: Hard fescue and sheep fescue.

On warm-season slopes: Blue grama grass or buffalo grass.

PAVE PARADISE

I've heard of places where angels fear to tread, but gardeners with children or grandchildren often have the opposite situation: They find themselves wishing their "angels" would tread elsewhere! As they go on

Super ★ Secret

Yankees Beware!

No matter where you live, you might see advertisements for zoysia grass that make it sound like the answer to a homeowner's prayers: drought-tolerant, weed-free, and needs little mowing. But Grandma Putt taught me to be wary of things that sound too good to be true, and this is one of those things. If you live where cool-season grasses are the rule, a zoysia grass lawn is something that you (and your neighbors) will live to regret. Zoysia's ability to spread and crowd out weeds also enables it to travel across property lines and into your neighbor's blue-grass lawn. When frost arrives, the zoysia turns brown, leaving dead-looking patches amid the green of the cool-season turf around it.

Yankee Doodle Data

Great Ground-Grabbers

When you're planting grass to prevent erosion, or even if you're just anxious to have a usable lawn, the speed with which a grass will take hold is important. Here's a look at some turf grasses and their rate of establishment.

COOL-SEASON GRASS	GROWTH RATE	WARM-SEASON GRASS	GROWTH RATE
Perennial ryegrass	Fast	Bermuda grass	Fast
Tall fescue	Fast	St. Augustine grass	Fast
Kentucky bluegrass	Moderate	Bahia grass	Slow
Bent grasses	Moderate	Centipede grass	Slow
Fine fescues	Slow	Zoysia grass	Slow

their carefree ways, kids and dogs (and other creatures of habit) can leave their mark—in the form of well-worn, grass-less pathways—on your lawn. The truth is, there may be some places in your yard where you can't grow grass because of traffic situations like these. And, unless you're looking for an uphill battle, you're better off giving up the grass in those spots and installing some sort of durable paving. Chapter 15 is full of helpful hints for all sorts of hardscaping, including structures to redirect the traffic, and a variety of paving materials for all kinds of landscapes.

TOP TURFS FOR TREADABILITY

If your yard's the kind that's actively engaged in family life, providing a place for picnics, a play area for backyard sports, and running room for Rover, you'll want to cover it with turf that can take a tromping and stand right back up for more. See what they're growing on the local soccer fields and refine that idea for your own use—anything that can stand up to an endless stream of kids in cleats should be able to handle your family's weekly croquet tournament! For cool-season lawns (and throughout most of the transition zone), tall fescue mixed with Kentucky bluegrass is a sports-field favorite, while warm-season athletes work out most often on Bermuda grass, usually overseeded with ryegrass for extended durability and color.

HOW DRY I AM

Thirst can send a turf into dormancy almost as quickly as extreme heat or cold, leaving your lawn looking sad and brown. If your landscape tends to be droughty, and especially if watering is limited by local restrictions or the depth of your well, you'll want to go with grasses that can make it through dry times on their own. Look for varieties that have been selected for drought resistance, and give them top-notch care to keep your lawn looking keen and green on what Mother Nature provides:

For warm-season lawns: Bermuda grass hybrids, blue grama grass, buffalo grass, zoysia grass.

For cool-season lawns: fine fescues, Kentucky bluegrass (selected varieties), perennial ryegrass (selected varieties), tall fescues.

MILDEW CHASER

Damp foliage—whether it's leaves of grass or of other landscape plants—is an invitation to the pesky fungi that cause powdery mildew. If your lawn develops a powdery white coating, take aim with this tonic to set things right.

4 chamomile tea bags
2 tbsp. Murphy's Oil Soap®
1 qt. of boiling water

Put the tea bags in a pot, pour the boiling water over them, and let the tea steep for an hour or so until the brew is good and strong. Let it cool, then mix in the Murphy's Oil Soap. Pour the tea into a 6 gallon hose-end sprayer, and treat the affected area with this tonic every week to 10 days until the mildew is history.

WHERE IT'S WET

Damp places in your landscape tend to cause less trouble in terms of immediate turf death—we're usually watering our lawns instead of drying them with a hair dryer! But some grasses, such as buffalo grass, perform better in dry soil than in wet. And constant moisture encourages all kinds of disease problems that you and your yard really don't need. In general, cool-season grasses are more tolerant of soggy sites, since they tend to need more watering than the drought-tolerant, warm-season turfs. As with shady spots,

★ CUSTOM COMBOS ★

IF you're having trouble finding a top-quality grass seed mix that's right for your yard, select the straight turf varieties that have the features you want. Then follow the percentages in my premium mix recipes to create the perfect custom seed combination for your lawn.

Cool-Season Premium Mix

This is my favorite combo for lawns on the north side of the "bluegrass line," the imaginary border between cool-season and warm-season regions.

- **40 percent Kentucky bluegrass**
- **40 percent perennial ryegrass**
- **20 percent creeping red fescue**

'Tweener Premium Mix

For lawns in that tricky ol' transition zone, I like to mix up some warm- and cool-season seeds for a yardful of green almost all year long.

- **25 percent Bermuda grass**
- **25 percent buffalo grass**
- **25 percent Kentucky bluegrass**
- **25 percent perennial ryegrass**

Warm-Season Premium Mix

Whipping up a seed mix for the sunny South can be a bit tricky—these warm-season grasses tend to be real ground-grabbers that don't always earn top marks for sharing. But this combo of Bermuda, carpet, and Bahia grass gets along pretty well, especially since they're all starting out together, and it grows into a durable, drought-tolerant lawn.

- **40 percent Bermuda grass**
- **30 percent carpet grass**
- **30 percent Bahia grass**

good culture is important to help grass survive in less-than-ideal conditions:

1 You may need to mow more fre-quently in moist areas to handle the increased growth of well-watered turf.

2 Remove clippings to keep them from matting down and keeping the grass wet, promoting disease problems.

3 Prune other plants in the area to improve air circulation to help the grass blades dry during the day.

4 If standing water is a common occur-rence, consider replacing the grass with more suitable plants. See Chapter 15 for some not-so-soggy ideas for planting in wet locations.

FIGHT PESTS WITH ENDOPHYTES!

For a lawn that bugs won't want to bite, grow grass that contains the fungi known as endophytes. Found in rye-grasses and fescues, endophytes produce a substance that repels some pests and is toxic to others. Chinch bugs, sod webworms, billbugs, and armyworms are among the pests that will leave your lawn alone if it's protected by endophytes. But, don't use endophyte-enhanced grasses in places where livestock will graze—they're toxic to cattle, sheep, and pregnant mares.

A WEED BY ANY OTHER NAME

One of the features that allows lawn grasses to form dense, soil-holding sod is their ability to spread. But plants that spread vigorously can also move into places where they're not wanted. Don't be surprised if you see your favorite turf type on a list of pesky weeds: After all—a weed's just a plant that's out of place, and some grasses' ground-grab-bing tendencies can earn them epithets instead of admiration when they roam beyond the lawn. Here's what to look out for:

Annual ryegrass. This one makes the list because of its coarse texture and clumping nature; it also grows quickly and needs frequent mowing. Useful in certain situations, but beware of seed mixes that contain more than 20 percent annual ryegrass, unless you want to deal with bare patches in years to come.

Bent grass. Even though it takes lots of pampering to keep it looking good, bent grass spreads aggressively via stolons and can crowd out other grasses, leaving bare patches in your lawn.

Bermuda grass. Tough and drought-tolerant, Bermuda grass can get into trouble for its pushy ways—especially if you have a Bermuda grass lawn and your neighbor doesn't (or didn't).

Starting from Scratch

I like to tell folks that starting a lawn is like baking a cake: When you follow the recipe, use quality ingredients, and perform all of the steps in just the right way, you're all but guaranteed to turn out a first-class product. Well, here's my down-home recipe for a lawn you'll be proud to call your own!

★ Out with the Old!

Have you just bought a spanking-new tract house on a lot that's been stripped as bare as a newborn baby's bottom? Then skip this section and proceed directly to "Prep That Plot!" on page 53. On the other hand, if you're faced with an ill-kept, weed-choked yard that's too far gone to save, you'll have to get rid of that unwanted cover before you launch your new lawn. Here's a slew of simple ways to make that very vexing vegetation vamoose.

CUT IT OUT!

One surefire way to bid good-bye to weeds and scruffy grass is to manually remove them to expose the bare soil underneath. There are several ways to perform this maneuver. Your best choice depends on how much time and energy you want to expend—or pay someone else to expend. Here's a rundown:

Dig it! If your future lawn is tiny—and you could use a little exercise—grab a sharp, square-ended spade and remove the old sod by hand. Just cut through the turf and lift it off in whatever size chunks you can manage easily. Then, use those slices to fill in any low spots in your yard. Just pile up as many as you need, upside down, sprinkling a handful of organic fertilizer or compost on each one, and saturate the finished pile with my Super Soil Sandwich Dressing (see page 53). When the time comes to plant your new lawn, sow seed or lay sod right on top. Over time, the old grass will decompose and enrich the soil.

A slicer is nicer. At least it's a whole lot easier than digging by hand! Just rent a sod cutter from your neighborhood equipment-rental establishment, and have at it. The machine will slice off the terrible turf just below the roots and leave you with a clean slate of bare soil— and of course, a nice supply of turf slabs to fill low spots.

Till we don't meet again. Rototilling can be a risky proposition because, rather than improving your soil, it can actually damage its structure (see "Serve a Super Sandwich" on page 52). Still, it *is* the quickest, easiest way to bid good-bye to weeds and battered turf grass. Just be sure to rent a tiller that has the rotating tines in the rear, behind the tires, because guiding a model with the tines in the front is like trying to control a runaway freight train! Till your lawn area to a depth of 6 to 8 inches, rake out all the old grass and weeds, then till again. Repeat the process until all the green stuff is gone.

OH, NO YOU DON'T!

If you're aiming to establish a lush crop of grass on a plot that was teeming with weeds, don't stop after stripping off the old cover. With just a little more time and effort, you can make sure those weeds don't make a return appearance in your new green scene. I've used both of these techniques with great success on fall-planted lawns:

Fallowing is an old-time farming trick, and the way it works is simple: You force dormant weed seeds to germinate, then kill the newly emerged plants. At the same time, you bring the roots and stolons of perennial weeds to the surface, where they quickly die of dehydration. Like a lot of classic methods, fallowing takes a little persistence, but it sure pays off in the long run! Here's all you need to do: In early to mid-summer, till your patch. Before you know it, weeds will sprout up all over the place. Till them under. When the next crop appears, till it under, too. Repeat the process until baby weeds no longer rear their little green heads above the soil. (One or two more times should be all it takes.)

Solarizing involves calling on a higher power—namely Ol' Sol—to kill off weed seeds and roots in the upper 6 to 8 inches of soil (the root zone for turf grass). As a bonus, you'll also kill soil-dwelling fungi and the larvae of many lawn and garden pests. Here's my simple five-step plan:

STEP 1. Till your lawn area to a depth of 6 to 8 inches.

STEP 2. Spread a 1- to 2-inch layer of fresh (not dried) manure on the site, and work it in well.

STEP 3. Water well, then let the ground settle overnight.

STEP 4. Cover the plot with a sheet of clear, 3- to 6-mil plastic, and pile rocks or soil around the edges to keep it in place. Patch any holes or tears that you find. Make sure the plastic has some slack in it, so it can puff up (instead of blowing away or even bursting) when the heat starts rising.

STEP 5. Wait about six weeks—longer, if the weather's cool. Then, take off the plastic and water the soil. Now sow your seed, spread your sod, or plant your plugs.

SERVE A SUPER SANDWICH

Of all the methods I know to prepare a plot for a new lawn—or any kind of planting, for that matter—this is the hands-down winner. Not only does it solve your old turf and weed woes with almost no effort, but it also gives your grass a good, rich starter bed that keeps improving over time. Here's how to gain new ground in seven easy steps:

1 Mark off your site. Use stakes and string if you want a straight-sided lawn; otherwise, just arrange a long rope or a garden hose in the shape you want. (Note: If your site needs serious grading or drainage improvement, have that work done *before* you make your "sandwich.")

Super ★ Secret

Waste Not, Want Not

No matter which method you use to banish unwanted grass and weeds, don't let 'em go to waste! Just toss 'em, clinging soil and all, into a compost bin. In no time, that debris will cook up into what gardeners call "black gold"—the best lawn food you could ask for. (For my super-simple compost-making method, see "Home Cookin'" on page 65.)

2 Mow down tall weeds and grass, but don't fuss with short growth—and don't do any digging.

3 Lay a 1-inch-thick layer of newspapers over the site, overlapping the edges as you go. Then wet them down so they don't blow away.

4 Spread 1 to 2 inches of organic matter over the papers. Whatever you can come by easily will do the trick; leaves, pine needles, dried grass clippings, seaweed, and shredded paper will all work like a charm.

5 Cover the organic matter with 6 to 8 inches of good topsoil and compost, mixed together thoroughly.

6 Saturate the lawn-to-be with my Super Soil Sandwich Dressing (at right) and go about your business.

7 Start your lawn! If you can let the "sandwich" cook over the winter, so much the better. But if it's spring and time's a-wastin', just wait two weeks, then sow your seeds, or lay your sod right on the papers.

The secret ingredient in this no-dig recipe is the bottom layer of newspaper. First off, it smothers the existing weeds and old, scruffy grass. More importantly, it draws earthworms by the zillions, and they will break down the organic matter into good, fertile, lawn-pleasing soil faster than you can say "Go to it, guys!"

SUPER SOIL SANDWICH DRESSING

When you've got your "ingredients" stacked up, top off your super soil sandwich with this zesty condiment. It'll kick-start the cooking process and get your new lawn off and running.

- **1 can of beer**
- **1 can of regular cola (not diet)**
- **½ cup of ammonia**
- **¼ cup of instant tea granules**

Mix all of these ingredients in a bucket and pour the solution into a 20 gallon hose-end sprayer. Then spray your "sandwich" until all the layers are saturated. Let it cook for at least two weeks (longer if you can), then get sowin'!

Prep That Plot!

If you're lucky, all you'll have to do to prepare the ground for your new lawn will be to rake away some rocks and rubble, and doctor up the soil (see page 96 for my super-simple soil-improvement plan). On the other hand, you may be, um, blessed with a site that won't produce more than a few scraggly blades without serious regrading and big-time drainage help. Whether your lot falls into one of those two extremes, or somewhere in between, you'll find the answers to all your pre-planting perplexities right here.

ON THE LEVEL— MORE OR LESS

You may *think* you'd like to have a lawn that's as flat as a pancake, but take it from me, you wouldn't—not even if you plan to host cutthroat croquet tournaments all summer long. What you really want is a lawn that slopes gradually away from your house on all sides. Otherwise, rainfall and water from your sprinkler will eventually find their way into your basement or, if you have no basement, into the walls and floorboards of your home, sweet home. And the money it'll cost you to repair that damage could buy a *lot* of croquet mallets!

So how gradual is gradual? Well, to ensure the optimum health and well-being of your grass and your home's foundation, your lawn should slope away from the house by no more than ¼ inch

for every foot, or roughly 2 feet for every 100 feet. Here's a simple way to figure out how well your ground measures up:

STEP 1. Starting at the base of your house, pound a 3-foot stake 1 foot into the ground.

STEP 2. Measure out 100 feet from that spot and drive a second 3-foot stake 1 foot into the ground.

STEP 3. Tie a string at the bottom of the stake by the house. Then stretch it to the second stake, and attach it so the string is level. (Use a carpenter's level to be sure.)

STEP 4. Now, at the second stake, measure the distance from the string to the ground.

STEP 5. Repeat the process in several places along your house wall if the slope varies. (And, of course, take measurements on each side of the house where you plan to install a lawn area.)

MAKE THE GRADE

If your measurements show that your ground is only slightly off-kilter (see "Do the Numbers" at right), you'll save a lot of money—and get some great exercise—by grading the soil yourself. But before you start moving your yard around, make sure you won't hit buried "treasure" in the form of power, water,

Yankee Doodle Data

Do the Numbers

So you've measured the lay of the land.
What does that information tell you? Here's what.

IF THE SLOPE:	IT TELLS YOU THAT:
Measures 3 to 6 inches upward and up to 2 feet downward	The ground needs only slight leveling. If you have the time and energy, you can easily do the job yourself.
Measures any distance upward and more than 2 feet downward	This is going to mean a lot of work, possibly with heavy equipment, and you'll probably want to hire a pro. At the very least, seek professional advice before you proceed.
Is so steep you don't even want to think about it	Forget about grass. Have the hillside carved into terraces, or plant soil-grabbing groundcovers (see Chapter 15 for some good candidates).

sewer, gas, or fiber-optic cable lines. If you're not sure of their location, call city hall or your local utility company: A representative will be delighted to come over and mark the routes for you. Likewise, if you have a private water supply, check your surveyor's map to pinpoint your well and septic tank, as well as all water lines and drain fields. Can't find your map? Mosey on over to your town's building department; they should have copies on file.

GEAR UP

Like any job, shaping the land goes a lot easier if you have the right tools. Whether you buy, borrow, or rent them, gather these handy helpers:

Gloves. Don't use your everyday garden gloves for this job. Instead, slide your paws inside the thickest, sturdiest leather work gloves you can find. Your local hardware store should have exactly what you need.

Level-checkers. A carpenter's level and an 8-foot-long, 2- by 4-inch piece of wood will do the trick here.

Rake. Forget the 18-incher that's hanging in your toolshed. Instead, get your hands on a special lawn rake that has a long handle and a 3-foot-wide steel head. You'll be able to move twice as much soil with each swoop.

Shovel. Or, maybe two. A sharp, squared-off blade is a must for scooping soil out of a wheelbarrow and for smoothing out rough spots on the ground. But if the soil you're moving is hard or compacted, a pointed shovel will make digging easier. Just make sure both your digging tools have long handles. Believe me, your back will thank you!

Super ★ Secret

Ah, Just Right!

Ground is easiest to level when it's moist and light. If you haven't seen rain in a while, water the soil slowly to a depth of 6 to 8 inches several days before you plan to start work. On the other hand, if your soil is soggy, sit back and wait a few days before you dig into it.

Wheelbarrow. You may be tempted to go with a big contractor's 'barrow because it will let you haul the soil away in larger batches, but take it from me: Unless you're used to heavy manual labor, pushing those monster loads will have you tuckered out in no time flat. The job will go faster if you use a smaller, garden-size model that you can easily handle.

GET TO GRADIN'

The process couldn't be simpler. All you do is dig up soil from the higher spots, toss it into your wheelbarrow, and move it to lower areas. (Depending on how steep your slope is, you may have to haul in new topsoil to level the site.) Then, once you've relocated the soil, use the big rake to smooth it out, and remove dirt clumps and any debris that you find.

As you go along, chart your progress by laying the two-by-four on the ground and setting the level on top. That way, you'll know whether or not you're getting the gradual slope you want. As an

extra guideline, I also like to leave the stakes and string in place from the initial testing phase (see "On the Level—More or Less" on page 54).

IS IT DRAINING YET?

Grading your soil will help ensure good drainage for your new lawn, but it may not be the be-all and end-all. To find out for sure, try this test: Water your newly sculpted soil thoroughly, or just wait until the end of the next good rain. Then two or three hours later, check back. If the H_2O hasn't drained away, you've got more work to do. Loading your soil with organic matter will solve minor drainage problems (for more about this garden-variety magic bullet, see page 65), but if you've got water hanging around for hours after a short, heavy rain, stronger measures are called for. How strong? That's a question best answered by a professional. Before you try any do-it-yourself tactics, get an opinion from a landscape architect or landscape contractor (see "Help!" on page 59). A short consultation now, at an hourly rate, could save you megabucks down the road.

TRY THIS AT HOME, KIDS

If your lawn-to-be has only a few isolated soggy spots, this 12-step program can work wonders.

STEP 1. Corral your supplies. You'll need: ★ agricultural fabric (available at farm-supply stores and garden centers) ★ carpenter's level ★ crushed stone or gravel ★ perforated, 4-inch-diameter pipe (either white PVC or black ADS) ★ shovel ★ string ★ tape measure ★ wooden stakes.

Star-Spangled
Lawn Lore

If all this hard lawn labor is starting to seem like more trouble than it's worth, here's a little incentive to keep you going (especially if you're planning to sell your house before too long): Statistics show that a well-maintained landscape adds as much as 15 percent to the value of a home!

STEP 2. Find a safe place below the level of your lawn for the water to drain. If you have a stream or pond on your property, that's perfect. Otherwise, a storm drain or roadside ditch will work just fine. If you have none of these dandy devices, build a dry well at the lowest spot in your yard (see "Oh, Well" on page 58 for the easy instructions).

STEP 3. Using rope or a garden hose, lay out a drainage pattern on your lawn, leading from the lowest point in the problem area to the drainage site. Then buy enough perforated pipe to cover the distance.

STEP 4. Dig a trench that's about 18 inches deep and 12 inches wide, sloping downhill between the two points. Aim for a drop of about ¼ inch for every foot, or roughly 2 feet for every 100 feet.

STEP 5. To test the slope, drive a stake into the soil at either end of the trench. Run a string between the two stakes, and use your carpenter's level to measure the drop between them.

STEP 6. When you've got the slope just so, add about 3 inches of crushed stone or gravel to the bottom of the trench.

STEP 7. Set the pipe on top of the stone, making sure any joints are fastened good and tight.

STEP 8. Cover the pipe with agricultural fabric to keep soil and other debris from clogging the perforations. (Tuck the cloth under the pipe at its uphill opening.)

STEP 9. Pour 6 more inches of stone or gravel over the pipe.

STEP 10. Refill the trench with the soil.

STEP 11. Water the area thoroughly to help the ground settle.

STEP 12. Check back in a week or so. If you find any low spots, fill them in before seeding or sodding your new lawn.

ENERGIZING ELIXIR

There's no doubt about it, installing a lawn is mighty thirsty business— and it always has been. Before fancy sports drinks came on the market, folks took a break from their outdoor chores by sitting under a shady tree and sipping this restorative drink.

> 2½ **cups of sugar**
> 1 **cup of dark molasses**
> ½ **cup of vinegar (either white or cider)**
> 1 **gal. of water**

Mix all of the ingredients together in a big jug. Then get your lawn crew out of the sun, and pour everyone a nice, tall, refreshing glass.

OH, WELL

You've got your drainage system all figured out. Now you need a safe harbor for all that unwanted water. (After all, you don't want it ending up in your neighbor's yard or in your cherished rose beds!) If nature hasn't blessed you with a ready-made repository, don't fret. Just trot off to the closest building-supply store, buy a 55-gallon drum, and cut off both ends. Then proceed as follows:

1 Pinpoint the spot, below the level of your lawn, where you want your drainage pipe to empty. Bear in mind that, in order for the well to function, the bottom of the drum needs to rest *below* any layer of rock or hardpan in the soil. If you're not sure whether your chosen location has this obnoxious stuff, test it by driving a metal pipe 4 or 5 feet into the ground. If you meet with no resistance, you're good to go.

2 Dig a hole that's wide enough to hold the drum, and deep enough so that its top will be below your drainage pipe.

3 Set the drum into the hole, pour in small stones and gravel up to the rim, and position the pipe so that it drains into the drum.

4 Fill the space around the drum with more stones and gravel. Then cover

Star-Spangled *Lawn* Lore

During World War II, our whole country pitched in for the war effort—including turf grass scientists. They spent a lot of time and money developing varieties that were tough enough to handle the wheels of an incoming plane, so our boys could have safe, grass-cushioned airstrips to land on.

the top with landscape fabric and about 2 inches of topsoil.

5 Let the soil settle for about a week, and you'll be ready to roll.

HELP!

If your yard is big, or your drainage woes are major, don't even think of tackling the problem yourself. Instead, turn the job over to a landscape architect or landscape contractor. So what's the difference between these two pros? Just this:

A landscape architect has a university degree in the subject, and a license to operate in your state. The best ones are also members of the Society of Landscape Architects. This is the person to call if:

★ Your lawn area covers 2,500 square feet or more

★ It includes very steep slopes, big boulders, or a lot of rock formations

★ You have a number of trees, walkways, or separate buildings that will remain in place

★ You want a comprehensive landscape plan

★ You suspect that your drainage problems are *really* serious, and/or

★ You lack the time, inclination, or experience to recruit and supervise a landscape contractor

A landscape contractor, whether hired by you or your architect, performs the actual work, or supervises a crew of sub-contractors. Your state may not mandate licensing, but make sure that anyone who does work for you *is* licensed and also bonded and insured to operate heavy equipment. Many landscape contractors provide design services and consultations, but don't expect the knowledge or sophistication of a landscape architect. This is the way to go if:

★ Your property is small- to mid-size and does not cover dramatic terrain

★ Your design aspirations are simple and straightforward

★ You know the nature of the problem and exactly what needs to be done

★ You feel comfortable negotiating with and supervising a contractor

GO WITH THE FLOW

Of course, you don't *need* to fix the low, wet spots in your lawn. Depending on the size, location, and degree of dampness, consider one or more of these options:

★ Forget growing turf grass in that spot and plant moisture-loving trees, shrubs, or perennials (for some dandy choices, see "Some Like It Damp" below).

★ Cover the area with a deck, gazebo, or elevated walkway.

★ Build a swimming pool.

★ Install a reflecting pool or fountain.

★ Go whole hog and turn the site into a water garden or fishpond.

For more on alternative lawns, for both dry and wet sites, see Chapter 15.

★ SOME LIKE IT DAMP ★

HERE'S a super-simple way to handle soggy spots in your lawn: Give grass a pass, and devote those mini-swamps to plants that thrive with wet feet. There are literally hundreds to choose from. Here's a small sampling of my favorites:

TREES

European larch (*Larix decidua*)

Pin oak (*Quercus palustris*)

Red maple, a.k.a. swamp maple (*Acer rubrum*)

Water oak (*Q. nigra*)

Weeping willow (*Salix babylonica*)

SHRUBS

Bog rosemary (*Andromeda polifolia*)

Red-twig dogwood (*Cornus stolonifera*)

Rosebay rhododendron (*Rhododendron maximum*)

Sweet pepperbush (*Clethra alnifolia*)

Winterberry (*Ilex verticillata*)

PERENNIALS

Bog arum (*Calla palustris*)

Cardinal flower (*Lobelia cardinalis*)

Goatsbeard (*Aruncus dioicus*)

Japanese iris (*Iris ensata*)

Marsh marigold (*Caltha palustris*)

Queen of the prairie (*Filipendula rubra*)

☆ The Key to It All

Like any other garden, that garden of grass that we call a lawn can only be as healthy as the soil it's growing in. Now, in this book I can't begin to tell you everything there is to know about soil. What I will do, though, is share some of my best secrets for giving your turf the best home its ever-lovin' roots could ask for!

THREE FOR THE SHOW

Before you start making up your lawn's future bed, it helps to understand a few terms that soil doctor-uppers toss around. After all, it's hard to fix a problem when you're not even sure what to call it!

Texture and structure. These refer to the relative amounts of sand, silt, and clay particles the soil contains. Sandy, or light, soil drains quickly and doesn't hold nutrients well. Clay, or heavy, soil holds nutrients like a dream, but it also holds water *too* well. When it gets wet, it sticks together like two sides of a peanut butter sandwich—and that's hostile territory for almost any plant's roots. Your average grass's dream soil is loam: a nicely balanced mix of sand, silt, clay, and organic matter. Loam holds a good supply of nutrients, doesn't dry out too fast, but doesn't stay soggy either. In other words, the perfect soil for great grass.

pH. Short for potential of hydrogen, pH measures acidity and alkalinity on a scale that runs from 0 (pure acid) to 14 (pure alkaline), with 7 being neutral. Turf grasses vary considerably in their pH preferences (see "pH Ranges for Grasses" on page 65), and it's crucial that you cater to their tastes. That's because when a plant is growing in soil that is either too acid (a.k.a. sour) or too alkaline (a.k.a. sweet) for its liking, it can't absorb the nutrients it needs.

Rich and lean. These have to do with fertility. Rich soil is chock-full of all the nutrients and trace elements that grass plants need for healthy growth. Soil that's lean has a low supply of nutrients. (For the complete story on serving your lawn a healthy diet, see Chapter 5.)

PUT IT TO THE TEST

The first secret to building lawn-pleasing soil is to know what you're starting off with. For just a couple of bucks, you can buy a do-it-yourself testing kit at any garden center. Don't do it! That approach is fine when you're planting a bed of annual flowers, but something as permanent—and expensive—as a new lawn deserves the red-carpet treatment. Send a soil sample to your Cooperative Extension Service or a private testing lab, and request a thorough analysis. If the guys and gals in white lab coats are up to snuff,

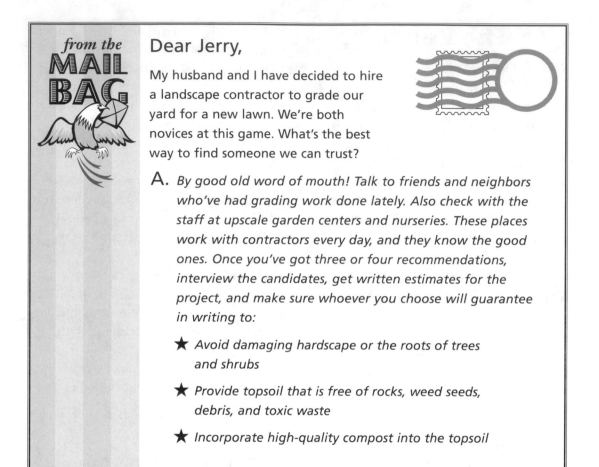

from the
MAIL BAG

Dear Jerry,

My husband and I have decided to hire a landscape contractor to grade our yard for a new lawn. We're both novices at this game. What's the best way to find someone we can trust?

A. *By good old word of mouth! Talk to friends and neighbors who've had grading work done lately. Also check with the staff at upscale garden centers and nurseries. These places work with contractors every day, and they know the good ones. Once you've got three or four recommendations, interview the candidates, get written estimates for the project, and make sure whoever you choose will guarantee in writing to:*

★ *Avoid damaging hardscape or the roots of trees and shrubs*

★ *Provide topsoil that is free of rocks, weed seeds, debris, and toxic waste*

★ *Incorporate high-quality compost into the topsoil*

---

they'll give you the full scoop on both major and minor nutrients, as well as soil texture, organic matter, and even the presence of toxic materials, like lead. (That won't make much difference for turf grass, but it's something you'll want to know about if you ever decide to convert part of your lawn area to a food garden. For more on that score, see Chapter 15.) The lab will send you complete instructions for taking your samples, but here's the basic, six-step routine:

STEP 1. Scrape away any gravel, vegetation, or litter from the test site.

STEP 2. Using a hand trowel or (easier yet) a bulb planter, remove a thin slice of soil about 6 inches deep.

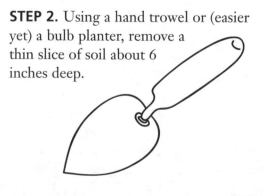

STEP 3. Collect samples from a dozen or so different places within your intended lawn area.

STEP 4. Pour all of the soil samples into a big bowl or tub and stir 'em up until they're well blended.

STEP 5. Scoop out a cup or two of soil and pour it into a plastic bag or the container provided by the testing lab.

STEP 6. Label the container with your name, address, phone number, and the date the sample was taken.

PASS WITH FLYING COLORS

As we all learned in high-school chemistry, the accuracy of any scientific test depends on the quality of the sample. These tips will put you on the honor roll:

Give them a hint. When you send in your soil sample, include a note saying what type, or types, of grass you'll be planting. That way, the lab folks can provide you with specific recommendations for nutrient and pH levels (see "pH Ranges for Grasses" on page 65).

Make it one of a kind. Take your samples only from places where you intend to grow turf grass. If your landscaping plans include other plants, such as trees, shrubs, or perennial flowers, have the soil in each of those areas tested separately—and label each sample accordingly.

Keep it clean. A stick, stone, or scrap of mulch can skew the test results. In fact, even using a trowel that has iron in it can throw off the nutrient reading. So work with a noniron tool, fish out all foreign objects before you pack up your samples, and don't take your sample for at least 30 days after you've added fertilizer or soil amendments of any kind.

Think "roots." You want to know what's in the soil that your grass's roots will be feeding from, so don't dig deeper than that. Stay within the top 5 to 6 inches of soil.

Super ★ Secret

A Snowball's Chance in...

When you want to find out in a hurry what kind of soil you have, use this simple test: Scoop up a handful of moist (not wet, not dry) soil and roll it into a ball, just like a snowball. Then squeeze it hard. If it crumbles into a little pile that looks like cake crumbs, count your blessings: You've got loam. If the ball just packs more solidly, like a cannonball, your soil is mostly clay. And if you can't even form a ball with your soil, it's too sandy.

Think "normal." Don't take a sample from an atypical spot, like the place your home's former owners had a compost pile, or a low area where puddles form after a rain.

THE RESULTS ARE IN!

When your soil test report comes back, it may show that you need to alter your soil's pH to grow the kind of grass you want. The standard fixer-uppers are ground limestone (generally referred to as "lime") to raise the pH, and sulfur to lower it. Whichever of these wonder "drugs" you use, apply it with a hand-held, broadcast spreader. And for best results, keep these tips in mind:

★ Add these soil adjusters only in the spring or fall, *not* during the lazy, hazy, crazy days of summer.

★ Don't apply more than 10 pounds of sulfur or 50 pounds of limestone per 1,000 square feet at any one time. If you need to add more than that, do it over two or more seasons, so the pH change is gradual.

★ Do the job on a calm day, and be sure to wear a mask, gloves, and protective eye gear. (You want that stuff in the soil, not in your eyes, mouth, and skin pores!)

★ When it comes to adding lime or sulfur, more is not better. Use only as much as you need to achieve the desired results. (See "pH Ranges for Grasses" at right and "The Quick-Change Artists" on page 66.)

FOR THE LONG HAUL

When you need to change your soil's pH, sulfur and limestone are surefire fixes, all right, and they work fast. But they don't last forever. Furthermore, they do nothing to improve the overall health of your soil. Eventually you'll have to crank up the old spreader all over again. You'll get longer-lasting results—and improve the content and structure of your soil at the same time—if you add the right kind of organic matter. Here are some of my favorite sweet and sour condiments.

To lower your soil's pH, add:

• Aged sawdust or wood shavings

• Coffee grounds

• Cottonseed meal

• Fresh manure

• Oak leaves

• Pine needles

To raise your soil's pH, add:

• Bonemeal

• Ground clam, oyster, or other seashells

• Ground eggshells

• Wood ashes

Yankee Doodle Data

pH Ranges for Grasses

You might think a soil pH that suits one kind of grass would suit 'em all. Not so! Just like any other plants, turf grasses differ in their preferences. Here's a rundown of optimum levels.

GRASS	PH RANGE	GRASS	PH RANGE
Bent grass	5.5–6.5	Fescue, chewings	5.5–7.5
Bermuda grass	5.0–7.0	Fescue, creeping red	5.5–7.5
Bluegrass, annual	5.0–7.5	Fescue, tall	5.5–7.5
Bluegrass, Canada	5.5–7.5	Grama grass	6.0–8.5
Bluegrass, Kentucky	6.0–7.5	Redtop grass	5.0-7.5
Bluegrass, rough stock	5.5–7.5	Ryegrass	5.5–8.0
Buffalo grass	6.0–8.5	St. Augustine grass	6.0–8.0
Centipede grass	4.0–6.0	Wheat grass	6.0–8.5
Clover, white	5.5–7.0	Zoysia grass	4.5–7.5

THE BE-ALL AND END-ALL

Any kind of organic matter works wonders for your soil. It helps sandy types retain water and nutrients better, loosens up clay, and keeps loam in tip-top shape. Best of all, it acts like a military recruiter, enlisting the aid of your lawn's allies, such as earthworms, beneficial bacteria, and all sorts of good-guy bugs.

HOME COOKIN'

Of all organic matter, compost ranks at the top of the heap. Gardeners have always sworn by this "black gold," and now scientific research is proving just how miraculous this stuff is. Not only does it provide nutrients for your plants, but it also kills foul fungi and bad bacteria while encouraging the good varieties of both.

You can buy compost by the bag or the truckload at most garden centers. And, in many communities, the public works department composts yard and garden waste and will give you all the finished product that you care to cart away. But, just like Mom's apple pie, your own home-cooked compost beats anybody else's, hands down. And the process is a lot easier than some folks make it out to be.

Yankee Doodle Data

The Quick-Change Artists

The easiest way to change pH is to add either sulfur (to make alkaline soils more acidic) or ground limestone (to make acidic soils more alkaline). This chart shows how much of either one you'll need, depending on the type of soil you've got.

LIMESTONE NEEDED (LB. PER 1,000 SQ. FT.) TO RAISE pH*			
pH CHANGE FROM/TO	SANDY SOIL	LOAM	CLAY SOIL
4.0–6.5	60 lb.	161 lb.	230 lb.
4.5–6.5	51 lb.	133 lb.	193 lb.
5.0–6.5	41 lb.	106 lb.	152 lb.
5.5–6.5	28 lb.	78 lb.	106 lb.
6.0–6.5	14 lb.	41 lb.	55 lb.

SULPHUR NEEDED (LB. PER 1,000 SQ. FT.) TO LOWER pH*			
pH CHANGE FROM/TO	SANDY SOIL	LOAM	CLAY SOIL
8.5–6.5	46 lb.	57 lb.	69 lb.
8.0–6.5	28 lb.	34 lb.	46 lb.
7.5–6.5	11 lb.	18 lb.	23 lb.
7.0–6.5	2 lb.	4 lb.	7 lb.

*If you need to add more than 50 pounds of limestone or 10 pounds of sulfur per 1,000 sq. ft. at any one time, apply it over two or more seasons.

First get yourself a commercial compost bin—it's neater, more attractive, and faster-acting than using an old-fashioned pile. (My favorite is my Speedy Spinning Composter—available at www.jerrybaker.com—which looks like a big tire on a stand.) Then toss in whatever yard waste, kitchen scraps, or other organic matter comes your way. Just be sure to keep the ratio at roughly three high-carbon ingredients (the "browns") for every one that's high in nitrogen (the "greens"). That's important, because if you have too much carbon, the compost could take donkeys' years to cook. Too much nitrogen, and it'll give off an odor that will make the neighbors show up at your door with clothespins on their noses. Once you've got your supply simmerin' along, give the bin a spin once a week to mix the ingredients. Every month or so open the bin door, and spritz your future treasure with my Compost Booster (at right).

COOL IT!

What's that? You say that balancing ingredients and spinning a compost bin is not your idea of fun, even if the end product is worth its weight in gold? Then try cold composting. In this method, anaerobic bacteria break down the organic material without the help of oxygen, so no turning is required. And there's no need to worry about the ratio of browns to greens. All it takes are some plastic garbage bags, yard waste or shredded grocery bags, and whatever "greens" your kitchen can offer up (see the list on page 68). Just one word of warning: When you open the bags, you'll be hit with a potent odor, but it will disappear as soon as the compost is exposed to the open air. Here's my cold-composting method:

STEP 1. Fill a large plastic garbage bag with a mixture of chopped leaves, grass clippings, and vegetable scraps. For every couple of shovelfuls of bulky,

carbon-rich material (see the browns and greens list on page 68), add some of my Compost Activator/Accelerator (available at www.jerrybaker.com), or a few cupfuls of my Compost Booster (below).

STEP 2. When the bag is nearly full, sprinkle a couple of quarts of water over the contents, and mix until all the ingredients are moist.

STEP 3. Tie the bag shut, and leave it in an out-of-the-way place where the temperature will stay above 45°F for a few months. For faster results, roll or shake the bag every few days. That's all there is to it!

BLUE PLATE SPECIAL

COMPOST BOOSTER

To give your compost a boost, spray it once a month with this bracing beverage.

- 1 can of beer
- 1 can of regular cola (not diet)
- 1 cup of ammonia
- ½ cup of weak tea water*
- 2 tbsp. of baby shampoo

Mix all of these ingredients together in a bucket and pour the solution into a 20 gallon hose-end sprayer. Saturate your compost to really keep things cookin'!

To make weak tea water, soak a used tea bag in a solution of 1 gal. of warm water and 1 tsp. of dishwashing liquid until the mix is light brown. Store leftover liquid in a tightly capped jug or bottle for later use.

THE WHOLESOME INGREDIENTS

Whether you use the hot or cold method to whip up your compost, here's your grocery list:

The browns: chipped twigs and branches ★ dead flower and vegetable stalks ★ dry leaves and plant stalks (including dry grass clippings) ★ hay ★ pine needles ★ sawdust ★ shredded paper ★ straw

The greens: coffee grounds ★ eggshells ★ feathers ★ flowers ★ fresh grass clippings ★ fruit and vegetable scraps ★ green leaves or stems ★ hair (pet or human) ★ manure ★ seaweed ★ tea bags ★ young weeds

Water, Water Everywhere

Of course, you don't really *need* a built-in irrigation system. It's perfectly possible to grow lush, green turf using only portable sprinklers or a garden hose. Heck, I even have a friend in Manhattan who waters her postage-stamp lawn with an old-fashioned watering can! Still, you *may* have plenty of good reasons for taking a systematic approach to delivering H_2O, and if you're going to go that route, the best time to install the equipment is *before* you plant your new lawn.

THINK IT THROUGH

An in-ground irrigation rig is a big investment, even if you do all the digging and set-up work yourself. In my humble opinion, if you have a small lawn, or you live in a place where you only have to water your grass a few times each summer during dry spells, an underground system is a waste of money. (For the complete lowdown on watering, see Chapter 6.) On the other hand, if you have a whole lot of grassy ground, or if summertime showers are few and far between in your neck of

---

Super ★ Secret

Calculating Compost

When you're starting a new lawn in good loam, you want to spread a 1-inch layer of compost over the entire area. For soil that's high in either sand or clay, go with a 2-inch layer. If you're taking that meal from your own cooker, it's a snap to figure out those serving sizes. But if you're buying your supply, you need to do a little calculating, because compost is generally sold by the cubic yard. Here's the equation:

3 cubic yards of compost = 1-inch layer per 1,000 square feet of lawn area.

the woods, this wonder of modern technology is a blessing from the gods. Here's why:

- It sends up a light, misty spray that the soil absorbs slowly. Conversely, above-ground sprinklers deliver water unevenly, and often in larger quantities than your grass really needs. The result: A *lot* of water gets wasted.

- With an in-ground system, you figure out exactly where the water needs to go, then set the output heads and forget 'em. But portable sprinklers are the very dickens to direct. It's all but impossible to position them so they don't send water gushing onto your driveway and sidewalks, or streaming off down the street. (Do you *really* want to pay good money to irrigate concrete?)

- The water from an in-ground system goes straight into the soil, where it's quickly absorbed by the grass roots. Much of the H_2O from sprinklers goes right into the air, where it evaporates faster than you can say "Holy cow! What a water bill!"

- With an automatic controller on your irrigation system, you can water your lawn wisely and well, even when you're off getting your kicks on Route 66. You can also install moisture-sensing devices that halt the flow when Ma Nature is quenching your turf's thirst just fine, thank you.

Star-Spangled *Lawn* Lore

Here's a not-so-trivial trivia question for you: How much water does an acre of actively growing grass need each week? For most varieties of turf grass, the sobering answer is 27,154 gallons. That's enough to fill a 20- by 30-foot swimming pool to a depth of 6 feet.

SOLD!

If you're planning to put your house on the market before long, here's another reason to consider investing in an irrigation system: Properly installed and maintained, it will add to the value of your real estate, just like a sunroom or a spankin' new kitchen.

WHO—*ME*?

Most likely, you'll want to leave the final part of an irrigation system installation to a pro. But if you enjoyed playing with Tinkertoys® as a kid, you can probably put the pipes in place with no trouble at all. Granted, the job is more complicated than grading soil and sowing grass seed, but the folks who make and sell the equipment can walk you through the process step by step. You can also find some excellent do-it-yourself manuals devoted entirely to installing and maintaining all kinds of watering systems. I'm not going to go into great detail here, but I will give you a brief overview. That way, even if you intend to hire a pro for this project, you'll be able to speak the language and ask savvy questions.

FIRST THINGS FIRST

Before you reach for the Yellow Pages to find an irrigation system dealer, a few preparatory steps are in order:

Call the authorities. Some communities have laws that regulate home irrigation systems. The folks at your town clerk's office or local utility company can tell you everything you need to know *before* you shell out cash for a lot of pipes and valves. And while you've got them on the phone, if you don't already know the whereabouts of any underground power or sewer lines, now's the time to ask.

Put on the pressure. To function successfully, an irrigation system needs water pressure of 40 to 50 pounds per square inch (psi). Your water company, or a plumber who's worked on your pipes, should be able to tell you whether your house's pressure measures up.

Figure the flow. In order to choose components that will work with your

plumbing, you need to know how much water flows through your pipes, measured in gallons per minute (gpm). To find the magic number, just set a 1-gallon bucket under an outdoor spigot, turn the water on full blast, and note how many seconds it takes the pail to fill up. Then divide that time into 60, and you'll have your gpm. For example, let's say it takes 30 seconds for the water to fill your bucket. Sixty divided by 30 equals 2, so your flow rate is 2 gallons per minute.

Map your territory. Before you (or anyone else) can install your irrigation system, you need a map that shows your yard and everything in it. Your drawing needn't be a work of art, but it must be drawn to scale on graph paper (for instance, 1 inch equals 10 feet), and be as accurate as you can make it. In addition to all your lawn areas and other plantings, be sure to include your house, garage, and other buildings, as well as sidewalks, driveways, and fences.

Share it. Whether you plan to install your own system or hire a pro to do the job, take your map to an irrigation equipment dealer (you'll find them listed in the Yellow Pages) and ask for help figuring out the most effective spray patterns and the placement for the lines and sprinkler heads.

Yankee Doodle Data

Bits and Pieces

With very few exceptions, when you've seen one irrigation system,
you've seen 'em all—at least as far as components are concerned.
Here's a roster of the usual working parts.

CRUCIAL IRRIGATION SYSTEM PARTS	WHAT THEY DO
Control valves	Regulate the water that flows from your home's water main through the pipes (see below) and on to the sprinkler heads. The valves, in turn, connect to the controller or timer (below).
Manifold	A group of valves that connect the water source to the system and control the flow of water to each circuit.
Controller or timer	Tells the control valves when to open and close. (Like a computer, though, the controller won't do what you want it to unless you program it properly. So make sure you know how to work the thing before you install it!)
Pipes	Carry the H_2O (of course). They're made of polyvinyl chloride (PVC), with one exception: the above-ground copper pipe that connects the system to your water meter. All the pipe you use should be the same diameter as that of your house's service line—generally either 3/4 or 1 inch.
Pipe fittings	Let you connect pipes in various configurations. For instance, some fittings turn corners, or send pipes up or down to avoid obstacles in the soil. Some fittings are designed to join two different materials, for instance, PVC and copper. (This is the gizmo you'd use to attach your underground lines to the one on your water meter.)
Risers	Vertical pipes that connect the underground lines to the sprinkler heads. They can be rigid or flexible, long or short, depending on the function of the sprinkler head.
Sprinkler heads	This is where the fun begins. They're the gadgets that actually send the water where you want it to go. They come in more shapes and sizes and adjust to more spray patterns than you can shake a garden hose at. You can buy all-purpose heads, or ones specially designed for vegetable gardens, flower beds, shrubs—and, of course, lawns.
Moisture sensors	Connect to the automatic controller, and they do exactly what their name implies: read the water content of the soil. So, for instance, if the controller is set to water on a particular morning, but it's just rained the night before, the sensor says, "None today, thanks!"

TOOL TIME

Once you have all the pipes, valves, and other working parts you'll need, assemble this collection of tools and supplies:

- Hacksaw
- Mallet
- Measuring tape
- Pipe tape
- Pipe wrench
- PVC primer
- PVC adhesive
- Stakes
- String
- Utility knife

DOWN TO BUSINESS

Once you know where all the pieces will go, getting them into the ground is a simple, seven-step process. Here's what you need to do:

STEP 1. Gather your gear. In addition to the working parts of your system, you'll need the supplies listed in "Tool Time" (above). You'll also need a good, sharp trenching shovel or, better yet, rent a trench-digging machine. (Look under Equipment Rental in the Yellow Pages.)

STEP 2. Check your pipe. To be extra-safe, lay out the PVC pipe in the configuration shown on your map. If you're a few feet shy of what you need, you want to learn that now, not when you're nine-tenths of the way through the job!

STEP 3. Make an outline. Using a mallet, drive stakes into the ground along the route your pipes will take, and run string from one to another.

STEP 4. Dig your trenches—or hire someone else to do it. The beds your pipes will lie in need to be 8 to 10 inches deep and 3 to 4 inches wide. Depending on how much ground you need to cover, that can mean a lot of work, even with the aid of a trench-digging machine.

STEP 5. Lay it out. Set all your pipes into the trenches and piece them together—but don't glue yet! At this stage, you just want to make sure everything fits the way it's supposed to.

STEP 6. Measure, cut, and fit. Using your hacksaw, cut the pipes to the right lengths, scrape off any rough edges with a utility knife, and clean both ends of each pipe.

STEP 7. Glue it all together. When you're sure everything fits as it should, brush primer on the outside of the standard pipe and inside the flared end. Then apply the adhesive to both primed areas, and shove the two ends together. Finally, give the pipes a one-quarter turn and hold themtogether for 20 to 30 seconds so they'll set.

HAND IT OVER

From this point on, the job gets a lot trickier, and a slipup or two could wind up costing you big bucks. My advice is to let a pro take it from here. This is what needs to be done:

★ Hook up the system to your water supply by tapping into an outside faucet, the main supply line, or the basement water meter.

★ Fasten all the pipes to the control valves at the manifold.

★ Install the risers. This entails cutting into the pipe at the site of each place where you want a sprinkler head, inserting a tee fitting, then attaching and adjusting the riser so that the sprinkler head will be at or just above ground level.

★ Flush the system to wash any dirt from the lines and check for leaks in the pipes and fittings.

★ Screw the sprinkler heads to the risers, and adjust them so they're pointed in the right direction.

Super ★ Secret

How <u>Not</u> to Do It Yourself

If you'd rather not install your own irrigation system, seek professional help in the same way you would for any other major home-improvement job: Gather recommendations, preferably from friends you trust, and interview at least three candidates. Ask each one for a price estimate and the names of three previous clients. Then call all of them! (After all, anybody can come up with *one* good reference.) And, of course, insist on a written contract, signed by you and the contractor.

★ Install the automatic controller or timer—a task that includes running electrical wires through a waterproof pipe.

★ Finally, test the system. If the water flows and the pipes don't leak, fill in the trenches and you're ready to roll.

☆ Ladies and Gentlemen, Start Your Lawns!

You've got your soil graded, amended, and draining like a dream. Your irrigation system is ready for action. Now all that hard work (or the outlay of all that hard-earned cash) is about to pay off. It's time to get that new lawn up and growing! In this section I'll walk you through the whole process for sowing seed, laying sod, and planting plugs or sprigs.

SEED LABEL LINGO

When you trot off to the garden center for your grass seed, you might get a kind of sticker shock—not from the price tag, but from the label on the bag. It's got enough confusing terms and numbers on it to make your head spin! Well, they're not idle words and phrases; once you understand what they mean, they'll help you get the best buy for your lawn, and your wallet. Here's how to decipher that label:

Type of grass. In big letters at the top, the label should tell you whether you're holding a bag of one species, such as red fescue or Kentucky bluegrass, or a blend of several.

PROFESSIONAL GREEN GRASS SEED MIXTURE

LOT# M55-8-006

PURE SEED		GERMINATION	ORIGIN
29.60%	FAMOUS KENTUCKY BLUEGRASS	85%	WASH.
27.86%	DASHER II PERENNIAL RYEGRASS	90%	OREGON
19.65%	VIVA KENTUCKY BLUEGRASS	85%	WASH.
19.48%	RED FESCUE CREEPING TYPE	90%	CANADA

AMS-527　　　　TEST DATE: 1/2005

01.64	%	OTHER CROP SEED
01.75	%	INERT MATTER
00.02	%	WEED SEED

NET WT. 1 LB. (0.45 KG.)

NOXIOUS WEEDS: NONE FOUND

Variety. In general, named varieties of grass are far superior to generic types, or strains. A quality blend won't simply list, for instance, bluegrass and perennial ryegrass. It will specify, say, 'Viva' Kentucky bluegrass and 'Palmer II' perennial ryegrass.

Origin. When the quantity of a seed measures more than 5 percent of a mixture, its state or country of origin must be declared. That's because traditionally, some regions produce better grass seed than others. Also, seed from certain locations may carry less risk of disease than seed from other places.

Germination percentage. This tells you the percentage of seed that germinates under optimal conditions. Steer clear of any seed that predicts less than 75 percent germination for Kentucky bluegrass and 85 percent for all other types.

Pure seed percentages. These numbers reveal the proportion of grass by weight. So, for instance "97 percent" on a 1-pound box means it contains 15.52 ounces of grass seed.

Other crop seed. Just like the rest of us mortals, lawn seed growers are not perfect. Generally, a tiny percentage of nongrass seed finds its way into any mixture, but a good one shouldn't contain more than 0.5 percent.

Weed seed. Like other crop seed, the proportion by weight should be less than 0.5 percent.

Inert matter. Chaff, soil, and other non-growing stuff fall into this category. It's harmless, but you sure don't want to pay good money for it! Don't buy a bag that contains more than 4 percent of it.

Noxious weeds. By law, manufacturers must 'fess up if their seed contains any notoriously bothersome weeds, such as field bindweed. In this case, the *only* number to settle for is a big, fat 0!

Test date. This is the equivalent of the freshness date on a carton of milk and, as with milk, fresher is better. You want a batch of seed that was tested no longer than a year ago.

IS IT TIME YET?

Just like any other kind of plant, grass germinates best and grows strongest within a certain temperature range. So what does that mean in terms of your calendar? Just this:

★ Plant warm-season grasses in the spring, as soon as the soil temperature hits 78°F, but before it reaches 85°F.

★ Plant cool-season grasses in late summer or fall when ground temps measure between 60° and 75°F. If that's the time you plan to be off seeing the U.S.A. in your Chevrolet, do the job between April and mid-May.

Star-Spangled *Lawn* Lore

Putting all that terminology on grass seed labels is not just a good idea—it's the law! And it has been since 1939, when the Congress of the United States decided that folks had a right to know what they were planting in their yards. The result was the Federal Seed Act, which decreed that every package of grass seed sold within our borders must contain the information you're reading about in this section.

NOT BREEZIN' ALONG

No matter how much you're itchin' to tickle your toes in your new turf, wait for a nice, calm day to do your sowing. Otherwise, before you know it, that seed will be breezin' along with the breeze!

FIRST THINGS FIRST

Before you sow your seed, you need to perform these preliminary maneuvers:

Give your soil a snack in the form of starter fertilizer. This is a sort of turf grass version of baby food that's designed to help new grass grow stronger, faster. If you've had your soil analyzed by a testing lab (see page 61), they may have advised you on the amount or type of starter fertilizer to use. If not, you'll find many good brands at the garden center. Just make sure the one you choose has roughly equal amounts of nitrogen, phosphorus, and potassium. Apply it according to the manufacturer's directions two or three days before seeding. Then follow up with a good dose of my Soil Prep Tonic (below).

Energize your seed with my Seed Starter Tonic (see page 187). Believe it or not, you'll speed up the germination rate by about 75 percent!

SOIL PREP TONIC

Two to three days before you sow grass seed, treat your soil to this terrific tonic. It'll get the seed off and growing in no time flat.

> **1 cup of fish emulsion**
> **½ cup of ammonia**
> **¼ cup of baby shampoo**
> **¼ cup of corn syrup**

After you've applied your starter fertilizer (see page 75) to the area, mix these ingredients in a 20 gallon hose-end sprayer and saturate the soil.

SUPER SOWING IN SEVEN SIMPLE STEPS

With your soil and your grass seed both jump-started, you're finally ready for the big day. So slather on the sunscreen, grab your spreader, and get going! Speaking of spreaders, if you've got just a pint-size lawn, a hand-held model will work just fine. For a bigger plot, use a rolling model. The garden center where you bought your grass seed may rent—or even lend—you one. Then, just fill 'er up with seed and proceed as follows:

STEP 1. Divide your seed in half, and sow the first batch in parallel rows across your prepared seedbed.

STEP 2. Sow the second half of the seed in rows at right angles to the first. The result will be a pattern of squares, like a checkerboard.

STEP 3. Lightly rake the whole area to make sure there's ample contact between seed and soil. Go easy, though! Otherwise, you'll bury some seed so deep it'll never come up, and you'll have bare spots in your new lawn.

STEP 4. Go over your newly seeded lawn with a water-filled roller. (The same outfits that rent spreaders may supply these dandy devices, too.) Or, if your lawn is tiny, just lightly tamp the seed with the back of your rake.

Yankee Doodle Data

How Much Seed Do You Need?

You might think that the more seed you sow, the thicker and lusher your lawn will be. Not so fast! Too many seeds in the ground will only result in too many baby grass plants fighting for life. Many of them will die, and the survivors will be weaker than if you'd planted fewer seeds and nursed them well. When you buy your seed, use this chart as a guide. It also tells you how long you'll need to wait before your little greenlings start poking their heads above the soil. (Bear in mind that times will vary, depending on the weather and location.)

GRASS TYPE	POUNDS OF SEED (PER 1,000 SQ. FT.)	DAYS TO GERMINATION
Bahia grass	6–10	18–28
Bent grass	½–1	6–14
Bermuda grass	1–2	10–30
Buffalo grass	2	14–30
Centipede grass	1–2	14–30
Fescue, fine	3–5	7–14
Fescue, tall	6–10	7–12
Kentucky bluegrass	1–2	6–28
Ryegrass, annual	6–8	5–10
Ryegrass, perennial	6–8	5–10

STEP 5. Give the whole plot a light misting with my Spot Seed Tonic (see page 103). Don't let the name fool you; this excellent elixir is not just for patching up bald spots; it provides get-up-and-grow power for new lawns, too, so mix up a batch and put it to good use.

STEP 6. Apply an appropriate mulch (see "Magical Mulch" on page 78 for some good choices).

STEP 7. Last but not least, bring on the H$_2$O! Either turn on your new, in-ground irrigation system, crank up your portable sprinklers, or haul out the garden hose. Whichever delivery method you use, turn the nozzle to a fine spray or mist, and soak the newly seeded area until the soil is moist to a depth of 6 inches. And don't guess about the distance—measure it with a ruler!

MAGICAL MULCH

Applying the right mulch to a newly seeded lawn is a crucial step. It helps conserve moisture in the soil; protects the small, frail seeds from harsh sun and drying winds; and helps keep weeds and bad bugs at bay. Later, as they decompose, organic mulches also provide food for young grass plants to grow on.

There are many good mulches to choose from. Like other facets in the lawn-tending game, the best one for you depends on your circumstances. Peruse the roster below, and pick the one that's right for your part of the country, your lawn's size and terrain, and your pocketbook:

Burlap, cheesecloth, or commercial mulching cloth. This is the way to go when you've seeded a steep bank. Unlike fine-textured stuff like compost or straw, they'll stay put on even the steepest slope (as long as you pin them in place, of course). The grass will grow right through any of these materials, and because they're organic, they'll break down over time. That means you won't have to scale the cliff to remove them!

Compost. As you might imagine if you've read the earlier parts of this chapter, this is my favorite organic mulch. Finely screened, it makes the best nursery a baby lawn could ask for.

Spun-polyester row covers. These do a terrific job of protecting seeds from wind and sun, as well as villainous insects, hungry birds, and floating weed seeds. Hold the sheets in place with pins made from old wire coat hangers, and remove the covering when the grass is 1 inch high. Row covers are expensive, but if you have a tiny lawn, in my opinion, they're well worth the investment. And they are reusable, so after they've performed their grassy guard duty, you can put them to work in your vegetable garden or pass them on to friends.

Straw. The classic baby blanket for newborn lawns. It's generally inexpensive and easily available. One 60- to 80-pound bale will cover a 1,000-square-foot lawn. Shake out the straw thoroughly before you spread it, then put down a layer that's no more than ¼ inch thick. That way, it will break down quickly and you won't have to remove it once the seeds have germinated. Just two words of warning: Make sure the straw you buy is guaranteed to be weed-free. And whatever you do, don't use hay—it's always chock-full of nasty weed seeds!

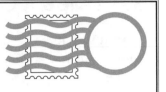

Dear Jerry,

I do a lot of woodworking, and I have a big supply of sawdust. Can't I use that to mulch my new lawn?

A. *Some folks like to mulch with sawdust, but I avoid it like the plague—and peat moss, too—for one reason: Both of them tend to form a crust that's very difficult, and often impossible, for young grass to penetrate. So, do those baby plants a favor and give them a softer blanket. Meanwhile, pour your sawdust into your composting bin! It's a top-notch "brown" (see page 68).*

WATER AND WAIT

From the time you've sown your seed until the grass starts growing, you need to keep the soil surface moist. That may mean you need to water two, three, or even four times a day. When you do that, just give it a light misting. Don't saturate the soil, or you'll issue an open invitation to foul fungi and other dastardly diseases (for more on that crowd, see Chapter 10). Once the green shoots appear, start giving them more water, less frequently. The exact timing will vary with the weather, but my basic watering routine is this:

★ Once a day for two weeks

★ Every other day for two weeks

★ Every third day for two weeks

After that, if the grass is growing well, begin watering it as you would a mature lawn. (You can read all about that routine in Chapter 6.)

As for the waiting, that's what you need to do until you can mow your fledgling lawn. If you cut into those plants before they've developed a good, healthy root system, you could kill them. At best, you'll give them a shock that will slow their rate of growth. You could also expose the tender tissue to too much sun, and the stems could be burned to a crisp. The right time for this rite of passage depends on what kind of grass you've got. Cool-season types, like Kentucky bluegrass, can be mowed when they're 2½ inches tall. Warm-season grasses, like Bahia, are ready for the first cut when they've grown to 3 inches high.

FIRST TIME'S A CHARM

At least it should be. When you're ready to mow your new lawn for the first time keep these pointers in mind:

Cut high. Adjust your mower's deck to a higher-than-normal level. You want to remove no more than ⅓ of the grass blade's height.

Cut sharp. Make sure your blades have a razor edge. A ragged cut from a dull blade can be fatal to new grass.

Cut dry. Always mow young grass when the soil is on the dry side. Otherwise you could end up pulling the roots right out of the ground!

For more on mowing, see Chapter 7.

☆ Starting from Sod

Although launching a lawn from sod is neither the cheapest nor the easiest way to do the job, it does have its advantages (see "Seed or Sod?" on page 82). For most folks, the biggest plus is the most obvious one: instant gratification. You can wake up in the morning with nothing but bare soil outside your window, and go to bed that night with the breeze wafting over fresh, beautiful turf. But that green scene won't leap into place all by itself. There are a *few* things you need to do to make it happen. For starters, you need to prepare the site exactly as you would for seed, beginning with clearing away any weeds and scruffy grass, and ending with grading the soil and installing an irrigation system if you want one.

A-SHOPPING WE WILL GO

Buying sod is a little trickier than buying grass seed. (For one thing, there are no truth-in-labeling laws for strips of sod.) To get the best batch possible, follow this plan:

Find your source. Either ask a good local nursery to recommend a supplier, or look in the Yellow Pages under Grass or Sod. When you make the call, ask what kinds of grass they sell, and which type or types they'd recommend for your location. (Be sure to describe your site, particularly in terms of sun and shade levels.)

Insist on fast service. Just like sweet corn, sod starts to go downhill the minute it's cut. If it's at all possible, find a sod farm that will cut the strips to your order and ship them to you immediately. Failing that, go with the supplier who will guarantee the freshest possible crop delivered to your doorstep at a time when you'll be there to receive it. (You don't want this stuff to arrive some morning while you're at work and sit around, high and dry, until you get home that evening.)

Take a trip. Unless your source comes so highly recommended that you have no doubts about the product, pay a visit to the grower and ask to see an order that's about to go out. Then compare its condition to those qualities in the Sod-Selection Checklist (below).

SOD-SELECTION CHECKLIST

Once you're face-to-face (so to speak) with a crop of sod, it's a snap to tell whether it's fresh and rarin' to grow in your yard. Here's what to look for:

★ Soil that's moist, but not sopping wet. Avoid sod with edges that are dry, cracked, or starting to curl up. Likewise, say no to anything with saturated soil; it'll be too heavy and messy to work with.

★ Grass that's consistent in length and an even shade of bright green. Yellowish or brownish patches and uneven grass height are both signs that the sod has been stored too long.

★ Sod that holds together when you handle it. The total thickness—including blades, roots, and soil—can vary anywhere from 1 to 3 inches, so don't just go by sight. Move it around as though you were working with it.

★ Sod that feels cool to the touch. If it's warm, that means it's been sitting around too long, and it's already starting to go belly-up.

★ IT'S WHAT'S DOWN ★ UNDER THAT COUNTS

IN theory, just about any kind of grass can be grown as sod, but how well it'll perform in your yard is another story. Of course, you want to get a type that's right for your region and your microclimate (see Chapter 2). Beyond that, bear in mind that the grasses that make the best sod are those that spread by stolons or rhizomes. Most warm-season grasses fall into this category. And on the cool side of the aisle, so do bent grass and Kentucky bluegrass. On the other hand, rye and fescues tend to make terrible sod because they spread by bunching and seeding.

Yankee Doodle Data

Seed or Sod?

If you want an instant lawn, sod is the way to go. But it will cost you plenty. On the other hand, not all grass types are available as sod, and then seed is your better choice. Confused? Don't worry—this comparison of pros and cons should help.

STARTING FROM SEED

PROS	CONS
It costs a whole lot less than sod.	To ensure good germination, you have a small weather window for sowing (see "Is It Time Yet?" on page 75).
You have an almost limitless choice of grass types.	Seed is fragile and easily lost to hungry birds, heavy wayward winds, or fluctuating temperatures.
Seed-sowing is light, easy work that just about anyone can do.	You need to wait two to three months before you can use a newly seeded lawn.
Seed will keep in its closed bag for up to a year after its testing date.	A lawn growing from seed demands almost constant care, including watering two or more times a day, for at least the first four weeks.

STARTING FROM SOD

PROS	CONS
You get almost instant gratification. Within two or three weeks you can romp and play on it.	Sod costs two to three times more than grass seed.
You can lay it any time, except during the dead of winter.	Laying sod is hard, heavy, grimy work. Installing even a mid-size lawn can require the labor of four or five people.
It stays put on a slope, rather than washing away as seed is prone to do.	Once sod is delivered, you need to install it within 24 hours—sooner if at all possible—and you need to water it thoroughly about an hour after it arrives on your doorstep.
Because it's already reached its teen years (lawnwise) when you buy it, it's dense enough to crowd out any weed seeds.	Although nearly all sod farms grow varieties suited to the local climate, most of them offer only two types: one suitable for shade and one for sun.

★ No bugs in sight! Even if you've gone to a sod farm with a world-class reputation, it never pays to take chances. Check the underside of a few strips for any signs of grubs or other insects.

TIMING ISN'T EVERYTHING...

But it *is* something to consider. Although sod can be installed at any time the ground is not frozen solid, you'll get the best lawn results if you follow this rule of green thumb:

Warm-season grasses: fare best when you lay the sod during either early spring or early fall.

Cool-season grasses: take hold best when planted in mid- to late spring, just before the temperature heads skyward.

HOW MUCH IS ENOUGH?

Sod comes in strips that are generally 6 to 8 feet long, 2 feet wide, and 1 to 3 inches thick, depending on the type of grass. It's sold by the square foot. Here's how to figure out how much to order:

For a square or rectangular lawn, simply multiply length times width. So, if your space measures 30 by 40 feet, you'll need 1,200 square feet of sod. Just to be on the safe side, though, order another 10 percent so you don't run short. In this case, that would be 1,200 + 120, for a total of 1,320 square feet.

To figure the area of an oddly shaped lawn, follow the directions on pages 114 and 116. And because it's all but impossible to measure weird shapes with total accuracy, order 10 to 20 percent more sod than you think you need.

SAVVY SODDING IN SIX SIMPLE STEPS

If it's at all possible, this is one job you want to do on a cool, overcast day, for two reasons: The sod will stay moist longer, and you'll stay fresh longer. And get as much help as you can—this is one labor-intensive job! Fortunately, though, it's a straightforward process. Here's all there is to it:

1 Two or three days before your sod's delivery date, give your soil a dose of starter fertilizer, followed by my Soil Prep Tonic (see page 76).

2 Lay the first strip along a straight edge, like a walk or driveway, pushing the edge of the sod tightly against the hard surface. If your lawn has no straight lines, run a string across the middle, attached to a stake at either end. Then line up the sod with the string.

3 Set the remaining pieces in what bricklayers call a "staggered bond," so that the joints of one row fall in the

middle of solid strips on each of the flanking rows. Push the ends of the strips together tightly, leaving no gaps where the sod could dry out. As you go along, pat down the sod with your rake to encourage good contact with the soil.

4 When you come to the end of a row—or encounter any obstacle, like a flower bed or walkway—cut the sod to fit using an ultra-sharp knife.

5 After you've arranged all of your sod strips, go back and fill the seams with compost or potting soil. Don't use tiny pieces of sod, which will dry out and die, or garden soil, which could contain weed seeds.

6 Roll your new creation with a roller that's filled halfway with water, working perpendicular to the sod strips.

AND THEN...

As new lawns go, sod might be low-care, but it's not no-care! For the first month or so, water every morning until the soil is soaked 6 to 8 inches below the surface. And every three weeks, give that turf a dose of my All-Season Green-Up Tonic (at right) to encourage faster, thicker growth. Also, avoid the temptation to romp on your new playground right away. In fact, you'll earn big-time dividends in the long run if you stay off the grass for four to six weeks. Crucial test: When you can't lift the corners, you've got yourself a *lawn!*

☆ Give Your Lawn a Plug

Plugging, also known as spot sodding or sprigging, is the process of planting small chunks of sod at intervals in the soil. It's used almost exclusively in the South, where the Princes of Plugs are Bermuda, St. Augustine, and zoysia grass.

Super★Secret

Steeply Does It

When you're dealing with an incline, lay the sod horizontally across the hill—never in the same direction as the slope. On very steep slopes, hold the sod to the soil with wooden pegs. Two pegs per strip should do the trick. Use 1- by 2-inch boards that are about 12 inches long, and pound each one 8 inches or so into the soil. That'll leave you a good handhold when you want to pull the stakes out, about four months later.

10 STEPS TO PERFECT PLUGGING

Here's everything you need to know to plant plugs:

STEP 1. Level and grade your ground, as you would for seeding or sodding (see pages 54–56).

STEP 2. Apply starter fertilizer and my Soil Prep Tonic (see page 76).

STEP 3. The day before planting, give the site a good soak with the hose.

STEP 4. Buy plugs in small plastic trays, or cut them from a piece of thick, healthy sod. Make sure that each plug is 2 to 4 inches in diameter, with plenty of soil on its roots.

STEP 5. On planting day, mist the soil lightly, so that it's damp but not sopping wet.

STEP 6. Stretch out strings, and fasten them to stakes to keep your planting rows straight.

STEP 7. Using a bulb planter, dig holes 6 to 12 inches apart along each row.

STEP 8. Set a plug into each hole and firm the soil around the root ball.

STEP 9. Level the ground with a rake, then roll with a water-filled roller.

ALL-SEASON GREEN-UP TONIC

This tonic will get your newly sodded lawn off to a sensational start—and supercharge the rest of your green scene.

> 1 can of beer
> 1 cup of ammonia
> ½ cup of dishwashing liquid
> ½ cup of liquid lawn food
> ½ cup of molasses or corn syrup

Mix all of these ingredients together in a large bucket, and pour the mixture into a 20 gallon hose-end sprayer. Then spray your lawn (and every other green, growing thing in your yard) to the point of run-off every three weeks throughout the growing season.

STEP 10. Keep the soil moist until the roots are established. Five weeks after planting, give those babies a drink of my Plug Feeding Tonic (below).

FEED THOSE PLUGS!

This Plug Feeding Tonic will get your plugs off to a flying start: Take 3 pounds of Epsom salts and mix with one bag of lawn food (enough for 2,500 square feet). Then apply at half the rate recommended on the fertilizer bag, using a hand-held broadcast spreader. *Note: If you're using a synthetic, slow-release fertilizer, spread the salts and lawn food separately (see "From the Mailbag" on page 120).*

Shape It Up

Have you just bought a house with a yard that's seen better days? Or maybe your old home ground is starting to lose its youthful good looks. (After all, lawns *are* like people and after a certain age, it doesn't take much to start that slide!) Unfortunately, you can't simply send your grass off to a fancy spa for a few weeks. But with my timely tips, you *can* put the healthy glow back in its cheeks, er, blades.

 ## Dispatch Thatch!

Of all the woes that can befall a lawn, thatch just might be the nastiest. Not only does it keep water, air, and nutrients from reaching the grass roots, but it also provides a dandy home for hordes of bad-guy bugs and dastardly diseases. (For more on that score, see Chapters 9 and 10.) Well, here's my foolproof plan for sending thatch to the Great Beyond—and keeping it there!

JUST WHAT *IS* THATCH, ANYWAY?

Contrary to what a lot of folks think, thatch is *not* a thick blanket of old grass clippings. Rather, it's a tightly woven layer of stems, roots, and crowns—both living and dead—that form between the grass blades and the soil line. These plant parts are high in *lignin*, a type of organic material that breaks down more slowly than most. But in a healthy lawn, it *does* break down. (Grass clippings, on the other hand, are made up mostly of cellulose, which decomposes in a flash.)

A little thatch is actually a good thing. A layer of half an inch or so cushions the turf, guards against soil compaction, and helps conserve moisture in the soil. The trouble starts when the stack of stuff builds up beyond that level.

HOW'D IT GET IN *MY* LAWN?

Before you attack the thatch that's in your lawn, it helps to know what caused it to get out of hand in the first place. That way, you'll be better able to keep it under control later. Any or (more likely) a combination of these factors can lead to big-time thatch trouble:

Frequent, shallow watering. It encourages both roots and organic debris to concentrate near the soil surface. For everything you need to know about watering, see Chapter 6.

Infrequent, too-high mowing. Whether you rake up the clippings or not, this practice contributes to thatch. I must confess that I don't entirely understand the reason, but research has

confirmed it time after time. Turn to Chapter 7 for the whole nine yards on mowing your yard.

Overfeeding. This makes for overly lush growth, especially if you're using potent chemical fertilizers. The lush growth then leads to thicker thatch. In particular, supplying more nitrogen than your grass needs will quickly lead to trouble. You can read all about good, healthy lawn diets in Chapter 5.

Herbicides, fungicides, and pesticides. All of these potent weapons kill the soil-dwelling critters (including droves of earthworms and billions of microscopic organisms) that break down organic material and prevent thatch buildup. For my commonsense pest, disease, and weed control policies, see Chapters 9, 10, and 11.

Improper soil pH. It prevents grass from absorbing the nutrients it needs, and can also discourage the presence of earthworms. See Chapter 3 for the lowdown on soil testing, and the pH preferences of popular turf grasses.

Heavy clay soil. Not only clay, but any type of soil that's become compacted lacks openings through which air, water,

Yankee Doodle Data

The Wrong Stuff

Thatch can build up on any lawn, in any part of the country.
But some grasses are more tangle-prone than others. Here's how the turf
grass gurus rate the various types.

THATCH RISK	WARM-SEASON GRASSES	COOL-SEASON GRASSES
High	Bermuda grass	Creeping bent grass
High	St. Augustine grass	Colonial bent grass
High to medium	Zoysia	Kentucky bluegrass
High to medium	Centipede grass	Fine fescues
Low	Carpet grass	Perennial ryegrass
Low	Bahia grass	Tall fescue

nutrients, and decomposing organisms can travel. That, in turn, means that grass roots migrate to the surface in search of sustenance, and the underground breakdown squad dies off. The result: big-time thatch, double-quick. My soil-doctoring procedures in Chapter 3 will help you conquer clay. For loosening up compacted ground, see "Boy, That's Hard!" on page 91.

THE CRUCIAL TEST

When you walk across your lawn, does it feel spongy underfoot? That's your first clue that thatch is beginning to build up. To find out how big the trouble is, grab a sharp knife or a bulb planter, and remove a slice of turf (blades, roots, and

soil). Then examine the thatch. You'll see a layer of brownish material that bears a striking resemblance to peat moss. If it's between $\frac{1}{2}$ and 1 inch thick, aerating—the same process you use to break up compacted soil—should solve the problem (see "Fork It Over!" on page 94). Anything thicker than that calls for full-scale dethatching.

TAKE IT OFF!

With dethatching, as with most lawn chores, you can choose from two modes of operation: manual and mechanical. These are the tools you'll need:

Thatching rake. This looks much like a normal rake, except that instead of tines, it has knifelike, double-ended blades. You can buy one at a large garden center or hardware store, and you use it in the same way you'd use a garden rake. There's just one difference: Raking up thatch is a whole lot tougher than raking bare soil! Unless you have a teeny-tiny lawn, take my advice and go the automated route.

Dethatcher. This power tool cuts through the thatch and yanks it out of the ground. It does the job with a fraction of the effort required with a thatching rake. Most equipment-rental yards can supply you with a fine machine. Bear in mind, though, that dethatchers are big, heavy machines, and they can be mighty tricky to handle. If you've never used one before, have the folks at the rental place walk you through the procedure, and follow their instructions *to the letter*. And if you're not accustomed to working with power equipment of any kind, do yourself a favor, and turn the task over to someone who is.

No matter who does the "driving," it's important to get the right dethatcher for your grass. There are two kinds. One has vertically rotating, steel blades; it's just the ticket for thick grasses, like Bermuda and zoysia. For finer grass types, like fescue and Kentucky bluegrass, use a wire-tined model. (If you're uncertain about which machine you need, put this on your questions-to-ask list before you head off to the rental yard.)

IT'S ALL IN THE TIMING

In addition to choosing the right tool for dethatching, you need to perform the chore at the right time, and that depends on where you live. In cool-season territory, you can dethatch your lawn in spring, late summer, or early fall. For warm-season lawns, the window runs from early to midsummer.

Super ★ Secret

Thatchaholics Anonymous

Plenty of garden-variety villains zero in on thatch-plagued lawns, but not one member of this quartet can resist the lure of that luscious layer:

★ Billbugs

★ Chinch bugs

★ Mole crickets

★ Sod webworms

For the full details on bad-guy-bug control, see Chapter 9.

THE GAME PLAN

Schedule your dethatching for a day when your lawn is moist—neither

Star-Spangled *Lawn* Lore

Here are a couple of questions that'll take you right back to grade school: Where's the most fertile, productive soil in this great land of ours? You got it: out there in Midwest farm country, a.k.a. the bread basket of the nation. And do you remember what the pioneers saw when they first reached those rolling prairies? Right again: endless waves of grass, glistening green and gold, and standing higher than an elephant's eye. Now, put two and two together, and consider this: Under all that grass were countless tiny critters, just going about their business and, in the process, creating deep, rich, black soil. And, given half a chance, that's exactly what their descendents will do in your lawn!

sopping wet nor bone dry. Or, if rain clouds haven't passed your way in a while, supply the needed moisture yourself. Then follow this six-step dethatching program:

STEP 1. Flag any permanent sprinkler heads or other immovable, hard-to-see objects that stick up above the ground. (You sure don't want to decapitate those things!) Don't worry about buried pipes or cable lines, though—the dethatcher's blades won't penetrate deep enough to touch them.

STEP 2. Mow the lawn ½ to 1 inch lower than normal.

STEP 3. Run the dethatcher across your lawn in parallel rows. Then make a second pass at a 90-degree angle to the first. If you don't think you got all the nasty stuff, repeat the process.

STEP 4. Rake up the thatch. (Use a garden-variety rake for this part of the job.) If you haven't used pesticides on your lawn, toss all of the debris into your compost bin, or simply dig a hole and bury it (see "Jerry Baker's Hole Improvement Plan" on page 96).

STEP 5. Add any fertilizers or amendments that your soil test called for (see page 64).

STEP 6. Water your lawn.

DON'T PANIC

A major dethatching will leave your lawn in a sorry-looking state, with more bare spots than you can count. Don't fret: As long as you performed the maneuver at the right time, the remaining grass will take off and fill in those gaps before you know it. But if you'd rather not wait for nature to take its course, reseed or plug the bare places now, following my simple seeding routine in Chapter 3.

AND DON'T COME BACK!

Keep thatch away by following this routine:

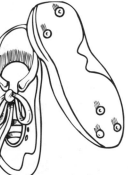

★ Wear golf spikes or aerating lawn sandals whenever you mow your lawn. That way, you'll break up the surface tension barrier between the soil and the blades of grass.

★ Mow on a regular schedule and at the right height for your grass type.

★ Apply my Thatch Blaster Tonic (on page 92) once a month starting in spring, as soon as temperatures stay above 50°F.

★ Water your lawn only when it needs it, and then deliver the H$_2$O slowly and deeply.

★ Don't overfeed. Serve up only the amount recommended for your grass variety. Too much chow of any kind invites thatch, and other problems, too.

★ Just say "No!" to herbicides, pesticides, and chemical fertilizers. They're a prime cause of thatch buildup.

★ Apply half an inch or so of finely sifted compost in spring and fall. It will supply important trace nutrients, improve the soil texture, and even help fend off nasty turf diseases.

★ Have your soil tested every few years. If the results show that it's either more acidic or more alkaline than your grass prefers, add the necessary amendments (see "pH Ranges for Grasses" on page 65).

★ Boy, That's Hard!

All kinds of things can make soil harden up and become what lawn and garden tenders call "compacted." And when that happens, it's bad news for your grass and every other plant that's growing in your yard. Fortunately, you don't need a degree in soil science to tackle the problem. All you need is this collection of tips, tricks, and tonics that are guaranteed to turn the most rock-solid soil back into root-friendly territory.

WHY, OH, WHY?

Just as we saw with thatch, before you set out to repair compacted soil, it helps to know what caused the problem in the first place. Here are some of the prime culprits:

Constant foot traffic. Perhaps the mailman is beating the same path to your box every day, or the kids are cutting across the same corner on their way to the school bus in the morning—and then back again in the afternoon!

Work in progress. Maybe you had a construction crew that spent the summer building your swimming pool—aided by a lot of heavy equipment—or the salt-and-cinder guys rolled their truck across your lawn's edges all winter long. After all, under that snow, how can they tell where the road ends and your grass begins?

Misguided TLC. Here I'm talking specifically about running a heavy roller over an established lawn. A lot of folks do this every spring to produce that velvet-carpet look.

Working with wet soil. Even walking on it makes the particles clump together. If you do it often enough, they stay that way.

Repeated tilling. It compresses the pores so much (especially in clay soil) that it can actually create hardpan—the most severe form of compacted soil.

THATCH BLASTER TONIC

This excellent elixir will help keep your lawn free of nasty thatch all season long.

1 cup of beer or regular cola (not diet)

½ cup of dishwashing liquid

¼ cup of ammonia

Mix all of these ingredients in a 20 gallon hose-end sprayer. Fill the balance of the sprayer jar with water, and saturate the entire turf area. Repeat once a month during the summer, when the grass is actively growing.

GIVE ME A CLUE

Of course, if you notice that your grass is wearing thin in places where people walk frequently, it's a sure bet that the ground below is on its way to rock-hardness. Here are three other clues that you've got a yard full of compacted soil:

1 After a rain, water puddles up on the surface and stays there for hours—maybe days.

2 After you've had the sprinkler on for only a few minutes, water runs off the lawn and down the street.

Yankee Doodle Data

The Old Eyeball Test

Long before there were fancy soil tests, our forefathers and foremothers had a way of telling what kind of soil they had simply by noticing what kinds of wild plants—including some of our peskiest weeds—were growing there. These handy wonders are called "indicator plants," and you can use them, too. Here's what to look for.

INDICATOR PLANTS	SOIL TYPE
Chickweed, plantain	Compacted
Chicory, dandelions	Well draining
Goosefoot, poison ivy	Alkaline
Joe Pye weed, mosses	Poorly draining
Sorrel	Highly acidic

3 The grass is turning brown and losing its get-up-and-grow power (because, of course, water isn't getting to the roots). And in some places, it just plumb disappears.

TALK TO THE TREES

Or rather, take a good look at their roots. If you can see surface roots on your lawn, that's a certain sign that your soil is compacted. How so? Well, normally, a tree's feeder roots roam through the top 4 to 8 inches of soil in search of air, water, and food—the same territory that grass roots call home. When that ground is compressed, the trees send their roots to the surface in their quest for oxygen—and who can blame them?

DRIVE THE POINT HOME

If your lawn shows any, or all, of the symptoms described in "Give Me a Clue" (at left), confirm the diagnosis with this simple test: Just poke a large screwdriver or a sturdy, pointed stake into the ground. If it goes in easily, your grass roots still have breathing room. But if you have to use muscle power to penetrate the soil, you've got work to do. As with other lawn-care chores, timing is important here. You want to test cool-season turf in the fall and warm-season lawns in the spring.

FORK IT OVER!

Your first response to compacted soil should be a technique called aeration. It simply involves poking holes in the soil so that air can reach the grass roots—followed quickly by food and water. On a small lawn, or in isolated spots of a large one, you can easily do the job with aerating lawn sandals, a garden fork or, better yet, a hand aerator. This useful gadget has a long, tined, horizontal bar at the bottom with a handle at either end. To use it, take hold of both handles, shove the tines 6 or 8 inches into the ground, and stand on the horizontal bar. Then rock back and forth a few times to make nice, wide holes in the soil. Pull up the fork, move it along 3 inches or so, and repeat the performance.

BIGGER GUNS

Larger spaces of compacted soil call for heavier gear. Instead of using muscle power, rent or buy a powered, walk-behind aerator that you maneuver just like a lawn mower. These dandy machines come in two types:

Open-tine, or spike aerators: simply punch holes in the soil, the same way the manually operated model does.

Core aerators: pull out small plugs, or cores, of grass and soil and toss them onto the ground. This is a more effective procedure than mere hole punching,

Star-Spangled *Lawn* Lore

Have you just settled into a newly built house? Or maybe you're planning to build one? Well, here's a statistic that will not be music to your ears: Studies show that during the construction process, about one-third of all lawns in the United States become so highly compacted that they have the same hydrologic (that is, water-absorbing) properties as concrete.

although, granted, it does leave your lawn littered with little bits of grassy soil. If these bother you, rake 'em up and toss 'em into the compost bin. Otherwise, just leave 'em be; they'll break down in a flash, adding (you guessed it!) valuable organic matter to the soil.

AERATING 101

No matter which type of aerator you choose to use, the basic operating procedure is the same—and it couldn't be simpler. Here's the process in four easy steps:

STEP 1. Just before you deliver air to your lawn, give it a good drink of my

Aeration Tonic (below). This will make the soil easier to penetrate.

STEP 2. Guide the aerator across your lawn, moving in parallel rows.

STEP 3. Make a second pass, at a 90-degree angle to the first. Aim for 3- to 4-inch spacing between the holes.

STEP 4. Spread a ½-inch layer of compost across the lawn, and brush or rake it into the holes. That's it!

WHAT—*AGAIN*?

Aeration is not a one-time event— not, that is, if you want to keep your soil's channels open and your grass growing great guns. So how often should you deliver fresh air? Well, different folks have different ideas about that, but here are my thoughts on the matter:

★ Any soil that's naturally high in clay should be aerated once a year, without fail.

★ All lawns, even those growing in good, loose soil, benefit from an annual airing-out. But if you follow my Guidelines for Great Ground (below), every other year should do the trick.

★ If your lawn sports a layer of thatch and you've chosen to aerate rather than dethatch (see "The Crucial Test" on page 88), haul out your hole puncher each spring and fall for two years in a row. After that, perform the chore once a year.

GUIDELINES FOR GREAT GROUND

In addition to aerating your lawn once a year, taking these simple measures will help produce soil that'll make your grass's roots think they've died and gone to lawn heaven:

• Mow regularly, on the best schedule for your grass type (see Chapter 7), and leave the clippings on the lawn. Then overspray with my Grass Clipping Dissolving Tonic (page 171).

BLUE PLATE SPECIAL

AERATION TONIC

This fabulous formula will help prevent soil compaction, so water, nutrients, and oxygen can penetrate deep into the turf.

1 cup of dishwashing liquid
1 cup of beer

Combine these ingredients in a 20 gallon hose-end sprayer, and fill the balance of the sprayer jar with warm water. Just before you aerate, spray your lawn to the point of run-off. From then on, spray once a month throughout the growing season to help keep the soil loose and fluffy.

• Spread a ½-inch blanket of compost over your lawn twice a year, in spring and fall.

• Serve up my Aeration Tonic (page 95) once a month during the growing season.

• For isolated trouble spots, or to improve the soil throughout your yard over time, implement my Hole Improvement Plan (below).

• Redirect traffic away from overly traveled routes; otherwise, that soil may never recover! Or simply give in to the passing parade and install paths or walkways (see "I Give Up!" on page 103).

JERRY BAKER'S HOLE IMPROVEMENT PLAN

When you want to provide a new lawn with five-star, grass-roots accommodations, my Super Soil Sandwich beats every other method I know, hands down (see Chapter 3). But what if you want to make your soil grass-pleasin' good *without* getting rid of the existing turf? The answer is simple: Implement my Hole Improvement Plan! This technique is so potent it'll even soften up hardpan. Here's all there is to it: Every time you have some organic matter on hand, dig a hole, toss in your stash, and refill the hole. Then scatter some grass seed on top, or pop in a home-grown plug (see

"Keep on Plugging" on page 102). Or simply wait for the surrounding grass to mosey on over and cover the bare spot.

HOLEY MOLEY!

My hole improvement method isn't just for soil with clay or hardpan headaches. It's a simple way to add get-up-and-grow power to any kind of soil. Best of all, any kind of organic matter will work, in any combination. You don't even need to think about carbon-to-nitrogen ratios as you do when you're cooking compost. (For the lowdown on that, see Chapter 3.) What do you toss into your holes? Of course, grass clippings, fallen leaves, and vegetable scraps are obvious choices, but here are some hole fillers that you might not think of:

★ Brown paper bags

★ Coffee grounds (filters and all)

★ Dead flowers

★ Dirty paper liners from the floor of a birdcage

★ Eggshells

★ Feathers

★ Hair from your (or your pet's) brushes

★ Leftover rice or pasta (minus sauces)

★ Matches (new or used, wooden or cardboard)

★ Newspaper (worms love it!)

★ Paper egg cartons

★ Paper towel and toilet paper rolls

★ Peanut and pistachio shells

★ Sawdust

★ Scraps of cotton, linen, or wool fabric (no synthetics!)

★ Shredded junk mail (skip the glossy paper)

★ Tea bags

★ Tree and shrub prunings

★ Wine corks

★ Wood chips

If you have hardpan, it's best if the hole reaches down to that layer, but if you don't have time to dig that far, don't bother; just go deep enough to cover whatever material you're planning to bury. The depth could range from an inch or so for a couple of tea bags to a foot or more for tree and shrub prunings. As the material decomposes, it will eventually make the soil fluffy, fertile, and rarin' to grow gorgeous green grass.

ANYBODY HOME?

Want to check on how your soil is progressing? Try this unscientific—but amazingly accurate—test: On a day when the ground is moist (not too wet, not too dry), dig up a block of soil that's roughly 12 inches wide and 12 inches deep, and ease the soil onto a board.

Very gently pull the clump apart with your fingers, and count the earthworms that you find. (Work as quickly as you can, so you can send the little fellers home before they dry out!) Here's how to analyze the results of your census:

5 earthworms per cubic-foot chunk. Your hole improvement plan is headed in the right direction. Keep at it!

10 or more slithering pink guys. You've succeeded in laying out the welcome mat for worms and, therefore, for all kinds of other soil-building organisms you can't even see. That's because where the worms wander, the microscopic marvels follow.

25 or more slinky heroes. WOW! Your soil has become heaven on earth for grass and just about every other plant you can think of. I say "just about" because, believe it or not, there *are* plants that perform best in so-so, or even downright poor, soil. Some of them make terrific stand-ins for turf grass. You'll find a small sampling on page 99, but you can read a lot more about these and other low-care winners in Chapter 15.

Yankee Doodle Data

What Happened to My Lawn?

Even on the best-tended lawns, brown patches can appear overnight, and for no good reason—or so it seems. Truth be told, though, there's always a reason. Here are some of the most common ones, along with where to go for the full details. In most cases, the only cure may be to dig up the dead grass, then reseed or resod. But knowing the cause will help you avoid future problems.

CULPRIT	HOW IT HURTS	YOUR BEST RESPONSE
Compacted soil	Foot and vehicle traffic make soil particles pack together so that roots can't grow as they need to.	Reroute traffic or install a footpath. If the entire lawn is compacted, aerate in spring, fall, or both (see "Boy, That's Hard! on page 91).
Dog urine	It delivers an over-concentration of nitrogen, which causes the grass to burn.	Within the first two or three days, flood the area with water (see Chapter 9).
Dull mower blades	They shred grass tips, making them dry out quickly.	Sharpen blades after every three to six mowings (see Chapter 7).
Overfeeding	It gives turf grass more nutrients (especially nitrogen) than it can handle.	Serve your grass as much as it needs for healthy growth, and no more (see Chapter 5).
Overwatering	It leaches away essential nutrients.	Deliver only as much H_2O as your lawn needs (see Chapter 6).
Reflected heat	Large windows, light-colored walls, and paved surfaces can reflect the sun's heat onto nearby grass—quickly drying the blades to a crisp.	Water sun-baked areas more frequently and deeply (see Chapters 6 and 12).
Scalping	Grass that's cut too short can't shield the soil from the sun. The soil dries out, and the grass follows.	Raise the blade before you mow in high spots (see Chapter 7).
Sloping ground	Water can run off a hillside before it has a chance to sink in.	Grade your soil properly, aerate so the water can penetrate the soil (see "Boy, That's Hard!" on page 91), or replace the grass with a groundcover that thrives in drier conditions (see Chapter 15).

What Happened to My Lawn?

CULPRIT	HOW IT HURTS	YOUR BEST RESPONSE
Spills and splatters	Gasoline, oil, and fertilizer spills cause dead, brown spots.	Be careful! (See Chapter 13.)
Thatch	It prevents water and nutrients from reaching the grass roots.	Dethatch your lawn, add organic matter, and avoid pesticides, herbicides, and chemical fertilizers (see "Dispatch Thatch!" on page 86).
Underground competition	Tree roots and buried debris, such as rocks, chunks of wood, or even lost toys, prevent roots from reaching into the soil for water. As a result, the roots—andsoon the grass blades—dry out.	Dig up the "treasure" and get rid of it. If the problem is tree roots, give up on grass and plant a less-thirsty groundcover (see Chapter 15).

FOR RICHER, FOR POORER

Here's a challenge: You have a piece of poor ground where grass won't grow, but you lack the time or inclination for a soil improvement project. Here's the simple answer: Plant one, or several, of these winners—they all thrive in poor soil:

Coltsfoots (*Petasites*)

Ivies (*Hedera*)

Pachysandras (*Pachysandra*)

Periwinkle (*Vinca minor*)

☆ Minor Repairs

Even when your soil is just fine, thank you, there are times when you need to patch up bare spots or fill low-lying areas in your lawn. When that time rolls around, you can find everything you need to know right here.

DIPPITY DON'T

If your lawn needs a major regrading, stop right here and flip back to Chapter 3, "Starting from Scratch." But if it's simply a matter of smoothing out a few gradual dips, just follow this eight-step remedial procedure:

STEP 1. Remove the grass in the low area with a sharp, square-ended shovel. Simply dig down about 2 inches, and lift out whatever size pieces you can manage easily.

STEP 2. If the sod is healthy, and you plan to finish the job within a day or so, tuck the pieces away in a shady spot and keep them moist. (But don't cover them with plastic—that's like throwing a party for all the foul fungi in town!) If this is a longer-term project, or the grass has seen better days, order new sod (see Chapter 3 for the lowdown on that procedure).

STEP 3. To lower a bump, simply shovel off enough soil to level the area; then work about an inch of compost into the soil. To raise a low spot, fill it with a half-and-half mixture of topsoil and compost.

STEP 4. Rake the area until it's smooth.

STEP 5. Water the site lightly to help the soil settle.

STEP 6. Replace the saved sod, or roll out your new strip that's been cut to fit the bare spot.

STEP 7. To get your newly installed turf growing on the right root, give it a good soaking with my Kick-in-the-Grass Tonic (at left).

STEP 8. Water the area lightly once a day for a week to 10 days, and tread lightly around the new turf until it's well-established and showing signs of new growth.

BLUE PLATE SPECIAL

KICK-IN-THE-GRASS TONIC

After you've given your lawn a sod "bandage," apply this timely tonic to get it off to a rip-roarin' start.

> **1 can of beer**
> **1 cup of antiseptic mouthwash**
> **1 cup of dishwashing liquid**
> **1 cup of ammonia**
> **½ cup of Epsom salts**

Mix these ingredients in a large bucket and pour the solution into a 20 gallon hose-end sprayer. Apply the tonic to your lawn-repair site to the point of run-off, wait two weeks, then administer another dose.

MICROMINI VALLEYS

To correct tiny irregularities in your terrain, just fill the low-lying areas with a half-and-half mixture of topsoil and compost. If the grass in residence is healthy, it'll grow right up through that topping faster than you can say "Jack and the Beanstalk."

10-STEP REPAIR PLAN: RESEEDING MADE EASY

Even in the world's best-tended lawns, bare spots happen. When they crop up on your home turf, don't panic. First, try to pinpoint the underlying cause and correct it, so you can head off further trouble. Then follow this simple patch-up plan:

1 Remove all dead grass, weeds, and debris from the area.

2 Loosen the soil, spread about 1 inch of compost on top, and work it in. Rake the site smooth, and at a level slightly higher than the surrounding ground. That way, when the soil settles, it'll be even with the rest of the lawn.

3 Two or three days before you intend to reseed, spray the area with my Soil Prep Tonic (see page 76).

4 Soak the replacement seeds for 24 hours in my Seed Starter Tonic (see page 187). Then, to speed the drying process, spread the seeds on a clean, flat surface, such as a freshly swept part of your driveway, and lightly run a broom back and forth over them.

5 Mix the seeds with a little compost and spread the combo on the bare spots. (If you have no "black gold" on hand, use professional potting mix.)

6 Tamp the seeds lightly with the bottom of a rake, so they make contact with the soil.

7 Apply an appropriate mulch (see "Magical Mulch" on page 78 for some good choices).

8 Overspray the area with my Spot Seed Tonic (see page 103).

9 Keep the soil surface moist (but not wet!) until the baby grass plants are about 3 inches tall. Then it's time for that toddlin' turf to rejoin your lawn's normal watering schedule.

10 Give yourself a big pat on the back! Once you've put this plan to the test, no one—not even *you*—will be able to find the former bald spots in your lawn!

FASTER PLEASE!

You say you need to fix a few bare spots *now*, and there's no time to grow a bunch of toupees? Don't fret! Just buy a piece of sod, then cut it apart into individual chunks of whatever sizes you need.

MOWER MORATORIUM

Once you've done your patching job, whether you've seeded or sodded the bare spots, hold off on mowing those areas for at least three, preferably six, weeks. That'll give the grass roots time to get a good, firm grip in the soil. Then, the first few times you mow, set the blade half an inch or so higher than normal. Also, go slow and make sure the soil is on the dry side, so the machine's wheels don't sink into the freshly tilled earth.

KEEP ON PLUGGING

My spot-reseeding plan works wonders all right, but I've got an even easier method for patching up small bald spots in my lawn. I keep a stock of home-grown plugs on hand, and whenever trouble comes my way, I just pop one—or sometimes half a dozen or more—into the problem plot. (I owe

Star-Spangled *Lawn* Lore

You think you've got a lot of lawn-repair work to do? Well, just be glad that you're not in charge of keeping the Great Lawn in Central Park looking its green and glorious best. This apple of the Big Apple's eye covers 15 acres—and I don't even want to think about how much foot traffic it gets!

this brainchild, and a whole lot more, to my old Boy Scout troop and the Scouts' motto, "Be prepared"!) To make your own plug platoon, here's all you need to do:

STEP 1. Collect a bunch of plastic flats, like the ones that many annual flowers and veggies come in. (Make sure there are holes in the bottom for drainage.)

STEP 2. Line each flat with aluminum foil, leaving about 2 inches of foil hanging out over one side. That will allow excess water to drain off and make the soil block easier to slide out later.

STEP 3. Fill each flat with potting soil or a half-and-half mixture of compost and garden soil.

STEP 4. Sprinkle grass seed on top—of the same type as you've got growing in your lawn, of course—and put the flats in a bright but sheltered place. (I keep mine by the back door so I never forget to water them.)

STEP 5. Keep the soil moist until the seeds sprout; after that, just give the grass a good drink twice a day.

Within a couple of weeks, you'll have nice, thick blocks of turf that you can use whenever a bare spot appears in your lawn. Just slide the soil out of the flat and pop it into place, either whole or broken into pieces first.

 I Give Up!

Sometimes, no matter what you do, you can't keep folks from walking (or maybe riding, running, or skipping) across certain parts of your lawn. So don't even try. Instead, turn those routes into paths, walkways, or even stairways. Read on for some dandy ways to save your turf, liven up your landscape, and add to your property's value in one fell swoop.

HOW WIDE IS WIDE?

A path or walkway that's too narrow for the job at hand can be a major pain in the grass—and sometimes it's even dangerous. Here's my rule of thumb for deciding how wide a path or walkway needs to be:

★ Path for slow and easy strolling: 2 feet minimum width

★ Route for lawn equipment, such as wheelbarrows and mowers: 3 feet minimum width

SPOT SEED TONIC

Make your lawn-repair job a super success with this sensational solution.

1 cup of beer
1 cup of baby shampoo
4 tbsp. of instant tea granules

Combine these ingredients in a 20 gallon hose-end sprayer, and lightly apply the mixture to the mulch covering your newly seeded areas.

★ Major walkway, like the one that goes up to your front door: 4 feet minimum width

MATERIAL MATTERS

Having trouble deciding what your lawn-saving walkway should be made of? Well, a lot of that boils down to personal preference. But aside from using a material that suits the style of your house, your taste, *and* your pocketbook, keep these guidelines in mind:

• A major corridor, like the one leading from the sidewalk to your front door, or the one that carries you from your car to the kitchen with arms full of groceries, should be so wide, safe, and level that people can move along at a good, fast clip without looking down. For this reason, very hard surfaces, such as concrete, brick, or mortared stone are usually the best materials for the job.

• For paths that simply meander from one part of your yard to another, speed doesn't matter so much. In fact, you may want to use a material that slows folks down just a tad, so they can relax and admire that green scene you've worked so hard on! Loose materials, such as finely shredded mulch or pebbles, may be just right, or you can install stepping stones flush with your grass so that you can mow right over them.

STEP LIVELY

When it comes to guarding your grass from too much foot traffic, you can't beat stepping stones. You can lay whole pathways, or just set individual stones or small groups of them, in especially trouble-prone spots. For instance, I made a mini- "patio" around the base of my mailbox post and another one in the place by the street where I set out the garbage can.

Of course, you can buy stepping stones in more styles, colors, and materials than you can shake a walking stick at. But it's easy—and a lot of fun—to make your own. (It makes a great craft project for youngsters.) This mix makes five "stones," each about 1 inch thick

and 12 inches in diameter. Here's your shopping list:

★ 5-gallon plastic bucket with straight sides

★ 60-pound bag of concrete mix

★ Band saw or sharp utility knife

★ Plastic drop cloth

★ Ruler or measuring tape

★ Scraper or straightedge

★ Wooden paddle for stirring

★ Decorations and trimmings (optional)

Once you've gathered your materials, proceed as follows:

STEP 1. Measure the height of the bucket and divide by 5. Then mark the sides of the bucket at those intervals, in at least three places around the circumference. (It's as though you were dividing a tall cake into five layers.)

STEP 2. Slice through the bucket crossways at each of your layer marks. You'll have five ring-shaped molds, including the bottom of the pail. (You can either remove the bottom or keep it attached.)

STEP 3. Spread your drop cloth on a flat surface, and lay the molds on top.

STEP 4. Mix the concrete according to the package directions, and pour about an inch of the mixture into each mold.

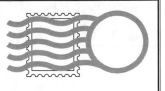

Dear Jerry,

A friend just offered me a load of bricks that came from an old house that was torn down in his neighborhood. I'd like to use them to make a walkway in my lawn. Will they work for that?

A. *Those old bricks should work just fine, but you need to give them a little TLC. First, clean them up as best you can using warm water and a wire brush, and lay them out in a sunny spot to dry. Then, before you start setting them into the ground, dip each one in a waterproofing solution. (Your neighborhood hardware or building-supply store should have several good brands to choose from.)*

STEP 5. Level the surfaces, using your scraper or straightedge, and decorate the damp concrete in any way you'd like (see "Art Underfoot" below).

STEP 6. When the concrete has set, push your stepping stones out of the molds, and pour in the next batch.

ART UNDERFOOT

To my way of thinking, concrete stepping stones look just fine in their unadorned state, but if you (or your grandkids) want to add a little pizzazz to the scene, consider these artful options:

- Make hand-, foot-, or paw prints. (Spritz the body part with cooking spray before you press it into the moist concrete; that way the stuff won't cling to skin or hair.)

- Insert marbles, shells, stones, or pieces of colored glass. Just make sure no sharp edges or rounded, slippery surfaces stick up.

- Sign your name or write a message. Either a stick or an old pencil will work for this job.

- "Draw" a design by pressing waterproof rope or cord into the concrete to create a pleasing pattern.

Chow Time

Just like any other plant, turf grass requires certain nutrients to help it grow strong and healthy, and to enable it to fend off trouble from wicked weeds, dastardly diseases, and pesky pests. But there's a lot more to feeding your lawn than just spreading a bag of fertilizer across the surface now and then. You need to serve up the right kind of food at the right times and in the right quantities. Otherwise, you'll have more trouble on your hands than if you hadn't fertilized at all. In this chapter, I'll give you the lowdown on your lawn's idea of gourmet dining.

★ What's on the Menu?

Your lawn's smorgasbord is made up of 12 essential nutrients. Too little or (in most cases) too much of any one of them can cause your grass to look sparse, coarse, yellowish, or stunted. But don't panic! Dishing up the right-size portions is simple once you get the hang of it. Here's everything you need to know.

THE MAIN COURSE

The most important essential nutrients are what gardeners and lawn keepers call "The Big Three": nitrogen (N on the fertilizer bag), phosphorus (P), and potassium (K). Here's the lowdown:

Yankee Doodle Data

When to Say "When"

Here's a rundown of nitrogen requirements for the most common turf grasses. The lower number indicates the amount needed for a low-maintenance lawn, or one in a place with a short growing season. The higher number represents the portion you'll want to serve up if you live in a warm climate, or if you want to maintain a lush (and therefore high-maintenance) lawn.

GRASS TYPE	NITROGEN NEEDED (LB. PER 1,000 SQ. FT.)	GRASS TYPE	NITROGEN NEEDED (LB. PER 1,000 SQ. FT.)
Bahia grass	2–4	Fescue, fine	1–3
Bent grass	2–6	Fescue, tall	1–6
Bermuda grass	1–6	Kentucky bluegrass	2–6
Blue grama grass	1–2	Perennial ryegrass	2–4
Buffalo grass	0–2	St. Augustine grass	2–5
Centipede grass	1–4	Zoysia grass	2–4

Nitrogen. Supplies the growing power for grass blades. When they get exactly the right amount, they develop at a steady pace into a lush, green lawn. Too little nitrogen and a lawn looks stunted and yellowish. Too much, and you're faced with rapid growth, delayed maturity, and weak, trouble-prone grass plants.

Phosphorus. Promotes the growth of strong, vigorous roots. If grass gets too little, the blades will have a reddish, purplish, or grayish cast. An overdose can interfere with the lawn's absorption of other essential elements and cause all manner of symptoms (see "Tasty Tidbits" on page 110).

Potassium. Supports the process of photosynthesis and the growth of strong plant tissue. It helps your lawn prepare for cold winters and protect itself against pathogens of all kinds. Too little potassium will cause grass to turn yellow, lose its get-up-and-grow power, and fall prey to plant diseases. Too much of The Big K interferes with the absorption of calcium and magnesium, which will also make the little plants grow poorly.

HOLD THE N!

You might think that you're doing your lawn a favor by giving it big helpings of nitrogen, but in fact, that's the worst thing you can do, for a couple of reasons. One is that with too much nitrogen in its diet, grass grows so fast that the blades develop only a weak, thin cuticle. (That's the outer layer of cells that stand guard against diseases and pests.) You can guess what happens then! Second, all that super-chow makes the grass plants send up more shoots than the roots can support. The turf might look thick and lush as all get-out, but the good times won't last—big trouble lurks just around the corner.

HOW MUCH IS TOO MUCH?

There is no concise answer to that question, because the amount of nitrogen that a lawn needs depends on three factors:

The type of grass. Some types just naturally consume more of The Big N than others. (For a rundown of the nitrogen requirements of common turf grasses, see "When to Say 'When' " on page 107.)

The length of your growing season. The longer the weather remains warm, the more nitrogen any kind of grass consumes.

LAST SUPPER TONIC

This soothing beverage is the equivalent of a bedtime cup of cocoa for your lawn.

½ **can of beer**
½ **cup of apple juice**
½ **cup of Gatorade®**
½ **cup of urine**
½ **cup of fish emulsion**
½ **cup of ammonia**
½ **cup of regular cola (not diet)**
½ **cup of baby shampoo**

Mix these ingredients in a large bucket, and pour the solution into a 20 gallon hose-end sprayer. Apply it to your lawn to the point of run-off, immediately after the last fall feeding. It'll soften up the ingredients in the dry fertilizer, so your grass's roots can absorb the nutrients all winter long.

The degree of lushness you demand in your lawn. As I've already said, the more nitrogen you feed your lawn, the greener, denser, and faster-growing it will be. But while a real overdose will do serious harm (see "Hold the N!" on page 107), a big, healthy portion will simply add to your chores because you'll have to mow more often. And the more you feed your lawn—especially if you opt for a chemical fertilizer—the more prone it will be to thatch, soil compaction, and other forms of nastiness. So, you can have that lush look if you want it, but be prepared to pay the consequences!

THERE'S GOLD IN THEM THAR CLIPPINGS

And food, too! In fact, by simply leaving the clippings in place when you mow your lawn, you can supply up to half the nitrogen that your grass needs—and it's absolutely free. But this only works if you don't use chemical fertilizers. Studies have proven that because these potent formulas hinder the work of the underground breakdown crew (including earthworms, fungi, and beneficial bacteria) they stall the decomposition of the grass clippings (see "Two for the Road" on page 112). The result not only robs the little plants of free food, but also contributes to thatch buildup. (For my surefire thatch removal and prevention plan, see "Dispatch Thatch!" on page 86.)

TAKE 'EM OFF!

Having delivered my free-food lecture, I will say that there are four occasions when you should remove your grass clippings. They are:

1 When you're switching to an organic lawn-care program after a period of using pesticides, herbicides, and chemical fertilizers—especially if you're battling a thatch problem.

from the **MAIL BAG**

Dear Jerry,

For years, I've been spreading compost on my lawn every spring and fall and my grass looks terrific! Then a neighbor told me that something called mushroom compost is even better than the "regular" kind. Exactly what *is* mushroom compost? And what's so great about it?

A. *It's the stuff that mushrooms grow in on mushroom farms. It's made of super-powered organic matter, like horse manure and straw, with a little gypsum and limestone tossed in. And your neighbor's right: You couldn't find a healthier snack for your grass! Just pick up a bag at a garden center or mushroom farm and apply it as you would any other compost (see page 116). Then, to get your lawn really growin' great guns, immediately spray your lawn with my All-Season Green-Up Tonic (see page 85).*

2 After giving your lawn its first haircut of the spring. Raking away the clippings will allow the sun to warm up the soil quickly and help the grass green up much faster.

3 After the final mowing in the fall. This will deprive pests and diseases of a cozy winter hideaway.

4 Anytime you've delayed mowing too long and you've had to cut off more than half of the top growth.

THE SECOND COURSE

In addition to The Big Three, turf grass needs a small, but steady supply of certain trace elements, a.k.a. micronutrients. Generally, they're present  in healthy soil, so you don't have to give them a thought. Once in a while, though, your grass roots may get a craving for a specific kind of snack—most often either iron (Fe) or magnesium (Mg). Both are key ingredients in chlorophyll (the stuff that makes your grass green), so if your turf starts turning yellow, suspect a lack of one of these elements. To find out for sure, you could have your soil tested by your Cooperative Extension Service or a professional testing lab. (For the full scoop on soil tests and building strong soil, see page 61.) Or you could

perform a simple do-it-yourself test (see "Test Time" at right).

TASTY TIDBITS

Besides the major and secondary elements, your grass needs small portions of these healthy side dishes:

Boron (B). Improves the absorption of all the other elements. If your soil is deficient in boron, your grass will have small leaf blades with dead spots on them. Too much will make the blades turn yellowish red.

Calcium (Ca). Builds strong grass blades by fortifying cell walls and ensuring normal cell division. Too little calcium puts the brakes on growth. Leaf blades begin to curl up or die at the tips, and the roots become weak and stubby. Too much can block a lawn's intake of potassium and magnesium.

Copper (Cu). An enzyme activator. When it's in short supply, you'll see a reddish brown, gummy substance oozing from the grass stems. Too much copper interferes with the absorption of iron and can stunt the roots.

Manganese (Mn). Another enzyme activator. When there's not enough in the soil, you'll see stunted growth and grass blades streaked with yellow. Too much manganese causes small dead

Yankee Doodle Data

Test Time

When your grass turns yellow, it could mean that your soil is lacking in either iron or magnesium. Here's a simple way to find out for sure. No matter which of the two has gone AWOL, once you remedy the situation, the turf will green up within 24 hours.

SOIL CONDITION	PROBABLE DEFICIENCY	TEST	REMEDY
Alkaline (pH higher than 7.0)	Iron	Buy a bottle of liquid fertilizer that contains iron, and spray it on a small section of your lawn according to the manufacturer's directions.	For a quick fix, spray the whole lawn with the same fertilizer you used in the test. For long-term relief, lower the pH of your soil (see page 64 for details).
Very sandy or highly acidic (pH much lower than 7.0)	Magnesium	Mix 1 tsp. of Epsom salts with 1 pint of warm water in a hand-held spray bottle. Shake it until the salts are dissolved, then spray the mixture very lightly on a small section of grass. (Do *not* apply it to the point of run-off!)	For each 1,000 sq. ft. of lawn, mix 1 lb. of Epsom salts with 3 gal. of water, and apply the mixture lightly with a hand-held sprayer. Don't use a stronger solution—too much magnesium interferes with the absorption of calcium and potassium.

patches in the lawn and yellow borders on grass blades.

Molybdenum (Mo). An ingredient in the enzymes that help grass utilize nitrogen. You'll probably never notice a shortage of molybdenum unless the nitrogen itself is lacking, but an overdose can be toxic to livestock. So whatever you do, don't even think about adding molybdenum supplements to your lawn if you have horses, cattle, or other grazing critters on the scene!

Sulfur (S). Helps build proteins (yes, grass needs proteins just as we do). Very few lawns suffer from a shortage of sulfur, but when the problem does occur, the grass will turn yellow or pale green. Too much can burn the grass, so don't try a do-it-yourself test. If you suspect a shortage, have your soil tested before you reach for a supplement.

Zinc (Zn). Essential for proper cell division. Too little zinc can turn your grass yellow and thin looking, with leaf blades small, distorted, and sometimes covered with tiny, white dead spots. Too much can be toxic, but symptoms rarely appear.

IT NEEDS EVERYTHING!

If your grass exhibits a number of the symptoms described above, chances are there's a simple, two-word answer to the problem: organic matter. Soil that's lacking in organic matter can neither hold nutrients nor allow them to be absorbed by plants' roots. One solution: Till in organic matter, and then reseed or resod. Any kind of organic matter will do the trick, including chopped leaves, straw, or (my favorite) compost. For more on adding life to tired soil, including my simple composting methods, see Chapters 3 and 4.

Fertilizers 101

When you stroll down the miles of aisles in a garden center, you'll see so many different kinds of lawn food that it'll boggle your mind. How can you possibly decide which one to buy? I'll tell you how.

TWO FOR THE ROAD

Lawn fertilizers come in different formulations to meet the specific nutrient needs of various grass types (see page 107), but every fertilizer on the market falls into one of two basic categories:

Chemical/inorganic fertilizers. These are made from synthetic substances that contain highly concentrated amounts of specific nutrients, primarily nitrogen, phosphorus, and potassium. When you apply a chemical fertilizer, you see almost instant results because the nutrients are immediately available to the grass roots. On the downside, this quick fix adds nothing to the soil itself. In fact, those potent chemicals actually destroy the beneficial organisms, including earthworms, that create the soil's natural nutrients and keep it in good shape. They also kill off the soil-dwelling critters that prey on bad-guy bugs. And, if used over time, the chemicals can build up in the soil and actually hinder the growth of your grass.

Natural/organic fertilizers. These don't feed your grass at all. Rather, they add essential nutrients, major and minor, to the soil, where they become available to the grass plants. They also improve the structure of the soil—and thereby improve living conditions for your underground hit squad. Organic fertilizers are made of naturally occurring substances, just like the ones I use in my

Blue Plate Specials. There are some excellent commercial brands, but it's easy to make your own healthy chow—check out Grandma Putt's Organic Fertilizer recipe at right.

RABBITS AND TURTLES

Besides the chemical/inorganic vs. natural/organic distinction, commercial fertilizers differ in another way—how fast they release their nutrients. There are three types:

Quick release. These fertilizers start dissolving the minute they hit the ground, because their ingredients (particularly nitrogen) are water-soluble. Your grass begins to feast immediately, and puts on a big growth spurt. The trouble is that the turf will clean its plate in a flash. Then, in a month or so, it'll be hungry again, and you'll have to serve up more chow. And then more. And then still more.

Slow release. These contain nutrients that do not dissolve in water. As a result, your grass dines at a slow, leisurely pace, so you don't have to feed it as often. Natural/organic fertilizers are, by definition, slow release because they consist of ingredients that must be broken down by earthworms and microorganisms in the soil. But in order to make synthetic foods perform slowly, the manufacturers have to coat the chemicals with a substance that holds back their usual, hair-trigger action.

GRANDMA PUTT'S ORGANIC FERTILIZER

Back in the good old days, folks couldn't just drop by the garden center for a sack of lawn fertilizer. They had to mix up their own brand of comfort food. This is the recipe Grandma Putt came up with to keep her lawn in tip-top shape—and it still works wonders today!

5 parts seaweed meal
3 parts granite dust
1 part dehydrated manure
1 part bonemeal

Thoroughly mix these ingredients in a large wheelbarrow. Apply the mixture evenly over your turf with a broadcast spreader, then stand back and watch that grass go to town!

Bridge, a.k.a. combination. These fertilizers are made from a combination of slow- and fast-acting ingredients, so you get both instant gratification and longer-lasting results.

IT'S IN THE BAG

All fertilizer manufacturers are required by law to list The Big Three elements—and the amounts of them—on the product package. This is what they call the "guaranteed analysis." It appears in the form of three numbers, which designate the percentage of nitrogen, available phosphorus, and water-soluble potassium in the mix. For instance, if the label reads "10-6-4 grade fertilizer," that translates into 10 percent nitrogen (N), 6 percent available phosphorus (P), and 4 percent water-soluble potassium (K).

DOING THE MATH

Let's say that you've bought a 40-pound sack of 10-6-4 fertilizer. Here's how that translates into weight:

★ 4 pounds of nitrogen (10 percent of 40)

★ 2.4 pounds of phosphorus (6 percent of 40)

★ 1.6 pounds of water-soluble potassium (4 percent of 40)

And just how far will those 40 pounds go? Well, since you want to apply no more than 1 pound of nitrogen per 1,000 square feet at any one time, and the bag contains 4 pounds of nitrogen, it will safely feed 4,000 square feet of lawn.

ACCEPT SUBSTITUTES

Can't find the ingredients for Grandma Putt's Organic Fertilizer (see page 113)? Then try my recipe! Just mix 2 parts alfalfa meal with 1 part bonemeal and 1 part wood ashes. Apply this formula at a rate of 25 pounds per 1,000 square feet of lawn area first thing in the spring and last thing in the fall. Then watch your

grass grow green and healthy—and your neighbors grow green with envy!

HOW BIG IS YOUR LAWN?

Figuring out the size of a square or rectangular lawn is a snap: You just measure the length and width and multiply the two. So, for instance, if your lawn is 80 feet long, and 60 feet wide, it covers 4,800 square feet. When you're dealing with other shapes, the process gets a little trickier. Here's how to figure square feet for odd-shaped lawns:

Circular areas. Measure the radius (the distance halfway across the center, or r) and multiply that number by itself (r^2), and then multiply that figure by pi (3.14). For a circular lawn that has a radius of 20 feet, the equation is: (20 x 20) x 3.14 = 1,256 square feet.

Triangular areas. Measure the longest length of your lawn, and consider this the "height" of your triangle. Measure the length of the side that's at a right angle to the height and consider this the "base" of your triangle. Multiply the height by the base and divide by 2. Here's a sample equation: 70 feet height x 40 feet base = 2,800 square feet. Divide by 2 and your final answer is 1,400 square feet.

Yankee Doodle Data

Slow or Fast?

Still not sure whether you want your
lawn food to be slow- or quick-acting? Here are the pros and
cons in a nutshell.

FERTILIZER RELEASE ACTION	PROS	CONS
Quick	☆ Shows almost immediate results ☆ Sports a low price tag	☆ Has no staying power; must be reapplied several times during the growing season ☆ Is likely to burn grass ☆ Destroys microorganisms in the soil ☆ Makes grass grow very quickly, so you'll have to mow more often
Slow	☆ Provides a steady supply of nutrients over a long period of time, so you need to fertilize only twice a year ☆ Helps build strong soil ☆ Is unlikely to burn grass ☆ Encourages underground enemies of pests and diseases ☆ Makes grass grow at a slower pace, so you'll have to mow less often	☆ Shows slower visible results ☆ Carries a higher initial price tag
Bridge/ combination	☆ Shows quick results ☆ Lasts longer than fast-response products ☆ Is less likely to burn grass	☆ Tends to be expensive ☆ In most cases, does nothing to improve the soil or encourage your underground hit squad

Irregular areas. Measure the distance across a wide area of lawn and call this your length line (L). Every 10 feet along this line, measure the width at a 90-degree angle to L. Now add all the widths and multiply by 10. You'll have your square footage, give or take 5 percent, and that's darn close. For example: If your widths measure 30 feet, 28 feet, and 22 feet, the area is (30 + 28 + 22) x 10 = 800 square feet.

Super★Secret

Pure and Simple

I have some friends who are real purists when it comes to feeding their lawns: They use no fertilizer at all. Instead, they just spread a layer of top-quality compost across the turf twice a year, in the spring and again in the fall. If you want to try this approach, you'll need a minimum of 50 pounds of compost for each 1,000 square feet of lawn area. As for the maximum, well, the sky's the limit—there's no such thing as an overdose of black gold! You'll find everything you need to know about making and serving this miracle chow in Chapter 3.

HOW DOES THAT TRANSLATE INTO FOOD?

Once you know your lawn's square footage, divide that number by 1,000 to determine how many pounds of nitrogen you need. Finally, multiply the pounds of nitrogen by 10 to determine how much fertilizer to buy. So, for instance, if you're using a 10-6-4 fertilizer on a 5,000-square-foot lot, the formula is 5,000 divided by 1,000 = 5, multiplied by (N) 10 = 50 pounds of lawn food.

☆ Jerry's Year-Round Feeding Program

Now that you've mastered the essentials of turf-grass nutrition, you know that old saying "You are what you eat" applies to lawns as much as it does to people! So does this old chestnut: "Timing is everything." Here's my foolproof feeding schedule that's guaranteed to keep your lawn well fed and free of both hunger pangs *and* those nasty tummy twinges caused by overeating.

FIRST THINGS FIRST

Even before you give your lawn a drink of my Spring Wake-Up Tonic (see page 123), get your whole yard off to a clean, fresh start with my Rise 'n' Shine Clean-Up Tonic (see page 122). It'll do for your lawn what a brisk morning shower does for you!

SPRING STARTUP

When the first balmy breezes float through the air, your lawn (like everything else in nature) wakes up rarin' to grow. That's the time to get it started on the right root with this four-step routine:

STEP 1. As soon as your grass starts rubbing the sleep out of its eyes, give it a rousing drink of my Spring Wake-Up Tonic (see page 123) followed immediately by a good, healthy dose of my Get-Up-and-Grow Tonic (see page 124).

STEP 2. Within two weeks of serving up that dynamic duo, give your lawn its first solid meal of the season. Add 3 pounds of Epsom salts to a bag of your favorite slow-release, dry lawn food (enough for 2,500 square feet). I like to use a 20-5-10 mix. Be sure to mix the salts in well. Apply half of this mixture at *half* the rate recommended on the label, with your spreader on the medium setting, moving from north to south in parallel rows across your yard. Set the other half of the mixture aside where you can get at it easily—you're going to need it soon!

STEP 3. No more than two days after you spread the fertilizer/Epsom salts mixture (see Step 2), give your turf a treat in the form of my Lawn Snack Tonic (see page 125). Apply this bracing beverage before noon—the earlier in the morning, the better.

STEP 4. One week later, haul out the remaining fertilizer/Epsom salts mixture from Step 2 and pour it into your spreader. This time, apply it in rows moving from east to west. This "checkerboard" trick guarantees that every square inch of turf gets fed, with no light green lines in your lawn where you missed.

Super★Secret

Dish and Dat

When you're shopping for dishwashing liquid to use in a tonic recipe, make sure you choose a brand that's made with pure, mild soap. Avoid any product that contains detergents or degreasing agents. They can harm your grass (or any other plants they touch). And whatever you do, avoid all products that boast antibacterial prowess. Not only will they damage your greenery, but they'll also kill off good bacteria along with the bad—and that can cause *big* trouble.

Yankee Doodle Data

Jerry's Lawn Smorgasbord

If you fancy yourself a creative cook, here's your chance to strut your stuff for a very appreciative eater: your lawn. Just mix up a batch of homemade fertilizer using these health-giving ingredients.

ESSENTIAL INGREDIENT	SOURCES	
Calcium	Aragonite	Eggshells
	Bonemeal	Gypsum
	Clam, oyster, or	Limestone
	other seashells	Rock phosphate
Iron	Iron sulfate, a.k.a copperas	Chelated iron
Magnesium	Dolomitic limestone	Epsom salts
Micronutrients	Alfalfa hay	Leaves
	Compost	Rock phosphate
	Eggshells	Soybean meal
	Granite meal	Wood ashes
	Grass clippings	Worm castings
	Kelp meal	
Nitrogen	Alfalfa meal	Fish emulsion
	Bird guano	Fish meal
	Bloodmeal	Manure (all kinds)
	Coffee grounds	Soybean meal
	Cottonseed meal	
Phosphorus	Bonemeal	Poultry manure
	Colloidal phosphate	Rock phosphate
	Fish emulsion	Seaweed
Potassium	Banana peels	Greensand
	Cow manure	Kelp meal
	Granite meal	Wood ashes
Sulfur	Epsom salts	Gypsum
	Ground sulfur	Manure (all kinds)

THROUGH THE GOOD OLD SUMMERTIME

Once you've given your lawn its hearty breakfast, it's time to begin the series of regular, but light meals that will carry it through to the first cold days of fall. (After all, not even turf grass wants to eat big, heavy meals when the weather's so hot you could grill a steak on the sidewalk!) Still, heat or no heat, those grass plants need sustenance, and for my money, the best way to provide it is with my All-Season Green-Up Tonic (see page 85). It delivers a light, refreshing combo of nutrients that give your little green plants the growing power they need without filling them up and slowing them down. Serve up this tonic every three weeks right through the first hard frost, and your lawn will romp like a pup through the dog days of summer!

If the heat gets you down so much that you'd rather not fuss with mixing up tonics, you can substitute a good liquid lawn food or fish emulsion. Whatever you use, just remember to keep it "lite."

GETTIN' ON TOWARD BEDTIME

Your final fall feeding should be a repeat of the spring routine, only this time use a 10-10-10 dry, slow-release fertilizer instead of the 20-5-10 version you used earlier. Once again, mix 3 pounds of Epsom salts into a bag of food (enough for 2,500 square feet) and apply half of the mixture at half the recommended rate, moving from north to south across your lawn. One week later, spread the remaining food/Epsom salts, going from east to west. Then, within two days after your second feeding, serve up a season's-end drink of my Lawn Snack Tonic (see page 125).

Finish up your turf's bedtime ritual by applying what I somewhat irreverently call my Last Supper Tonic (see page 108). This excellent elixir softens up the dry fertilizer mix so that your lawn can easily digest the nutrients, even during its long winter's nap.

SYNCHRONIZE YOUR WATCHES

Calendars, rather. Although all turf grasses need to be fed in spring and fall, exactly what part of spring and fall depends on where you live. Here's a rundown:

★ Warm-season grasses like St. Augustine and Bermuda perform their best when they're fed in late spring and again in early fall. The reason: If you serve up the chow too early in the spring, you're likely to fill the bellies of wicked weeds. And if you wait too long in the fall,

from the
MAIL BAG

Dear Jerry,

I tried your feeding program for the first time this spring, but something went haywire—when I combined the Epsom salts with my lawn fertilizer, the mixture got all wet, and it wouldn't spread at all. What's going on here?

A. *I'm glad you brought this up, because it's a question I've been hearing a lot lately from folks who are using synthetic, slow-release fertilizers. These products work the way they do because the chemicals are coated so the nutrients are released gradually over time (see "Rabbits and Turtles" on page 113). And that coating—particularly the one used in some of the newer brands—reacts with Epsom salts to form a damp mess that you can't get through a spreader for love nor money. My best advice: Switch to a natural/organic fertilizer. Their natural ingredients team up just fine with Epsom salts—and all of my other tonic makings. If you'd rather stick with a synthetic product, simply divide Steps 2 and 4 (see "Spring Startup" on page 117) into substeps: Spread your lawn food first, then clean your spreader to remove any fertilizer residue, and spread the Epsom salts.*

your grass won't have time to absorb all the nutrients in the food. As a result, it'll go into the winter unprepared to fend off cold-weather damage. (For more on coping with Old Man Winter and other environmental, um, adventures, see Chapter 12.)

★ Cool-season grasses such as tall fescue and Kentucky bluegrass need their substantial meals in early spring and late fall. Being Johnny-on-the-spot in the spring is especially important with these turf types, because you want to give them their get-up-and-grow power while the weather's still cool. If you wait too long, you'll trigger a super growth spurt just as the temperatures skyrocket.

Yankee Doodle Data

The Secret Behind My Tonics

So far, you've seen a whole passel of my terrific tonics—all made from common household products. And as we go along, you'll see a lot more of them. You may be thinking, "Is this tonic business just a lot of mumbo jumbo?"

Well, friends, it's not mumbo jumbo. The powerful ingredients in my tonics really do give your lawn get-up-and-grow power—and help it in a whole lot of other ways. Here's how.

NUTRITIONAL POWERHOUSE	HOW IT HELPS YOUR LAWN
Ammonia	Provides an instant, easily digestible form of nitrogen to your grass.
Antiseptic mouthwash	Does the same thing in your lawn that it does in your mouth—wipes out disease germs before they do their dastardly deeds.
Beer	Acts as an enzyme activator to stimulate the health and growth of the beneficial microorganisms in the soil—which in turn ensure that your grass's roots can take up the nutrients they need.
Cola	Serves a big dose of sugar to bacteria that help condition the soil. Skip the diet brands—artificial sweeteners don't work like the real thing!
Dishwashing liquid, baby shampoo, and Murphy's Oil Soap®	Clean the grass blades and soften the soil so the plants can absorb nutrients through both their roots and foliage.
Epsom salts	Are a potent source of magnesium, which improves the root structure of your grass—and that's essential for good, steady growth.
Garlic	Sends pesky pests scurryin' and acts like an antibiotic that can help sickly grass plants get growing on the right root again.
Sugar, molasses, and corn syrup	Stimulate chlorophyll formation in your grass plants and help feed the good soil bacteria.
Tea	Provides tannic acid, which helps your grass plants digest their food faster so your lawn can leap into its spring growth.
Tobacco	Poisons bugs when they ingest it, or when they simply come into contact with it. (For the lowdown on lawn pests, see Chapter 9.)
Urine	Gives your grass a jolt of nitrogen to keep it green and lush.
Whiskey	Whether it's bourbon, Scotch, rye, or plain old rotgut, provides nutrients for your grass and also keeps bugs and thugs away.

EARLY TO RISE

Whatever kind of lawn fertilizer you use—whether it's liquid or dry, organic or synthetic—apply it as early in the morning as you can. That way, the food can sink into the soil before the sun gets hot. That's important because high temperatures plus fertilizer equals burned grass!

NOT RIGHT NOW, THANKS

When a lot of folks are stressed out, a good, healthy meal makes them feel better. But the same does *not* apply to grass plants. When your lawn is under stress of any kind, don't feed it! Many things can trigger "emotional" turmoil in a lawn, including pest and disease attacks, drought, extreme heat waves, and other natural calamities. No matter what's troubling your turf, get rid of the cause and *then* offer it some comfort food.

DON'T WEED AND FEED

We all know that lawns have to be fed and weeds have to be controlled—but don't try to do both at the same time. In spite of the fact that weed-and-feed

RISE 'N' SHINE CLEAN-UP TONIC

First thing in the spring, spray down your lawn, and everything else in your yard, with this powerful potion. Besides getting your whole green scene off to a squeaky-clean start, it'll stop bad bugs in their tracks.

1 cup of Murphy's Oil Soap®
1 cup of tobacco tea*
1 cup of antiseptic mouthwash
¼ cup of hot sauce
Warm water

Mix the Murphy's Oil Soap, tobacco tea, mouthwash, and hot sauce in a 20 gallon hose-end sprayer, filling the balance of the jar with warm water. Apply to everything in your yard to the point of run-off.

* To make tobacco tea, place half a handful of chewing tobacco in an old nylon stocking and soak it in a gallon of hot water until the mixture is dark brown.

products sell like hotcakes, they're not the wonder workers they're cracked up to be. In fact, they can actually do more harm than good. That's because, in order to kill weeds, you have to use so much of this double-dip stuff that you feed your lawn way too much nitrogen. And you know how much trouble that can cause! But if you try to avoid a Big N overdose by serving up less weed-and-feed, you won't put much of a dent in your unwanted-plant population.

AND THAT'S NOT ALL

Here are a couple more reasons for making weeding and feeding two separate items on your to-do list:

1 Weed-and-feed combos are expensive. A sack of a dual-action product will set you back considerably more than separate packages of commercial fertilizer and weed killer—and a *whale* of a lot more than the ingredients for my feeding and weed control tonics. (For my surefire strategy for winning the war on weeds, see Chapter 11.)

2 They're made from synthetic chemicals. And, as we've already seen, these potent substances contribute to soil compaction, thatch, and big-time pest and disease problems.

HOW DRY IT IS

Or at least it should be. If you have fertilizer left over after your last fall feeding, be sure to guard it from any dampness in your garage or workshop. If moisture seeps into the bags, it will ruin the food. Either put the sacks on boards or wooden pallets to raise them off the cold, concrete floor, or tuck the bags into plastic trash cans and cover them tightly. That way, the chow will be as good as gold when it's time to dish it out in the spring.

SPRING WAKE-UP TONIC

As soon as possible in the spring, issue a wake-up call to your lawn with this marvelous mixture.

50 lb. of pelletized gypsum
50 lb. of pelletized lime
5 lb. of bonemeal
2 lb. of Epsom salts

Mix these ingredients in a wheelbarrow, and apply to your lawn with a broadcast spreader no more than two weeks before fertilizing. This will help aerate the lawn, while giving it something to munch on until you start your regular feeding program.

☆ Ways and Means

Serving the right food at the right time is a crucial part of lawn care, all right. But in order for your grass plants to take full advantage of that chow, you also need to dish it up in the right way, using the right tools. (After all, you wouldn't try to ladle out chicken soup with a fork, would you?) Don't worry: You don't need to spend a fortune, or clutter up your garage with a lot of fancy gadgets. Here's everything you'll need, and how to use it.

START SPREADIN' THE NEWS

The food, rather. The best way to serve up dry fertilizer is with a spreader. There are a number of brands on the market, but only two basic types:

Drop spreaders. These do exactly what their name implies: They drop fertilizer through small, adjustable holes at the bottom of the bin in a neat, orderly fashion. Because most drop spreaders cover about a 2-foot-wide swath of ground, they're ideal for small- to medium-size lawns. They're also just the ticket for situations where accuracy matters—for instance, if your yard contains trees, shrubs, or flower beds that could be harmed by lawn food.

Broadcast, a.k.a. rotary, spreaders. These come in both hand-held and wheeled models. They consist of a fertilizer hopper on top, with a horizontal, whirling wheel mounted beneath. If you've got a big lawn, it's hard to resist one of these babies because, with a spreading distance of up to 6 feet, they let you finish your feeding chores a lot faster than you could with a drop spreader. Unfortunately, though, what you gain in time you lose in accuracy. You need to gauge your passes very carefully to avoid feeding the nongrass plants in your landscape—not to mention patios, walks, and driveways, which don't need to be munching on fertilizer of any kind!

GET-UP-AND-GROW TONIC

After applying my Spring Wake-Up Tonic (see page 123) to your lawn, overspray it with this tonic to kick it into high gear.

1 cup of baby shampoo
1 cup of ammonia
1 cup of regular cola (not diet)
4 tbsp. of instant tea granules

Mix these ingredients in a 20 gallon hose-end sprayer, and apply to the point of run-off. This tonic will get all that good stuff working to help your grass off to a super start—so get ready for the most terrific turf in town!

DON'T PINCH PENNIES

There are plenty of inexpensive spreaders on the market but, as with other tools, you generally get what you pay for. In this case, a cheap spreader can actually cost you money because most likely, it won't spread its contents evenly. At best, you'll wind up wasting fertilizer; at worst, you'll underfeed some parts of your lawn and burn others. Whether you opt for a drop or broadcast type, buy the best one you can afford. Or, if you don't care to invest in equipment that you use just a couple of times a year, rent a top-notch spreader when it's feeding time at your place.

EVEN STEVEN

Using good equipment is the first step toward uniform spreading, but your technique is important, too. Fortunately, it's not hard to get a nice, even flow. Here's all you need to do in six simple steps:

STEP 1. With your spreader resting on a flat, nonliving surface to avoid burning the grass, turn the settings to correspond with the amount of fertilizer you need to apply. You should find this information in your spreader's instruction manual or on the fertilizer bag; if not, see "How Does That Translate into Food?" on page 116.

STEP 2. Pour in the fertilizer. If you spill any, sweep it up immediately before the stuff can be washed into drains or sewers. (For the full scoop on handling lawn-food spills and other mishaps, see Chapter 13.)

STEP 3. Moving at your normal walking speed, start by spreading fertilizer over the edges of your lawn. If it's a neat square or rectangle, make a back-and-forth pass over each end. On the way back, be sure to overlap the wheel path by a couple of inches so you don't miss any ground. On an oddly shaped lawn, simply go once around the perimeter.

STEP 4. Walk back and forth, in parallel rows across your lawn. Again, overlap the wheel path to ensure complete coverage. When you reach the end strips, or your meandering border, turn the spreader off as you're turning around to avoid dropping too much food in any one spot. (Likewise, turn off the flow anytime you pause in the action.)

STEP 5. As soon as you've covered the whole lawn, water it thoroughly. That way, the fertilizer won't burn the grass blades, and nutrients will seep into the soil where the roots can begin absorbing them.

BLUE PLATE SPECIAL

LAWN SNACK TONIC

Served as a chaser to your lawn's spring and fall feedings, this tasty tonic will give you better-looking turf than you've ever imagined.

1 can of beer
1 cup of dishwashing liquid
Ammonia

Mix the beer and dishwashing liquid in a 20 gallon hose-end sprayer, filling the balance of the jar with ammonia. Overspray your lawn to the point of run-off. Apply this tonic in the morning, within two days of putting down your lawn's main meal of dry fertilizer and Epsom salts (see page 117).

Super★Secret

Have a Ball

Here's a neat trick I learned a long time ago: Always keep a golf ball in your 20 gallon hose-end sprayer. It acts as an agitator while you're spraying, keeping the ingredients thoroughly mixed up and allowing for nice, even application.

STEP 6. When you're finished, set the spreader on the lawn, hose it off thoroughly, and then let it dry before you put it away. Don't skip this step, no matter how much you may want to move on to the lawn-care equivalent of the 19th hole! (Over time, even small amounts of fertilizer residue can corrode the metal parts of your spreader.)

A LIQUID DIET

With liquid fertilizers, the delivery process is a little different. For starters of course, instead of a spreader, you need to use a hose-end sprayer. But here are a few other tips to keep in mind:

Mix it up. Follow the mixing directions on the package to the letter, and make sure all of the ingredients are completely dissolved before you start spraying. Otherwise, the early sprays will deliver weak doses of nitrogen, and the later ones will be too strong.

Walk the line. Start in a corner of your lawn, or along one edge if there are no corners. Then walk backward in a straight line, spraying as you go. When you reach the end, turn off the sprayer, twirl around, and walk a second line parallel to the first.

Don't overlap! Whatever you do, don't overlap your spray patterns. If you do, the strips that have been double-dosed will grow more quickly, and you'll wind up with a wavy lawn.

MY BAKER'S DOZEN RULES FOR SPRAYING SUCCESS

Whether you're applying a commercial liquid fertilizer or one of my tonics, you need to use and store it properly. So, no matter whether the spray you're using is meant for feeding, wiping out weeds, or battling pests and diseases, always heed these 13 commonsense rules:

1 Use the right sprayer. To apply a commercial liquid fertilizer, buy the kind of sprayer recommended on the package. And don't pinch pennies—buy the best product you can afford. A high-quality model will not only last longer than a cheap one, but it will also give you better control of the spray mix and application. When you're serving up my tonics, it's a different story. Then, you want to use my hose-end sprayers,

which are specifically designed to mix the ingredients with the proper amount of water and deliver the goods in exactly the right way.

2 Read before you spray. Study the instruction booklet that comes with your sprayer, and then, for good measure, give it a "test drive" before you get down to serious business. How do you do that? Just fill 'er up with a simple recipe like my Wild Weed Wipeout Tonic (see page 243), find a patch of weeds you want to get rid of, and let 'er rip! That way, even if the sprayer is defective, or it takes you a while to master your technique, you won't risk delivering too much food to your lawn.

3 Follow the tonic instructions to the letter. You may enjoy improvising in the kitchen, but when it comes to feeding your lawn (or giving it any other kind of TLC), you need to stick to the script.

4 Select the right pressure. For most purposes, set the dial on high for a fine, penetrating mist. Use the low-pressure setting for delivering a heavy, saturating spray (like a weed-killing tonic) that you don't want to drift.

5 Spray only to the point of run-off. Never drench your lawn. At best, you'll be wasting valuable ingredients; at worst, you could serve up an accidental overdose that could do some serious damage to your lawn.

6 Aim carefully—especially when you're targeting trouble spots, like a lawn area that needs extra nourishment, or weeds that you want to put out of your misery. (For the whole scoop on wiping out wicked weeds, see Chapter 11.)

7 Adjust for distance. Use a fine, cone-shaped mist for close-up applications, and a coarser spray for long-range targets.

8 Keep it cool. Do your spraying early in the day, before Ol' Sol heats things up. It's best for your grass and for you—no need to sweat in the sun!

9 Keep it calm. Never spray on a windy day. Those bracing breezes can cause your tonic to drift off target onto plants that don't need it—or maybe right into your face!

10 Dress for success. Even nontoxic products like vinegar, ammonia, and citrus oils can irritate your skin. As for urine, which appears in a number of my tonics—well, you sure don't want to get *that* on yourself! So play it safe. Whenever you're working with any spray, wear a long-sleeved shirt and pants, along with a hat, gloves, and goggles.

11 Drain for gain. As soon as you're through, drain your sprayer completely, wash it with mild soap and warm water, and wipe it dry. That way, residue from the tonic you've just used won't hang around to mingle with the next one.

12 Put 'em away. Store all tonics and ingredients (and any store-bought sprays and dusts) well out of reach of children and pets—preferably under lock and key.

13 Show it off. Keep store-bought sprays in their original containers with the labels intact. When you have some leftover tonic, put it into a clean, tightly capped container, labeled with the name of the tonic and its ingredients, and the date you mixed it.

SPEAKING OF TONICS

Sometimes folks tell me they have trouble with their sprayers clogging up while they're applying tonics. Well, it's a snap to avoid that problem. Here's all you need to do:

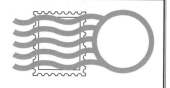

Dear Jerry,

Do I really need to plan a lawn? Can't I just buy some grass seed and toss it around where I want my yard to be?

A. *No, you don't have to plan—if you're willing to risk creating a high-maintenance monster. But my Grandma Putt taught me that anything worth doing is worth doing right. By planning your lawn before you start tossing around the grass seed, you can head off problems like weeds, poor soil, and hard-to-mow spots before they have a chance to cause you even a minute's misery.*

Give 'em a look-see. Before you start mixin' up any tonic, inspect your sprayer, as well as the container you're using to mix the ingredients. They need to be spotlessly clean, because it only takes one tiny particle of dirt to clog the sprayer's siphon tube.

Mix, then pour. Always mix your ingredients thoroughly in a pail or bucket before you add them to the sprayer jar. This way, they'll flow more freely through the tube.

Warm 'em up. Bring thick, sticky ingredients, such as molasses, corn syrup, and honey, to room temperature before you add them to any recipe. Don't use them right out of the fridge! If they're cold, they'll clog the tube. And make sure they're mixed thoroughly with the other ingredients.

Add dishwashing liquid last. Because it has a heavy consistency, especially if it's concentrated, this ingredient is easier to mix (and therefore flows better) if you add it at the end of the process.

Dissolve it all. Make sure that granular substances, such as Epsom salts and instant tea, are completely dissolved in the tonic liquid.

Star-Spangled *Lawn* Lore

Like most garden plants, many of the best turf grasses have been bred from wild parents. But some of them, including three popular varieties of Kentucky bluegrass, were first discovered growing in not-so-wild places. 'Mystic' got its start on a golf course near New York's Kennedy Airport. The forerunners of 'Banner' were plucked from the grounds of Fort McHenry in Maryland. And 'Midnight' traces its family roots to the Mall in Washington, D.C.—just a stone's throw from the White House.

Strain first. When you're using tobacco tea in a recipe, pour it through a sieve first to eliminate any small particles that could clog the tube.

Strain last. To be extra sure of successful delivery, strain all tonics through a sieve (or a piece of old pantyhose) into your sprayer jar. This way, you'll snag any tiny bits of stuff before they can clog up the sprayer and cause you a lot of grief.

GREAT BALLS O' BUBBLES!

Water that has a high concentration of chlorine can make baby shampoo (or my Plant Shampoo) foam up like a bubble bath—clogging the sprayer in the process. If this happens to you, just remove the tonic from the jar, mix a small amount of antiseptic mouthwash with water, and run this solution through the sprayer to cut the foaming action.

 ## Easy Does It

You say you'd like to have a gorgeous, green lawn but you lack the time—or maybe just the inclination—to do the necessary feedin', weedin', and waterin'? So don't do it. Hire somebody else to provide that TLC. But no matter how eager you may be to trade in your fertilizer spreader for a bag of golf

clubs, don't just call the first lawn-care company that pops out from the Yellow Pages. A mission as important as maintaining your home's green scene demands a top-notch caregiver. Here's how to find that superstar.

WHO'S BEHIND THAT SPREADER?

Find out who handles the tending chores for friends and neighbors who have good-looking lawns. Or ask the folks at a local garden center for recommendations. Try to get referrals for at least

BLUE PLATE SPECIAL

POLLUTION SOLUTION TONIC

Over the winter, a lawn tends to accumulate a load of dust, dirt, and other crud, and that can add up to trouble in the spring. So give your turf some relief by applying this mighty mixture as soon as the snow melts.

50 lb. of pelletized lime
50 lb. of pelletized gypsum
5 lb. of Epsom salts

Mix these ingredients together in a big tub, and spread the mixture over your lawn, using either a drop or broadcast spreader. Then wait at least two weeks before giving your lawn its first spring feeding (see "Spring Startup" on page 117). This recipe makes enough for 2,500 sq. ft. of lawn area.

three companies. Interview them all, and be sure to ask each one for at least three references. Then quiz those customers, too—don't just assume that because you were given their names they'll give you glowing reports about the company.

Of course, you'll want to know whether the fellas and gals on the job deliver all the services they're hired to perform, and do them well. But don't stop there. Ask how these people are to work with. For instance, are they pleasant and polite? (After all, who wants a bunch of grumps around the place?) Are they alert and careful when any children, pets, or elderly folks wander onto the scene? (Of course, it's your job to supervise your brood, but we all know what can happen if you turn your back for two seconds!) And what about their personal habits? Are they neat and tidy, or do they leave your yard littered with sandwich wrappers and cola cans?

GET IT IN BLACK AND WHITE

Once you've found a couple of likely lawn-care candidates, ask the head honcho of each company to give you two written documents:

1 An itemized listing of services and costs. Any company that's worth its salt will have this at its fingertips. If you

Star-Spangled *Lawn* Lore

If you'd rather leave the yard work to somebody else, don't think you're a rare duck: At last count there were roughly 70,000 lawn-care companies in the United States, with an average of nine full-time and three part-time employees.

find one that doesn't, take your business elsewhere. Otherwise, hidden costs could send the price tag soaring.

2 A full explanation of the service contract. In particular, note the length of the contract and whether it automatically renews itself each year. If you haven't worked with a company before—even if your best friend has given you glowing reports about it—my advice is don't tie yourself to a multiyear agreement.

SHOW AND TELL

Having written estimates and contracts in hand will ensure that your lawn-care service doesn't cost more than you bargained for. But a few other pieces of information could be crucial to your financial well-being. Ask to see copies of these documents:

Licenses and permits. In most places, a business must be licensed by the town or state (or both) to do the work it does. Don't sign any contract until you know your lawn-care outfit is operating legally.

Insurance policies. Make sure the company has insurance that covers both workers' compensation (landscaping has one of the highest claims rates) and any damage caused to your neighbors' property. This is especially important if the company uses pesticides or herbicides, which are becoming a big legal issue all across the country. If, for instance, chemicals drift across your property line and kill your neighbor's flowers, you could be held liable (and take it from me: this *does* happen more than you'd think). Mishandled equipment causes problems, too. In the blink of an eye,

an inexperienced worker can destroy a tree or a bed of prize roses.

Proof of membership in a professional association. The Professional Lawn Care Association of America is the biggie, but there are also state associations. This is important to you for three reasons: First, these groups have codes of ethics that their members must agree to follow. Second, they generally have lawyers or resolution counselors on retainer to handle any problems that arise between their members and homeowners. (In extreme cases, this could spare you the hassle and expense of going to court.) Third, you can usually figure that only a company that is capable and serious about its business will go to the bother and expense of joining an association.

Super★Secret

It's Electrifying!

Have you ever noticed how your lawn looks greener right after a thunderstorm? Well, that color change is not just your mind playing tricks on you. It's electroculture in action. In simple terms, here's how it works: Every time there's a bolt of lightning, the electrical energy causes airborne nitrogen and oxygen atoms to combine, forming nitric oxide. This, in turn, dissolves in water to form nitrates, which fall to earth in the form of raindrops. They seep into the soil, and bingo— your grass greens up!

KEEP IT NATURAL

One way to make *sure* that your lawn-care company doesn't put you in hot water with your neighbors (or their lawyer) is to look for one that uses only organic methods. In the old days, these outfits were about as common as giraffes in Alaska, but now they're springing up all across the country. And they rarely keep a low profile, so you should have no trouble finding one in your neck of the woods.

CHAPTER 6

Give It a Drink

Every living thing on earth needs water to survive, and turf grass is no exception. But, just as we saw with food in Chapter 5, too much H_2O can lead to all kinds of problems, ranging from thatch buildup to root rot. Finding the right balance can be tricky; so can delivering that life-giving elixir at the right times, and in just the right way. But fear not, my friends: In these pages, I'll let you in on my tricks for quenching your lawn's thirst in a way that'll keep it in the pink of health.

☆ Less Is More

If you're like most of the folks that I hear from across this great land of ours, you're watching your water bills climb higher every year. And unless I miss my guess, you're wondering how you can curb your lawn's drinking habits, but still keep it healthy, happy, and handsome. So before we move on to the ways and means of delivering H_2O, I'll tell you how to help your turf live better on less. (P.S. It's easy!)

A GRASS-ROOTS MOVEMENT

The road to a water-thrifty lawn starts with a strong, healthy—and deep—root system.

How Much Water Does My Lawn Need?

To stay in peak form, most lawns need roughly 1 inch of water each week during the growing season, whether it's supplied by you, rainfall, or a combination of both. But that's a general guideline, *not* a hard-and-fast rule. Your turf may need either more or less than that, and its thirst can even change from one week to the next. That's because a lawn's water requirements depend on many factors, including the type and variety of grass, where you live, how well your soil retains moisture, and even current weather conditions such as temperature, wind, and humidity. Fortunately, there are a number of simple ways to tell when your lawn is thirsty, and you'll find them right here in this chapter, so keep on reading!

Johnny-on-the-spot you'll have to be with the H_2O when a dry spell hits.

TOUGH LOVE

Ready for a pop quiz? True or false: On the first hot day of spring, you should haul out the garden hose or crank up the sprinklers and give your lawn its first nice, cool drink of the season. The answer: A resounding FALSE! That's because if the water's flowing freely early in the year, life will be easy in the top few inches of soil—and that's where the grass roots will stay. (After all, why would they bother to go lower? Like most of us folks, plants generally don't work any harder than they have to!) But,

Although most of a grass plant's roots grow in the top 6 to 8 inches of soil, many thirsty plant parts will dive a whole lot deeper if you give them a chance. How do you do that? Well, for starters, you do it by providing the kind of loose, healthy, teeming-with-life soil that we talked about in Chapters 3 and 4. To see how your soil stacks up, er, stacks down, in terms of grass-roots hospitality, just grab a shovel and dig up a clump of turf (don't worry: you can tuck it back in later with no harm done to the grass). Then, look at the roots. The longer they are, the more moisture they can grab from deeper in the soil, and the less water you'll have to give them. Conversely, the shorter they are, the more

if you let that soil dry out some, those underground parts will scurry down to deeper, damper territory. And the moisture they find at those levels will sustain the plants when Ma Nature turns up the heat later on in the summer.

DOWN, PLEASE

When you water your lawn, always make sure the H_2O seeps down to the full depth of the roots. The exact distance varies (see "A Grass-Roots Movement" on page 133), but in most cases it will be in the range of 6 to 8 inches. Shallow watering actually does more harm than good because it encourages the roots to stay in the soil's upper reaches—making for weak grass with a thirst that won't quit. When you water deeply, you create a reservoir that the underground legions can tap into. The more moisture they have at their disposal, the more they'll expand, and the more soil the roots occupy, the stronger, and more hose-independent, your lawn will be.

DELIVER DRIBS AND DRABS

Instead of serving your grass its full ration of water all at once, go at it slowly. Give it about ¼ inch of water, wait 10 minutes, then give it another ¼ inch. Continue this water-then-wait approach until you've moistened the soil all the way down to the bottom of the

Star-Spangled *Lawn* Lore

Here's something to ponder at your next barbecue: Whom do we have to thank for introducing us to this all-American pleasure? The answer: none other than Christopher Columbus. When he and his crew landed in the Caribbean in 1492, they encountered folks cooking fish and meat on a framework of sticks raised above a fire. The locals called the method "barbacoa." Chris and the boys took the custom back home to Spain, and before long it was all the rage in Europe. The English called it "barbecue," and when they set sail for Virginia and Massachusetts, they brought their favorite recipes with them.

roots (see "See for Yourself" on page 145). When you put in just a little water at a time, the soil absorbs it more efficiently and sends it to deeper levels.

HIGH TIME

One of the easiest ways to encourage long grass roots is to set your mower deck higher. That's because, as with

Yankee Doodle Data

Deep, Deeper, Deepest

Grasses differ greatly in their diving prowess, but even the most shallow-rooted ones can send their roots much farther down than you probably think possible. Here's a comparison of some common types.

GRASS TYPE	DEPTH
Bent grasses	Deep (1 to 8 in.)
Kentucky bluegrass, perennial ryegrass, red fescue, St. Augustine grass	Deeper (8 to 18 in.)
Bermuda grass, tall fescue, zoysia grass	Deepest (down to 5 ft.)

most other plants, the height of the blade is directly related to the length of its underpinnings. (Just think of a tree, which normally has a root system that reaches to the edges of its canopy, or even beyond.) The reason is that the upper part of the plant produces carbohydrates, which make roots grow longer and larger. If you routinely give your lawn a crew cut, you'll deprive the roots of needed nourishment, and they'll stay short. But if you keep those green tresses on the long side— 2 inches or higher—you'll give them a chance to produce plenty of carbohydrates and the parts belowground will stretch downward to the best of their ability.

Besides encouraging deep roots, mowing high helps conserve water in another way: Because taller grass shades and cools the soil, less moisture is lost to evaporation.

THAT'S NOT ALL, FOLKS!

Helping your grass grow long, strong roots is a crucial step in reducing your lawn's water needs (and your monthly bills). But there's a lot more you can do to curb your turf's drinking problem. Here's a roundup of terrific tactics that could actually wean your grass from the garden hose—at least in years when the clouds are generous with their output:

Sow smart. When you're starting from scratch (see Chapter 3) or renovating an existing lawn (see Chapter 4), choose the most drought-resistant grasses that will thrive in your neck of the woods (see "Is There Any Drought?" on page 138).

Look sharp. Never mow your lawn with a dull blade. That'll leave the grass with frayed, ragged edges that quickly release moisture to the air. Sharp cuts result in clean, even tips that hold water inside the plant, where it belongs. How often you need to sharpen your blade depends on the type of mower you have and how often you mow. For the full details on the cutting edge, see Chapter 7.

Dispatch thatch. This nasty stuff makes it difficult—and in extreme cases, all but impossible—for water to reach the grass roots. See Chapter 4 for my surefire thatch removal and prevention method.

Cool it. Don't dethatch or aerate your lawn in hot, sunny weather. Save those chores for cool, overcast days (see Chapter 4). And forget about feeding, weeding, and even battling bad bugs when the temperature skyrockets. All these chores put stress on grass plants—and a stressed plant is a thirsty plant.

Don't dig it. And don't till it either—at least not any more than absolutely necessary (for example, if you're starting a new lawn and have to get a lot of organic matter into the soil pronto). Tilling and cultivating cause the soil particles to clump together, making it harder for the grass roots to tunnel through in search of moisture. (You can read all about lawn-friendly soil in Chapters 3 and 4.)

Star-Spangled Lawn Lore

We've been talking a lot about roots, and for good reason: Under your lawn, there are a lot of them! To be specific, just one little ol' grass plant has as many as 13 million roots, and if you stretched them out on the ground in a single line, they'd go for 300 miles. That's roughly the distance from Hartford, Connecticut, to Baltimore, Maryland.

THE DIET SQUAD RIDES AGAIN

Chalk up yet another reason for giving your lawn the amount of food it needs, and not one speck more: Grass that gets just enough nutrients develops a healthy, water-thrifty root system. Overfeeding causes all manner of problems that lead to greater water consumption. Especially beware of serving up an overdose of nitrogen. It triggers rapid growth up above the normal mowing height and into the air currents, where moisture is quickly wicked away from the blades. For everything you need to know about turf grass diets, see Chapter 5.

Yankee Doodle Data

Is There Any Drought?

As we've seen, you can improve the water-holding power of any soil and encourage any kind of grass to grow longer, more drought-resistant roots. But the fact remains that some kinds of grass just naturally handle dry conditions better than others. Here's how the major types react when Mother Nature turns off the faucet.

WHAT DROUGHT?	WE'LL GET THROUGH THIS!	WATER NOW!
Bermuda grass	Bahia grass	Annual ryegrass
Buffalo grass	Canada bluegrass	Bent grass
Fine fescue	Kentucky bluegrass	Carpet grass
Tall fescue	Perennial ryegrass	Centipede grass
Zoysia grass	St. Augustine grass	Rough bluegrass

DON'T FORGET MY MAGIC BULLET!

Throughout this book I've been telling you all the ways that adding heaping helpings of organic matter to your soil can make your lawn healthier. Well, that's not all my favorite magic bullet can do: It can also help you cut back on your watering. That's because soil that's made up of 3 to 5 percent organic matter retains water two to three times longer than soil that hasn't been treated to this healthiest of health foods.

YES, BUT...

No matter how much organic matter you add, the real-time water-retention ability of any soil depends on its type. For example, heavy clay soil can hold up to three times as much moisture as sandy soil—and therefore, go without water from you *or* Mother Nature for up to three times as long.

IT ALL DEPENDS ON YOU

Well, maybe not *all*, but to a large extent, how much water your lawn consumes depends on how green you insist on keeping it. By nature, all northern grasses go dormant in the summer unless they get a steady supply of moisture, either from rain or from your sprinkler. They don't die; they just turn brown and stop growing until the flow starts up again. Of course, no grass can survive all summer long without *some* liquid refreshment (see "Is There Any Drought?" at left). But, except in extremely dry years, most lawns in the Northeast and Midwest can survive just fine on rainfall alone, though there's a chance they'll look pretty ugly for a good part of the time.

I have to admit that to my way of thinking, this hands-off approach makes about as much sense as hauling a dead, brown tree into the house at Christmastime—after all, summer is the very time when you want soft, green, toe-ticklin' turf to romp on. But don't skirt the law if your community is under water restrictions due to drought. In other words, don't get caught with the hose in hand while your neighbors comply and their lawns turn brown. Remember that letting your lawn fend for itself is usually a safe option, at least for a while. For more on coping with drought and other natural nuisances, see Chapter 12.

Sprinkle, Sprinkle, Liquid Star

A garden hose works fine for serving up my tonics or washing down a driveway, but at watering time, you need equipment with real star power—namely, a top-notch sprinkler. You have many shapes, operating styles, and price ranges to choose from. Here's the lineup.

SPEAKING OF SPRINKLERS

Before you set out to shop for a sprinkler, it helps to know a little technical lingo. That way, you'll be able to understand the numbers on the sprinkler box and talk turkey with the sales clerk at the garden center.

Distribution pattern. The shape of the area covered by the sprinkler. It may be a square, rectangle, circle, or semicircle. Some types can be adjusted to spew out their water in several different configurations—definitely a feature to look for if your lawn has nooks and crannies created by nonturf elements like flower beds, patios, or pathways. That way, you can water (let's say) the

---

Super ★ Secret

Down Under

Aboveground, portable sprinklers are all well and good if you have a small-to-middlin' lawn, or if you live in a place where rain provides most of the water your grass needs. On the other hand, if your green scene covers several acres, or you rarely see clouds from spring through fall, consider forking out some bucks for an in-ground irrigation system. It's not a small investment, but it could save you big bucks in water bills. For the whole lowdown on these down-low marvels, see "Water, Water Everywhere" on page 68.

circle of grass inside your curving drive-way without irrigating the concrete.

Flow rate, a.k.a. precipitation rate. Measures the amount of water the sprinkler spews out in an hour, and that can range from ¼ to 1 inch. Here, look for the label that sports the lowest number you can find. That's because the lower the flow rate, the more time the water has to seep into the soil and down to those roots I talked so much about earlier.

Throw radius. This tells you the size of the area the spray reaches. Depending on the model, the distance will be anywhere from 25 to 75 feet. Buy a device that gives you the coverage you need, but don't go overboard: You don't want to send water flying beyond your lawn and into the street!

Uniformity. A comparison of how much water falls at various points along the throw radius. No sprinkler can boast 100 percent uniformity, but the closer it can come to that impossible dream, the better it'll serve you *and* your lawn.

IT TAKES ALL KINDS

Aboveground sprinklers come in five basic types. Each has its pros and cons, and within each type, quality varies considerably. (It's the same old story: By and large, you get what you pay for.) Here's the quintet:

1 Fixed. This is the least expensive of the bunch, and for good reason: Fixed sprinklers generally have a short throw radius and poor uniformity. They're also prone to leaking around the head, which means that the ground within a couple feet of the sprinkler gets a lot more water than it should. On the plus side, they have no moving parts to break or get stuck (water simply shoots out of holes in the head). And some models are adjustable, so you can vary the spray pattern.

2 Impulse. No doubt you've seen big agricultural sprinklers at work as you've traveled our country's highways and byways. Well, these guys are scaled-down, domestic versions, and they function in the same way: As a strong jet of water shoots out from a nozzle, a spring-loaded arm whacks against that stream, shattering the water into tiny droplets and, at the same time, making the nozzle revolve in a circle. As you might expect from equipment that's modeled on serious farm machinery,

Super ★ Secret

It's Raining Cats and Dogs!

Throughout this chapter, I've been sharing my best secrets for helping your lawn thrive on very little water. But what about those times when it rains so much for so long that you start surfing the Net in search of ark-building plans? Well, I can't make the clouds dry up. But I can offer you some terrific tips, tricks, and tonics to help mop up the mess once the sun returns. You'll find them all in Chapter 12, beginning on page 268.

impulse sprinklers do a first-rate job. They have a good throw radius and the best uniformity of any sprinkler (including the in-ground systems). On the downside, like any nontraveling sprinkler, even these irrigation marvels can leave puddles of water at the base.

3 Oscillating. This is the most popular of all sprinkler types, but that's not because of its watering prowess. The reason is that it delivers water in a rectangular pattern that's tailor-made for the typical suburban lawn. Oscillating sprinklers have a pretty good throw radius, and the pricier models rate high in uniform delivery. At the lower end of the dollar spectrum, though, uniformity plummets. As they rock back and forth, they drop more water on the downside of each swing, forming mini-lakes in the process. The result: prime breeding ground for weeds, diseases, and (yes) mosquitoes. So buy accordingly.

4 Revolving. These babies sport a rotating arm that spins around faster than a speeding bullet, shooting water from a nozzle at each end. As any kid will tell you, there's no better way to spend a hot summer afternoon than running back and forth through that cold spray. Unfortunately, although "planting" a revolving sprinkler in your lawn will make you a hero of the under-10 set, it won't do your grass much good. As with fixed sprinklers, you can expect a short throw radius and lousy uniformity. In fact, most of the water pools up around the base of the sprinkler.

5 Traveling. If you loved playing with model trains as a kid (or maybe still do), this is the irrigation device for you! The business end is a standard revolving sprinkler that's mounted on a wheeled base that moves along a hose that you've laid out on the ground (much as you'd lay out a model train track). It has the same low throw radius as any other revolving sprinkler (see above), but because this sprayer goes anywhere you send it, its spewing distance becomes a moot point. And, because most traveling sprinklers are very well made, they deliver excellent uniformity. Granted, a traveler will cost you a pretty penny, but the upside is that it'll reward you with a job well done—not to mention the fun factor!

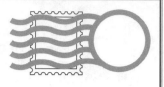

Dear Jerry,

We went on a month's vacation and left our neighbors' teenage son in charge of watering our lawn. When we came home, the grass was full of brown patches. What went wrong? And how can we get rid of the spots?

A. *Sounds like your young helper was workin' the night shift! Watering in the evening—and even late afternoon—lays out the welcome mat for brown patch and other diseases caused by foul fungi. To get rid of the spots, spray your turf with my Lawn Fungus-Fighter Tonic (see page 225). And from now on, make sure no one gives your grass a drink after 2 P.M. To play it extra safe, water between 5 A.M. and 8 A.M. (For the full scoop on dastardly diseases, see Chapter 10.)*

WHAT A CAN CAN TELL YOU

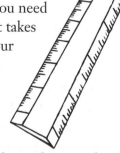

Once you've got your spankin' new sprinkler home, you need to find out how long it takes to deliver the water your lawn needs (which, in most cases, is 1 inch a week when the grass is actively growing). The all-American, traditional method of doing this is with the can test. Just set empty soup or coffee cans around your lawn in the sprinkler's spray path, and run the sprinkler for about 15 minutes. Then stick a ruler into each can, and measure the amount of water inside. Then get to figurin'. Let's say your measuring stick is wet up to the ¼-inch mark. How long would you need to keep the faucets on to give your lawn an inch of H_2O? If you said 1 hour, give yourself an A! If you didn't, well, don't worry about it. I understand that Professor Einstein was lousy at math, too.

By the way, it usually takes between 30 minutes and an hour to deliver 1 inch of water to your lawn.

HONEY, I FLOODED THE NEIGHBORHOOD!

Unless you've got a better memory than anybody *I* know, I all but guarantee this scenario will happen to you one day: You'll turn on the sprinklers, go about your business, and come back hours later to find your lawn flooded and a stream of water gushing down the street—or into your neighbors' yards. Fortunately, there's an easy way to avoid this sort of, um, adventure: When you buy your sprinkler, also pick up a timer that you hook up between your faucet and your hose. Prices vary depending on the degree of sophistication. Some models will turn off the water flow at a given time, and that's that. Other types can be programmed to turn the sprinklers on and off whenever you want.

THE HOSE KNOWS

Or perhaps I should say, the hose can spell the difference between a sprinkler that does the job you bought it for, and one that just fizzles off. Take it from me: Buy the highest quality hose your budget will allow. If you try to economize with a bargain-basement brand, you'll waste a lot of time and energy fussing with (and cursing over) cracks, kinks, and leaks. The best models are generally made of high-grade rubber or laminated filament. But new, high-tech materials are springing up all the time, so before you make a final decision, ask the folks at your local hardware store or garden center what they'd recommend.

If you have both a front yard and a backyard to water, do yourself a favor and buy two hoses. That way, you won't have to drag that long, rubber snake from one faucet to the other.

SIZE IT UP

Before you head off on your hose shopping trip, measure the distance from your outside faucet to the farthest point in your lawn. Then, make sure you buy a hose that's long enough to reach it. In terms of diameter, generally ¾ inch works just fine, but if your house has low water pressure (see "First Things First" on page 70), opt for ⅝-inch diameter; it'll give you wider sprinkler coverage.

SUMMER SOOTHER TONIC

Automatic sprinklers provide a simple, efficient way to water your lawn. But every now and then, I like to take hose in hand and do the job the old-fashioned way. When I do that, I soothe my whole yard with this nice, relaxing shower.

2 cups of weak tea water*
1 cup of baby shampoo
1 cup of hydrogen peroxide

Mix these ingredients in a 20 gallon hose-end sprayer, and give everything in sight a good soaking. Your yard will thank you for it!

* To make weak tea water, soak a used tea bag in a solution of 1 gal. of warm water and 1 tsp. of dishwashing liquid until the mix is light brown. Store leftover liquid in a tightly capped jug or bottle for later use.

AH, GO SOAK!

For watering very narrow areas, like a grass strip between your driveway and flower beds, you can't beat a soaker hose. There are two types: One is made of porous material that "sweats" water for its entire length. The other is a flat, rubber hose that's pricked with tiny holes through which the water seeps. Whichever kind you choose, just stretch it out down the middle of your skinny-mini lawn, turn on the faucet, and let the moisture ooze right into the soil. You'll lose almost no H_2O to evaporation, and none at all to run-off.

SEEING DOUBLE

While you're at the hardware store, pick up a two-headed Siamese faucet attachment for every outside water hookup you've got. These contraptions are the cat's meow when it comes to lawn and garden chores, because they let you hook up your hose to one of the heads and leave the other open for the times you need to fill a bucket or watering can. Just think—no more screwing the hose off and on a zillion times each summer!

BLUE PLATE SPECIAL

LAWN FRESHENER TONIC

When your lawn tells you it needs a drink, serve it this refreshing, restorative cocktail.

1 can of beer
1 cup of baby shampoo
½ cup of ammonia
½ cup of weak tea water*

Mix these ingredients in a 20 gallon hose-end sprayer, and apply the elixir to the point of run-off. Then watch your tired-looking lawn spring back to life!

To make weak tea water, soak a used tea bag in a solution of 1 gal. of warm water and 1 tsp. of dishwashing liquid until the mix is light brown. Store leftover liquid in a tightly capped jug or bottle for later use.

☆ Watering Wisdom

So now you know how to get your lawn drinking less and enjoying it more. And you know how to choose gear that'll serve up liquid refreshment in just the right way. Now let's look at all the other whys and wherefores of wise watering.

CARE FOR A DRINK?

There's really no great skill involved in knowing when to water your lawn. When your turf is thirsty, it'll speak up loud and clear! Well, not in English, of course. Like all plants, grass communicates in sign language. Here are three signs that translate into "Give me a drink—please!"

1 The grass plants turn from a healthy green color to a dull, grayish blue. At the same time, the blades curl up or fold in along the edges.

2 The soil changes. Heavy soil hardens into a solid block; lighter soils turn tan-colored and crumbly.

3 When you walk across your lawn, the grass doesn't spring back. Instead, your footprints remain for a long time—often for several hours.

THE TURN OF THE SCREW(DRIVER)

Here's a simple—and foolproof—way to tell whether it's time to water your lawn: Just push a long screwdriver into the

ground. If you have to struggle to get the tool 6 inches or so into the soil, turn on the sprinklers and give that turf some liquid refreshment.

SEE FOR YOURSELF

Of course, you don't really want to let your lawn get dehydrated. The key to keeping it green and healthy is to water it just *before* it starts showing symptoms. "How on earth can I do that?" you might ask. "I'm not psychic!" Maybe not, but you can still learn to read your lawn's mind. Just get a shovel and dig up a block of turf, in the same way you'd check the root length (see "A Grass-Roots Movement" on page 133). Only this time, grab a fistful of soil from the turf block. If you can still feel some moisture, it's not time to water yet. Keep sampling throughout the summer until you get a good sense of how long it takes the soil to dry out. And be sure to take samples from different parts of your yard, because moisture vanishes at different speeds, depending on many factors. Here are some of them:

Slope. Soil at the top of a hill can be bone dry when the ground at the bottom is still damp. As for the soil along the way down—how it's holding up will vary depending on the steepness of the incline.

Super★Secret

Super Sod

If you're starting a new lawn and saving water is a high priority, go with sod rather than seed. According to the folks who study such things, lawns started from sod can absorb 10 to 12 times more water than those started from seed—even after they've been growing for two years.

Yankee Doodle Data

Sippers and Gulpers

How long you need to keep your sprinklers running depends on the kind of soil you've got. This chart shows how long it takes for water to reach a depth of 4 to 6 inches. If the roots of your grass are longer than 6 inches (see "A Grass-Roots Movement" on page 133), just increase the watering time accordingly.

SOIL TYPE	INFILTRATION PER HOUR (IN.)	TIME REQUIRED FOR 1 IN. OF WATER TO REACH A DEPTH OF 4 TO 6 IN.
Sand	2	30 min.
Sandy loam	1	1 hr.
Loam	0.5	2 hr.
Silt loam	0.4	2 hr., 15 min.
Clay loam	0.3	3 hr., 20 min.
Clay	0.2	5 hr.

Sunlight. The more there is, the faster the soil will dry out.

Wind. Wide open spaces will lose moisture much more quickly than areas on the leeward side of a fence or wall.

IN THE SHADE OF THE OLD APPLE TREE

Or maybe it's a maple—no matter. On a hot summer day, there's nothing like lying back on the grass in the shade of a big ol' tree. And you can bet the soil in that cool, cozy spot is nice and moist, too, so you don't have to water that part of the lawn so often, right? Wrong! Turf grass that's growing under a tree or a big-bruiser shrub needs to be irrigated *more* frequently than grass that's basking in full sunshine. In fact, a lawn area that has a lot of trees or shrubs growing in it may need up to three times as much water as a spot without any woody plants. How come? Two reasons:

1 When light rains fall, they're often blocked by a tree's leafy canopy. As a result, the soil below gets cheated out of its fair share of natural moisture regularly.

2 Trees and shrubs are big drinkers. And when they go root to root with grass for the same water supply, they usually win.

TREE-TIME STRATEGY

To hear some folks talk, you'd think that keeping tree-shaded lawn areas well-watered and healthy was as complicated as putting a man on Pluto. Well, it's not. Here's all you need to do:

★ When you suspect that it may be time to water, check tree-shaded spots first, because they'll be the first to dry out.

★ When you do water, remember these three operative words: slow, easy, and deep. Let your hose or sprinkler run at a gentle pace for at least an hour. That way, the moisture will reach down to the deepest levels of the soil. The last thing you want to do is supply water only to the top 6 or 8 inches of soil because that'll encourage the tree to produce shallow roots. And that could mean big-time bad news because, although shallow-rooted grass can send your water bill soaring, a shallow-rooted tree could crash through your roof!

ON THE OTHER HAND

In areas where the turf is shaded by something that does not have a competing root system—say a tall fence or a vine-covered arbor—it's a different story altogether. Grass plants growing in those dim sites do need less water than their brothers on the sunny side of the lawn. How much less depends on the degree of shade and, of course, on all those other variables I've been warning you to watch for, such as slope, type of soil, and weather conditions. My best advice here: Experiment until you find the amount and the right delivery schedule for your trouble spot (see "See for Yourself" on page 145). Bear in mind, though, if the shade is really intense, trying to grow even the most shade-tolerant grass will just be a waste of time, money, and effort (see Chapter 2 for the lowdown on shady characters).

WHY BOTHER?

Besides shady spots, there are two other lawn sites that are so hard to keep well-watered that you may not want to bother growing turf grass in them at all:

Very steep slopes or hillsides. These tend to be a huge waste of both time and water. That's because the water's natural tendency is to run downward rather than soak in (after all, just like everything else on earth, it has to obey the law of gravity). In order to get any moisture to the grass roots, you have to use sprinklers or a hose that delivers water *very* slowly, and apply it in short cycles, a few minutes on and a few minutes off. Plus, sloping ground is the very dickens to mow. (Moderate slopes, while still trickier to deal with than level ground, are at least doable. For the lowdown on sowing grass on tilted territory, see Chapter 3.)

Don't Let It Burn, Baby!

Super ★ Secret

Some of the trickiest places to keep grass well-watered and thriving are areas adjacent to patios and driveways, light-colored walls, or large expanses of glass. That's because all of these structures capture sunlight and radiate heat to their surroundings. At best, the grass in these spots will need a lot of water. At worst, those little blades could burn to a crisp. If you live where summers get really hot, consider getting your grass out of the "kitchen" and replacing it with plants that can take the heat. Many flowers and herbs—including lavender, verbenas, lantana, and portulaca—put on their best show in hot, dry sunlight.

Semi-public ground. In particular, I'm thinking of the narrow strip of land between the sidewalk and the street. For one thing, it's all but impossible to set up a sprinkler to water the grass without sending gallons of H_2O gushing onto the street and sidewalk. And, unlike narrow spaces closer to your house (see "Ah, Go Soak!" on page 144), it may be a royal pain in the grass to keep a soaker hose in operation. Furthermore, in order to get your grass to survive at all, you need to engage in a constant battle with compacted soil, reflected heat from the concrete, and often the roots of street trees.

My advice in both these cases: Give up on turf grass and plant an attractive, unthirsty groundcover. You'll find some dandy choices in Chapter 15.

HELP US, ET!

No, I'm not suggesting that you phone home and talk to that cute little movie star from outer space. In this case, ET doesn't stand for extraterrestrial. It's short for evapotranspiration. Try *that* as a tongue-twisting challenge at your next barbecue! I know this is starting to sound intimidating, folks, but it's not. So please bear with me while I explain.

In recent years, scientists have been trying their darnedest to help all of us reduce water waste while still keeping our lawns lush and lovely. One big breakthrough has been adapting the use of ET for lawn care. (It's a concept that's been used in commercial agriculture for years.) It's the measurement, in inches, of the amount of water that evaporates from the soil, combined with the amount of water that transpires (or "sweats") from the leaves of a specific plant over a particular period of time. And it's turned out to be an amazingly accurate way of figuring out how much H_2O turf grass needs, based on the local weather conditions.

So just what does this mean for you? Well, for one thing, in traditional low-water states, such as Arizona, New Mexico, and California, municipal water departments and Cooperative Extension Services keep seasonal ET estimates at their fingertips. All you need to do is pick up the phone, call the office closest to you, and ask for the info. And if you live in farm country anyplace in the U.S.A., you can probably find daily figures in your local newspaper. Most likely, these will be calculated for cash crops rather than lawns, but the folks at your Cooperative Extension Service can give you a simple conversion factor.

DON'T GET *TOO* EXCITED

The ET formula provides the best system yet devised for calculating a Mama Bear lawn drink (not too much, not too little—*just* right). But you can't simply take the published statistics at face value. Here are some things you need to keep in mind:

★ When you read a water-needs figure for plants in general, it's usually 20 to 40 percent higher than your lawn's requirements (depending, respectively, on whether you have warm- or cool-season grass).

★ To compensate for the uneven distribution of most lawn sprinklers, you need to bump the number up a tad. How much depends on the uniformity of your sprinkler. I can't give you a hard-and-fast number because sprinklers vary so greatly. (This is why it's so important to perform the test described in "What a Can Can Tell You" on page 142.)

★ Even when ET figures are calculated for lawns, they're only general guidelines. They're not tailor-made to suit your yard. You will need to make alterations to compensate for individual characteristics such as sloping ground, compacted soil, and shady nooks.

from the **MAIL BAG**

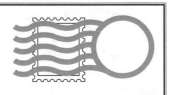

Dear Jerry,

I just got a new water softener, and I'm concerned about the salt it adds to my water. Is it true that it's harmful to grass?

A. *Yep, it's true, all right. Too much salt can make a lawn go belly-up. Fortunately, the answer to your problem couldn't be simpler: Just make sure your outdoor faucets—or the lines that run to your underground sprinklers—are not connected to the water-softener system. (Besides saving your grass, you'll save money on water-softener salt!)*

Super ★ Secret

It Just Ain't So

Contrary to what a lot of folks think, brown spots in your lawn are *not* a sign of dry soil. In fact, those patches could signify that you're watering too much. But they could also be caused by any number of other factors. For the whole roster, see "What Happened to My Lawn?" on page 98.

WATER EARLY

No matter how much water your lawn needs, serve it up as early in the day as you can. First thing in the morning is best, but whatever you do, avoid these two times:

Midday. From roughly 10 in the morning until 2 in the afternoon, the sun is generally at its hottest and brightest. And that means you'll lose a lot of water to evaporation before it has a chance to seep into the soil.

Evening. Grass that stays wet overnight is a prime target for all sorts of fungal diseases.

AA-CHOO!

If you suffer from allergies, you have another reason for being early to rise on watering day—or setting your sprinkler to go on at the crack of dawn. Turf grass releases its pollen between 3 A.M. and 8 A.M. (don't ask me why; I don't make the rules). By giving your lawn a good soaking during that time, you'll put most of the pollen out of commission...at least for a while.

WHO ORDERED MUSHROOMS?

Are mushrooms popping up all over your lawn? Well, I'll bet pennies to pepperoni that it's not because the pizza-delivery guy dropped the box. Instead, it's probably a sign that one of two things is going on: Either you're giving your lawn too much water or, more likely, you're watering too often.

To get rid of the 'shrooms, just pluck 'em up by hand and toss 'em in the trash can— *not* the compost bin. And if you have a dog on the scene, don't dawdle! If Rover gobbles up those foul fungi, they'll make him sick as a dog—or worse. Then

let that soggy turf dry out thoroughly before you give it another drink.

WORSE YET

Another clue that you may be letting the sprinklers work too hard is the sudden appearance of fungal diseases. These foul felons thrive in damp conditions, and once they've taken hold, some of them can be the very dickens to get rid of. In Chapter 10, you'll find my strategy for diagnosing and dispatching dastardly diseases of all dispositions.

BUT JUST MAYBE...

There's also a third possibility for the appearance of mushrooms or fungal diseases: You could have poor drainage. For my guidelines on testing your soil and correcting drainage problems, see Chapter 3. Or, if the soil is so soggy you'd just as soon give up on growing grass in that spot, check out some great alternatives in Chapter 15.

KEEP OFF THE GRASS

Unless it's absolutely necessary, don't walk on your lawn when it's wet, whether the water came from rain showers or your sprinklers. And don't let kids or pets romp on the grass before it's had a chance to dry. Foot

Star-Spangled *Lawn* Lore

If your town fathers and mothers are constantly after you to cut back on your lawn watering, it's no wonder: Statistics show that, depending on the city, 30 to 60 percent of the freshwater supply is used for watering lawns.

traffic on damp ground will put your soil in the fast lane on the road to compaction. (If your soil is already compacted, you can loosen it up by following my tips in Chapter 4.)

GIVE IT A NIGHTCAP

Many types of grass start to go dormant when the first frost hits in the fall. So, just before you expect Jack Frost to land on your doorstep, give your turf one last, thorough soaking. A lawn that goes into the winter with a bedtime drink in its belly will always wake up in better shape than one that didn't get that extra bit of pampering.

THE MATERNITY WARD

Brand-new lawns, whether they're started from seed or sod, demand much

BUZZ BUSTER LEMONADE

If mosquitoes are making your lawn watering chores a nightmare, send 'em packin' with this citrusy beverage. There's nothing skeeters hate more than the scent of lemon! (For more on conquering these vile vampires, see Chapter 9.)

1 cup of lemon-scented ammonia
1 cup of lemon-scented dishwashing liquid

Put these ingredients into a 20 gallon hose-end sprayer, and hose down everything in your yard three times a week, preferably early in the morning.

different treatment than established plots of grass. You can read all about starting a new lawn in Chapter 3, but here's the watering routine in a nutshell:

Newly seeded lawns. For the first two to three weeks, keep the top ¼ to ½ inch of soil moist, but not wet. If the seed is allowed to dry out, it won't germinate. On the flip side, if it gets too much water, the little tykes will float off or fall prey to foul fungi. Turf professionals solve that dilemma by lightly misting the seedbed anywhere from three to five times a day. If you have sprinklers with sophisticated timers (see "Honey, I Flooded the Neighborhood!" on page 142), you can (and should) follow their example. Otherwise, just do the best you can. Water before you leave for work, and the minute you get home. If you can possibly do it, water at midday, too, or hire someone else to do the job—that's actually the time the seeds need refreshment the most.

At the toddler stage. Once the seeds germinate, start supplying more water, less frequently. The exact timing will vary with the weather, but my basic watering routine is this: once a day for two weeks; every other day for two weeks; every third day for two weeks.

Newly sodded lawns. Sod, too, needs to be kept constantly moist until its roots have tunneled into the ground beneath. For the first month or so, water every morning until the soil is soaked 6 to 8 inches below the surface. And keep a close eye on the intersections where strips of sod come together, and the edges next to driveways, sidewalks, and other paved areas. These spots will all dry out more quickly, so you may need to water them more often. Once the grass is actively growing, you can switch to the same routine you use for a mature lawn.

WATCH THOSE BABIES!

Missing just one day of watering grass seed can reduce germination by 30 percent or more. Skip two days, and you can kiss half of those seeds good-bye. And freshly laid sod will dry to a crisp if it's not kept moist. So water, water, water!

Jerry's 10 Commandments for Wise Watering

In this chapter, I've gone into a lot of detail about the whys, ways, and wherefores of watering. This box boils it all down to 10 can't-miss rules for keeping your lawn healthy, happy, and hydrated:

1. Honor your roots. Help your grass develop long, strong roots, because the deeper and more robust those under-pinnings are, the more moisture they'll absorb from the soil—and the less water you'll have to provide.

2. Know your soil. Find out whether you've got clay, sand, loam, or a combi-nation thereof, and water accordingly.

3. Learn the signs of thirsty grass. When your lawn is overdue for a drink, the blades turn grayish blue, the soil hard-ens up, and your footprints linger on the surface.

4. Water before symptoms appear. Fig-ure out how long it takes for your lawn to dry out so you can deliver moisture before the grass starts crying for help (see "See for Yourself" on page 145).

5. Know the territory. Even the smallest lawn contains places that need less water than others. Find out where these microclimates are in your yard and water accordingly.

6. Water early. Watering early in the morning, before Ol' Sol heats up, will ensure that the maximum amount of moisture sinks into the soil, rather than disappearing into thin air. This timing will also help you fend off fungi and other disease-causing troublemakers.

7. Water deep. Always saturate the soil to the full depth of the grass roots. In most cases, that's at least 6 to 8 inches.

8. Watch the weather. You'll need to provide more water during periods of warmer temperatures, bright sun, brisk breezes, or (of course) no rain. Your lawn will need less help from you in times of rain showers, cool tempera-tures, cloudy skies, or calm air.

9. Get to know ET. Ask your Cooperative Extension Service to give you the evapo-transpiration figures for your area, and set your sprinklers by them (see "Help Us, ET!" on page 148).

10. Know when to say when. In some places, growing turf grass may take more time, effort, and expense than it's worth to you. When that's the case, give up the struggle. You have plenty of eas-ier options (see Chapter 15).

The Kindest Cut of All

On the face of it, cutting your grass seems about as straightforward as a yard chore can get: You just crank up the ol' mower and off you go. But in reality, mowing is *the* most important part of lawn care. Your timing, your technique, and even the equipment you use can all spell the difference between a beautiful, healthy, trouble-free lawn, and one that gives you nothing but grief—and could even go belly-up. Here are my time-tested tips for trimming that turf in a way that'll keep it lush and lovely, and (believe it or not) reduce your water and fertilizer bills.

So What's the Big Deal?

I know: It seems impossible that something as simple as taking a little off the top can affect your lawn's health. So let me explain mowing from a grass plant's point of view. That way, when I start making a big deal about when, how, and with what gadgets you should mow your lawn, you'll understand the reason.

UNNATURAL ACTS

The most important thing to remember about mowing

is that your lawn doesn't like it one bit. If that grass had its druthers, it would go through life doing what Mother Nature intended: growing straight up, maturing, and setting seed for the next generation. Turf grasses can tolerate mowing simply because they are what scientists call "basal-growing" plants, meaning they grow from a point in the crown, close to the soil line. When you cut off the tips (which are actually the oldest parts of the plant), new growth shoots up from the crown. But the fact remains that having growing tissue suddenly whacked off takes its toll on the plants in several ways:

There go the groceries! Through the process of photosynthesis (remember this from high school biology class?), grass, like other green plants, takes carbon, oxygen, and hydrogen from the air and, with the help of the sun's energy, turns them into food. When you cut the blades, you reduce the plant's ability to snag those airborne elements. The result: less nourishment for the grass—both above and below ground.

Look out below! As we saw in Chapter 6, the height of the grass blades is directly related to the depth and vigor of the roots. The shorter you cut the blades, the shorter and weaker the roots will be. And grass without a strong root system not only has a constant thirst, but it's also a sitting duck for pests and diseases. In fact, if you remove more than

Star-Spangled *Lawn* Lore

If baseball is the American pastime, then lawn mowing is the American chore—at least if you consider time as the criterion. On average, we Yanks spend 40 hours each year mowing our lawns. Think about it: That's a typical workweek—or a full week's vacation!

40 percent of the top growth at any one time, the roots simply stop growing.

The door's open! Every time you cut the grass, you create openings that work like a wide-open door. Moisture inside the plant goes out and, given half a chance, diseases come in.

It's bright in here! Cutting the grass too closely (as a lot of folks tend to do) ushers in the sunshine, which both dries out the soil and causes those nasty weed seeds to germinate.

HAVING SAID THAT...

The fact that cutting grass isn't *natural* doesn't mean it's *bad*. In fact, if you go at it the right way, you'll actually

Yankee Doodle Data

How High I Am

The optimum mowing height for any lawn depends on the kind of grass and the time of year. Although turf types differ in how long they like to wear their tresses, they all like to keep a little more on top during hot weather, and a little less in spring and fall (or in regions where the weather stays cool all summer long). Here's a rundown of preferences.

TYPE OF GRASS	COOL-WEATHER HEIGHT (IN.)	HOT-WEATHER HEIGHT (IN.)
Bahia grass	2	3
Bermuda grass	½	1
Buffalo grass	2	3
Carpet grass	1	2
Creeping bent grass	¾	1¼
Fine fescue	2	2½
Kentucky bluegrass	2	3
Perennial ryegrass	1½	2½
St. Augustine grass	2	3
Zoysia grass	½	1

produce turf that's thicker, stronger, and more resistant to weeds and drought. That's because when a grass plant is cut, it responds in the same way many garden plants do when you prune them: In an effort to reproduce itself, it sends out side shoots—a process known in lawn circles as "tillering." Furthermore, when you mow, you admit light that lets those baby shoots grow and develop into a lush carpet of turf. And that's just what every lawn wants to see. (For my handy primer on grass anatomy, see page 21.)

WHAT DO YOU MEAN, "THE RIGHT WAY"?

There are a number of steps you can take to ensure that your grass bounces back like a champ every time you cut it (and I'll get to them all in a minute). But the four most important words to remember are these: Mow high, mow sharp. As for the first part of that rule, the classic rule of green thumb—and an easy one to remember—is to never cut more than one-third of the height of the grass at any one time. What that means in terms of actual inches depends on the type of grass and the time of year (see "How High I Am" at left). "Mow sharp" simply means that you need to keep a razor edge on your mower blade. That way, it'll slice cleanly through the grass, leaving as little wiggle room as possible for escaping moisture and invading germs. (For the lowdown on sharpening mower blades, see "Look Sharp" on page 162.)

HIGH IS GOOD, BUT HIGHER ISN'T BETTER

Having delivered my mow-high lecture, I must tell you that it is possible to let your grass get too high. Turf grasses that grow much over 3 inches tall tend to get thin and stringy; they don't form that nice, uniform look that we love in our lawns. Overly tall grass also tends to fall over, and to get all matted in wet weather. Then it may take a long time to dry out, and fungal diseases can set in.

YOUR GUESS IS AS GOOD AS MINE

You know how high your grass prefers to be, and you know that you should remove no more than one-third of the blade, but how do you know when it's reached that one-third-over-the-limit

stage? You measure it, that's how! Let's suppose you have Kentucky bluegrass, which likes to be kept at 2 inches in cool weather. Just grab a ruler, and mark it at the 3-inch line. Then when you suspect that it may be time to mow, hold the ruler upright on the ground. If the grass brushes your line, haul out the mower and trim off an inch.

To make your height check even easier, "plant" a few measuring sticks here and there around your yard. Then all you have to do is glance at them now and then. (It's important to have guide sticks in several places because grass grows faster in some parts of your lawn than others, depending on such factors as soil fertility, moisture level, and degree of shade.)

CHILLIN' OUT BREW

Mowing the lawn can be mighty hot work. So before you start, mix up a batch of this cooling spray, and tuck the bottle into your pocket. Then, every once in a while, as you're goin' about your yard chores, give yourself a few spritzes. You'll stay as cool as a cucumber!

> 2 tsp. of witch hazel tincture
> 12 drops of lavender essential oil
> 10 drops of peppermint essential oil

Mix these ingredients with enough water to fill an 8-ounce spray bottle, and use it to keep cool.

Super ★ Secret

Spray Your Troubles Away

Are you sick and tired of scraping grass clippings off your mower blades? Well, stop scraping! Instead, before you crank up the engine, just coat the underside of the mower with any of these lubricants:

★ Cooking spray

★ Household oil spray, such as WD-40®

★ Liquid car wax

IT'S OVER THE LINE!

It happens to all of us now and then: Life takes a turn for the busier and our attention wanders away from the lawn. Or we go away on vacation and come home to find grass so long that we can't even see the measuring sticks (see "Your Guess Is as Good as Mine" on page 157). When you're confronted with overly high grass, don't panic. Just cut it in small stages, no more than an inch at a time, and let the turf rest for a day or two between mowings.

★ Not So Fast

I know: It's Saturday morning, there's a golf course waiting, and you just want to crank up your mower and get the job done. But, like any other important endeavor, mowing a lawn demands a little preparation. Here's the routine that I follow.

IT'S A JUNGLE OUT THERE!

Your lawn may not seem like a dangerous place, but chances are it's full of booby traps that, if you hit them, can damage your mower—and even injure you or innocent bystanders. So before you start mowing (every single time) take a slow stroll around your yard scouting for hazards. Here are the things I look for:

Sticks, stones, and dog bones. And maybe those pruning shears that vanished last week. Pick 'em all up and toss 'em well out of the mower's path. If they're caught in the whirling blades (and you're lucky), they'll damage the machine. If you're not so lucky, those objects could be hurled through the air like a Roger Clemens fastball—maybe right through a window or at someone strolling by.

Stray mulch. If it's big and hard enough, it'll nick your blade. But even if it's too soft or small to do real damage, the chunks can fly all over your nice, neat lawn. Toss those wood chips and gravel pieces back on the flower beds where they belong.

Litter. If your yard is anything like mine, it seems to attract a strange assortment of paper and plastic—candy bar wrappers, plastic bags, fast-food boxes—you name it. Heaven knows where the stuff blows in from, but once it's been shredded by the mower blade, your lawn will look like the aftermath of a New Year's Eve party. Just collect it all in a plastic grocery bag and throw it into the trash can.

Anthills. These seem to pop up overnight, and if your mower hits one, the ants may retaliate by stampeding up your pant legs. That can be a big nuisance if the little swarmers are regular ol' picnic ants. If they're fire ants, you could find yourself racing to the emergency room. In Chapter 9 you'll find my foolproof tips for saying "toodle-oo" to both types of tiny terrors.

Yankee Doodle Data
Your Home Health Club

If you're like most folks I know, you could stand to lose a pound or two. Well, don't go out and spend good money on health-club dues—you've got a world-class gym in your own backyard! Here's a rundown of the calories you can burn up just by doing routine lawn and garden chores—and then enjoying the fruits of your labor afterwards. (The figures shown here are for a 150-pound person; the number of calories you burn will be higher if you weigh more, and lower if you weigh less. But you'll see the same results when you look in the mirror!)

LAWN CHORE	CALORIES BURNED PER HOUR
Mowing with a manual push mower	400
Digging, clipping, and other yard work	300–450
Raking your lawn	280
Mowing with a power mower	250
Mowing with a riding mower	175
AND THEN AFTERWARDS...	**CALORIES BURNED PER HOUR**
Playing badminton	350
Square dancing at your barbecue	350
Playing volleyball	300
Strolling around admiring your handiwork	120
Sitting in a lawn chair admiring your handiwork	84

Frogs and toads. These garden-variety heroes usually leap out of the way when they hear a mower approaching, but it doesn't pay to take chances. Find out in advance where their hidey-holes are, so you can give them a gentle heave-ho if you have to.

DRESS FOR SUCCESS

For most occasions, shorts and sandals make a fine summer uniform. But that's not what the well-dressed lawn tender wears on mowing day. For that chore, put on your golf spikes or other sturdy, closed-toe shoes with nonslip soles—not flimsy sneakers. And be sure to wear long pants, just in case you get hit with a piece of flying debris that you missed on your inspection tour (see "It's a Jungle Out There!" on page 158). Put on a good pair of gardening gloves if your hands are prone to blistering. And don't forget your sunglasses: Besides filtering out the sun's rays, they'll form a barrier between your eyes and airborne debris. Finally, if you're concerned about the effect of sun on your skin, add a broad-brimmed hat and long-sleeve shirt to your wardrobe list.

Whatever you do, leave all your jewelry in the house, and avoid any clothes that are loose or dangling. They can easily get tangled in the blades or other moving parts, and the results can be grisly—and sometimes fatal. (Trust me on this, folks: It happens more often than you'd think.)

CHECK YOUR MOWER

When I first started cutting the lawn at my Grandma Putt's house, she always insisted that I give the mower a thorough going-over before I started out. At the time, of course, I thought that was just about the most boring chore on earth. But now—many moons and thousands of mowings later—I know that the most important part of the job comes *before* you start the engine. Here's what to look for:

Super ★ Secret

What? I Can't Hear You!

The next time you see somebody wearing ear protectors while he's mowing his lawn, don't scoff. In fact, I wear them myself. The reason: Tests have shown that short-term exposure to as few as 100 decibels of noise can cause hearing loss. Gasoline-powered lawn mowers run in the range of 95 to 120 decibels. If you decide to follow my example, don't just stuff your ears with cotton or those foam things they sell in drugstores. Get yourself the kind of heavy-duty protective gear that sharpshooters wear at firing ranges. Is it cheap? No. But how much is it worth to hear "Happy Birthday" being sung at your (or your grandchild's) next milestone?

★ **Air filter.** If it isn't clean, replace it, *pronto*. Otherwise, dirt can sneak into the engine, wearing down vital parts and making starting a real hassle.

★ **Belt.** Check the condition and tension. If it's a little slack, tighten it; if it's showing signs of wear, replace it. (I like to keep a spare belt or two on hand for just those circumstances.)

★ **Blade.** If it's not razor sharp, sharpen it *now* (see "Look Sharp" on page 162), or replace it with a new one. (A blade that's badly nicked or very dull is definitely ready for retirement.) I keep at least two sharp blades hanging on a nail in the wall of my garden shed—well away from anything that could dull or nick their edges.

★ **Cooling fans.** They should be spotlessly clean and free of debris that could clog the works.

★ **Hardware.** Inspect all nuts, bolts, screws, and cotter pins. If anything's loose, tighten it now—don't wait until something starts to wobble.

★ **Oil.** Make sure it's at the full mark. Running your mower with too little oil in its tank is like begging for a blown engine. And at least once a year, change the oil and the filter. (I always do this

job on July 4, just because it's an easy date to remember.)

★ **Safety controls.** I shouldn't have to tell you why it's important to make good and sure these are in smooth working order!

★ **Underside.** If a mass of grass clippings or other debris has built up, clean it all out. Otherwise, it'll prevent the blade from turning smoothly.

LIVING BETTER ELECTRICALLY

If you have a cordless electric mower, don't forget to plug it in after every mowing to recharge the batteries. After the final cut of the fall, charge it overnight one last time, then unplug the cord and tuck the machine away until it's time for your lawn's first spring haircut.

AND EVERY NOW AND THEN

Once a month or so, wipe down all your mower's rubber and plastic parts with Armorall® to keep them from drying out, cracking, and even disintegrating before your very eyes. And every few weeks, give all chrome and metal parts a good rubdown with WD-40® or a similar lubricant. That'll prevent rust, corrosion, and sticking.

Look Sharp

There's almost nothing worse you can do to grass than cut it with a dull mower blade. In fact, a dull blade doesn't really cut at all. It tears the grass, leaving it with frayed tips that I like to think of as revolving doors: Water goes out; sun damage and diseases come in. How often a blade needs sharpening depends on the size of your lawn, how often you mow, and the type of mower you use. I like to do the job after every three mowings. Here's the routine for a standard, rotary mower:

Step 1. Gather your gear. You'll need:
- ★ Adjustable wrench
- ★ Block of wood or blade-locking tool
- ★ Bench vise
- ★ Blade balancer (optional)
- ★ Dowel or screwdriver
- ★ Flat medium file
- ★ Large can or other container with a tight lid

Step 2. Drain out the gas into the lidded container.

Step 3. Disconnect the spark plug wire so the motor doesn't turn over while you're working. This step is critical, because just a few drops of gas in the tank could be enough to make the motor kick over when you move the blade.

Step 4. Tilt the mower on its side, and wedge a block of wood between the blade and the mower deck to keep the blade from turning. (Or buy a tool that's made just for this purpose; most garden centers and many hardware stores carry this item.)

Step 5. Using your adjustable wrench, remove the bolt from the center of the blade. Then pull off the blade and clamp it in the bench vise.

Step 6. Carefully inspect the blade edges for small nicks, and remove them using your flat file.

Step 7. Sharpen the blade by filing toward the cutting edge with smooth, even strokes, following the original bevel. Be sure to make the same number of strokes on each edge. (If you take more metal off of one side than the other, the blade will be out of balance.)

Step 8. Balance the blade on a dowel or the handle of a screwdriver. If one side points up, sharpen the other until the blade lies flat. (Or use a blade balancer, which you can buy at garden centers and hardware stores.)

A word of warning: Don't try to save time and energy by sharpening mower blades—power or manual—with a power grinder or an electric drill with a grinding-wheel attachment. Either one can destroy the temper of the metal.

Look Sharp, Part II

All across the country, old-timer manual push mowers are staging a big comeback, for all kinds of good reasons (see "The Reel Deal" on page 175). One good reason is that, to a large extent, they sharpen themselves simply because of the way they work: As you push the mower, the revolving blades scrape over the cutter bar, and the action tends to make both blades keener. But every year or two, even these marvels need sharpening. You do it with this process, called "backlapping":

Step 1. Round up your supplies. You'll need:

- ★ Automotive valve-grinding compound
- ★ Flat medium file
- ★ Newspaper
- ★ Screwdriver
- ★ Soap
- ★ Soft paintbrush (optional)
- ★ Water

Step 2. Prop up the mower so you can turn the reel by twirling the wheels.

Step 3. Inspect the blades for burrs or nicks. If you find any, remove them by holding a file flat against the blade and pushing away from the edge.

Step 4. Examine the cutting bar. It should just meet the blades along their entire length. (To make sure it's in the right spot, grab hold of a wheel and turn it forward; if it's A-OK, you'll hear a whispery sound as the blades pass the bar.)

Step 5. If the bar is out of alignment, adjust it using the screws on the ends of the bar. (There are two at each end; you'll know at a glance which one will move the bar closer to the blades.)

Step 6. Using your fingers or a soft paintbrush, cover the blades with a thin, even coat of automotive valve-grinding compound (you can buy a can at any auto-parts store).

Step 7. Grab a wheel and turn it slowly backward so that the grinding compound is squeezed between the blades and the cutting bar. As the cutting edges pass each other, both will be sharpened. Just be sure that each blade touches the bar as you rotate the wheel.

Step 8. Make a dozen or so turns, applying more grinding compound as needed.

Step 9. Examine the blade edges. If they look sharp, wash off all the valve compound with soapy water, and rinse thoroughly.

Step 10. To test your work, insert a sheet of newspaper between the blades and the cutting bar, and rotate the reel forward. (It may take a few tries to get the paper in just the right position.) When the blades cut the paper as easily and as cleanly as a sharp pair of scissors would, you're ready to roll.

NO MO' ALLERGY WOES

Over the course of a week or two, between one lawn mowing and the next, huge amounts of pollen, dust, and dirt get blown onto the grass from who-knows-where. And, as every allergy-suffering lawn keeper knows, a lot of that crud flies up into your face every time you mow. Heck, even if you're not the one manning the mower, you still get clobbered by particles that drift into your house through the open doors and windows. Well, you don't have to pave your whole yard to alleviate your allergy woes. Here are a couple of easy ways to ease your discomfort on mowing day—and all summer long:

Mow low. Keep your grass cut to a height less than 2 inches. Of course, that means choosing a variety that can thrive with a crew cut (see "How High I Am" on page 156).

Shut 'em up. Close your windows before you (or your lawn-care crew) start mowing, and leave them closed for a few hours after the job is done. And this means *all* windows, not just those on the ground floor.

GO WITH THE GIRLS

Another simple way to cut back on your sneezin' and wheezin' is to plant female trees and shrubs. ("*Huh?*" I hear you saying.) Here's the deal: Many of our country's favorite trees and shrubs are *dioecious*, which means that each individual plant is either male or female. In order to reproduce their kind, the males release huge amounts of pollen into the air. When a female of the same species is close by, her flowers snag most of those particles. But when your yard (or, as is often the case these days, your whole neighborhood) is an old boys' network, the pollen just floats around—until it reaches your sinuses. So do yourself a favor: When you're shopping for woody plants, tell the folks at the garden center that you want a female. (Don't let anyone sell you a so-called seedless variety. These are actually male clones, and although they don't produce seeds, fruits, or flowers, they still produce pollen—and plenty of it.) Here are some of the most popular dioecious landscape plants:

Ashes (*Fraxinus*)

Bittersweets (*Celastrus*)

Cottonwoods (*Populus*)

Hollies (*Ilex*)

Honeylocust (*Gleditsia triacanthos*)

Junipers (*Juniperus*)

Kentucky coffee tree (*Gymnocladus dioica*)

Maples (*Acer*)

Mulberries (*Morus*)

Poplars (*Populus*)

Smoke tree (*Cotinus coggygria*)

Spice bush (*Lindera benzoin*)

Sumacs (*Rhus*)

Willows (*Salix*)

Yews (*Taxus*)

Star-Spangled *Lawn* Lore

Between 1960 and 2000, the percentage of Americans who suffer from allergies skyrocketed from roughly 3 percent to a whopping 38 percent. Many scientists now attribute that increase to a misguided landscaping trend: Over that same 40-year period, cities, towns, and a whole lot of homeowners began planting only male trees because, unlike females, they produce no "messy" fruits, flowers, and seedpods. That left us with millions of woody boys offering up tons of pollen—and very few girls to trap it in their blossoms.

⭐ The Fine Art of Mowing

Well, by now you've learned enough about grass to know how important a first-rate cutting job is. And you know how to get yourself and your mower ready for the task at hand. So let's move on to the ins, outs, dos, and don'ts of this all-American ritual.

SAFETY FIRST

Just like a gun or an automobile, a power lawn mower is a dangerous weapon. In fact, every year in our country, roughly 60,000 to 70,000 people are severely injured by lawn mowers. So play it safe and follow these simple tips:

Read all about it. Study the owner's manual that came with your lawn mower, and make sure you know how to maintain and operate the machine.

Don't touch that dial! Never disconnect any of the safety features—the manufacturer installed them for a very good reason.

Take a hike. Before you start mowing, take an inspection tour of your yard, scouting for potential hazards (see "It's a Jungle Out There!" on page 158).

Clear the decks. Shoo children and pets off the lawn, and keep them off until you're finished. And for good measure, clear away any movable objects that could be damaged by flying debris—inflatable swimming pools, for example. (Your inspection jaunt may not have turned up every single stick, stone, or wayward toy.)

Remember the dress code. Heavy, nonslip shoes and long pants are the uniform of the day (see "Dress for Success" on page 160).

Carry no passengers. Never—and I mean *never*—give a child a ride on a riding lawn mower. A sudden stop or a bump in the ground could put that youngster under the blades in the blink of an eye. (For more on riding mowers and tractors, see "Giddy-up!" on page 174.)

Push, don't pull. Don't ever pull a walk-behind lawn mower toward you when the motor's running. But what if your lawn has niches that are too narrow for you to walk in? Turn the mower around, and walk out. Then cut those mini-plots with a trimmer, or replace the grass with something that doesn't need to be mowed at all. (You'll find oodles of great options in Chapter 15.)

Fuel with care. Add fuel only when the engine is cool and the mower is on a level, nonliving surface (gas and oil kill

from the **MAIL BAG**

Dear Jerry,

My 10-year-old daughter is begging me to let her mow the lawn, but I just don't know whether she's old enough. At what age do you think it's safe to let kids do this job?

A. *Only you can decide whether your daughter is ready for this all-American rite of passage, because it's not a matter of chronological age. To my way of thinking, a child is ready to mow the lawn when he or she is tall enough and strong enough to handle the equipment, mentally mature enough to understand sound mowing techniques, and emotionally mature enough to practice them faithfully. (I've met a few 40-year-old "kids" whom I wouldn't trust with my lawn mower!) So let your conscience be your guide.*

grass, and other plants, too). When it's time for a second round of go-juice, turn off the machine and let it sit for 10 minutes or so before you fill 'er up. (In Chapter 13 you'll find my timely tips for dealing with fuel spills and other messy mishaps.)

Stop! Before you cross a nongrassy area, turn off the engine. Otherwise, you could send gravel, dirt clods, and who-knows-what flying through the air. And always shut off the power if you have to leave the mower unattended, even for a few seconds.

A HILL OF A DEAL

As I've said before, a steep hillside is a difficult place to grow grass, and it's definitely *no* place to be using a lawn mower! Even gentle slopes need to be handled with more care than level ground. Tackle them only with a walk-behind mower. Riding models are prone to flipping, and believe me, you don't want to be on one of those babies when it topples! And, to make the job both safer and easier, mow across the slope, not up and down.

CALLED ON ACCOUNT OF RAIN

…and a wet playing field. Regardless of the season, don't mow wet grass. How come? I'll give you half a dozen good reasons:

1 Wet grass cuts unevenly, so no matter how careful you are, you're all but guaranteed to wind up with a sloppy-looking lawn.

2 A lot of the clippings will bunch up on the underside of your mower, clog the blades, and most likely make the engine stall—again and again.

3 The clippings that stay on the ground will clump together and sit on top of the lawn, making a matted, yucky mess, instead of settling onto the soil, out of sight, as dry clippings do.

4 Your trampling feet and your mower's wheels will compact the wet soil. And if you recall Chapters 3 and 4, you know the trouble that can cause!

5 Cutting wet grass, like fussing with any other wet plant, encourages the growth and spread of diseases.

Save Those Trees!

Just a nick or two from a lawn mower can usher in diseases and bad bugs that may eventually kill a tree (though it might be years before the damage becomes visible to the human eye). So do your trees a favor—and make mowing easier on yourself at the same time: Replace the grass under those leafy branches with a shade-loving groundcover, or simply lay down a wide circle of organic mulch. (Just be sure to keep the stuff at least 4 inches from the trunk; otherwise, you'll be giving little bark-munching rodents a cozy winter hideaway.)

6 Wet grass tends to be very slick. You could easily slip and fall, and especially on a slope, the results could be nasty.

CHANGE IS GOOD

With some chores (scrubbing a floor or shoveling snow, for instance), it's fine to do the work in exactly the same way, time after time. Not so with mowing your lawn. In this case, you want to change directions each time you do the job. For instance, proceed on a north-south axis one week and east-west the next. Or move in straight lines this time and curvy swaths the following go-round. This variety of motion accomplishes two things: First, it helps keep the grass growing straight up, which makes for a more even cut.

Second, it puts less pressure on the soil, thereby reducing the risk of compaction. What's more, depending on how creative you are in your choreography, you could wind up with a nifty pattern on your lawn!

SPEED IS IMPORTANT, TOO

The speed of your blades, that is. Anytime you're mowing, always adjust the throttle to its fastest setting, for two reasons:

• Fast-moving blades make cleaner cuts, thereby causing less stress on the grass plants—and, as we've seen before, reducing water loss and barring the door for dastardly diseases.

• When you're going full throttle ahead, you save wear and tear on the engine.

SCALP PROBLEMS?

Is your lawn turning a whiter shade of pale? Or maybe a sickly yellow or brown? Can you see bare ground here and there? If you answered yes to any or all of those questions, there's a good chance that you're scalping your lawn. If the symptoms are generalized (as the docs like to say), most likely you're mowing too low or too often. But if the trouble spots are few and far between, chances are the problem stems from one of these two causes:

★ You're making sharp turns when you mow. This is a prime scalping maneuver. The solution is obvious: Stop making sharp turns on the grass. Instead, swing around in the driveway or on another paved surface, or change your landscaping layout to allow for easy maneuvering (see "Don't Cut Corners" at right).

★ Your lawn has bumps that get creamed every time your mower rolls over them. In this case, too, your mission is clear: Smooth out the terrain (see "Dippity Don't" on page 99).

GRASS CLIPPING COMPOST STARTER

Every time you add a new batch of grass clippings to your compost pile or bin, speed up the decomposition process with this magical potion.

> 1 can of regular cola
>   (not diet)
> ½ cup of ammonia
> ½ cup of liquid lawn food
> ½ cup of dishwashing liquid

Mix these ingredients in a 20 gallon hose-end sprayer and soak each new layer of grass clippings and other yard fodder.

DON'T CUT CORNERS

Maneuvering a lawn mower in and out of corners is annoying, time-consuming, and likely to result in scalped spots. So do what I did: Get rid of the corners. Rather, get the grass out of there and fill those angular spaces with flower beds, groundcovers, trees, or shrubs. And give all their living quarters gentle, curving edges. That way, you'll spend less time mowing and reduce the risk of scalping your lawn by making tight turns.

TO EVERYTHING THERE IS A SEASON

And that includes your mowing schedule. Here's my four-season routine:

Spring. Resist the temptation to rev up your mower the minute you see the first robin hopping across the lawn. Instead, let the grass grow just a little taller than one-third over the recommended height (see "How High I Am" on page 156). This way, it'll have time to wake up and gather some strength after its long winter's nap. When it's time to mow, trim it back by about one-third. Then, with each trim after that, gradually lower the mower deck until you're cutting at the right height for your type of grass.

Yankee Doodle Data

Be a Speed Demon

On some lawn mowers, you can adjust the wheel speed to match the condition of your grass. If your model came equipped with this neat feature, follow the guidelines in this chart. (For more about mowers, including how to choose the best one for you and your lawn, see "Lawn Mowers 101" starting at right.)

GRASS CONDITION	BEST WHEEL SPEED
Tall or thick	1 or 2
Normal	3 or 4
Thin	5 or 6

Summer. This is the time when your grass is most vulnerable to sunburn and water loss. So always let it grow beyond its maximum height by one-third. Then cut it back to its maximum, *not* its minimum, height.

Fall. To prepare your lawn for the long winter ahead, cut the grass to its maximum recommended height until it stops growing or goes dormant. Then drop the blade a notch and mow one last time.

Winter. This may be sleepy time for northern lawns, but there's no rest for you folks in the Sun Belt! Still, depending on where you live, you probably won't have to cut so often because your grass may grow more slowly. Just keep an eagle eye on it, and keep it at the recommended height for your current temperature range (see "How High I Am" on page 156).

GREEN GOLD

Simply by leaving the clippings on your freshly mowed lawn, you can cut the amount of fertilizer you need by as much as 25 percent. Furthermore, leaving those trimmings in place actually helps prevent thatch (for the full explanation of that miraculous process, see Chapter 4). But what about those times when you've been delinquent in mowing, and you've got so many clippings you could build a little grass hut (if only the strands were a tad longer...)? Don't worry: You've still got a chance to win your neighborhood's Environmental Hero Award. Actually, you've got three chances:

1 **Compost 'em.** Just rake 'em up and toss 'em into your compost bin or onto your pile. Then follow up with a good dose of my Grass Clipping Com-

post Starter (see page 169). Before you know it, that green gold will turn into black gold that, in turn, will enrich your whole landscape.

2 **Mulch 'em.** Spread the clippings around your trees, shrubs, flowers, and vegetables. They'll slow down water loss, reduce the soil temperature, and suffocate wicked weed seeds.

3 **Share 'em.** Offer your extra clippings to friends and coworkers, especially those who garden in cities. These folks are usually thrilled to receive gifts of what many suburbanites consider useless trash. In fact, I have a well-heeled friend who actually goes around soliciting grass clippings and banana peels to feed her tiny, walled garden in Boston. (It's a real showplace, I might add.)

DON'T LEAVE 'EM BE

Grass clippings are one thing. Fallen leaves are another. Left on the lawn, they can block sun and moisture from reaching the grass. So before the first snow flies, rake up the leaves and add them to the compost pile. To speed up the decomposition process, mow them over several times first, chopping them into nickel-sized pieces.

GRASS CLIPPING DISSOLVING TONIC

If you leave your grass clippings in place (whether your mower mulches them or not), spray your lawn twice a year with this timely tonic. It'll help the clippings break down more quickly and give your lawn a chance to breathe better, too.

> **1 can of beer**
> **1 can of regular cola (not diet)**
> **1 cup of ammonia**
> **1 cup of dishwashing liquid**

Mix these ingredients in a bucket and pour the solution into a 20 gallon hose-end sprayer. Apply to the point of run-off. Those clippings will decompose almost before your very eyes!

☆ Lawn Mowers 101

Lawn mowers come in so many shapes, sizes, and price ranges that my brain aches just thinking about it! And every season, manufacturers come out with newer, glitzier models with more bells and whistles. So what's the best mower for you? That's exactly what I'm going to talk about in this section.

THE ROTARY CLUB

Just drive around any suburban neighborhood on a Saturday morning and

Star-Spangled *Lawn* Lore

If I ever get around to starting a Lawn and Garden Hall of Fame, the first inductee will be William Beazley. How come? I'll tell you: In 1933, Mr. Beazley, of St. Petersburg, Florida, received a patent for the first ever gasoline-powered rotary lawn mower—and Saturday mornings haven't been the same since!

you'll see—and hear—dozens upon dozens of lawn mowers at work. And the vast majority of them will be rotary types. They cut with a single long, horizontal blade beneath a plastic, metal, or fiberglass housing called a deck. The operating principle is simple: The blade spins so fast that it creates a slight vacuum, lifting the grass for a split second before whacking it off. It's a good system (these babies didn't become suburban icons for no reason). Generally speaking, rotary machines are simple to maneuver, easy to maintain, and able to tackle even the toughest grass blades and most wicked weeds. Furthermore, they offer you plenty of choices in the showroom (we'll get to those in a

minute). Rotary mowers do have some downsides, though:

- They can't cut effectively below 1 inch, so they're all but useless on grasses that prefer the low life (see "How High I Am" on page 156).

- They don't cut as cleanly as a reel mower (see "The Reel Deal" on page 175), especially when the "victim" is a stiff, wiry customer like Bermuda grass.

- On a bumpy or uneven lawn, no matter how careful you are, a rotary blade is likely to scalp the turf (although some larger models feature "oscillating" or "floating" decks that are better able to navigate rolling terrain).

THE FAMILY TREE

Rotary mowers come in models ranging from bargain-basement basic to souped-up-spiffy, and the prices vary accordingly. These are the basic categories:

Gas-powered push mower. If you want plenty of power at a reasonable price, and you have a normal-size lawn, this is the machine for you. Many models come with bagging attachments mounted on either the side or the rear. Side-baggers tend to be less expensive, but don't let that be your deciding factor. Choose whichever type that you feel more comfortable maneuvering and that suits your landscape. (For instance, if you have to mow close to a lot of obstacles, a bag sticking out of the side could be a real pain in the grass.)

Self-propelled gas mower. This type provides easy maneuverability because pulleys and gears connect the engine to either the front or back wheels. Models with front-end drive are generally easier to handle: To stop forward motion, all you do is lift the front wheels off the ground. These machines tend to be more expensive than push mowers, but if your lawn is on the large side, you've got a few slopes to cut, or you just don't have the muscle power you once had, you'd be wise to overlook the higher price tag.

Mulching mower. The blade of this baby is designed to trap the cut grass blades inside the deck longer, so they get diced into tiny pieces before falling to the ground, where they decompose in a flash. You pay a pretty penny for this feature: A mulching mower can cost up to twice as much as a nonchopping version. Is it worth it? It is if you want to leave your clippings on the ground, but it drives you nuts to look at them lying

TERRIFIC TURF TONIC

No matter what mower you use, or how carefully you mow, having that little bit taken off the top is a shock to your grass. To help it recover, apply this gentle, but effective elixir once a month.

1 cup of baby shampoo
1 cup of ammonia
1 cup of weak tea water*
Warm water

Mix the shampoo, ammonia, and tea water in a 20 gallon hose-end sprayer, filling the balance of the jar with warm water. Then, just after you mow your lawn, apply the solution to the point of run-off.

* To make weak tea water, soak a used tea bag in a solution of 1 gal. of warm water and 1 tsp. of dishwashing liquid until the mix is light brown. Store leftover liquid in a tightly capped jug or bottle for later use.

there, even for a few days. One word of warning, though: Mulching mowers tend to choke on long, thick grass, so you need to cut frequently and slowly.

Electric rotary mower. Ah, the lovely sound of silence! And the nostalgic aroma of fresh, grass-scented air! Not to mention the delightful feeling in your pocket of dollars not being spent at the gas pump. Those are the three beauties of these mowers. The downside is the cord. Unless it can reach to the farthest edges of your yard, you're out of luck (or stuck lugging around a very long, heavy-duty outdoor extension cord). Then there's the risk of running over it and slicing it in two.... (As long as you don't grab on to the live end, there's no danger involved, and you can easily splice it back together. Still, it's a nuisance.)

GIDDY-UP!

If you've got a Ponderosa-size plot to mow, you want to sit down while you do it, and if you're willing to shell out some big bucks for the privilege, you've got a trio of options. (As you'd expect, the price tag rises with each increase in size, power, and versatility.)

Option 1. The Baby Bear of sit-on mowers, a.k.a. the riding mower, does nothing but cut grass. Generally, the mowing deck is out in front; the engine, with power generally ranging from 8 to 13 horsepower, is in the rear; and your saddle is somewhere in between. You can mow a path that's anywhere from 30 to 40 inches wide, which means you can make a lot better time than you could with any walk-behind machine.

Option 2. Mama Bear comes in the form of the lawn-and-garden tractor.

Super★Secret
Present and Accounted For

Don't even think of buying a ride-on mower that's not equipped with an operator presence switch. This dandy device halts blade movement when the operator leaves the driver's seat—or in some cases, won't allow the motor to start if the seat is unoccupied.

The 12- to 18-horsepower engine is out in front, under a hood that makes this model look kinda-sorta like a real farm tractor. You sit on a seat directly over the mowing deck. Sizes vary, but generally you can expect to cut 38 to 48 inches of grass in a single swipe. Some models can double as snow-removal helpers. (Blades, blowers, and throwers cost extra, of course.)

Option 3. Papa Bear is the true garden tractor. It's a scaled-down version of the workhorse farmer's tractor, with a 12- to 20-horsepower engine and the ability to cut 38 to 60 inches of grass at once. What's more, it accepts just about any attachment a weekend farmer could want, including chippers, tillers, earth-moving blades, and snow-removal gear—just the ticket for a multi-acre spread.

The one downside (not counting the price tag): You don't want to use any of these big bruisers on a slope because they can flip over faster than you can say "Whoa, Nellie!"

THE REEL DEAL

If the only reel mower you've ever known was the one you muscled around your parents' lawn on Saturday mornings, you could be in for a treat. That old dinosaur has been reborn, with a lighter body, smoother-working parts—and even a new, trendy image. The reasons are many:

Precision. These babies work like scissors, with curved, spinning blades whizzing over a fixed-bed knife. They cut sharp, they cut clean, and they cut close. (That's why they've never stopped being the darlings of the folks who tend golf courses, ball-parks, and fancy estates from Maine to California.)

Simplicity. Fewer moving parts equals fewer maintenance hassles.

Low cost. The initial price is below that of almost any powered machine; there's no gas or oil to buy; and the blade never needs replacing. Scrooge himself couldn't ask for a better bargain!

Cleaner air. Depending on whose statistics you read, and the age of the machines in question, running a gas-powered lawn mower for one hour produces the same amount of noxious fumes as driving a car for anywhere from 20 to (yes, you're reading this right) 350 miles. Fumes produced by a manual reel mower: zero.

Better health. Mowing your lawn with a push mower burns up as many as 400 calories an hour—besides toning your muscles and revving up your heart rate far beyond what you'd achieve with a powered machine.

Silence. If your entire mowing pleasure comes from picturing yourself at the wheel of a roaring racing car, this may be a major drawback to a reel mower. But if (like me) you love nothing better than listening to the sound of the birds and the bees and the wind in the trees.... well, I've made my point.

Star-Spangled *Lawn* Lore

If you like the idea of having a robot mow your lawn, you're in some pretty high-powered company: My informed sources tell me that the CIA has several of these cut-ting-edge cutters on the job at their headquarters in McLean, Virginia.

Mower Shopper's Checklist

Lawn mower quality and price tags range all over the ballpark. And this is one case where you don't always get what you pay for. For example, some big-name, rock-solid brands that used to be made in the good old U.S.A. are now being made overseas. As a result, their quality has plummeted—but in most cases, the price tag hasn't. Whether you're shopping for a new machine, or you think you've found a steal of a deal on a used model, always run through this checklist before you shell out your hard-earned cash. And be sure to try all these recommended maneuvers yourself, because when you get the machine home, the person running it will be *you*—not the big, hefty expert who wants to sell it to you. Here goes:

☐ Does the mower have a blade shut-off switch? (This safety feature is a *must* in my book!)

☐ Can you easily raise and lower the mowing height?

☐ Does the mower start right up when you pull the cord or flick the switch?

☐ If it's a push model, can you push it easily? (On your lawn's own contours, that is—not just on the pancake-flat showroom floor!)

☐ Can you maneuver it easily? (Put it through the kind of turns you'll have to make on your lawn.)

☐ Does it feel too heavy to handle, too light for stability, or just right?

☐ Is the catch bag in a convenient place for you?

☐ Is the catch bag easy to put on and take off?

☐ Will the mower be easy to clean, both up above and under the deck?

☐ Is the mower easy to take apart, so you can make minor repairs or sharpen the blade?

☐ If the mower is a cordless electric model, how long can you mow between battery charges?

☐ If it's a self-propelled machine, does it have enough power to get you over hilly terrain? (Generally you need a minimum of 5 to 6 horsepower.)

☐ If it's a ride-on type, is the seat comfortable?

☐ Can you get on and off of the thing easily?

☐ Last, but certainly not least, is the mower a name brand that can be serviced locally or—if it turns out to be a lemon—returned to the store where you bought it? (You don't want to be stuck with some obscure make that you may have to send halfway across the country—at your expense.)

YES, BUT...

Even I have to admit that a manual reel mower is not the right choice for every lawn. It does its best work on level lawns planted with soft grasses, like ryegrass, fescues, bent grasses, and Kentucky bluegrass. Also, unless you want to spend a *lot* of time mowing, you don't want to use a manual push model on turf that covers much more than 1,000 square feet.

GEE WHIZ, MR. SCIENCE!

Engineers, equipment manufacturers, and technological tinkerers are constantly working to give us new and better ways to mow our lawns. Two up-and-comers are the cordless electric mower and (believe it or not) the robotic mower.

Cordless electrics. These have been around for quite a while, but only in the past few years have they gone from being little more than pricey toys to solid tools that I can honestly recommend. They still don't come cheap, but if you'd love to have the benefits of an electric mower without the hassles of a cord, you owe yourself a test drive. Battery life, run time between charges, and general performance vary

considerably, so shop around before you buy (see my Mower Shopper's Checklist at left). As of now, only a few models are self-propelled, but with progress marching on as it is, that's likely to change soon. Also, bear in mind that, like reel mowers, cordless electrics perform best on level lawns consisting of soft, cool-season grasses (but look for advances in this department, too).

Robotic mowers. These have finally left the laboratories and hit the open market. They work just like those battery-powered cars that you played with as a kid, except that you don't have to follow them around, clicking a switch to guide their movements. All you need to do is bury some electromagnetic grids to mark the borders of your lawn. Then you turn the little guys loose, and off they go. The mowing pattern tends to be a tad erratic, but hey, nobody's perfect! And they do get the whole lawn covered—while you just sit there in your easy chair. The price? A lot more than most walk-behind mowers, but less than you're likely to pay for a ride-on

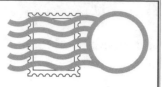

Dear Jerry,

I just moved to a new house, and I don't have the faintest idea what kind of grass is growing in the yard. So, of course, I don't have a clue how high to cut it. How can I find out what it is?

A. *It's simple, my friend: Just dig up a small clump from an out-of-the-way spot in your lawn. Then take it to a good garden center or your closest Cooperative Extension Service. The folks there will be happy to give you a positive ID.*

machine (in fact, a *lot* less than you'd pay for one of the big boys).

IS THAT OLD MAN WINTER I HEAR?

If you follow my pre-mowing ritual religiously (see "Check Your Mower" on page 160), your machine should stay in tip-top shape all season long. Then, when it's gettin' on toward hibernation time, all you need to do is perform this bedtime routine:

1 Empty the gas tank. Over time, old gasoline turns into a varnish-like film that can wreck your carburetor.

2 Drain and replace the engine oil. Replace the filter, too, if you haven't done that earlier in the year. That way, you'll be ready to roll next spring.

3 Remove the spark plug. Then squirt about 15 drops of lubricating oil into the hole. Crank the engine a few times to spread this oil all over the inside of the engine.

4 Check the spark plug. If it's in good condition, clean and regap it; otherwise, replace it.

5 Sharpen the blade. For my easy how-to directions to get 'em in tip-top shape, see "Look Sharp" on page 162.

6 Dip a soft cloth in oil. Then rub it over the blade and all exposed metal parts to keep rust from forming.

7 Finish by greasing all moving parts. This'll keep 'em from freezing up in the cold.

Then, tuck that baby into your garage and let it sleep in peace until next spring.

JUST A TRIM, PLEASE

Virtually every lawn has a few places that a mower can't reach, or can't cut neatly. Enter edgers and trimmers. These two tools do similar jobs, but there is a slight difference between the two:

Edgers are designed to cut grass that's growing along a hard surface like a sidewalk or driveway. The classic model consists of a wheel-blade combo at the end of a broomstick-like pole. You set the wheel on the pavement with the blade hanging over the edge. Then you simply roll it back and forth. Powered models make the job faster and easier, but with their exposed, rotating blades, they can be dangerous. If you choose this route, follow all the precautions you would with a mower—and then some!

Trimmers do the work of edgers, and a lot more besides. You can use them next to raised decks or flower beds, or in nooks and crannies where your mower won't fit—you can even whack down tall, tough weeds. The most basic trimmers are old-fashioned hand-held clippers. They come in both manual and battery-powered versions,

and for my money, you can't beat them for precision work around flower and vegetable beds. They're also inexpensive and blessedly quiet.

String trimmers use a piece of rotating nylon, plastic, or sometimes metal cord to whack the tops off tall grasses and weeds. The least expensive are the electric models with power cords. They're lightweight, quiet, and efficient, but as with a traditional electric mower, you still have that cord to deal with. Battery-powered trimmers cost a little more, but they give you unlimited room to roam. Running time between charges varies, but it's increasing all the time. Gas-powered trimmers have more power than electrics, so you can get your work done faster. On the downside, they're heavier, need more maintenance, make enough noise to wake the dead, and (of course) have to be kept filled with that liquid gold—gasoline.

String Along

Always keep a spare reel of trimmer cord on hand. That way, if your supply runs out when you're in the middle of yard duty, you won't have to call time-out and rush to the store. (Guess how I learned this timesaving tip!)

All-American Lawn-Care Calendar

Well, friends, now that you know everything you need to do to have the toe-tick-linest turf in town, there's only one thing left to tell you: when to offer up all that tender lovin' lawn care. With this at-a-glance calendar, you'll be able to plan your lawn chores season by season, no matter what part of our great land you live in.

☆ Early Spring

• As the snow melts, repair any winter damage to drives and walkways. Remove piles of soil and scraped-up grass, rake the area clean, and water well to remove any road salt. Then reseed or resod as needed, following the directions on pages 101–102.

• Test your soil for pH and nutrients, if you didn't do it last fall, and make any adjustments recommended by the results (see page 64).

• Give your whole yard a wake-up drink of my Rise 'n' Shine Clean-Up Tonic (see page 122). This bracing beverage will rouse your lawn from its winter slumber and nail any pesky pests that managed to survive the winter.

Follow this Five-Step Spring Feeding Program (also see page 117):

STEP 1. Apply my Spring Wake-Up Tonic (see page 123) just as your grass is waking up—*before* you apply any fertilizer or other tonics.

STEP 2. Follow up with a dose of my Get-Up-and-Grow Tonic (see page 124) to get your lawn up off its grass!

STEP 3. Within two weeks of applying the Spring Wake-Up and Get-Up-and-Grow tonics, feed your lawn with a mixture of 3 pounds of Epsom salts per bag of premium dry lawn food (enough for 2,500 square feet). Apply at half the rate recommended on the package label, going first north to south, then east to west. **Note:** If you're using a natural/organic lawn food, go ahead and mix the salts and fertilizer together as described here. If you're going with a synthetic type, though, spread the fertilizer and Epsom salts separately.

STEP 4. Within two days of putting down the Epsom salts and fertilizer (see Step 3 above), kick your lawn into action by applying my Lawn Snack Tonic (see page 125).

STEP 5. One week later, apply the other half of the salts and fertilizer as described in Step 3.

• Whack annual weed seeds before they sprout by applying corn gluten (see page 246) or my Brussels Sprouts Weed Brush-Off (see page 248). For broadleaf perennial weeds, use my Wild Weed Wipeout Tonic (see page 243). First, though, spray the turf with

Super★Secret

Is It Spring Yet?

As you peruse this calendar, you'll see that I'm not giving you dates to go by. That's because spring doesn't start on the same day, or even the same month, everywhere in this great big land of ours. Why, when my friends down in Texas are watchin' tulips pop up in their yards, folks in New England are still shoveling snow—and will be for quite a while yet! So how do you know when spring has sprung? It's easy: Just keep your eyes and ears open. For instance, when I hear the sound of spring peepers, I know it's early spring. When the grass starts greenin' up, it's a sign that midspring has arrived in my neck of the woods. A little later on, in late spring, the lilacs burst into bloom. The signals may be different where you live, but if you pay attention to Mother Nature, you can't go wrong!

1 cup each of dishwashing liquid and ammonia poured into a 20 gallon hose-end sprayer.

• As new grass growth begins, spread screened compost over your lawn, particularly in any weak, thin, or scraggly areas.

• Clean up below your bird feeders: Remove any debris before it grows into weeds, and reseed or resod if needed (see pages 101–102).

• Sow cool-season grasses if you didn't do that last fall. Be sure to use my Soil Prep Tonic (see page 76) before sowing, followed by my Seed Starter Tonic (see page 187) to get the grass off to a rip-roaring start.

• Lay warm-season grass sod, followed by a dose of my All-Season Green-Up Tonic (see page 85) to jump-start the growth.

• Plant warm-season grass plugs, then apply my All-Season Green-Up Tonic (see page 85). Five weeks later, fertilize with a 20-5-10, slow-release, dry lawn food and Epsom salts (3 pounds of salts per bag of fertilizer with 2,500-square-foot coverage). (See Note in Step 3.)

☆ Spring

• Overseed to repair any damaged areas of the lawn (see Chapter 4). Then treat each of those new mini-lawns to a dose of my Spot Seed Tonic (see page 103).

• Be sure to water those newly seeded areas at least twice a day, and preferably three or four times daily, until the little sprouts poke their heads above the soil.

• If you didn't do it last fall, sharpen your mower blade, or replace it with a new one, so you'll be all set for the first cut of the season.

• After you give your lawn its first haircut, rake up the clippings to let the sun shine in and warm up the soil. This'll help the grass green up faster. Then toss that green gold onto the compost pile, and saturate it with my Grass Clipping Compost Starter (see page 169).

• Remove thatch from cool-season lawns. Then spread screened compost over the dethatched turf, followed by a dose of my Kick-in-the-Grass Tonic (see page 100). To keep the nasty stuff from coming back, apply my Thatch Blaster Tonic (see page 92), and follow my thatch-prevention guidelines in Chapter 4.

• If Japanese beetles were a problem last summer, apply milky spore to your lawn now. (See Chapter 9 for the details on this and other grub-and-beetle-control measures.)

• As soon as the weather warms up, look for new mole tunnels, along with telltale signs of other ornery critters (see Chapter 9). Apply my All-Purpose Pest Prevention Potion (see page 218) to tunnels, runs, and holes.

• Issue a No Trespassing sign to dogs, cats, and deer by spraying my All-Purpose Pest Prevention Potion (see page 218) in their target areas.

• Lay cool-season grass sod, and follow up with my All-Season Green-Up Tonic (see page 85). And for the first month or so, water every morning until the soil is soaked 6 to 8 inches below the surface. (You can read all about watering in Chapter 6.)

• Plant groundcovers on steep slopes or other places where you don't want to fuss with turf grass. And get them off and running fast with my Groundcover Starter Chow (see page 327).

Yankee Doodle Data

Friend or Foe?

When a critter wanders onto your lawn, don't just assume that he's up to no good. In fact, if you let him get on with life as he knows it, he could be one of your truest allies in your war on bad-guy bugs and other lowlifes. Let me give you a few of the best examples.

TRUE-BLUE ALLIES	GO GUNNIN' FOR
Foxes	Mice, mole crickets, voles
Moles	Beetles, grubs, slugs and snails
Opossums	Gophers, grubs, mice, rats, snails
Raccoons	Grubs, mice, mole crickets
Skunks	Armyworms, baby rats, grubs, insects and insect eggs, mice, slugs, voles

 # Late Spring

• If roving canines have been visiting your yard, or your own pooch has been doing his duty where you don't want him to do it, apply my Lawn

TIRE-TRACK REMOVER TONIC

When your lawn is damp, anything on wheels can leave its mark in the turf—delivery trucks, cars, bicycles, wheelbarrows, and even your lawn mower. The good news is that, regardless of what caused them, getting rid of those ruts is simple. Just wait for the soil to dry out a little, and then stroll across the area with your aerating sandals, or punch holes in the ground with a garden fork. Spread gypsum over the damaged area at the recommended rate, and overspray it with this timely tonic.

> **1 cup of ammonia**
> **1 cup of beer**
> **½ cup of baby shampoo**
> **¼ cup of weak tea water***
> **Warm water**

Mix the ammonia, beer, shampoo, and weak tea water in a 20 gallon hose-end sprayer, filling the balance of the jar with warm water. Apply to the point of run-off. Repeat this treatment every three weeks to get your lawn on the road to recovery!

* To make weak tea water, soak a used tea bag in a solution of 1 gal. of warm water and 1 tsp. of dishwashing liquid until the mix is light brown. Store leftover liquid in a tightly capped jug or bottle for later use.

Saver Tonic (see page 212) to the affected areas.

• To keep unwelcome doggy guests away, mix up a batch or two of my Dog-Be-Gone Tonic (see page 218) and sprinkle it around the perimeter of your yard.

• Keep felonious felines at bay by spraying their target areas regularly with my Hit the Trail Mix (see page 218).

• Sow seed for warm-season lawns now, so the grass can benefit from the hot weather that's coming up. Before you start, get the seedbed ready by using my Soil Prep Tonic (see page 76). And don't forget to energize the seeds by soaking them in my Seed Starter Tonic (see page 187) for 24 hours before you sow them.

• Test for grubs in the soil (see page 203) and apply milky spore or beneficial nematodes if needed. (For the low-down on grubs and other lowlifes, see Chapter 9.)

 # Early Summer

• Make your time in the yard more enjoy-able—and safer, too—by declaring it off-limits to mosquitoes and fire ants. (See my fail-safe battle plan in Chapter 9, as well as the recipe for my Buzz Buster Lemonade on page 152.)

• Change the oil and oil filter in your lawn mower on or before July 4 or another easy-to-remember date.

• Start using your edger and string trimmer to keep the grass neat and tidy around trees, shrubs, and flower beds, and along walks and driveways.

• If you're growing any ornamental grasses, give them a morning shower once a week with my Rust Blocker Tonic (see page 324).

Summer

• Give your groundcover plants a midsummer boost by treating them to a dose of my Just Desserts Tonic (see page 330).

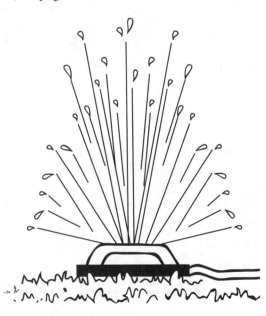

Star-Spangled *Lawn* Lore

At last count, 53 million households in the United States had lawns to look after. That's a lot of folks out there feedin', weedin', waterin', and mowin'!

• If slugs are running roughshod through your shady groundcover beds, serve 'em a batch of my deadly Quack-Up Slug Cookies (see page 259).

• Anytime you water your lawn by hand, use my Summer Soother Tonic (see page 143). It'll keep the turf perky on even the doggiest of the dog days.

• When you and Mother Nature have both slipped up, and your lawn is overdue for a drink, serve it a big "glass" of my Lawn Freshener Tonic (see page 144).

• When drought threatens, apply my Drought Buster Brew (see page 262) to help your lawn shoulder the tough times ahead. After the rain clouds have moved back in again, treat your grass to my Drought Recovery Tonic (see page 264).

• Keep the skeeter population in check with regular applications of my Buzz Buster Lemonade (see page 152).

• Check regularly for symptoms of fungus among us. If you find any, diagnose the dastardly disease (see Chapter 10), then choose your medicine: Fairy Ring Fighter Tonic (see page 224), Lawn Fungus-Fighter Tonic (see page 225), or Lawn Mildew-Relief Tonic (see page 228).

• If moss appears, and you don't like it one bit—or even worse, if hot, humid weather is making mold form on your grass—deliver regular doses of my Moss Buster Brew (see page 255). On the other hand, if you like the looks of this soft, green, and ultra-low-maintenance groundcover, encourage its growth by applying my Moss-Grow Tonic (see page 332). (For more on moss from both points of view, see Chapter 11.)

 **Early Fall**

• Sow cool-season grasses now so the plants can build strong root systems before winter sets in. Be sure to use my Soil Prep Tonic (see page 76), and soak the seeds for 24 hours in my Seed Starter Tonic (at right) so they'll get off to a rip-roarin' beginning.

• Don't forget to keep the seedbed constantly moist until the seeds germinate. After that, follow my new-grass watering guidelines on page 79.

• Lay warm-season grass sod, and jump-start growth by applying my All-Season Green-Up Tonic (see

Dear Jerry,

I live out West, where wildfires are a constant threat in the summer and early fall. Are there any lawn grasses that are less of a fire hazard in hot, dry weather?

A. *Yes, indeedy! Many native grasses can reduce the risk of fire. In fact, the folks at your local garden center probably have a fire-retardant lawn seed mix that's been custom blended for your region. If they're sold out (these things sell like hotcakes!), ask them to recommend a good blend of nonnative grasses that will provide some protection (see Chapter 12 for some suggestions).*

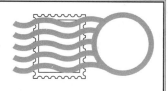

SEED STARTER TONIC

This powerful potion will have your grass seed popping out of its jacket in no time flat!

¼ cup of baby shampoo
1 tbsp. of Epsom salts
1 gal. of weak tea water*

Mix these ingredients in a large container. Drop in your grass seed and put the mixture into the refrigerator for 24 hours. Then strain out the seed, spread it on paper towels to dry, and sow as usual.

* Soak a used tea bag in a solution of 1 gal. of warm water and 1 tsp. of dishwashing liquid until the mix is light brown.

page 85). And remember to water deeply once a day until the roots are well-established.

Fall

- Fertilize your lawn with 3 pounds of Epsom salts per bag of premium slow-release lawn food (enough to cover 2,500 square feet). If you're using a natural/organic type, mix the two together, but with a synthetic fertilizer, always spread the chow and the salts separately (see page 120 for the full explanation).

- Two days after fertilizing, apply my Lawn Snack Tonic (see page 125) to activate the dry food mix.

- Have your soil tested for pH and nutrients. Correct any deficiencies by adding lime, sulfur, or other sweet or sour condiments, along with whatever nutrients the test results suggest (see Chapter 5).

- Remove fallen leaves pronto, before they smother the grass. Chop them up with your mower, add them to your compost pile, and spray it with my Compost Booster (see page 67).

- Now that the weather's cooled down, tackle big projects like regrading slopes, repairing drainage problems, and adding garden beds to your lawn. (See Chapter 3 for the lowdown on grading soil and improving drainage.)

- If the weatherman's predicting a drier-than-normal winter, apply my Drought Buster Brew (see page 262) to help your lawn ride out the rough times ahead.

- Use my Fall Clean-Up Tonic (see page 276) to prepare your lawn for the cold weather to come and also to fend off snow mold, fungus, and other wintertime nasties.

- If you're going to need a new mower or other lawn gear next spring, start shopping for it now. Merchants are eager to clear out the old equipment to make way for the new spring models, and chances are you'll get a whale of a deal.

 ## Late Fall

- Keep cutting your grass to its maximum recommended height until it stops growing or goes dormant. Then drop the blade a notch and mow one last time.

- After your final mowing, rake up the clippings. This'll deprive pests and disease germs of a cozy winter hide-away. Then toss those trimmings onto the compost pile, and saturate the pile with my Grass Clipping Compost Starter (see page 169).

- Also after you mow your lawn for the final time, apply my Last Supper Tonic (see page 108) to keep it munching happily all winter long.

- Before you tuck your mower into bed for its long winter's nap, give it the pre-hibernation TLC recommended in "Is That Old Man Winter I Hear?" on page 178.

Super★Secret

When a Bargain Isn't a Bargain

There is one time when an end-of-season markdown may not be to your advantage. That is when you know the new spring models will have improvements that you'd be happy to pay for— longer between-charge running time on a cordless electric mower, for example, or a quieter engine on a gas-powered trimmer. So always do your homework before you head off to the garden center. That way, you'll know when to bide your time and when to say, "It's a deal!"

• Wash all sprayers and tonic-mixing containers thoroughly with soap and water, and rinse well with clear water. Then dry and store them in a cool, dry place until you need them next spring.

• Clean up your manual trimmers and other hand tools by wiping off any dirt with a moist rag. Then follow up with a light coat of oil to help keep rust from forming.

• Look for new mole tunnels before the ground freezes. If you find any, pour my All-Purpose Pest Prevention Potion (see page 218) into the openings.

• Store all leftover tonics and tonic ingredients in tightly closed, labeled containers, well beyond the reach of children and pets. Make sure all unused, dry lawn food is raised off the floor on wooden pallets, or tucked into clean plastic garbage cans with good, tight lids.

• Overseed warm-season grasses with annual ryegrass to keep your lawn green all winter long.

Winter

• If you live in the Sun Belt, your mowing chores will continue, though your grass may grow more slowly. Just eyeball it regularly, and keep it

Star-Spangled Lawn Lore

If you've got a riding mower, and you just can't get enough of toolin' around on that baby, you might want to get in touch with the United States Lawn Mower Racing Association (USLMRA) in Glenview, Illinois. These folks stage more than a dozen races a year across the country, and all it takes to enter is a gung-ho spirit and a riding mower with the blade pulled off. To find out more, check out the USLMRA website at www.letsmow.com.

at the recommended height for your current temperature range (see "How High I Am" on page 156).

• In warm climates, apply my Stress Reliever Tonic (see page 190).

• Before Old Man Winter arrives in earnest, carefully clean and roll up your garden hoses, then store them in the garage or basement. And be sure to turn off the water to the outside spigots so the pipes don't freeze!

• Apply my All-Purpose Pest Prevention Potion (see page 218) as needed to keep

STRESS RELIEVER TONIC

BLUE PLATE SPECIAL

For those of you who live in the Sun Belt states, winter is feeding time for your lawn. First, apply any premium dry lawn food at half of the recommended rate, adding 1 pound of Epsom salts to each 25 pounds of lawn food. (If you're using a synthetic fertilizer, rather than a natural/organic type, spread the lawn food and the salts separately.) Then follow up with this tonic to keep your lawn relaxed through the winter months.

> **1 cup of baby shampoo**
> **1 cup of antiseptic mouthwash**
> **1 cup of tobacco tea***
> **¾ cup of weak tea water****
> **¼ cup of ammonia**

Mix these ingredients in a 20 gallon hose-end sprayer, and apply once a month to the point of run-off.

* To make tobacco tea, place half a handful of chewing tobacco in an old nylon stocking and soak it in a gallon of hot water until the mixture is dark brown.

* *Soak a used tea bag in a solution of 1 gal. of warm water and 1 tsp. of dishwashing liquid until the mix is light brown. Store leftover liquid in a tightly capped jug or bottle for later use.

deer and other unwelcome critters from dining on your trees and shrubs.

• Keep the grass around walks and driveways in good shape by spreading gypsum on the turf and following up with my Winter Walkway Protection Tonic (see page 294).

☆ Late Winter

• In warm climates, continue applying my Stress Reliever Tonic (at left) once a month to keep your lawn growing great guns.

• Remove thatch from warm-season lawns, then spread screened compost over the dethatched turf. (See Chapter 4 for my no-fail thatch removal and prevention plan.)

• After dethatching, apply a dose of my Kick-in-the-Grass Tonic (see page 100). To prevent the reappearance of this nasty stuff, use my Thatch Blaster Tonic (see page 92).

• As snow melts from lawns in cold-weather regions, check for snow mold growing on grass blades. (See my treatment guidelines in Chapter 10.)

• Watch for critters waking up from their long winter's naps, and if they're causing trouble, send them scurryin' using the tactics spelled out in Chapter 9.

Super★Secret

And Don't Forget!

Throughout the growing season, remember these important lawn-care duties:

★ Check your lawn regularly for any signs of insect, varmint, or disease damage. If you spot any, treat it pronto! (See Chapters 9 and 10 for my timely techniques.)

★ Keep an eagle eye out for weeds, and clear 'em out fast, while they're still small and puny. (See Chapter 11 for my all-time best weed-fighting strategies.)

★ Get to know when your lawn is ready for a drink so you can deliver just the right amount of moisture at just the right times. (See Chapter 6 for my wise watering guidelines.)

★ To help keep your lawn breathing freely, wear your golf spikes or lawn aerating sandals whenever you're working in your yard. (But when you're mowing, stash the sandals and wear the spikes or other closed, sturdy, and nonslip footgear.)

★ Keep your mower, mower blades, and all other tools clean, sharp, and in tip-top shape.

★ Before and after you mow, take a walk around your lawn and scout for hazards and pick up any debris (see "It's a Jungle Out There!" on page 158).

★ After mowing, give your lawn a drink of my Terrific Turf Tonic (see page 173) to help it recover faster.

★ To make grass clippings vanish like magic, spray your newly mowed lawn with my Grass Clipping Dissolving Tonic (see page 171). If you compost the clippings, saturate the pile with my Grass Clipping Compost Starter (see page 169).

★ Whenever you water your lawn with a hose rather than letting your sprinklers do the job, use my Lawn Freshener Tonic (see page 144).

★ Every two weeks, apply my All-Season Clean-Up Tonic (see page 218).

★ Every three weeks, apply my All-Season Green-Up Tonic (see page 85) and rub your mower's metal parts with WD-40® to prevent rust, corrosion, and sticking. **Note:** Every once in a while, Clean-Up and Green-Up weeks will overlap. When that happens, allow a day or so in between the applications.

★ Once a month, slow down soil compaction by applying my Aeration Tonic (see page 95), and wipe your mower's rubber and plastic parts with Armorall® to keep them from drying out and cracking.

Get Outta Here!

It can take a lot of money, time, and good old-fashioned elbow grease to keep a lawn looking its best. So the last thing you need is to have it dug up or eaten alive by a bunch of pesky pests. Well, folks, you don't need to put up with those mischief-makin' trespassers anymore. I've got a wheelbarrow of ways to kick 'em outta Dodge—and *keep* 'em out!

★ Insect Invaders

When it comes to lawn villains, these multilegged menaces rank right at the top of a lawnkeeper's Most Unwanted List. Read on for my advice on how to keep 'em under control.

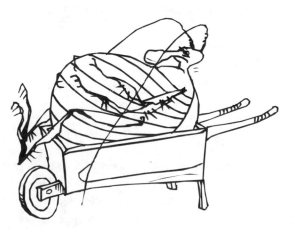

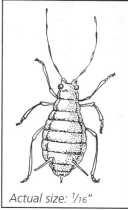

★ VILLAIN ★

Actual size: ¹/₁₆"

APHIDS

Unwanted for: Sucking the life-giving juices out of grass blades and leaving them covered with sweet, sticky honeydew. Your clues that they've arrived: The grass blades turn yellow-orange and grow poorly, and ant hills suddenly appear. (That's because ants are so crazy about the honeydew the aphids produce that they actually farm the little suckers.)

Description: Lawn aphids, a.k.a. green-bugs, are about ¹/₁₆ inch long with soft, wingless, pear-shaped bodies that are translucent green.

Most likely victims: A greenbug's idea of heaven is a midwestern lawn chock-full of Kentucky bluegrass—and the shadier the site, the better.

How to kick 'em out: Mow your lawn, and then spray it with my All-Season Clean-Up Tonic (see page 218). Repeat the process every two weeks during the growing season. Meanwhile, set about controlling ants (for the details on that maneuver, see page 204).

How to keep 'em out: Encourage their two biggest enemies: lacewings and lady-bugs. And whatever you do, avoid overfeeding. In particular, keep an eagle eye on the nitrogen level (see "When to Say 'When'" on page 107).

Super ★ Secret

One More Reason to Hold the N

When aphids tap into a plant, they're after just one ingredient in the sap: nitrogen. Once their systems have extracted it, they secrete the excess liquid in the form of their famous honeydew. So, of course, the more nitrogen you feed your grass, the more attractive the blades will be to the tiny terrors—and to the ants who crave their disgusting by-product.

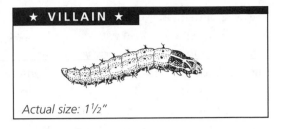

Actual size: 1½"

ARMYWORMS

Unwanted for: Gobbling up every grass blade in their path. They dine after dark, and a large horde can destroy a small lawn in a single night. Armyworms generally strike in late summer or fall, leaving round, bald spots in the turf.

Description: These vile villains are slightly hairy caterpillars, about 1½ inches long, with black heads marked with a white Y. Three thin, yellowish white stripes stretch along their backs from head to tail. On either side is a dark stripe and, below that, a wavy yellow line splotched with red. The main body color can be green, brown, or nearly black.

Most likely victims: Armyworms conduct maneuvers from coast to coast, sparing only very cold regions of the country. But they do the most damage on warm-season grasses in southern Florida and along the Gulf Coast. (They're especially partial to Bermuda grass.)

How to kick 'em out: If you can be on the scene just after dusk when the worms slither out to feed, blast 'em with my Caterpillar Killer Tonic (see page 194). For this treatment to be effective, it has to make direct contact with the target. Or, if you prefer a hands-off approach, treat your lawn with either Btk (*Bacillus thuringiensis* var. *kurstaki*) or parasitic nematodes of the species *Neoaplectana carpocapsae*—they've been specially bred to polish off armyworms. For more on these two magic bullets, see "The Dynamic Duo" on page 199.

How to keep 'em out: Dig up the dead turf, and reseed with a grass that's resistant to armyworms. New varieties come on the market almost every year, so check with your Cooperative Extension Service to find the best type for your territory. (For the lowdown on one kind of pest-resistant grass, the endophytic crowd, see page 49.)

CATERPILLAR KILLER TONIC

This potent brew means death on contact to armyworms and any other cantankerous caterpillars.

½ lb. of wormwood leaves
2 tbsp. of Murphy's Oil Soap®
4 cups of water

Simmer the wormwood leaves in 2 cups of the water for 30 minutes. Strain, then add the Murphy's Oil Soap and the remaining 2 cups of water. Pour the solution into a 6 gallon hose-end sprayer jar, and saturate your lawn in the early evening, when armyworms (and other grass-munching caterpillars) come out to dine. Repeat this treatment until the varmints are history.

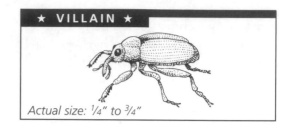

★ VILLAIN ★

Actual size: ¼" to ¾"

BILLBUGS

Unwanted for: Chewing holes in grass blades (at the adult stage), or (during their juvenile delinquent phase) eating the whole plant—roots, blades, and all. Small, distinct circles of brown or yellowish grass are a good clue that billbugs are at work. You'll know for sure if the discolored turf pulls up in a mat, and the roots are covered with a light brown powder that looks like sawdust.

Description: The larvae are white, legless grubs with bright, burnt-orange heads. The grownups are brown or black weevils, with a distinctive snout, or "bill," that gives them their name. (You'll sometimes see them strolling along sidewalks and driveways in early spring.)

Most likely victims: Any lawn that has a thick layer of thatch, or that's growing in poorly drained soil, is a magnet for billbugs. But these wicked weevils cause the most trouble in southern coastal regions.

How to kick 'em out: Launch an attack force of beneficial nematodes. They'll polish off the grubby babies pronto. For the whole scoop on these all-but-invisible warriors, see "The Dynamic Duo" on page 199.

How to keep 'em out: Improve your soil's drainage, control thatch, aerate your lawn regularly, and keep your soil well-stocked with organic matter, especially compost. (Besides improving drainage, the "black gold" will supply important trace nutrients and help fend off diseases.) Do everything you can to encourage songbirds to camp out at your place. They eat billbugs by the barrelful, at both the adult and grubby stages. Finally, when you reseed or resod, choose billbug-resistant grass varieties. Your Cooperative Extension Service can clue you in on the best ones for your region.

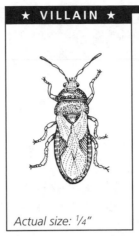

Actual size: ¹⁄₄"

CHINCH BUGS

Unwanted for: Sucking the sap from grass blades and, at the same time, injecting a poison that kills the plants; Blame these guys if your lawn is full of round, yellow patches that quickly turn brown and die.

Yankee Doodle Data

Hey, Kids! What Time Is It?

When you're trying to protect your turf from multilegged marauders, it helps to know when they're most likely to show up. Here's a schedule you can copy and pin to your toolshed wall. (Note: The time you need to be looking for the bugs is not necessarily the same time that you notice the damage to your lawn.)

INSECT INVADER	APPEARS IN WARM CLIMATES	APPEARS IN COOL CLIMATES
Aphids	———	March–October
Armyworms	June–August	June–August
Billbugs	March–August	March–October
Chinch bugs	March–October	March–October
Cutworms	April–May	April–May
Mites	April–May	———
Mole crickets	March–August	———
Scale	June–August	———
Sod webworms	April–August	March–May; September–October
White grubs	March; June–August	March; June–October

Description: Nymphs are bright red with a white band across their backs. Adults have dark brown bodies with a black triangle between white, folded wings.

Most likely victims: Any turf grass is a likely target, but varieties of St. Augustine and Kentucky bluegrasses are especially vulnerable.

How to kick 'em out: Make a solution of 2 tablespoons of dishwashing liquid to 1 gallon of water, and pour it on the area, using a sprinkling can for even coverage. Put a soft, white cloth on top of the grass. Wait 15 to 20 minutes, then peek under the fabric. It should be teeming with chinch bugs who've crawled toward the surface to escape the soap. Gather up the cloth, and dunk it into a bucket filled with soapy water. Then, hose down your lawn to remove the soap residue.

How to keep 'em out: Control thatch, keep your lawn watered, and avoid overfeeding.

CHINCH BUG TONIC

If problem areas are too big for the white-cloth treatment described above, make up a batch of this brew.

1 cup of Murphy's Oil Soap®
3 cups of warm water
Gypsum

Combine the soap and water in a 20 gallon hose-end sprayer, and saturate your lawn. After it dries, apply gypsum to the bug-infested areas at the recommended rate.

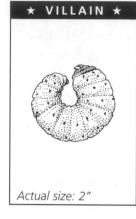

★ VILLAIN ★

Actual size: 2"

CUTWORMS

Unwanted for: Slicing off grass blades at ground level. The result: a lawn that's littered with 1- to 2-inch-diameter spots of close-cropped, dead turf.

Description: Cutworms are fat, soft, bristly, greasy-looking caterpillars that range in color from brown, gray, or black to red and greenish white. If you find one and you want a positive ID, poke it lightly with a stick. If it curls up in a ball, it's a cutworm.

Most likely victims: These malevolent munchers favor new lawns all across the country, except in the very coldest climates. Furthermore, they believe in eating a balanced diet, so you'll want to protect your young flower and vegetable seedlings, too. Just surround each one with a collar sunk about 2 inches into the ground with about 3 inches showing above. (Good collar makings include aluminum foil, toilet paper rolls, and aluminum cans with both ends removed.)

How to kick 'em out: Mix 3 tablespoons of dishwashing liquid with 1 gallon of water, and pour it on the troubled spots. The soap will bring the cutworms to the surface. Then you have two choices: Let hungry birds gobble them up (which they'll do in a flash), or spray the creepy crawlers with my Squeaky Clean Tonic (see page 219). Whichever method you choose, be sure to haul out the hose and rinse the soapy residue off of your lawn afterwards.

How to keep 'em out: If you live in warm-season grass territory, replace your current turf with either zoysia or Bermuda grass, which cutworms don't much care for. No matter where you live, encourage the worms' enemies, including birds, toads, tachinid flies, parasitic wasps, and bats (they eat the egg-laying adults, which are small, night-flying moths). Entice these good guys to your yard with bird feeders, bat houses, and a variety of flowers (see "Y'all Come!" on page 198).

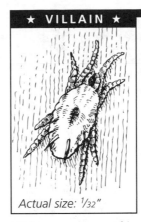

★ VILLAIN ★

Actual size: 1/32"

MITES

Unwanted for: Sucking the sap from your grass. If the pest population is small, the result will be yellow or straw-colored blades. But a major mite invasion can kill large sections of lawn, leaving it an unattractive brown and thinned out.

Description: Several species of mites attack turf grass. Most are so small that you need a magnifying glass to see them, but they all resemble tiny spiders.

Yankee Doodle Data
Good Guys to the Rescue

A hit squad of beneficial insects can end your lawn's bad-bug problems, once and for all. To call these heroes to your aid, just plant a variety of flowers that are rich in pollen and nectar, and keep a source of water handy. (A nonporous plant saucer filled with pebbles and sunk into the ground is perfect.) And, of course, don't use pesticides, which will kill off the good guys along with the bad.

HERO BUG	LAWN VILLAINS TARGETED
Assassin bugs	Aphids, armyworms, beetles (a.k.a. grubs' parents), mole crickets, sod webworms
Big-eyed bugs	Aphids, armyworms, chinch bugs, sod webworms
Ground beetles	Ants, aphids, armyworms, cutworms, grubs, mites, mole crickets
Ladybugs	Aphids, chinch bug larvae, mites, scale
Spined soldier beetles	Sod webworms

Most likely victims: Although the various mite species differ in their menu preferences, any kind of grass can fall prey to their voracious appetites. The most vulnerable lawns are those that have been treated repeatedly with chemical pesticides, or that are unhealthy or suffering from stress of any kind.

How to kick 'em out: If you catch the damage in the early stages, you can give them the cold shoulder. Simply haul out the hose, and give the tiny tykes a cold shower. (Do the job first thing in the morning, before the sun has a chance to heat up the hose.) Or, if you have a very small lawn, or only a few plagued patches, just fill a hand-held sprayer with ice water, and let 'er rip. To halt a serious infestation, haul out stronger ammunition in the form of my Mite Not Tonic (see page 219).

How to keep 'em out: Keep your lawn in the pink of health by following the tips you'll find throughout this book, and do everything you can to encourage good-guy bugs to set up camp in your yard (see "Y'all Come!" below). They'll help keep a lid on the mite population.

Super★Secret

Y'all Come!

Birds, bats, ground beetles, and a whole lot of other good guys will join your pest control posse if you make your yard and garden a hospitable place for them to spend some time. Just follow these basic guidelines and you'll have all kinds of helpful critters flocking to your property.

Lay off pesticides. They kill the good guys right along with the bad ones. Think beyond grass. Plant as many different kinds of flowers, herbs, vegetables, fruits, and even trees and shrubs as you have room for. That way, you'll attract a whole lineup of helpers.

Give them shelter. Make sure your yard includes shrub borders, perennial flower beds, hedgerows, and even a few clumps of weeds where your allies can set up housekeeping.

Give them a drink. It doesn't have to be a big pond. A few old plant saucers sunk into the ground and filled with pebbles will work fine. Then just pour water in, and let some of the rocks stick up above the surface.

Don't panic. You can't have "good guys" unless they have some "bad guys" around to munch on. So don't reach for your hose-end sprayer at the first sign of a billbug or an armyworm. Instead, just think of the little creep as lunch for your heroes.

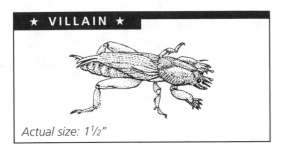

★ VILLAIN ★

Actual size: 1½"

MOLE CRICKETS

Unwanted for: Tunneling through the soil, eating grass roots as they go along, and leaving your lawn "decorated" with irregular brown streaks of dead grass. And on warm nights, when the soil is moist, the crickets venture aboveground to munch on grass blades.

Description: Mole crickets look much like their aboveground cousins, except their heads are bigger, and they have short, powerful front legs with shovel-like feet.

Most likely victims: These undercover culprits pillage turf grasses throughout the South, from the Atlantic Coast to Texas. And there's nothing they like better than a lawn with a nice, thick layer of thatch.

How to kick 'em out: Go at 'em underground by releasing one of these four hired guns: Bt *(Bacillus thuringiensis)*, predatory nematodes, a beneficial wasp *(Larra bicolor)*, or the Brazilian red-eyed fly *(Ormia depleta)*.

Yankee Doodle Data

The Dynamic Duo

When it comes to pickin' off pesky lawn pests, beneficial nematodes and Bt *(Bacillus thuringiensis)* are two of the best helpers you could ask for. They're deadly to bad bugs, but harmless to other living things, including you, your children, and pets. You can find them in many garden-supply catalogs and some garden centers. But bear in mind that you need to get the species of nematode or Bt that's been bred to tackle your resident bad guys, and you need to launch the attack in exactly the right way at exactly the right time. The catalog description or package label should give you all the details.

HIT MEN	WHAT THEY ARE	PRIME LAWN TARGETS
Beneficial nematodes	Almost-microscopic critters that demolish some of the most feared felons in all of lawn- and gardendom.	Armyworms, beetle grubs, cutworms, mole crickets
Bt *(Bacillus thuringiensis)*	A beneficial bacterium that kills pests galore, but almost no beneficial insects. There's just one down side: Bt can't tell butterfly larvae from enemy caterpillars—so use it with caution.	Armyworms, billbug larvae, mole crickets, mosquito larvae, sod webworms

If you can't find your weapon of choice in a garden-supply catalog, call your local Cooperative Extension Service. Don't stop with this list, though. Ask about the best time to plan your attack (it can vary from one region to another, and from one year to the next).

If your lawn is small, or you don't have time for posse-shopping, simply flush the area with a solution made of 3 tablespoons of lemon-scented dishwashing liquid per gallon of water. Within two or three minutes, the entire mole cricket population will rise to the surface. Then, let 'em have it with my Hot Bug Brew (see page 219). Once the villains have bitten the dust, haul out your hose and rinse the soapy water away.

How to keep 'em out: First, control thatch by following my routine in Chapter 4. And lay out the welcome mat for the dastardly diggers' natural enemies. They have many, both below and aboveground, including ground beetles, assassin bugs, toads, snakes, raccoons, foxes, and birds.

the damage at the start of the spring growth season: The grass will appear thin, weak, and simply unable to get its show on the road. Some of the little plants may look like they've been done in by winter damage.

Description: If you have houseplants, chances are you've had plenty of close encounters of the scale kind. The adults are legless insects with yellowish white, waxy shells that protect them while they feed and lay their eggs. The teeny-weenie, reddish brown youngsters, a.k.a. crawlers, generally appear in June and July, and when the population skyrockets, your lawn will actually look rusty.

Most likely victims: Scale primarily targets southern lawns that are stressed out from environmental causes or poor care. In addition, grass that's growing in shady areas or sporting a thick layer of thatch is especially prone to attack.

How to kick 'em out: My Hot Bug Brew (see page 219) will wipe out the young crawlers fast. To deal a death blow to both generations at the same time, whip up a batch of my Super Scale Scrub (see page 219), and let 'er rip.

How to keep 'em out: Control thatch, keep an eagle eye on your lawn's health and well-being, especially in times of environmental upheaval (see Chapter 12), and encourage ladybugs to take up residence. They think scale is the tastiest snack this side of buttered popcorn!

★ VILLAIN ★

Actual size: 1/32"

SCALE

Unwanted for: Sucking the juices from grass blades. In small numbers, scale insects are harmless, but if the invasion force is large, it's a different story. Most likely, you'll notice

A String of Pearls

If you live in the Southeast or a warm-winter part of Arizona or California, your lawn could fall prey to pearl scale, a.k.a. ground pearls *(Margarodes meridionalis)*. They attack only warm-season grasses, specifically Bermuda, centipede, St. Augustine, and zoysia. Instead of draining the juices from grass blades, as other scale insects do, these villains attack the roots, robbing them of nutrients and water. Their calling card is the same as that left by many pests and diseases: a lawn littered with circular dead patches. To pinpoint the culprit, pull up a section of grass on the edge of a

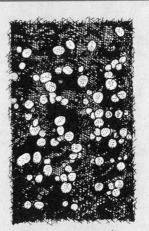

Nodules less than 1/16"

dead area, and inspect the roots. If pearl scale is the culprit, you'll see small, pearly white cysts—the equivalent of the waxy covering on aboveground scale. (But don't confuse these bumps with the larger white nodules on the roots of clover, which are made by beneficial, nitrogen-fixing bacteria.)

Unfortunately, your only effective course of treatment is to dig up and replace the infested turf, along with the foot or so of grass surrounding it. When you're shopping for your new sod, examine the roots carefully, and if you see any sign of pearls, take your business elsewhere. Then, to head off future trouble, apply beneficial nematodes to your lawn in the spring. They'll attack the crawlers when they emerge from their coverings. Check with your Cooperative Extension Service for the timing in your area.

★ VILLAIN ★

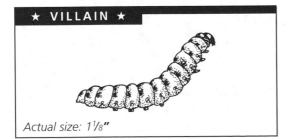

Actual size: 1⅛"

SOD WEBWORMS

Unwanted for: Chewing off grass blades at the crown and pulling them into silk-lined tunnels in the ground to eat them.

The damage first appears as small dead patches (1 to 2 inches in diameter) in early spring. By July or August, they've usually developed into *big* dead patches.

Description: The worms are sleek, tan caterpillars with black spots on their backs and a beaklike projection on their heads. Their parents are small, white moths. (You'll know for a fact that webworms have come to call when these little critters rise up in clouds in front of your lawn mower.)

Most likely victims: Sod webworms wander here and there and yonder, and gleefully chow down on any kind of grass. But their favorite stomping, er, crawling ground is out there in America's heartland. And their idea of a genuine fine-dining experience is a lawn full of bent grass or Kentucky bluegrass, covered with a thick, cozy layer of thatch.

How to kick 'em out: First, mow your lawn while wearing your golf spikes or lawn sandals, and follow up with a dose of my Aeration Tonic (see page 95). That way, your weapon of choice can better penetrate the thatch layer. Then, apply the "coup de grass" in one of two forms: either Btk (*Bacillus thuringiensis* var. *kurstaki*) or my All-Season Clean-Up Tonic (see page 218). Whichever weapon you choose, be quick about it, because with sod webworms, a small problem can turn into a big one in the blink of an eye. And be aware that you may need to repeat the process several times before you see results—but be patient, keep at it, and see results you will!

How to keep 'em out: Do everything in your power to control thatch (where have you heard *that* line before?), and encourage the slimy monster's natural enemies. Many good-guy bugs and other critters consider sod webworms a tasty treat, but birds and spined soldier beetles gobble 'em up like there's no tomorrow.

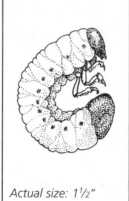

★ VILLAIN ★

Actual size: 1½"

WHITE GRUBS

Unwanted for: Eating the roots of your grass, and leaving you with a lawn full of irregular, brown patches that look burned. If you tug on one of the dead clumps,

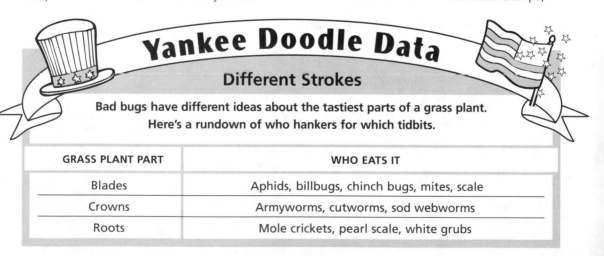

Yankee Doodle Data

Different Strokes

Bad bugs have different ideas about the tastiest parts of a grass plant. Here's a rundown of who hankers for which tidbits.

GRASS PLANT PART	WHO EATS IT
Blades	Aphids, billbugs, chinch bugs, mites, scale
Crowns	Armyworms, cutworms, sod webworms
Roots	Mole crickets, pearl scale, white grubs

What—Me Worry?

A few grubs are no cause for panic. The trouble comes when too many of them start munching on the same piece of turf. Here's a simple way to take a census: Cut both ends off of several soup cans and sink each one up to its rim in the soil, spaced about 10 feet apart. Then fill the cans close to the top with water. After 5 or 10 minutes, count the grubs that you find in each can. That number will equal the number of grubs per square foot of lawn. If there are 8 to 10 per can, don't sweat it. Birds can keep that crowd under control without harming your lawn in the process. More than 10 grubs means you've got a major invasion on your hands and you need to strike back—hard!

How to kick 'em out: For fast-acting relief, drench your turf with beneficial nematodes (see "The Dynamic Duo" on page 199). They'll burrow into the villains, reproduce, and at the same time deliver bacteria that'll kill the grubs, but harm no other critters. Unfortunately, the results are temporary, so it's likely that you'll have to repeat the maneuver the following spring.

To ease your grub woes and aerate your turf at the same time, strap on a pair of spiked sandals (available from garden-supply catalogs) and stroll back and forth across your lawn. The spikes will skewer enough grubs to turn a big problem into a no-worry situation in no time at all.

If you know for sure that the grubs in your lawn are baby Japanese beetles (because the grownups are chewin' the daylights out of your shrubs, flowers, and veggies), get some milky spore disease (*Bacillus popilliae*), available in catalogs and many garden centers. All you do is sprinkle it onto your freshly mowed lawn according to the package directions, and it stays in the soil for years, killing baby grubs as soon as they hatch, but harming nothing else. Unfortunately, milky spore takes a few years to achieve its full effect, but once it gets up to speed, your grub woes will be gone for good.

it'll come right up like a piece of loose carpet—often exposing the culprits in action. Grubs start feeding in early spring, and the damage becomes apparent any time from late spring through early fall, usually during dry spells.

Description: White grubs are the larvae of many different beetles, including chafer, Japanese, June (a.k.a. May), and Asiatic garden beetles. It's all but impossible to tell them apart: They all have fat, whitish bodies that tend to curl up into a C shape.

Most likely victims: White grubs are not fussy eaters. As a matter of fact, any kind of grass in any part of this great land of ours is fair game for these greedy gluttons.

How to keep 'em out: Snatch the adult beetles before they have a chance to fill up the maternity wards—and encourage your neighbors to do the same. Your best options: Start handpicking the beetles early in the season, and send a warm invitation to beetle-eating helpers like birds and toads. You can also trap the buggers with commercial or homemade devices, but I wouldn't advise you to go that route. The reason: A whole lot of studies have shown that traps attract more beetles than they polish off. So you could wind up trading a fair-to-middlin' annoyance for a giant headache!

☆ The Bothersome Brigade

None of this quartet will harm your grass, but when they set up camp in your yard, they can be first-class nuisances—or, in some cases, life-threatening menaces.

ANTS

Unwanted for: Farming aphids that plague turf grass and landscape plants, building unsightly mounds in lawns, and making nuisances of themselves at picnics and barbecues.

Description: I don't have to tell you what ants look like—or what it feels like when you step on one of their mounds as you're mowing the lawn, and the little monsters swarm up your pant legs, nipping all the way!

Most likely victims: Ants will cheerfully set up camp in any lawn, anywhere. But, because they find honeydew irresistible, they cause the most trouble in the same places that attract aphids: lawns that are getting too much nitrogen in their diets.

How to kick 'em out: Most of the time, ants do far more good than harm in a lawn (see "Hold Your Horses!" at right), but if you really must declare war on a colony, the simplest way I know of is to sprinkle instant grits on top of the anthill. The worker ants will carry the grains into the nest, where they and the queen will have a feast. Then the grains will swell up inside their little bodies. Within about 48 hours, the whole colony will be history.

Super ★ Secret

Hold Your Horses!

Unless ants are running a major aphid ranch in your lawn, don't be too quick to send the little guys packin'. Ants don't damage grass or any other plants. In fact, they're some of the best yard and garden helpers you could ask for. Here are a few of the chores they tackle:

★ Breaking down organic matter into soil-building humus

★ Aerating the soil by digging thousands of miles of tunnels

★ Pollinating flowers and in some cases, such as peonies, helping the blossoms to open fully

★ Waging war on termites and taking over their nests

★ Preying on mealybugs, scale insects, cockroaches, and other pests

★ Eating mosquito eggs by the millions

How to keep 'em out: Plant tansy, spearmint, pennyroyal, or southernwood (*Artemisia abrotanum*) in your yard—ants keep their distance from all of those great-smelling herbs. And keep an eagle eye on your lawn's nitrogen intake. That way, you'll make it uninviting to the ants' aphid cronies.

★ VILLAIN ★

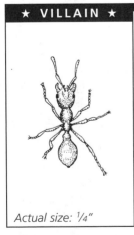

Actual size: ¹⁄₄"

FIRE ANTS

Unwanted for: Attacking humans, pets, and other animals (sometimes with fatal results); building high, hard mounds that damage lawn equipment and even cars; and destroying young trees and other landscape plants.

Description: Fire ants are almost dead ringers for the garden-variety picnic pests, but there's no mistaking a mature colony: You'll see a rock-hard dome that's up to 1½ feet high and 2 feet in diameter—a disaster-in-waiting for any car or piece of machinery that runs over it. What's more, the excavation often extends 3 feet or more belowground, and flitting around inside, there can be as many as a quarter of a million ill-tempered ants.

Most likely victims: Fire ants plague lawns and gardens throughout the South and Southwest, including Texas and southern California. They're especially partial to warm, sunny areas, and they flock to yards that have raised beds or compost piles.

How to kick 'em out: In the case of a major invasion, don't even contemplate do-it-yourself measures. Call a professional pest control operator who will go at the villains with an insect growth regulator such as abamectin, or avermectin, a naturally occurring soil fungus that's lethal to fire ants.

If your resident colony is so new that its mound is just a slight bump in the ground—and if you're not allergic to insect bites—you can wipe out the nest by dousing its residents with my God-Sink-the-Queen Drench (at right). Enlist a helper for this ambush, and make sure you both wear the uniform of the day: gloves, a long-sleeved shirt, and long pants that are tucked into high boots. To be extra-safe, wear rubber boots that you've smeared with a sticky substance like petroleum jelly. Finally, plan to attack early in the morning, or on a cool, sunny day (that's when the queen is usually near the top of the mound), and follow all of my instructions to the letter.

How to keep 'em out: Avoid raised planting beds and compost piles (instead, cook your supply in a commercial composting bin, and keep it raised a few inches off the ground). If you already have enclosed, raised beds or big planters in your yard, wrap the bottom of each one in a sticky trap made from a strip of plastic sheet or flexible cardboard that's about 6 inches wide and long enough to reach around the container. Tack or tape the strip on, then coat it with any sticky substance, such as petroleum jelly, spray adhesive, or Tanglefoot®. Just remember to keep the strip clear of "bridges" that

BLUE PLATE SPECIAL

GOD-SINK-THE-QUEEN DRENCH

When fire ants are driving you up a wall, serve their boss-lady this fatal cocktail.

4 cups of citrus peels
3 gal. of water
1 willing helper
1 long, sharp stick

Toss the peels into a pot with the water, bring the mixture to a boil, and let it simmer for about 10 minutes. Grab the pot, and with your partner, tiptoe as softly as you can up to the mound—fire ants are ultra-sensitive to ground vibrations. Have your cohort poke the entrance with the stick. *Immediately* pour the boiling solution into the hole. Then turn around and run like the dickens! The boiling water will polish off any ants it reaches, and the citrus-oil fumes will send more to the gas chamber. Repeat the procedure every two or three days, until there's no sign of life in the mound.

the ants could scramble over, like twigs, leaves, or dead bugs.

Cover paths and unpaved walkways with 2 or 3 inches of sand or pea gravel to keep the ants from tunneling into the soil. Better yet, pave them!

Remember, fire ants are real sun worshipers. So if you're on their hit list, do whatever you can to make your yard shadier: Plant trees and tall shrubs; build walls or fences; or grow vines on arbors and trellises.

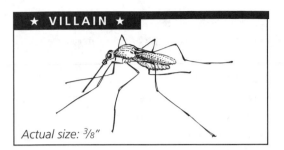

★ VILLAIN ★

Actual size: ³⁄₈"

MOSQUITOES

Unwanted for: No surprises here—sucking the blood from humans and pets and, in the process, often transmitting deadly diseases, including yellow fever, encephalitis, West Nile virus, and heartworm in dogs and cats.

Description: In the mosquito clan, it's the females who are out gunnin' for our blood. The males just go around sipping nectar from flowers; they don't sink their chops into anybody. One of the biggest challenges in dealing with skeeters is that, like many bad bugs, they've been so bombarded with chemical pesticides that they've grown immune to nearly all of them. But that doesn't mean you have to let the vile villains spoil your summertime fun. It just means ya gotta outwit 'em!

Most likely victims: *You* and your four-footed pals.

How to kick 'em out: For temporary relief when you're working or playing in your yard, here's what you can do: Sweep the vampires up with a hand-held vacuum cleaner; set out oscillating fans to keep the air moving (mosquitoes don't like that one bit); or simply eat a lot of fresh garlic, which

from the MAIL BAG

Dear Jerry,

Mosquitoes are driving us crazy, and my husband wants to get one of those electric bug zappers. I've heard that they don't really work well, and I'm afraid that all it's going to zap is our peace and quiet. Who's right?

A. *You both are. Those contraptions zap bugs all right—just about every kind except mosquitoes, including a whole lot of the good guys. That's because most of them use light to attract their "prey," and mosquitoes couldn't care less about light. They zero in on the scent of carbon dioxide, which humans and other mammals give off. What you want is a machine like a Mosquito Deleto® that uses CO_2 to lure skeeters to their deaths—and quietly, too.*

seems to repel them. And why not? After all, they are vampires!

How to keep 'em out: Eliminate their breeding grounds, which are anything that holds water—especially stagnant water. Fill in low-lying areas where rain collects, and keep rain barrels covered. Throw away water-collecting debris, like old tires or discarded buckets. Change the water in birdbaths and pet bowls every day, and empty portable wading pools just as soon as the kids are through using them.

To make water gardens and other permanent water features off-limits, your best bet is to use Laginex® or Bti (Bacillus thuringiensis var. israelensis). Both kill mosquitoes without harming any other living things. You can order them from garden-supply centers or catalogs. Just one word of advice: If you go with Bti, make sure you look for slow-release tablets like Mosquito Dunks™; some brands lose their effect after about three days, and you'll have to add more.

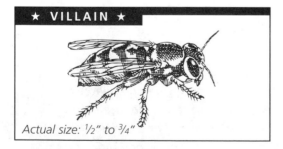

★ VILLAIN ★

Actual size: ½" to ¾"

YELLOW JACKETS

Unwanted for: Showing up uninvited at picnics, barbecues, and any other outdoor, summertime event where refreshments are served—and planting their stingers into innocent human bystanders at the drop of a hat.

Description: With their torpedo-shaped, yellow-and-black-striped bodies, yellow jackets look a little like honeybees. But they sure don't *act* like honeybees! Those kinder, gentler buzzers rarely sting unless they're provoked; and once they've implanted their barbed stingers into a target, they die. The Y guys, on the other hand, can shove their smooth weapons into you again and again—and, given half a chance, they will!

Most likely victims: Although yellow jackets will travel miles for a good party, they're more likely to set up permanent quarters in your yard if you grow fruit of any kind, or if your grass or other plants are plagued by aphids. The reason: They just can't resist anything sweet, whether it's ripe fruit or the sapsuckers' honeydew.

How to kick 'em out: Trap visiting yellow jackets with this simple device: Cut the top third off of a plastic soda bottle and spritz it with cooking spray. Tuck some meat scraps or chunks of canned pet food into the lower part of the bottle, then invert the top over the bottom. The old yellers will zoom in, and they'll stay there.

As for resident populations, heading off a colony-in-the-making is a snap. Just keep your eyes open in the early spring, when young queens are establishing their households. To encourage Her Majesty to build elsewhere, repeatedly knock down her nest while she's out gathering construction mate-

Ouch!

No matter how careful you are, sooner or later you're bound to wind up on the wrong end of some stinging insect. When that happens, remove the pain and itch by dabbing the bitten spot with one of these wonder "drugs": white vinegar, antiseptic mouthwash, white wine, vodka, or a thick paste made from baking soda and lukewarm water. (And, of course, if you've ever had an allergic reaction to a bee sting or other insect bite, get to a doctor, pronto!)

rial. If you really want to put an end to her reign, just whack her with an old-fashioned fly swatter or give her a blast of All-Season Clean-Up Tonic (see page 218).

To my way of thinking, removing an active colony that's fastened to a building or a tree branch is a job for a pro. (To find one who specializes in relocating wasp and bee colonies, check the Yellow Pages under Pest Control Services, or call your Cooperative Extension Service.) An in-ground nest is a different story. All you need to do is go out just after dusk, set a big, clear plastic or glass bowl upside down over the entrance hole, and push the edges into the soil. In the morning, when the workers see daylight streaming in, they'll try again and again to fly out, but they won't dig an exit hole. Before long, they'll starve to death. Just two words of warning: If you need extra light, set a lantern or flashlight on the ground well off to the side. Don't shine it directly on the nest! It'll get the workers all riled up,

and they'll come swarming out at you. Also, dress as you would for a fire-ant foray (see page 206). Add a hat with a beekeeper's veil, or drape an old net curtain over it, and tuck the edges snugly into your collar.

How to keep 'em out: Keep garbage cans tightly covered, clear away ripe fruit when it falls from trees, don't feed pets outside, and don't leave soft drink cans lying around. Also, if you have a swimming pool or hot tub, hang up damp towels where they'll dry quickly—wasps find moist fabric extremely attractive.

☆ The Bigger Bunch

This crowd isn't gunnin' for you *or* your grass. But they sure can make a mess of your lawn in the process of chasing what many of them do hanker for: bugs lurking in the soil.

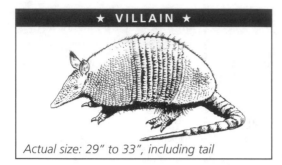

★ VILLAIN ★

Actual size: 29" to 33", including tail

ARMADILLOS

Unwanted for: Digging up your lawn in search of dinner. And I *do* mean digging. These determined little guys sometimes tunnel down 25 feet or more when they're hot on the trail of a tasty morsel—namely, subterranean insects.

Description: With their armored coats, big, floppy ears, and innocent-as-a-baby expressions, armadillos are as cute as all get-out (that is, when it's not *your* lawn they're demolishing). Because they have almost no hair to protect them from the elements, their dining schedule varies with the time of year: In the summer, they venture out in the cool of the evening. In the winter, you're more likely to spot them during the warmest part of the day, which is generally midafternoon.

Most likely victims: Armadillos primarily roam through the South and Southwest, but in recent years, they've been showing up as far north as Nebraska. Like any other wild critter, they'll go anywhere they can get a good meal, but their prime targets are lawns that are badly infested with grubs (because that's their very favorite

food), and those growing in light, sandy soil (because that's where the digging is by far the easiest).

How to kick 'em out: Scrub the grubs! (See my foolproof grub-getting guidelines on page 203.) And if you find that the 'dillos are also helping themselves to your flowers or shrubs, which happens now and then, spray the target plants with my Hot Bite Spray (below).

How to keep 'em out: Do everything you can to control adult beetles and their grubby offspring (see page 204).

HOT BITE SPRAY

When armadillos or other ornery critters wander out of your lawn and into your flower beds, whip up a batch of this timely tonic.

> 3 tbsp. of cayenne pepper
> 1 tbsp. of hot sauce
> 1 tbsp. of ammonia
> 1 tbsp. of baby shampoo
> 2 cups of hot water

Mix the cayenne pepper with the hot water in a bottle, and shake well. Let the mixture sit overnight, then pour off the liquid without disturbing the sediment. Mix the liquid with the other ingredients in a hand-held sprayer. Keep a batch on hand, especially when tender shoots and new buds are forming, and spritz the plants as often as you can to keep them hot, hot, hot! No critter who tastes the stuff will come back for a second bite.

★ VILLAIN ★

CATS

Unwanted for:
Using your freshly seeded lawn-in-the-making as their personal privy, eating or trampling ground-cover plants, or, worst of all, gunning for winged warriors at your birdfeeder.

Description: Mischief-making felines fall into one of three categories: homeless strays, who are just trying to make a living; cats whose misguided owners allow them to roam at will; and your own kitty, who spends most of her time running your household, but now and then ventures outdoors for a little hunting trip or a romp in the grass.

Most likely victims: Cats can show up on any lawn at any time—and usually, it seems, at the worst possible times.

How to kick 'em out: To protect newly seeded areas, cover the soil with thorny canes cut from rosebushes or bramble fruits, and keep them in place until the baby grass plants have grown big enough to cover the loose ground. Or, if you don't have any prickly branches on hand, use my flashy feline-foiling fence

(below). For added protection, sprinkle my Hit the Trail Mix (see page 218) around the perimeter of your yard, or around Fluffy's specific targets. Those furry felons'll scurry in a hurry! (Just bear in mind that you'll have to renew the supply after every rain, or after your sprinklers have diluted the firey scent.)

How to keep 'em out: When your own cat is the culprit, avoiding cat-astrophes is a snap: Just keep your frolicking felines indoors! With neighborhood roamers, it's a little trickier, because there's almost no vertical fence that a cat can't scale. So what do you do? Build a flat fence! Just plant seeds of a low-growing groundcover, like creeping thyme or sweet alyssum, around the area you want to declare

Super ★ Secret

Foil 'Em with Foil

Cavorting cats can destroy a freshly seeded lawn in no time flat. But this flashy foil "fence" will make the felons flee fast! And it's as easy as 1, 2, 3. Here's all you need to do:

Step 1. Fill empty 2-liter soda bottles halfway with water, and add a few drops of bleach, just to keep smelly algae from growing.

Step 2. Put two or three long, thin strips of aluminum foil into each bottle.

Step 3. Set the bottles every few feet around the area you want to protect. The constantly changing reflections from the foil will scare the daylights out of any cat who comes prancing onto your turf.

off-limits. Then, on top of the newly seeded soil, lay 2- to 3-foot-wide strips of chicken wire. When the plants grow up, they'll cover the flat fencing, so you'll hardly notice it. But when Fluffy's paws touch that sharp wire, she'll be outta there! Note: If you use this trick to safeguard birdfeeders or nesting boxes, just make sure that those shelters are well out of leaping range of tree limbs, porch overhangs, or other handy platforms—or your fence will be bypassed!

★ VILLAIN ★

DOGS

Unwanted for: Answering nature's call on your lawn, leaving it "decorated" with unsightly souvenirs.

Description: The brown, burned-looking patches that we call "dog spots" are simply the result of too much of a good thing—namely, nitrogen and salts. The same damage would occur if you spilled fertilizer on the grass. (By the way, it is not true that the urine of female dogs is more potent than that of males. It causes more damage only because females tend to urinate all at once, in one spot, while males generally spray a little here and a little there.)

Most likely victims: Dogs relieve themselves when they must, where they must; they don't give a hoot what kind of grass is growing on your lawn. However, Bermuda grass and Kentucky bluegrass are especially sensitive to dog urine. So is any lawn that's getting high concentrations of nitrogen, like you'll find in chemical fertilizers.

How to kick 'em out: If you reach the scene while the deed is being done, or shortly thereafter, just grab the hose and flush the site thoroughly; that should stop any damage in its tracks. There's still hope even after a day or so. Just lightly sprinkle gypsum over and around each spot to dissolve accumulated salts, then pour 1 cup of baby shampoo or dishwashing liquid into your 20 gallon hose-end sprayer and overspray the lawn. One week later, overspray the turf with my Lawn Saver Tonic (below). Later, when the grass is dead and brown, your only option is to dig up the affected areas, and reseed or resod. And use fescue or perennial ryegrass if either is suitable for

BLUE PLATE SPECIAL

LAWN SAVER TONIC

When bad things happen to good grass (courtesy of a pooch who didn't know better), reach for this liquid safety net.

½ **can of beer**
½ **can of regular cola (not diet)**
½ **cup of ammonia**

Combine these ingredients in a 20 gallon hose-end sprayer. Then saturate your grass to the point of run-off.

your climate; they're the most urine-resistant types. (See Chapter 4 for my reseeding and resodding routine.)

How to keep 'em out: Teach your dog to go where his offerings won't hurt anything. While he's learning to use his privy, add Yeast & Garlic Bits® to his daily treat menu. They seem to alter the chemistry of dog urine, making it less damaging to turf grass. What's more, they help repel fleas. The only sure way to keep neighborhood roamers out of your yard is to erect a good, solid fence. For a temporary solution, though, spray my Dog-Be-Gone Tonic (see page 218) in places where Spot isn't welcome. This same potent potion will also keep your dog and any roving canines from digging up your turf. (Just be sure to spray again after rain or your sprinklers have washed away the scent.)

★ VILLAIN ★

Actual size: 6" to 12"

GOPHERS

Unwanted for: Tunneling through your lawn, killing your grass in the process, and eating just about any plant they encounter.

Description: Because gophers operate underground, it's unlikely that you'll see them at work. And at first glance, it's easy to mistake their dirty work for that of moles. To make a positive ID, just eyeball the tunnel entrance. You'll know you've got a gopher on your hands if you see a U- or crescent-shaped mound of moist soil that looks as though it's been sifted. Moles make round mounds at their entrance holes. The damage in your yard will give you another clue: Moles eat no plants at all, so if greenery is being munched on, you can pin the blame on gophers.

Most likely victims: Gophers can strike any lawn in any part of the country, but they tend to cause the most trouble in the stretch from Indiana west to the Pacific Ocean. But they're not really gunnin' for grass. They want more substantial vegetation in the form of flowers, vegetables, and the roots of fruit trees or grapevines. And the more of those plants your yard contains, the more vulnerable it is.

How to kick 'em out: Gophers hate strong scents. So gather up a bunch of odor emitters, and stuff one into each hole. Be sure to wear gloves so you don't transfer your scent to the repellent, and seal all the entrance holes you can find, so the tunnel gets good and smelly. Gophers will flee from any of these fragrant offerings: rags soaked in ammonia, sticks of Juicy Fruit® gum, rotting garbage, paper towels soaked in rancid oil, dog or cat hair, or used cat litter. (Note: Don't use this last one anywhere near vegetables, herbs, or other edibles!)

Then, to be extra-safe, sprinkle my Gopher-Go Tonic (see page 214) around all the plants in your yard. When the little

GOPHER-GO TONIC

When your lawn has more tunnels than the New York subway system, it's time to reach for this remarkable recipe.

4 tbsp. of castor oil

4 tbsp. of dishwashing liquid

4 tbsp. of urine

½ cup of warm water

2 gal. of warm water

Combine the oil, dishwashing liquid, and urine in ½ cup of warm water, then stir the solution into 2 gallons of warm water. Pour the mixture over any problem areas, and the greedy gluttons will gallop away!

an acrid, milky juice that gophers can't stand. One whiff, and they'll find another dining establishment!

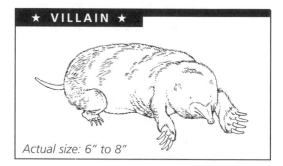

★ VILLAIN ★

Actual size: 6" to 8"

MOLES

Unwanted for: Burrowing through the soil in search of food, damaging grass roots in the process, and leaving the plants vulnerable to drought, diseases, and other pests.

Description: Like gophers, moles spend most of their lives deep in their tunnels, and their construction projects bear a close resemblance to those of gophers. But chances are, you'll notice a big difference in the damage. Both of these vivacious vandals leave your lawn riddled with streaks of dead grass. But when moles are at work, there's a good chance that's the only destruction you'll see. Gophers, on the other hand, will probably mosey on to your flower beds and vegetable garden, too.

Most likely victims: Moles conduct maneuvers throughout the United States and southern Canada, but their favorite targets are lawns that are growing in loose, moist loam—and are well-stocked with grubs.

varmints pop up out of their tunnels and smell the "coffee," they'll scurry in a hurry.

How to keep 'em out: Line the bottom and sides of planting beds, or individual planting holes, with ½-inch galvanized wire mesh. Lay the screen about 2 feet under the surface, and make sure it covers the sides all the way up to a few inches above the soil surface. Don't leave any gaps, because I guarantee these little contortionists can squeeze through even the teeniest openings.

You can also plant a protective barrier. Just run down to the garden center and buy as much gopher spurge (*Euphorbia latyrus*) as you can afford. Then plant it all around the perimeter of your garden—or even your whole lawn. The roots produce

How to kick 'em out: Stuff each tunnel entrance with a stick of Juicy Fruit® chewing gum and a partially crushed garlic clove, several scoops of used kitty litter (but don't get it near any plant that you intend to eat), a few squirts of pine-based cleaner, or half a cup or so of my Mole-Chaser Tonic (see page 219). Whichever one you choose, you might have to repeat it a few times, but eventually, the moles will give up and move on.

How to keep 'em out: You probably don't want to hear this, but the only sure way to get moles out of your yard and *keep* 'em out is to banish their food supply—namely grubs. Over the long haul, milky spore disease *(Bacillus popilliae)* is your best bet, but you won't see the full results for several years. For more immediate measures, see my anti-grub tactics on page 203. Just beware that once you've sent the grubs packin', your mole problems could get worse for a while before they get better. That's because the little guys, suddenly finding themselves without their favorite food, will charge around frantically in search of dinner before they head for grubbier pastures.

Star-Spangled *Lawn* Lore

Here are a couple of things you might not know about one of America's most unwanted lawn pests:

1. Moles are not rodents, as a lot of folks think. They belong to the biological order Insectivora, *which, in scientific lingo, means insect eaters.*

2. Moles do not eat grass, or any other plants. They fully live up to their scientific moniker. In fact, every day, a mole eats close to his own body weight in grubs, beetles, other bad bugs, and even a snail now and then. If they could only operate aboveground, instead of below, that would put them right up there with the best of the good guys!

★ VILLAIN ★

Actual size: 24" to 40", including tail

RACCOONS

Unwanted for: Robbing birdfeeders, snatching fish from ponds and eggs from birds' nests, stealing your pets' food, helping themselves to the fruits and veggies in your garden, and emptying your trash cans—all while making a royal mess of your lawn in the process. And sometimes, they carry roundworms and a number of diseases that can be transmitted to people and pets (the worst of which is rabies).

Description: These masked bandits are some of the cleverest and most conniving critters who ever cavorted across a lawn. And once they've added your yard to their must-visit list, they can be the very dickens to outwit.

Most likely victims: To a hungry coon, any yard in the country, the suburbs, or even the heart of a major city is fair game.

How to kick 'em out: Set electric fans around the coons' targets. (Be sure to use outdoor-grade extension cords.) Then, just before you go to bed, turn 'em all on. The raccoons will hightail it for calmer pastures. To make sure the message sinks in, perform this trick every night for a week or so.

Super★Secret

Go Vegetarian

At least as far as your compost is concerned. Adding meat, fish scraps, or cooking oils to the pile will attract raccoons from far and wide—and other varmints besides. What's more, those fats and proteins will slow down the pile's decom position and make it smell like, well, rotten meat.

Another ploy: Surround your yard (or its most vulnerable area) with a 3-foot-wide strip of stuff that's sticky, slippery, sharp, or just plain strange-feeling. Because raccoons have hairless and very sensitive feet, they won't walk across that "moat." Good choices include plastic sheeting, nylon netting, wire mesh, broken pot shards or jagged stones, leaves with Tanglefoot® sprayed on them, and thorny rose or bramble fruit canes.

To protect your birdfeeder, rig up a motion detector to a lawn sprinkler, and set it at the base of the pole. The birds will be able to fly in from above, but when the coons try to scamper up, they'll get sent to the showers!

How to keep 'em out: Stash your garbage in tightly sealed containers, and if coons are a persistent problem in your neighborhood, keep the trash indoors until collection day. And don't feed your pets outside; even a few scraps of leftover food are a coon's idea of an invitation to a never-ending dinner party.

For really serious coon control, erect a fence around your yard (any kind will do), and run three strands of electric wire around the base on the outside. (You can buy electrified fencing at most hardware and farm-supply stores.) Put the bottom wire 3 to 4 inches off the ground, then follow with two more, 3 to 4 inches apart. When the coons start to scamper over the top, they'll get a hot foot they won't soon forget! Of course, if your yard is already fenced, all you need to do is add the juiced-up wire!

★ VILLAIN ★

Actual size: 24" or more, including tail

SKUNKS

Unwanted for: Running roughshod through lawns and shrub beds in their quest for grubs (their food of choice), and issuing a fragrant calling card every now and then.

Description: Contrary to what a lot of folks think, a skunk sprays only when he's cornered or feels threatened. When you've got one in that position, he'll stiffen up his front legs, stomp them, and shuffle backward a little. He may also hiss and growl. Your job then is to back off quickly and quietly, and the skunk may retreat, too. Otherwise, the little acrobat will throw his body over his head and—still facing you—let 'er rip. If that happens, reach for my Skunk-Away Pet Bath (at right). (Don't let the name fool you: It works as well on humans as it does on Fido or Fluffy.)

Most likely victims: Skunks can show up just about anywhere except desert areas. But they prefer lawns that are on the edges of woodlands, or that feature dense shrub borders. They'll also find your place welcoming if it offers four-star lodgings like abandoned groundhog holes, old tree stumps, or a porch with nice, cozy crannies underneath.

How to kick 'em out: Just grab your garden hose, stand at least 20 feet away from the trespasser, and blast away. If you'd rather not get even *that* close, spray your yard and everything in it with my All-Purpose Pest Prevention Potion (see page 218).

How to keep 'em out: Because skunks rarely climb fences, you can make an effective barrier using ¼-inch wire mesh that's 3 feet wide. To keep the rascals from tunneling under, bend the bottom 6 inches outward at a 90-degree angle, and bury it at a depth of 6 inches. Then disguise the 2 feet left above the ground by tacking it to a picket fence or other decorative model.

BLUE PLATE ★ SPECIAL

SKUNK-AWAY PET BATH

There's almost nothing worse than getting up close and personal with a skunk. Fortunately, you can rely on this super de-skunking solution to save the day—whether the victim is Rover, Fluffy, or you.

2 cups of hydrogen peroxide
¼–½ cup of baking soda
1 tbsp. of mild dishwashing liquid

Mix these ingredients in a bowl, and apply the solution to your pet's coat (but don't get it on his head or near his eyes or ears). Rub the mixture in, then wash it out. Presto: Your best pal will smell fresh and clean again. If a human being was the recipient of the skunk's offerings, follow the same procedure.

PEST PROTECTION

Throughout this chapter, I've given you lots of tips and tricks to outsmart lawn pests. But we're not done yet—here are more tonics to add to your arsenal in the war against these menacing marauders.

ALL-PURPOSE PEST PREVENTION POTION

Skunks and just about any other critters I can think of will run away when they get a whiff of this powerful potion.

> **1 cup of ammonia**
> **½ cup of urine**
> **½ cup of dishwashing liquid**
> **¼ cup of castor oil**

Mix all of these ingredients in a 20 gallon hose-end sprayer. Then, thoroughly saturate the places where you don't want the little varmints venturing.

ALL-SEASON CLEAN-UP TONIC

This is the one tonic that you absolutely need to use religiously throughout the growing season. The shampoo cleans the plants and helps the other ingredients stick better; the mouthwash kills bad bacteria and discourages insects; and the tobacco tea contains nicotine, which does a double whammy on those pesky pests.

> **1 cup of baby shampoo**
> **1 cup of antiseptic mouthwash**
> **1 cup of tobacco tea***

Mix these ingredients in a 20 gallon hose-end sprayer, and give everything in your yard a good shower every two weeks in the early evening throughout the growing season. You'll have the healthiest yard in town—guaranteed!

To make tobacco tea, place half a handful of chewing tobacco in an old nylon stocking and soak it in a gallon of hot water until the mixture is dark brown. Pour the liquid into a glass container with a tight lid for storage.

DOG-BE-GONE TONIC

Whether it's a beagle bashing your bluegrass, a poodle peeing on your pachysandra, or a St. Bernard making an unsightly mess of your St. Augustine, the pitter-patter of pet paws can mean real trouble for your lawn. The simple solution: Lay out the unwelcome mat with this untantalizing tonic.

> **2 cloves of garlic**
> **2 small onions**
> **1 jalapeño pepper**
> **1 tbsp. of hot sauce**
> **1 tbsp. of chili powder**
> **1 tbsp. of dishwashing liquid**
> **1 qt. of warm water**

Chop the garlic, onions, and jalapeño pepper finely, and combine them with the rest of the ingredients. Let the mixture sit and marinate for 24 hours, strain it through cheesecloth or old pantyhose, then sprinkle the resulting liquid on any areas where dogs are a problem. This spicy potion will keep man's best friend from becoming your lawn's worst enemy!

HIT THE TRAIL MIX

When cats are cuttin' capers in your lawn, or gunnin' for your feathered friends, put up a Keep Out! sign in the form of this zesty potion.

> **4 tbsp. of dry mustard**
> **3 tbsp. of cayenne pepper**
> **2 tbsp. of chili powder**
> **2 tbsp. of cloves**
> **1 tbsp. of hot sauce**
> **2 qt. of warm water**

Mix all of the ingredients, and sprinkle the solution around the perimeter of your yard, or any place where Fluffy isn't welcome. She'll get her kicks elsewhere!

HOT BUG BREW

This potent beverage will deal a death blow to mole crickets or any other bug that's buggin' your lawn.

>   3 hot green peppers (canned or fresh)
>   3 medium cloves of garlic
>   1 small onion
>   1 tbsp. of dishwashing liquid
>   3 cups of water

Purée the peppers, garlic, and onion in a blender. Then pour the mixture into a jar, and add the dishwashing liquid and water. Let stand for 24 hours. Strain out the solids, pour the liquid into a spray bottle, and blast the mole crickets to kingdom come. **Note:** You probably won't get all the varmints on the first try, so you may need to repeat the process a few times.

MITE NOT TONIC

When mites are making a mighty mess of your lawn, reach for this simple, but fabulous formula. It's a powerful mite killer and mild fertilizer all in one.

>   1 cup of ammonia
>   ½ cup of dishwashing liquid

Mix these ingredients in a 20 gallon hose-end sprayer. Then spray your beleaguered lawn every five days for three weeks, and you'll moan over mites no more!

MOLE-CHASER TONIC

Moles will pack up and head outta town (or at least out of your yard) when they get a taste of this potent potion.

>   1½ tbsp. of hot sauce
>   1 tbsp. of dishwashing liquid
>   1 tsp. of chili powder
>   1 qt. of water

Mix these ingredients in a bucket, and pour a small amount of the solution into each mole hole. The little guys will get a taste they won't soon forget!

SQUEAKY CLEAN TONIC

This powerful tonic deals a mighty blow to cutworms and other bad guys who are buggin' your lawn.

>   1 cup of antiseptic mouthwash
>   1 cup of tobacco tea*
>   1 cup of chamomile tea
>   1 cup of urine
>   ½ cup of Murphy's Oil Soap®
>   ½ cup of lemon-scented dishwashing liquid

Mix all of these ingredients in a large bucket. Then pour the solution into a 20 gallon hose-end sprayer, and apply it to your lawn to the point of run-off.

To make tobacco tea, place half a handful of chewing tobacco in an old nylon stocking and soak it in a gallon of hot water until the mixture is dark brown. Pour the liquid into a glass container with a tight lid for storage.

SUPER SCALE SCRUB

This double-barreled potion works two ways: The soap kills the unprotected scale babies, a.k.a. crawlers, and the alcohol cuts right through the grownups' waxy shells.

>   1 cup of 70% isopropyl (rubbing) alcohol
>   1 tbsp. of dishwashing liquid
>   1 qt. of water

Mix these ingredients in a hand-held sprayer, and treat your scale-stricken grass every three days for two weeks. The scale will sail off into the sunset.

Cures for What Ails It

When it comes to defeating lawn diseases, half the battle is knowing what you're dealing with. Often the trouble isn't a disease at all, but an insect invasion, cultural problem, or even the result of an accident, such as spilled fertilizer. Here's how to tell when your grass is really in sick bay—and how to get that turf up and growing on the right root again.

 ## Dastardly Diseases

Don't let this roster throw you into a state of panic! Chances are, none of these menaces will raise their ugly heads on your lawn. (Their targets of choice are golf courses and similar playgrounds that are highly fertilized, closely mowed, and constantly being bombarded with insecticides, herbicides, and fungicides.)

Still, it's important to recognize trouble when you see it. That way, if it does strike, you can fight back—hard.

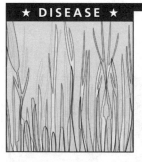

★ DISEASE ★

ANTHRACNOSE

Symptoms: After a period of hot, humid weather, yellow patches appear, ranging from an inch or two across to several yards. ★ Grass turns from yellow to bronze, then (just before dying) khaki tan. ★ Individual grass blades sport small yellow lesions with pinhead-size black centers (the fruiting bodies of the fungus).

Prime victims: Annual bluegrass and, usually with less severe results, Kentucky bluegrass and red fescue.

How to cure it: Aerate the soil, spread compost across the lawn, and raise your mower deck. Make sure your grass is getting all the nutrients it needs (see Chapter 5), and whatever you do, avoid watering in the evening.

How to avoid sick bay: If your brand of grass is prone to anthracnose, lightly mist your lawn twice a day during hot, humid weather: once in midmorning, and again in midafternoon. (The aim here is not to deliver water to the grass roots, but simply to cool the area, thereby preventing fungal spores from developing.)

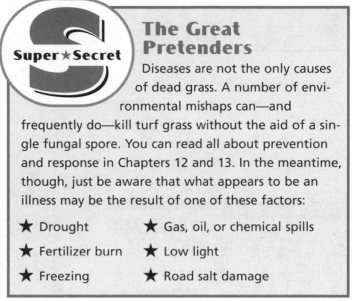

Super ★ Secret

The Great Pretenders

Diseases are not the only causes of dead grass. A number of environmental mishaps can—and frequently do—kill turf grass without the aid of a single fungal spore. You can read all about prevention and response in Chapters 12 and 13. In the meantime, though, just be aware that what appears to be an illness may be the result of one of these factors:

★ Drought   ★ Gas, oil, or chemical spills
★ Fertilizer burn   ★ Low light
★ Freezing   ★ Road salt damage

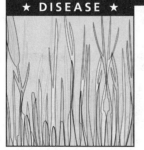

★ DISEASE ★

BROWN PATCH

Symptoms: Circular patches appear, ranging in size from a few inches to several feet in diameter. ★ Grass first looks dark and water-soaked, then dies and turns brown. ★ On coarse grasses, such as ryegrass, the circles may be light in color with brown edges. ★ Occurs during humid weather, when temperatures are between 80° and 85°F. ★ Generally strikes during the summer on cool-season lawns, and in spring and fall on warm-season turf.

Prime victims: Highly fertilized lawns, especially those with poor drainage or thick layers of thatch. Bent grass in the North and St. Augustine grass in the South are susceptible.

How to cure it: Spread compost over the damaged areas, and go cold turkey on nitrogen until symptoms subside. Blast thatch (see Chapter 4). Water deeply and infrequently, letting the soil dry out between waterings. Test your soil for calcium, phosphorus, and potassium, and correct any imbalances. If the troubled turf is shaded by tree branches, prune them to improve air circulation and let in more sunlight. If brown patch strikes your lawn repeatedly, it means you probably have a drainage problem; correct it using the methods in Chapter 3. Don't even *think* of applying a fungicide—it'll only make matters worse by wiping out the breakdown squad that aerates the soil.

How to avoid sick bay: During prolonged periods of hot, humid weather, drag a rope or garden hose across the grass first thing every morning. This will remove the dew, where fungal spores tend to multiply like crazy.

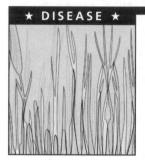

★ DISEASE ★

CROWN AND ROOT ROT

Symptoms: Grass blades develop purplish brown spots, and then the entire plant takes on a purplish tinge. ★ The turf thins out and slowly begins to die off in regularly shaped patches.

Prime victims: Any lawn that is poorly nourished, is growing in compacted soil, or has been treated repeatedly with herbicides.

How to cure it: For a quick fix, apply my Fungus-Fighter Soil Drench (above) to the affected areas. If the troubled spots are small, the remaining grass should quickly cover them up; if they're large, reseed or resod according to my damage control plan on page 231. For long-term results, test your soil for nitrogen and potassium, and add any necessary amendments. Loosen up your soil following the procedure in Chapter 4. (See "Boy, That's Hard!" beginning on page 91.)

BLUE PLATE SPECIAL

FUNGUS-FIGHTER SOIL DRENCH

When foul fungi are fussin' around in your soil, makin' a mess of your lawn, polish 'em off with this potent potion.

> 4 garlic bulbs, crushed
> ½ cup of baking soda
> 1 gal. of water

Mix these ingredients in a big pot and bring them to a boil. Then turn off the heat, and let the mixture cool to room temperature. Strain the liquid into a watering can, and soak the ground in the problem areas (remove any dead grass first). Go VERY slowly, so the elixir penetrates deep into the soil. Then dump the strained-out garlic bits onto the soil, and work them in gently.

How to avoid sick bay: Keep your soil well-fed (but not overly fed!) and do everything you can to avoid compaction.

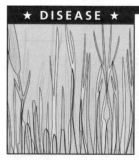

★ DISEASE ★

CURVULARIA BLIGHT

Symptoms: Irregular patches and streaks appear in the lawn. ★ Leaves turn yellow and brown from the tips all the way down to the sheath. ★ Most often strikes during the hottest part of summer.

Prime victims: Annual bluegrass, bent grasses, and fescues, especially when they have a thick layer of thatch, or they're suffering from heat stress or other cultural problems.

How to cure it: Raise your mower height to reduce turf stress, and get rid of any thatch on your lawn.

How to avoid sick bay: Simply give your grass good growing conditions by following my feeding, watering, and mowing tips in Chapters 5, 6, and 7.

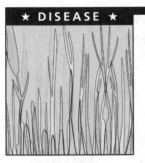

DOLLAR SPOT

Symptoms: Tan spots, from 2 to 6 inches in diameter, appear in the lawn, usually in late spring (so you know it's not a sign of winter damage). ★ Leaves are marked with hourglass-shaped blotches that extend across the blades. Each mark has a lighter center with a darker border of brown, black, or purple. ★ A fine, white, cottony fungus appears on the afflicted blades early in the morning, but disappears as the sun heats up.

Prime victims: Poorly nourished lawns with Bermuda grass, centipede grass, bluegrass, ryegrass, zoysia grass, and fine fescues.

How to cure it: Give your lawn a good meal (see Chapter 5), and water it well. Then spray with liquid seaweed (available in catalogs and many garden centers). That should put it on the rebound fast.

How to avoid sick bay: Feed your lawn a good diet (see Chapter 5). Water as needed to avoid drought stress, and give the grass time to dry out between waterings. Aerate to prevent thatch, and mow at the right height (no crew cuts).

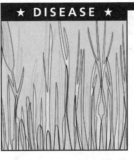

FAIRY RING

Symptoms: Circles or semi-circles of lush, dark green grass appear, usually in spring. ★ Gradually, the grass dies, and mushrooms or puffballs appear on the outer reaches of the circle.

Prime victims: Poorly nourished lawns with a thick layer of thatch, or a lot of buried, woody material, such as dead tree roots or debris from construction projects. Bluegrass, red fescue, and bent grass are the highest-risk targets.

How to cure it: First, pluck and discard the mushrooms (don't compost them, and don't let your dog eat them!). Then, puncture the turf by walking around in your golf shoes or aerating sandals, and apply my Fairy Ring Fighter Tonic (see page 224).

How to avoid sick bay: Feed your grass a well-balanced diet (see Chapter 5), and keep the soil well-stocked with compost—it contains microorganisms that fight fairy ring—and every other kind of foul fungus, for that matter!

★ DISEASE ★

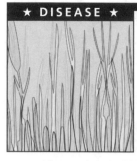

LEAF SPOT

Symptoms:
Usually in warm weather, grass blades develop small, elongated spots in shades of brown or tan, with purplish red borders. ★ The spots may extend over the width of the whole blade. ★ Grass tips may die, giving the lawn a brown tinge. ★ Eventually, the entire plant dies, leaving thinned-out patches of turf that appear slimy and withered.

Prime victims: Lush lawns filled with Bermuda grass and older varieties of Kentucky bluegrass.

How to cure it: If you reach the scene when the spots have first appeared, administer my Lawn Fungus-Fighter Tonic (at right). Otherwise, dig up the infected plants and reseed according to my damage control guidelines on page 231.

How to avoid sick bay: Go easy on the nitrogen, control thatch (where this fungus spends the winter), and never water in the evening—leaf spot spreads like lightning on wet leaves. When you reseed, use resistant grass varieties.

FAIRY RING FIGHTER TONIC

When circles of mushrooms sprout in your lawn, leap into action with this timely tonic.

Dry, mild laundry soap* (1 cup for every 2,500 sq. ft. of affected lawn area)

1 cup of baby shampoo

1 cup of antiseptic mouthwash

1 cup of ammonia

First, pour the dry laundry soap into a hand-held spreader, and spread it over the affected area. Then mix the remaining ingredients in a 20 gallon hose-end sprayer and apply to the point of run-off. Those 'shrooms will be history!

* Such as Ivory Snow®

★ DISEASE ★

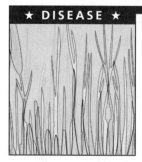

MELTING OUT

Symptoms: Elongated, straw-colored spots with reddish brown to black borders appear on the grass blades. ★ As the disease progresses, stems, crowns, and roots rot. ★ Dead grass appears wilted and slimy, as though it had been melted under a broiler. ★ In advanced stages, the lawn is littered with dead patches, irregular in shape and varying in size from a few inches to several yards across. ★ Most often appears in spring or fall, during periods of cool, moist weather.

Prime victims: Bermuda grass, Kentucky bluegrass, and fine fescues.

How to cure it: As soon as you see the first spots, apply my Lawn Fungus-Fighter Tonic (below). In later stages, dig up the infected plants, and reseed according to my damage control guidelines on page 231.

How to avoid sick bay: Avoid big doses of nitrogen, and don't fertilize in very hot weather. Remove thatch. Mow high (1½ to 2½ inches), and rake up the clippings. Plant resistant varieties.

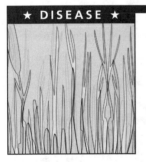

★ DISEASE ★

NECROTIC RING SPOT

Symptoms: In warm weather, dead spots suddenly appear on a lawn that seems as healthy as can be. ★ Grass may not die, but simply become stunted and turn red or yellow. ★ Roots may be killed during cooler weather, while foliage remains unaffected until extreme heat or other environmental stress hits. ★ When you dig up a chunk of turf, you'll see strands of black fungus on the roots and crowns. ★ Disease may strike any time from May to October, but most often appears between July and September.

Prime victims: Any kind of grass may be affected, but bent grass, Bermuda grass, bluegrass, and fine fescues are most at risk. And, for reasons that are beyond me, necrotic ring spot is especially troublesome in Washington state and Wisconsin.

How to cure it: Apply an organic fertilizer that contains *actinomycetes* (for the low-down on these helpers, see page 112).

How to avoid sick bay: Mow at the correct height, feed a balanced diet (watch the N!), and keep your soil at the proper pH level for your grass type (see "pH Ranges for Grasses" on page 65). During periods of extreme heat, give your lawn a light misting at midday. (For more on keeping your lawn stress-free during environmental hard times, see Chapter 12.)

BLUE PLATE SPECIAL

LAWN FUNGUS-FIGHTER TONIC

At the first sign of foul fungi, fight back *fast* with this fabulous formula.

1 tbsp. of baking soda
1 tbsp. of instant tea granules
1 tbsp. of horticultural oil or vegetable oil
1 gal. of warm water

Mix all of the ingredients in a large bucket. Then pour the solution into a hand-held sprayer, and lightly spray the affected turf. Do *not* apply to the point of run-off! Repeat in two to three weeks if necessary.

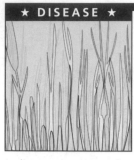

★ DISEASE ★

PINK PATCH

Symptoms: Grass begins to die off in irregularly shaped patches that, from a distance, appear (you guessed it) pink. ★ In severe cases, the whole grass plant may die, but generally only the leaves, sheaths, and stems are affected. ★ Most often strikes when temperatures are between 65° and 75°F.

Prime victims: Unlike most diseases, this one generally strikes lawns that are receiving too little maintenance, rather than too much. Any kind of grass can fall prey to pink patch, but perennial ryegrass and fine fescue are the ones that tend to suffer the most damage.

How to cure it: Have your soil tested for both nutrients and pH, then dish up whatever sustenance the results call for—and be quick about it!

How to avoid sick bay: Take better care of your lawn! Feed it a healthy, balanced diet; mow it at the proper time and at the proper height; water it wisely and well; and control thatch.

What's Up, Doc?

You say that all these diseases sound an awful lot alike? Well, there's a good reason for that: Most of them do produce very similar symptoms. In fact, sometimes the only way to positively diagnose a lawn malady is to send a "biopsy" to (guess who?) your Cooperative Extension Service, or a specialist it might recommend. Take your sample from an area where the trouble is just starting to take hold, with about half of it healthy turf, and half showing early symptoms. Dig down about 2 inches, and try to lift up a section that's roughly 1 foot square. Then pack it up carefully (ask for instructions when you call the Extension Service), and send it off to the lawn docs with a cover note telling everything you know about the problem (see "Show and Tell" on page 230).

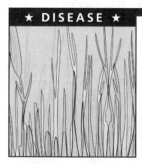

★ DISEASE ★

PINK SNOW MOLD, A.K.A. FUSARIUM PATCH

Symptoms: Fungus takes hold in the summer and fall, and attacks grass blades over the winter. ★ Strikes hardest under cover of snow but will grow without it. ★ When the snow starts to melt (or in very early spring if there's been no snow), reddish brown patches, from 1 to 12 inches across, appear, with fuzzy pink around the edges. ★ As leaves die, they turn tan and clump together in an ugly mat. ★ The good news: Snow mold usually affects only the blades and not the crown or roots of the plants; when warm, sunny weather arrives, the grass quickly turns green and lush again.

Prime victims: Lawns that have a thick layer of thatch, that have too little potassium in their diet, or that get too much nitrogen going into the fall. The combination of cool air temperatures and humid conditions in the early spring seems to kick snow mold into high gear.

How to cure it: Have your soil tested for nutrients. If the results show a potassium deficiency, give your lawn a healthy dose of the Big K (some excellent organic sources include banana peels, cow manure, and wood ashes—see Chapter 5 for more information). And for goodness sake, get out there and blast that thatch!

How to avoid sick bay: Don't apply any nitrogen within six weeks of the time your grass normally goes dormant. Make sure your grass gets as much potassium as it needs. In the fall, rake up leaves, grass clippings, and other debris where the fungal spores thrive in the winter. Try to reduce shady areas by pruning trees and shrubs to let in more sunshine.

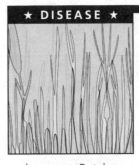

★ DISEASE ★

POWDERY MILDEW

Symptoms: Tiny, superficial patches of white to light gray fungus appear on leaves. ★ Patches get bigger and turn powdery as more fungal spores are produced. ★ In advanced cases, the leaf tissue turns yellow, then tan, and finally brown before dying. ★ Generally strikes only shady parts of a lawn during periods of high humidity and temperatures between 60° and 72°F.

Prime victims: Bluegrass is most susceptible, but any grass that's growing in a shaded area (like the north or east side of your house or garage) is a candidate for powdery mildew.

How to cure it: Relieve the symptoms by applying my Lawn Mildew-Relief Tonic (see page 228) at the first sign of trouble. Then set about treating the underlying cause—otherwise, the fungus will return to your lawn again and again.

How to avoid sick bay: Replace bluegrass with a more shade-tolerant type (see Chapter 2 for some good choices). Try to reduce the amount of shade in your yard by pruning or removing trees or shrubs to let in more sunshine. And practice all of my good TLC guidelines in Chapters 5 through 8.

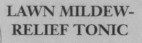

LAWN MILDEW-RELIEF TONIC

When your grass shows the first signs of powdery mildew, whip up this remarkable recipe, and let 'er rip.

1 cup of baby shampoo
1 cup of hydrogen peroxide
4 tbsp. of instant tea granules
Water

Mix the shampoo, peroxide, and tea granules in a 20 gallon hose-end sprayer, filling the balance of the jar with water. Spray the affected area every week to 10 days, and your lawn will soon be spotless once more.

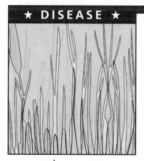

★ DISEASE ★

PYTHIUM BLIGHT

Symptoms: During hot, humid weather, dark, slimy-looking patches appear; they're about 2 inches across. ★ After a rain, or in the morning when the dew is on the grass, the water-soaked leaves collapse and mat together, and a white, cottony fungus becomes visible. ★ As the grass blades dry, they turn brown, wither, and die. ★ Dead patches often form streaks in the direction of your mowing pattern, because the mower spreads the fungal spores.

Prime victims: Any grass that's growing in an area with moist soil, hot days, and warm, humid nights. Bent grass, bluegrass, and perennial ryegrass are most susceptible, and lawns with soil that's compacted or has a high pH are high-risk targets.

How to cure it: Pythium blight kills the grass crowns, so your only option is to remove the turf in the dead spots and apply a good dose of my Fungus-Fighter Soil Drench (see page 222). Then follow my damage control plan on page 231. Be quick about it, because once this nasty stuff takes hold, it spreads like lightning.

How to avoid sick bay: Water infrequently and deeply, and *never* water at night. If pythium has reared its ugly head before, try to avoid watering or mowing when the temperatures go above 82°F.

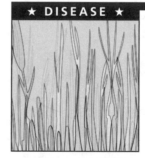

★ DISEASE ★

RED THREAD

Symptoms: In the fall, just as the lawn is going dormant, irregular, reddish or pinkish brown patches appear. ★ Oval spots appear on the blades, eventually girdling and killing the leaves. ★ Grass wilts and turns yellowish tan. ★ In advanced stages, a pinkish red, gelatinous mass grows from the ends of the grass leaves. ★ In severe cases, the crown rots and the whole plant dies.

Prime victims: Any poorly fertilized lawn in the North, but especially perennial ryegrass and fine fescues.

How to cure it: If whole grass plants have gone belly-up, replace them by following my damage control plan on page 231. Otherwise, simply mow regularly to remove infected leaf tips, and make sure your lawn is getting all the nitrogen it needs (see Chapter 5).

How to avoid sick bay: Feed your lawn a good diet, and water only during the day, so the grass leaves stay as dry as possible.

Stop Spreadin' the News

Super ★ Secret

Once a disease has set up camp in your lawn, it can spread like wildfire—and if you're not careful, you can give those fungal spores a free ride. So, while you're getting the disease under control, take these two simple precautions to fend off hitchhikers:

★ As much as possible, avoid walking on the lawn, and try to keep kids and pets off of it, too.

★ After you've been working with infected grass, clean your mower, rake, hose, and any other tools before you move on to healthy turf. A simple rubdown with either 70 percent rubbing alcohol, or a solution of 1 part household bleach to 3 parts water will do the trick.

★ DISEASE ★

RUST

Symptoms: Yellow-orange spots the size of pinheads appear on blades and grow into brick-red pustules.

★ Eventually, leaves turn reddish brown or yellow, and die. ★ Most often strikes when daytime temperatures are between 85° and 95°F and nighttime temps are between 70° and 75°F. ★ Rarely kills the infected lawn area, but may weaken it, making it more likely to be killed by winter cold or other stress.

Prime victims: Any grass in any part of the country can get rust, but perennial ryegrass and Kentucky bluegrass are most at risk. A diet that's too low in nitrogen contributes to the problem.

How to cure it: Mow every four or five days to remove the damaged leaves (and don't be surprised if your mower or catcher bag turns yellowish orange!). Water infrequently and deeply. Make sure your grass is getting the nitrogen it needs. And to get rid of really stubborn rust problems, bathe your lawn every two weeks with my All-Season Clean-Up Tonic (see page 218).

How to avoid sick bay: Feed your lawn a well-balanced diet, and water early so the grass can dry before nightfall. If you grow perennial ryegrass or Kentucky bluegrass, over-seed your lawn with a rust-resistant variety.

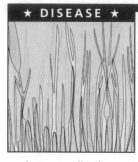

★ DISEASE ★

SCLEROTIUM, A.K.A. SOUTHERN BLIGHT

Symptoms: Circles of grass up to 3 yards in diameter turn reddish brown and eventually die. ★ In advanced cases, the lawn takes on a whitish cast caused by the white *sclerotia* (seedlike objects known as fungus resting bodies) at the base of the stems.

Prime victims: Bent grass, bluegrass, fescues, and ryegrasses with a thick layer of thatch. Lawns in hot, moist climates are most at risk.

How to cure it: Apply my Lawn Fungus-Fighter Tonic (see page 225) at the first sign of trouble, and get rid of thatch.

How to avoid sick bay: Feed your lawn the right amounts of food at the right times, control thatch, and practice good lawn hygiene. (See "Fundamentals for Foiling Foul Fungi" on page 234.)

Yankee Doodle Data

Show and Tell

Many lawn diseases are hard to diagnose accurately, even for professional turf grass scientists. So, when you send off a sample for analysis, the more information you can provide, the more likely it is that you'll get a positive ID and an effective treatment plan. Here are the general categories.

CATEGORY	IMPORTANT DETAILS	
Patient's bio	☆ Age of the lawn	☆ Type and variety of grass
Symptoms	☆ Overall appearance of the lawn	☆ Appearance of individual grass blades (i.e., streaked, spotted, wilted)
	☆ Size, shape, color of the affected areas	
	☆ Location of the damaged spots (e.g., along your normal mowing path, at the base of your sprinkler heads, or on a slope)	☆ Root condition (e.g., Does the turf pull up in a mat? Have the roots rotted?)
History	☆ When the problem first appeared	☆ Recent activity in your yard, such as construction or house painting
	☆ Weather conditions at the time	
Routine	☆ Soil pH and nutrient levels care	☆ Any pesticides, herbicides, and fertilizers you've used
	☆ Your mowing, watering, and feeding routine	

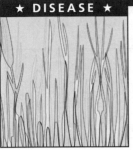

★ DISEASE ★

SLIME MOLD

Symptoms: A white or grayish powder, resembling cigarette ashes, covers grass leaves. ★ The affected area may be a few inches to several yards across. ★ Generally appears during warm, wet, or humid weather and vanishes when the temperatures rise and the humidity goes down.

Prime victims: When the climatic conditions are right, any grass, anyplace, is a likely target.

How to cure it: Just haul out the hose and wash your troubles away, or mow off the affected parts of the grass leaves, being careful not to break the one-third rule (see "What Do You Mean, 'the Right Way'?" on page 156).

How to avoid sick bay: The best you can do is hope for good weather!

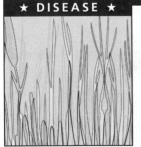

★ DISEASE ★

SPRING DEAD SPOT

Symptoms: In the spring, just as the lawn is starting to green up, circular dead patches, about 3 to 4 feet in diameter, appear. ★ The grass eventually grows back, but it may take several months. ★ The problem usually recurs each year in the same spots.

Prime victims: Highly maintained lawns of Bermuda grass and zoysia grass.

How to cure it: In the fall, give your lawn a healthy dose of potassium (see Chapter 5

Super ★ Secret

Damage Control

No matter what felonious fungus has run roughshod through your lawn, here's a simple, three-step plan that'll green it up again.

Step 1. Sprinkle cornmeal over the damaged area at a rate of 50 pounds per 2,500 square feet. Scientists have found that this common supermarket product makes a whole lot of fungus diseases vanish like magic. They haven't figured out exactly how it works, but from what they can tell, it attracts and feeds the good guys who hang around to eat the fungal spores.

Step 2. Buy the highest-quality grass seed you can find—preferably one that's resistant to the disease that's been plaguing your lawn. Then, sow it thickly, so that the seeds are almost, but not quite, touching each other.

Step 3. Spread ¼ inch of good compost over the seedbed, and water well. And remember: As with any newly seeded area, you'll have to keep the seeds constantly moist until they sprout.

for some good sources) and apply my Lawn Fungus-Fighter Tonic (see page 225).

How to avoid sick bay: Feed your lawn a balanced diet, being very careful not to overdo the nitrogen. And dethatch every year, because that nasty layer is where this foul fungus spends the winter.

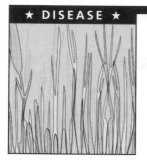

★ DISEASE ★
STRIPE SMUT

Symptoms: During cool weather (between 50° and 60°F), grass blades develop long, yellow-green streaks that turn gray and then black. ★ The black streaks rupture, releasing fungal spores and making the leaves look torn and tattered. ★ The leaves curl downward at the tips, then turn brown and die. ★ The symptoms disappear when the weather heats up.

Prime victims: Creeping bent grass and some varieties of bluegrass, most often in lawns that are a little low on nitrogen.

How to cure it: Give your lawn a good dose of nitrogen, water slowly and deeply early in the day, and reseed any dead spots according to my damage control plan on page 231.

How to avoid sick bay: Sow resistant varieties of grass, and keep your lawn in the pink of health by following my "Fundamentals for Foiling Foul Fungi" on page 234.

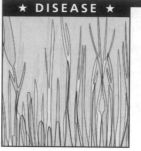

★ DISEASE ★
SUMMER PATCH

Symptoms: During hot, dry weather, scattered, elongated patches appear. They're generally 6 to 12 inches across, start out light green, then quickly turn to a straw-brown color. ★ Grass blades die back from the tip. ★ As the grass dies, weeds may move into the patches.

Prime victims: Bluegrass and fine fescues that are heat-stressed, mowed too short, or growing in compacted soil.

How to cure it: At the first sign of trouble, administer Jerry's Anti-Summer-Patch Tonic (at right). If you've reached the scene too late for that, dig up the dead turf and reseed the affected areas with a tall fescue or a resistant variety of Kentucky bluegrass, such as 'Bristol', 'Rugby', or 'Wabash'.

How to avoid sick bay: Go easy on nitrogen, mow at the right height, and fend off soil compaction following the guidelines in Chapter 4.

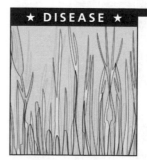

★ DISEASE ★
TAKE-ALL PATCH

Symptoms: Circles or rings of dead grass appear, ranging from a couple of inches to several feet

across. ★ Grass roots rot and are covered with dark strands of fungus.

Prime victims: Bent grasses, fescues, and ryegrasses that are growing in soil that's either sandy, damp, lacking in organic matter, highly alkaline, or poorly nourished.

How to cure it: Administer my Fungus-Fighter Soil Drench (see page 222) in the fall. Then, figure out which of the above problems is plaguing your soil, and set about correcting it. You'll find plenty of advice in this book. (See Chapter 3 for the lowdown on drainage and soil improvement; Chapter 5 for my lawn-dietary guidelines.)

How to avoid sick bay: Replant with resistant varieties, feed them a top-notch diet, and keep your soil in good shape.

JERRY'S ANTI-SUMMER-PATCH TONIC

Summer patch is caused by a fungus that aggressively attacks grass during periods of wet, warm weather from late spring to late summer. This remarkable recipe will help send it packin'!

    1 cup of dishwashing liquid
    1 cup of tobacco tea*
    1 cup of antiseptic mouthwash
    1 cup of ammonia
    3 tbsp. of saltpeter

Combine all the ingredients in a large bucket and pour the solution into a 20 gallon hose-end sprayer. Apply it to your lawn to the point of run-off every three weeks during the growing season.

* To make tobacco tea, place half a handful of chewing tobacco in an old nylon stocking and soak it in a gallon of hot water until the mixture is dark brown. Pour the liquid into a glass container with a tight lid for storage.

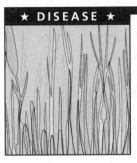

★ DISEASE ★

TAKE-ALL ROOT ROT

Symptoms: Patches of grass turn yellow and thin out. ★ When you dig up a clump of turf, you'll see that the roots have decayed and rotted. ★ Usually strikes in summer or fall, during periods of hot, moist weather.

Prime victims: St. Augustine grass, centipede grass, and Bermuda grass that's been injured by underground insects, or that's stressed out from environmental trouble or poor care—especially scalping (i.e., repeatedly mowing the grass to short).

How to cure it: Mow high to reduce stress, and replace the dead grass (see "Damage Control" on page 231).

How to avoid sick bay: Do everything you can to keep your lawn stress-free (in other words, give it the best possible TLC). For my tips on handling turf stress when Mother Nature dumps trouble in your lawn's lap, see Chapter 12.

Fundamentals for Foiling Foul Fungi

With the exception of one viral infection (see "That's SAD!" on page 238), all of the major lawn diseases are caused by fungi of one kind or another. And once they take hold, they can be very tricky to get rid of. Fortunately—like many of life's problems—they're a lot easier to avoid in the first place. Here's my foolproof (well, *almost* foolproof) plan for keeping these fearsome felons from fouling your favorite field of green:

Give it great groundwork. Whether you're starting a lawn from scratch, or doctoring up an existing one, your grass will only be as strong and healthy as the soil it's growing in. For the full lowdown on soil, including how to ensure good drainage (most fungi love poorly drained soil), see Chapters 3 and 4.

Go for the gold. Black gold, that is—compost. Scientists at Cornell University and other horticulture schools have found that this wonder drug works in three ways to keep your lawn (and all your other plants) strong and healthy: It produces chemicals that kill fungi and bad bacteria, feeds microorganisms that eat fungi, and provides essential nutrients in a safe, slow way.

Know your territory. Assess your climate and the growing conditions in your yard, including not only temperature and humidity, but also such factors as light level, soil type, and the amount of foot traffic your lawn gets.

Then choose a type and variety of grass that's been bred to thrive (not merely survive) in that environment. The reason: Any grass that you plant on the edges of its comfort zone will be under constant stress. And stressed grass is a sitting duck for diseases.

Know the enemy. Find out what lawn diseases are most prevalent in your area, and plant resistant varieties of grass. Your best sources of intelligence: your lawn-tending neighbors and the folks at your closest Cooperative Extension Service.

Water right. Most lawn diseases take off like gangbusters in moist or humid conditions. Although you can't do anything about the weather, you can head off a whole lot of trouble with these two simple steps: Water early in the day, so the grass can dry off before nightfall; and water deeply but infrequently, so the grass dries out between waterings. (For more on watering, see Chapter 6.)

Feed right. Many diseases target overfertilized lawns (especially those that are getting too much nitrogen). Others prefer turf that's underfed. Your mission: Follow the dietary guidelines in Chapter 5. And test your soil's pH frequently, because when that's out of whack, your grass plants can't properly absorb all the nutrients they need. (See Chapter 3 for the lowdown on pH levels.)

Mow right. By that I mean mow at the maximum recommended height for your type of grass, and keep your mower blades razor sharp. How come? Because (as I explained in Chapter 7) cutting your grass short weakens the plants, making them easy targets for diseases; and dull blades make ragged cuts, through which fungal spores swarm like ants at a picnic.

Dispatch thatch. Any disease worth its salt craves this stuff. You'll find my thatch removal and control strategy in Chapter 4.

Keep a weather eye out. You can't control Mother Nature—or the local road crew that dumps salt on the edges of your lawn all winter long. But you can help your grass cope with the inevitable stress that results, thereby making it less vulnerable to fungus attacks. (See Chapters 12 and 13 for the game plan.)

Don't take "cides." When bad bugs, weeds, or foul fungi are driving you to drink, it's awfully tempting to reach for a potent insecticide, herbicide, or fungicide—and in most cases, you will get relief. And fast, too. But it won't last long. Before you know it, you'll have to load up the old spray gun and march into battle again. And the more you use these chemical killers, the more damage you do to your lawn's true heroes: earthworms, good-guy bugs, and zillions of invisible organisms that keep diseases and pests in check. As a result, you'll find yourself in a never-ending war with germs and bad-guy bugs. Is that really how you want to spend your precious time and hard-earned money?

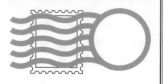

Dear Jerry,

I asked my Cooperative Extension Service to suggest a good disease-resistant grass for my area, and they recommended a mixture of several types. I sowed the seed and it came up just fine, but my lawn is still being clobbered by foul fungi. Have those folks taken leave of their senses? Or is this whole disease-resistance business just marketing hype?

A. *Neither, my friend! What we have here is a misunderstanding of the terminology. The word "resistant" doesn't mean that a particular variety of grass is immune to trouble. It simply means that it's less likely to fall victim to a particular disease (or pest) than its nonresistant counterparts are. If it doesn't get all the TLC it needs from you, or if it's under stress from harsh weather or other environmental woes, any turf can wind up on the casualty list.*

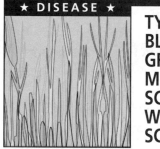

★ DISEASE ★

TYPHULA BLIGHT, A.K.A. GRAY SNOW MOLD, SNOW SCALD, AND WINTER SCALD

Symptoms: Right after the snow melts, sections of grass appear bleached.

Prime victims: All cool-season turf grasses in areas where snow stays on the ground for three months or longer.

How to cure it: Rake the affected areas and get rid of any debris, which will help the grass dry out faster. In spots where damage is light, simply apply a little well-balanced fertilizer to encourage new top growth. Give severely injured patches my full-scale damage control treatment (see page 231).

How to avoid sick bay: Because this fungus attacks over the winter, you need to take preventive action in the fall. First, discourage the growth of new, lush foliage by going cold turkey on nitrogen six weeks before you expect the first frost. Second, don't let up on mowing—keep at it until the grass stops growing in the fall. And control thatch—like most foul fungi, this one loves the stuff!

★ DISEASE ★

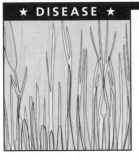

WHITE PATCH

Symptoms: Round, white patches appear, ranging in size from 6 to 12 inches in diameter. ★ Often, small, tan mushrooms grow up around the circles.

Prime victims: New lawns planted in areas recently cleared of trees. Any type of grass can come under attack, but fescues seem the most prone to trouble.

How to cure it: Test your soil for pH and nutrients, and apply whatever amendments the results call for. Correcting any imbalance is usually all you need to do solve the problem.

How to avoid sick bay: Just feed your lawn a well-balanced diet (in particular, make sure it's getting enough phosphorus), and keep the soil at the recommended pH for your type of grass (see "pH Ranges for Grasses" on page 65).

★ DISEASE ★

YELLOW PATCH

Symptoms: Patches of grass, 2 to 3 inches across, turn light green or a sickly yellow-

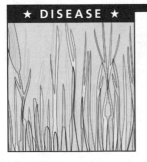

green. ★ The spots turn light brown and increase in width to 2 feet or more. ★ Grass at the outer reaches of the dead patches may be reddish, with darker brown spots. ★ Sometimes, a clump of grass continues to grow inside the dead area.

Prime victims: Kentucky bluegrass and any grass growing in heavy clay soil. Sod that's been recently laid on clay soil is especially at risk, because it must be kept constantly moist—exactly the conditions this fungus loves best.

How to cure it: There is no cure, so your only option is to replace the dead turf according to my damage control plan on page 231.

Star-Spangled *Lawn* Lore

Do you know that, if you're like most folks in the good old U.S. of A., you eat grass several times each day? Yep, I kid you not. Just about all of our breads, breakfast cereals, and pastas are made from grass plants, such as corn, oats, wheat, barley, and rye. In fact, even if you pass up those other carbs in favor of dessert, it's all but guaranteed that you're still eating grass in the form of sugarcane.

How to avoid sick bay: Do whatever you must to improve drainage (see Chapter 3), and aerate your lawn regularly following my directions in Chapter 4.

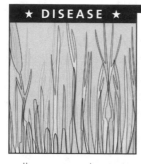

★ DISEASE ★

ZONATE LEAF SPOT

Symptoms: During periods of hot, humid weather (over 85°F), the lawn starts turning yellow over a large area. ★ Grass leaves develop spots and begin to die in circular and semi-circular sections that get bigger almost before your very eyes.

Prime victims: Bermuda grass and St. Augustine grass in hot, humid climates and getting too much nitrogen.

How to cure it: Reduce the nitrogen load. If you've been using a quick-release fertilizer, switch to a slow-release type—preferably a natural/organic food that delivers the Big N in smaller doses. Water early in the day, and supply only as much moisture as the grass needs (see Chapter 6). To avoid infecting healthy turf, stay off the lawn as much as possible.

How to avoid sick bay: Spread compost over your lawn twice a year, deliver a balanced diet, and follow my "Fundamentals for Foiling Foul Fungi" (see page 234).

Super★Secret

That's SAD!

St. Augustine decline (SAD) is the only major lawn disease that's caused by a virus, rather than a fungus. Despite its name, SAD attacks both St. Augustine and centipede grass. It's most widespread in Texas, but sometimes appears in Arkansas and Louisiana. Infected grass is slow to get going in the spring. When it does start to grow, the leaves turn a mottled yellow (unlike the solid yellow, or yellow with green veins, that indicates iron deficiency). The plants weaken, the lawn thins out, and weeds move in. There is no cure, but a jolt of iron (see Chapter 5) in the summer will revive the green color temporarily. For permanent results, get some plugs of a SAD-resistant variety, and plant them at 2- to 3-foot intervals across your lawn. Within a few years, they'll crowd out the weak, infected plants, and you'll be back in business.

Yankee Doodle Data

The Specialists

A handful of lawn diseases plague only one type of grass. The victims are all of the warm-season variety, so if you live in cool-turf territory, read no further. For those of you in balmier climes, here's what to look for and how to respond if you spot it.

DISEASE AND VICTIM	WHAT TO LOOK FOR	WHAT TO DO
Bermuda grass decline: Bermuda grass	Grass thins out and turns yellow in 1- to 2-foot-diameter patches. Feeder roots rot, causing the remaining roots to die of starvation. Prime target: lawns that are mowed too low.	Raise your mower deck! And faithfully follow my Fundamentals for Foiling Foul Fungi (see page 234).
Centipede decline: Centipede grass	Round dead spots begin appearing in the spring and grow throughout the summer. Grass on the outer edges of the circles turns yellow before it dies. Prime target: stressed-out lawns.	Serve up only as much food as your lawn needs (see Chapter 5), and keep the soil's pH between 5.0 and 5.5. Also, mow high, and follow my stress-avoidance tips in Chapter 12.
Leaf blotch: Bermuda grass	Tiny reddish or purplish spots appear on leaves of seedlings (never on older grass), which soon wither and die. Dead patches may be anywhere from a few inches to 3 feet across. Prime target: seedlings growing in thatch-covered lawns.	Keep your lawn free of thatch, go easy on the nitrogen, and follow all of my tips for good grass health.
Nigrospora blight: St. Augustine grass	Leaves and stolons dry out and turn yellowish brown, and brown lesions appear on the stolons. The resulting yellow patches resemble those left by chinch bugs. Prime target: lawns that are weak and poorly cared for.	Apply my Lawn Fungus-Fighter Tonic (see page 225) at the first sign of trouble. Then simply start taking better care of your turf!

Winning the War on Weeds

Botanically speaking, there is no such thing as a weed. But as lawn-lovers know all too well, there *is* such a thing as a plant that's growing where it's not welcome. In this chapter, I'll share my surefire secrets to send those gate crashers packin'!

☆ Turf-Trashing Trespassers

Unlike the diseases we talked about in Chapter 10, weeds can—and do—show up in even the best-kept lawns. Here's an

"Unwanted" list of the troublemakers you're most likely to see in your yard, along with my tips and tricks for getting rid of them—fast!

★ WEED ★

BINDWEED, A.K.A. WILD MORNING GLORY
(Convolvulus arvensis)

Distinguishing features: Twining vines, with white or pinkish, trumpet-shaped flowers that wither by midday. The leaves resemble either hearts (in the case of hedge bindweed) or shields (as in field bindweed, shown in the illustration at left).

Modus operandi: Warm-season broadleaf perennial. Spreads by seed and strong, vigorous roots that may reach as far as (yes, you're reading this right) 20 feet underground!

★ WEED ★

BROADLEAF PLANTAIN
(Plantago major)

Distinguishing features: Wide, gray-green, egg-shaped leaves with wavy edges. It looks a little like miniature rhubarb.

Modus operandi: Cool-season broadleaf perennial. Spreads by seed and grows easily in moist, compacted soil. It quickly moves into bare spots and will overrun a thin lawn.

★ WEED ★

BURCLOVER, A.K.A. BLACK MEDIC
(Medicago lupulina)

Distinguishing features: Light green, cloverlike leaves, bright yellow flowers, and prickly seedheads (known as burs, which give the plant one of its names).

Modus operandi: Cool-season broadleaf annual. Appears in late spring or summer, grows by leaps and bounds, and can easily take over a weak lawn.

Super ★ Secret

High Mow, High Mow...

It's off to play we go. What on earth do I mean by that? Just this: Simply by keeping your lawn mowed at the maximum recommended height for your type of grass, you can wipe out a whole lot of worrisome weeds—thereby leaving yourself more time to spend on the golf course or down at the old fishin' hole. This easy trick works for a couple of reasons:

1. Tall grass shades and cools the soil, making it harder for those pesky weed seeds to get a toehold.

2. As we saw in Chapter 7, mowing high makes for deep-rooted, healthier grass that's better able to crowd out any weeds that do develop.

High mowing is especially effective at controlling low-growing troublemakers, such as annual bluegrass, crabgrass, witchgrass, and yellow nut sedge.

Super ★ Secret

Coming to Terms with Weeds

Before you set out to wage war on wily weeds, it helps to know a little terminology. That's because your best battle strategy depends in large part on which category—or rather, combination of categories—your resident troublemakers fall into. Here's the breakdown:

1. Appearance.

★ Narrowleaf, a.k.a grassy, weeds look like, well, grasses, and most of them are exactly that. In fact, the grassy "weeds" in your lawn may be somebody else's idea of first-rate turf grass. (For more on that score, see "Friend and Foe" on page 258.) But some of these intrepid intruders are grass look-alikes called sedges.

★ Broadleaf weeds include all of our uninvited green guests that are *not* grasses or sedges—even though some of them have leaves that are downright skinny.

2. Reproductive styles.

★ Annual weeds germinate, mature, flower, set seed, and die in a single year. In fact, some especially prolific procreators complete that cycle several times each year. (In serious gardening circles, these overachievers are known as *ephemerals*.)

★ Perennial weeds live for two or more years.

3. Prime troublemaking period.

★ Cool-season weeds germinate in spring or fall. Up North, that's when they raise the biggest ruckus. In the South, they go on the rampage in winter, when temperatures are mild, and lawns are dormant.

★ Warm-season weeds germinate in late spring or summer, and grow like blazes as long as the hot weather lasts. Come winter, the annuals die (leaving their seeds behind to launch the next generation), and the perennials go dormant (to rise again, bigger and stronger, in the spring).

Having all these categories to choose from means that weed control demands a multi-pronged approach: For instance, there are warm-season narrowleaf annuals, cool-season broadleaf perennials, and so on. For a look at your most effective combat plan for each feisty foe, see "Battle Tactics at a Glance" on page 247.

★ **WEED** ★

CANADA THISTLE   (*Cirsium arvense*)

Distinguishing features: Rosette of crinkle-edged leaves held just above the soil on a single stem and armed with pliable, but (*ouch!*) needle-sharp spines. Flowers are hairy tufts about ¼ to ½ inch across, usually rosy purple in color, but sometimes white or lavender. If you pull up a plant, you'll see a short, stout taproot that's attached to a thinner, horizontal root.

Modus operandi: Cool-season broadleaf perennial. Plants start appearing in early spring and spread like gangbusters from the wandering taproot. Causes the most trouble in heavy, moist soil, but can show up in any lawn, thanks to fluffy seedheads that can float on the wind for miles.

★ **WEED** ★

CARPETWEED   (*Mollugo verticillata*)

Distinguishing features: Ground-hugging stems with tufts of smooth, green, oblong leaves at roughly 1-inch intervals. From each of these bunches, tiny, five-petaled, white flowers grow on slender stems, followed by green seedpods containing small, orange, kidney-shaped seeds.

Modus operandi: Warm-season broadleaf annual. Appears when the soil has warmed up and loves loose, sandy soil. Quickly forms a green carpet (hence its name) over areas, but shallow roots make it easy to rake or pull up.

BLUE PLATE ★ ★ SPECIAL

WILD WEED WIPEOUT TONIC

When you've got weeds that won't take no for an answer, knock 'em flat on their backs with this potent potion.

    1 tbsp. of gin
    1 tbsp. of white vinegar
    1 tbsp. of baby shampoo
    1 qt. of very warm water

Mix these ingredients together, and pour the solution into a hand-held sprayer. Then, drench the weeds to the point of run-off, taking care not to spray any plants that you want to keep.

Yankee Doodle Data

Got It!

You can spend a fortune on fancy weeding tools, but some of the handiest of all are right in your kitchen drawer, or maybe your toolbox. Here's my can't-do-without-'em list.

UNFANCY TOOL	WHAT I USE IT FOR
Curved, serrated grapefruit knife	Scooping out seedlings, or shallow-rooted weeds of any age
Broad, round-ended knife	Prying out weeds from gaps between pavers or stepping stones
Flat-ended screwdriver	Getting into really tight spaces, like cracks in pavement
Pliers	Pulling out tough, deeply rooted weeds that tend to break off right at ground level when you use your bare hands (Just grab on to the stem where it meets the soil, and twist gently as you pull up.)

★ WEED ★

CHICKWEED (Stellaria media)

Distinguishing features: Stems form a low, tangled mat in cool weather, but reach upward when temperatures warm up. Leaves are about ½ inch long, oval, and pointed at the end. Small, white flowers open fully on sunny days, but only partially when skies are cloudy.

Modus operandi: Cool-season broadleaf annual. Extremely cold-hardy plant that will often bloom all winter long in mild climates. Most common in new lawns, and prefers soil that's moist and rich, with a near-neutral pH (7.0 on the scale).

★ WEED ★

CHICORY (Chicorium intybus)

Distinguishing features: Grayish green, toothed, lance-shaped leaves, and many-petaled flowers that are usually clear blue, but occasionally white or pink.

Modus operandi: Warm-season broadleaf perennial. Sends its large taproot far and wide, and loves soil that's high in clay.

★ WEED ★

CLOVER *(Trifolium repens)*

Distinguishing features: Three- or (on your lucky day) four-part emerald green leaves with white, crescent-shaped markings and globular flowers in white or pink.

Modus operandi: Cool-season broadleaf perennial. Technically speaking, this plant is considered a "creeper," but when it takes hold in a spot it likes, it doesn't creep—it gallops! Its favorite home: poorly nourished turf that gets plenty of moisture.

★ WEED ★

CRABGRASS *(Digitaria sanguinalis)*

Distinguishing features: Stems spiraling out from a central crown in a sort of (you guessed it) crablike manner, with short, hairy, light green leaves that can rise more than 2 feet if they're left undisturbed. The "flowers" consist of anywhere from three to nine short spikes, reaching out like birds' claws from the stem, with each spike containing dozens of tiny, seed-filled capsules.

Modus operandi: Warm-season narrowleaf annual. Zeroes in on bare spots and lawns that are closely cropped or thinning, and grows faster than almost any other weed.

from the **MAIL BAG**

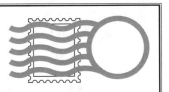

Dear Jerry,

I've just bought an old house with a big, beautiful Kentucky bluegrass lawn. The grass is growing great, but unfortunately, so is a whole lot of crabgrass. Is there a way to get rid of this ugly stuff without resorting to chemicals?

A. *There sure is, and it couldn't be easier! Just cover the crabgrass with either black plastic or black paper mulch (available at most garden centers), and leave it in place for 10 days. When you pull it off, that ol' crabgrass should be dead as a doornail. The bluegrass will be yellow, but it'll green up again fast.*

★ WEED ★

CREEPING CHARLIE, A.K.A. GROUND IVY
(Glechoma hederacea)

Distinguishing features: Square, spreading stems with round, scallop-edged leaves and funnel-shaped, lavender flowers that bloom in the spring and sometimes into summer.

Modus operandi: Cool-season broadleaf perennial. Spreads rampantly, often forming a solid mat, with roots forming at every node (the place where a leaf meets the stem). When mowed, it responds by sending out more plants from the stems left behind. Will grow happily anywhere, but loves moist soil in partial shade.

★ WEED ★

CURLY DOCK   *(Rumex crispus)*

Distinguishing features: Enormous leaves, up to 2 feet long, curl around the base of the plant, forming a rosette that's about a foot high. A 1- to 4-foot stalk shoots up from the center, with smaller, sparser leaves, and curled side branches of tiny, greenish flowers that turn reddish as they age.

Modus operandi: Cool-season broadleaf perennial. Generally targets lawns that are not very well cared for. Grows from a long, woody taproot that can reach 2 feet in length, and spreads rampantly if seedheads are allowed to develop. A single plant can produce up to 40,000 seeds each year, and—here's the sobering part—those seeds have been known to remain viable for 70 years!

Super★Secret

How Corny Can You Get?

When weeds are driving you to drink, don't reach for the corn liquor. Instead, run down to the garden center and buy a big sack of corn gluten meal. It's a highly effective preemergent herbicide that zaps scads of troublemakers, including crabgrass, dandelions, plantain, and creeping bent grass. Unlike chemical weed killers, it won't harm the teeny life-forms that keep your soil healthy and your grass growing great guns. And best of all, it's perfectly safe to use around toddlers and pets. Just apply 25 to 50 pounds per 2,500 square feet of lawn area before weeds start to sprout in spring.

Yankee Doodle Data
Battle Tactics at a Glance

The best method for whipping weeds depends on which kind of tenacious trespassers you're dealing with. Here are the routines I follow when I march into battle. (For descriptions of the various weedy categories, see "Coming to Terms with Weeds" on page 242.)

TYPE OF WEED	YOUR BEST PLAN OF ATTACK
Cool-season annuals	☆ In the North, avoid feeding your lawn in the spring; in the South, hold the chow in the winter! You'll deprive the weeds of sustenance when they need it most.
	☆ In the North, mow high in spring and fall, so the grass can shade the soil and keep seeds from germinating.
	☆ In the South, mow high in late summer to deprive seeds of light. Then, in the fall, overseed your lawn with a cool-season grass like perennial ryegrass or Kentucky bluegrass, and keep it mowed high through the winter.
Cool-season perennials	☆ Early in the season, scrape the plants out with a metal rake.
	☆ Immediately after raking, mow your lawn to its shortest recommended height (see Chapter 7), rake up the clippings, and get rid of them fast, before the stems can root again.
	☆ After the first frost in the fall, feed your lawn according to my guidelines in Chapter 5, and follow up with a dose of my Last Supper Tonic (see page 108). That way, the grass will grow like blazes in the spring, and crowd out weeds before they get a toehold.
Warm-season annuals	☆ Mow at the maximum recommended height, and if you've whacked off a lot of seedheads in the process, remove the clippings.
	☆ Avoid summertime feeding, and follow my guidelines for healthy watering (see Chapter 6).
	☆ Aerate your soil, and do whatever else is necessary to reduce compaction (see Chapter 4 for that routine).
Warm-season perennials	☆ Dig out the clumps, toss organic matter into the hole, and reseed. (See Chapter 4 for the lowdown on reseeding and my Hole Improvement Plan.)
	☆ Mow high.
	☆ Avoid summertime feeding.

★ WEED ★

DALLIS GRASS *(Paspalum dilatatum)*

Distinguishing features: Clumps of light green leaves that can reach as high as 5 feet if left unmowed, with seedheads that bear a slight resemblance to rattlesnake tails.

Modus operandi: Warm-season narrowleaf perennial. Appears most often in warm climates, where it spreads like crazy in the summer, by both seeds and underground rhizomes. Its favorite home: poorly drained, infertile soil.

★ WEED ★

DANDELION *(Taraxacum officinale)*

Distinguishing features: Circular clusters of toothed, dark green leaves with golden flowers, which give way to white, fluffy clouds, made of zillions of tiny, seed-filled parachutes. Children adore them and that makes grown-up lawn keepers say, "@#*%&!*^%#!!"

Modus operandi: Warm-season broadleaf perennial. Dandelion seeds sail on the wind to any small bare patch of sunny ground, where they send their tenacious taproots down deep—and then deeper and deeper. Their favorite targets are thin, poorly cared for lawns. Up North, they go dormant in the winter, like other perennials, but in warm climates, the plants carry on business as usual all year long.

BLUE PLATE SPECIAL

BRUSSELS SPROUTS WEED BRUSH-OFF

This marvelous mix delivers a knock-out punch to weeds. Serve it up in early spring, before the weed seeds germinate.

1 cup of Brussels sprouts*
½ tsp. of dishwashing liquid
Water

Blend the Brussels sprouts with just enough water to make a thick mush. Then add the dishwashing liquid, and pour the mixture into cracks in your sidewalk or driveway, or anyplace you want to stop weeds before they pop up. (Just don't use it in places where you want flower, herb, or veggie seeds to grow.)

* Or substitute cabbage leaves.

A Weed Warrior's Bag of Tricks

Super ★ Secret

There's more than one way to wipe out nasty weeds. Here's a roundup of my favorite techniques for battling bad plants, both big and little:

Boil 'em alive. One of the oldest tricks in the book is still one of the best: Just boil a kettle of water, and pour it over the weeds. This works best on shallow-rooted weeds, because the danged things will keep coming back unless the boiling water reaches the roots.

Give 'em a blast. Load up your hand-held spray bottle with rubbing alcohol and take aim at those wicked weeds. They'll be dead in no time.

Smother 'em. Got a high-traffic area where the soil is so compacted that nothing but weeds will grow there? Then install a walkway. But first, smother the weeds by laying cardboard, brown paper bags, or newspaper over the soil. Then spread on pea gravel, shredded bark, pine needles, or any other topping.

Suck 'em up. A vacuum cleaner makes a dandy anti-dandelion weapon. Just put the nozzle over each seedhead, and presto—those menaces-in-the-making will be goners. (Either a wet/dry vacuum or a hand-held model will work.)

Let 'em eat veggies. Members of the Brassica family, which includes Brussels sprouts, cabbage, broccoli, and kale, all contain thiocyanate, a chemical that's toxic to newly germinated seeds, especially small ones. Brussels sprouts pack the biggest dose, which is why I made 'em the star ingredient in my Brussels Sprouts Weed Brush-Off (at left). Just whip up a blender full of the super stuff, pour it on the soil in early spring, and your weed woes will soon be history. It's especially useful for weeds that spring up in hard-to-get-at places, like cracks in your driveway and gaps between the stones in your terrace. Remember, though: Don't use this stuff on a newly seeded lawn, or your baby grass plants will never see the light of day!

Get 'em while they're down. Perennial weeds are at their weakest just before they flower. That's the time to give 'em a lethal dose of my Wild Weed Wipeout Tonic (see page 243).

Pickle 'em. Plain old vinegar—either cider or white—kills weeds fast, especially if you use it on a sunny day. Just pour the stuff into a hand-held spray bottle, and fire away. But be sure to aim carefully, because vinegar will kill any plant it touches.

★ WEED ★

FOXTAIL *(Seteria viridis)*

Distinguishing features: Long, flat leaf blades springing from a single cluster of roots, with long, arching, bristly seedheads that look just like (surprise!) a fox's tail.

Modus operandi: An aggressive warm-season narrowleaf annual. Foxtail primarily targets poor, patchy lawns and rarely competes with healthy turf.

★ WEED ★

GOOSEGRASS *(Eleusine indica)*

Distinguishing features: Spiraling, ground-hugging stems and finger-like seedheads bear a close resemblance to those of crabgrass. The differences: Goosegrass stems are flat at the base and nearly white, while crabgrass stems are rounded and purplish. Also, goosegrass rarely grows taller than 2 feet; crabgrass often soars beyond that height in rich, moist soil. Seedheads are also similar to those of crabgrass (see page 245), but each goosegrass "finger" sports a heavy, black beard.

Modus operandi: Warm-season narrowleaf annual. Seeds travel all over creation with the aid of wind, water, birds, insects, and even the soles of your shoes. The first seedlings generally appear about six weeks after crabgrass makes its unwelcome entrance—which is yet another way you can tell these two copycats apart.

Super★Secret

Goin' for the Gold—Again

Chalk up yet another reason to spread compost over your lawn. Actually, make that two reasons:

1. Weeds perform their best dirty work in soil that's deficient in trace elements—of which compost supplies heaping helpings. By keeping your lawn well supplied with nutritional nuggets, you discourage weeds, and give your grass the *oomph* it needs to crowd out the weaklings.

2. Weed seeds can only germinate when they land on bare soil. Make sure that they don't by spreading a ½- to 1-inch layer of compost over your lawn in spring and fall.

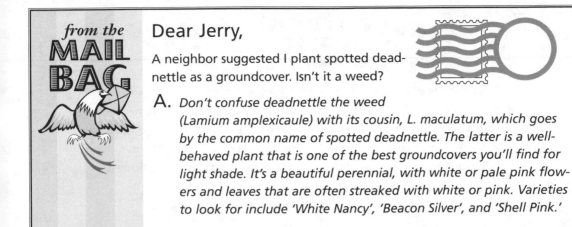

from the **MAIL BAG**

Dear Jerry,

A neighbor suggested I plant spotted dead-nettle as a groundcover. Isn't it a weed?

A. *Don't confuse deadnettle the weed (Lamium amplexicaule) with its cousin, L. maculatum, which goes by the common name of spotted deadnettle. The latter is a well-behaved plant that is one of the best groundcovers you'll find for light shade. It's a beautiful perennial, with white or pale pink flowers and leaves that are often streaked with white or pink. Varieties to look for include 'White Nancy', 'Beacon Silver', and 'Shell Pink.'*

★ WEED ★

HENBIT, A.K.A. DEADNETTLE
(Lamium amplexicaule)

Distinguishing features: Square stems (declaring its membership in the mint family), with coarse, round, scalloped-edged leaves. In mid-spring, small clusters of light purple, trumpet-shaped flowers appear among the topmost leaves. The plant reaches about a foot in height if it's not mowed down.

Modus operandi: Cool-season broadleaf annual. Seeds sometimes sprout in early spring, but more often in early fall. Henbit thrives in rich, moist soil, and causes the most trouble in newly seeded lawns in late summer or fall. Fortunately, it sends down very shallow roots that make it a snap to pull up. (For the lowdown on getting weeds out of a lawn before you sow seed or lay sod, see "Oh, No You Don't!" on page 51.)

★ WEED ★

KNOTWEED   *(Polygonum aviculare)*

Distinguishing features: Circular mats of slender, wiry, nonrooting stems, with smooth, bluish green leaves and tiny white flowers.

Modus operandi: Cool-season broadleaf annual. Germinates in late winter and appears aboveground about the time the grass is beginning to green up in the early spring. Can appear anywhere, but it favors lawns in cool climates—especially when it can sink its roots into compacted soil.

Yankee Doodle Data

If Ya Can't Beat 'Em, Eat 'Em!

Who says weeds are good for nothin'? A lot of them make mighty
fine eatin'! Here's a small sampling of some of my favorites. Just remember:
Some of these winners can cause allergic reactions if you consume large quantities.
So enjoy them as occasional treats, not as part of your daily diet. And avoid any
weeds from lawns that have been treated with herbicides or pesticides!

TASTY WEED	PART TO EAT	FLAVOR	HOW TO ENJOY IT
Burdock	Leaves and stems of first year's growth	Nutty and mildly sweet	Steam and serve with butter; sauté and add to soups and casseroles.
Chickweed	Leaves and stems	Mild spinach	Steam lightly and serve with butter; toss in salads.
Chicory	Young leaves and roots	Tangy and bitter	Toss leaves in salads; boil or bake young roots and eat like potatoes; roast and grind roots for New Orleans–style coffee.
Dandelions	Young leaves, young, tight flower buds, and roots	Mild and lettuce-like	Toss leaves and flowers in salads.
Mallow	Green seedpods	Slightly sweet, with a crisp texture	Munch 'em like candy.
Pigweed	Leaves and seeds	Mild leaves; nutlike, crunchy seeds	Toss young leaves in salads or use on sandwiches; steam or boil older leaves; sprinkle ripe black seeds on sweet breads or muffins.
Purslane	Leaves and stems	Sweet and sour	Toss in salads.
Queen Anne's Lace, a.k.a. Wild Carrot	Roots	Mild carrot	Chop and add to soups or salads.
Shepherd's Purse	Basal leaves	Peppery	Chop and add to salads.

★ WEED ★

MALLOW, A.K.A. CHEESEWEED *(Malva neglecta)*

Distinguishing features: Loose mounds of round leaves that are very similar to those of bedding geraniums *(Pelargonium)*, with flowers the shape of miniature hollyhocks (this plant's more well-bred cousins), in shades of white, pale pink, or pale blue. Flowers are followed by seed-pods shaped like flattened disks that, when mature and brown, break into a wheel of segments resembling a wheel of cheese that's been cut into wedges—hence the name "cheeseweed."

Modus operandi: Cool-season broadleaf annual. Targets stressed-out lawns with fertile soil, into which it sends down a thick, but blessedly short taproot.

★ WEED ★

NARROWLEAF PLANTAIN, A.K.A. ENGLISH OR BUCKHORN PLANTAIN *(Plantago lanceolata)*

Distinguishing features: Thick, low-growing rosette of long, slender, sometimes dusty-looking leaves, with prominent veins. A single cone-shaped flower cluster grows at the top of each stem, with fuzzy, white blooms opening from the bottom up.

Modus operandi: Cool-season broadleaf perennial. Seedlings begin appearing in the spring and keep sprouting—and producing large quantities of seeds—all summer long. Meanwhile, the persistent and long-lived roots keep on spreading. Plantain causes the most trouble in moist soil and partial shade.

Star-Spangled
Lawn Lore

When I was a lad, before the days of television—and long before the days of computer games—buckhorn plantain gave me and my pals hours of summer-time fun. We used to challenge each other to "fencing matches," using the stems as swords. The winner was the kid who knocked the flower tip off his opponent's stem.

Carry No Passengers

Weed seeds can travel for miles in search of a good home. Some just catch a breeze and fly off like tiny hot-air balloons. Dozens of other kinds get help from unintentional co-conspirators—like you. Here are two simple ways to foil the felons:

★ Anytime you borrow a mower or other lawn equipment, clean the machine with a good, stiff broom before you start to work. And if you hire folks to tend your lawn, make sure they follow the same routine.

★ At the end of an outdoor excursion, inspect your clothes, the soles of your shoes, and the grille of your car before you head for home. These are all favorite clinging spots for Queen Anne's lace, pigweed, and other prickly seeds.

★ WEED ★

PIGWEED   *(Amaranthus blitoides)*

Distinguishing features: Sprawling mats of many-branched stems with oblong, pointed, wavy-edged leaves that grow to about 1 inch long. In late summer, spiky clusters of teeny green flowers appear, each one filled with thousands of tiny seeds.

Modus operandi: Warm-season broadleaf annual. Multiplies like crazy from seeds carried by the wind, and by birds and other small critters, who love to eat the tiny black specks. Prefers dry soil, but will quickly move in and take over any sun-warmed space in your lawn, or even in a gravel driveway.

★ WEED ★

PRICKLY LETTUCE   *(Lactuca scariola)*

Distinguishing features: Loose spirals of long, narrow, prickly leaves that stay close to the ground, with a single, hollow stem rising from the center. The flowers resemble tiny dandelions, but they seldom appear in lawns (stems rarely bloom before they're 6 inches high, and the norm is 3 to 5 feet).

Modus operandi: Warm-season broadleaf annual. Seeds travel long distances, thanks to plumes of downy white hairs that function like sails. They keep arriving all summer long and will gleefully plant themselves in any kind of soil—moist or dry, rich or poor, acidic or alkaline.

★ **WEED** ★

PURSLANE   *(Portulaca oleracea)*

Distinguishing features: Mats of smooth, fleshy stems sprawling out-ward from the main root, with plump, glossy leaves appearing singly along the stems but clustered at the tips. Pale yellow, five-petaled flowers, about ¼ inch across, open for only a few hours in the morning.

Modus operandi: Warm-season broadleaf annual. Targets any warm, sunny soil, and multiplies prolifically by seed (of which a single plant produces as many as 50,000!) as well as less orthodox methods: Broken pieces of leaves and stems often take root and grow if they fall on bare ground. What's more, moisture stored in those plant parts allows purslane to sail right through the worst of droughts. Talk about survivors!

★ **WEED** ★

QUACKGRASS   *(Agropyron repens)*

Distinguishing features: Thin, flat leaf blades emerge alternately (rather than opposite each other) on slender stems that curl upward from the base. Other stems, trailing along the ground, root at each joint. When not mowed, produces flat, narrow flower spikes about 6 inches long and packed with upward-facing bristles.

Modus operandi: Cool-season narrowleaf perennial. Spreads rampantly by way of long, shallow, underground rhizomes that send up new plants like there's no tomorrow.

BLUE PLATE SPECIAL

MOSS BUSTER BREW

Does moss keep cropping up, no matter how many times you rake it away and sow grass seed in its place? Moss thrives in shady, often poorly drained sites with acidic soil, while grass prefers neutral to slightly alkaline soil, excellent drainage, and a lot of sunshine. This brew is the perfect temporary remedy, but for long-term results, you need to doctor up your soil (see Chapters 3 and 4) and add more light to the scene.

   1 cup of antiseptic mouthwash
   1 cup of chamomile tea
   1 cup of Murphy's Oil Soap®

Mix these ingredients in a 20 gallon hose-end sprayer, and apply to your lawn to the point of run-off every two weeks until the moss is history.

Two Can Play This Game!

Super★Secret

If you have places in your yard where weeds won't take no for an answer, sow one or more of the following self-seeders in those problem spots, and you'll have a beautiful, low-maintenance flower garden:

Asters (*Aster*)

Columbines (*Aquilegia*)

Coreopsis (*Coreopsis*)

Forget-me-not
(*Myosotis sylvatica*)

Johnny-jump-up
(*Viola tricolor*)

Morning glories (*Ipomoea*)

Poppies (*Papaver*)

Sweet alyssum
(*Lobularia maritima*)

★ WEED ★

QUEEN ANNE'S LACE, A.K.A. WILD CARROT
(*Daucus carota*)

Distinguishing features: Foliage that's a dead ringer for (you guessed it) carrot tops, and lacy, white flowers on tall, branching stems that are attractive to butterflies.

Modus operandi: Warm-season broadleaf biennial. Produces a low mound of deep green, ferny foliage in its first year. The following spring, stems grow up to 3 feet or so, and flowers appear from summer through fall. Fuzzy seedheads hitch rides by latching on to human clothes, and the fur, feathers, and feet of critters. The seeds generally get a good foothold only in thin, patchy lawns, gravel driveways, or cracks in pavement (and, of course, in flower beds and other garden areas).

★ WEED ★

RED SORREL, A.K.A. SOUR GRASS
(*Rumex acetosella*)

Distinguishing features: Clumps of slender, arrowhead-shaped leaves that rarely reach more than a few inches high, and slender flower stalks growing to a foot or more, each topped with separate spikes of male and female buds. As the blossoms develop, the female flowers take on a reddish tint, while the males stay green.

Modus operandi: Cool-season broadleaf perennial. Grows prolifically via spreading roots that meander along, just underground. Prefers poor soil that's highly acidic, and generally targets lawns that are seriously lacking in TLC.

★ WEED ★

SANDBUR *(Cenchrus longispinus)*

Distinguishing features: Smooth, twisted leaf blades rising from stems that lie flat against the ground, often forming mats. Seedpods are covered with little spikes, or burs (hence the common name "sandbur").

Modus operandi: Warm-season narrowleaf annual. Seeds germinate in the spring and grow through the summer in any dry, sandy soil.

★ WEED ★

SHEPHERD'S PURSE *(Capsella bursa-pastoris)*

Distinguishing features: Ground-hugging rosettes of leaves (deeply lobed when young; arrow-shaped later on), with flower stalks anywhere from 4 to 20 inches long growing from the central crown. Tiny, four-petaled flowers in white, pink, or yellow appear in spring, but quickly give way to brownish seedpods that look exactly like the tote bags that shepherds use to pack their bread, cheese, and wine.

Modus operandi: Cool-season broadleaf annual. Spreads by seed, with each plant sending down a long, slender taproot that can squeeze through narrow cracks in the pavement and penetrate the most compacted soils. The good news: It's as easy to pull out of the ground as a shepherd's crook is from an umbrella stand. Well, *almost* as easy!

Star-Spangled Lawn Lore

Quick: Picture your dream lawn. If you're like most of us, the image that popped into your head was a lush, velvety carpet of grass with nary a weed in sight. But in our country's earlier days, folks had a slightly different idea of what the well-dressed yard should wear. In fact, in the mid-1880s, when the novelist Nathaniel Hawthorne visited England, he was distressed to see one pristine, green lawn after another. He wrote home that he longed for American yards, with their colorful array of nettles, clovers, and dandelions.

★ WEED ★

SMUTGRASS *(Sporobolus indicus)*

Distinguishing features: Clumping grass with stems that can reach as high as 4 feet in a very short time. The flowers are flat, dark green spikes, often covered with a black fungus (hence the name "smut-grass") that causes contact dermatitis in some people.

Modus operandi: Warm-season narrowleaf perennial. Targets lawns in the South, where it's common along roadsides and vacant lots, and can take over a neglected lawn in the blink of an eye (a plant can grow from seedling to seed producer in two weeks or less).

★ WEED ★

SPURGE *(Euphorbia maculata)*

Distinguishing features: Stiff, but fleshy, stems that radiate from a central taproot and contain a milky juice that's highly irritating to human skin. Leaves are small and oblong, with a green top surface and reddish underside. Tiny, cup-shaped, white flowers, with even tinier green seed capsules on top, appear at the tips of branches and in the tight angles where the leaves meet the main stem.

Modus operandi: Warm-season broadleaf annual. Seeds start sprouting after the first warm rains in spring, and new plants keep coming all summer long. Spurge thrives in any kind of soil, as long as it gets plenty of sun.

Super ★ Secret

Friend and Foe

As the old saying goes, "Beauty is in the eye of the beholder"—which explains why some of the "weeds" that you're cursing may be the grass that your neighbors planted in their yard. The best way to handle these wanderers is simply to dig them up, and reseed with your own variety. And, of course, follow all of my tips for keeping your lawn strong, healthy, and better able to crowd out emigrating seeds of any kind. These are some of the grasses that most often stray away from their home turf. (You can read all about them in Chapter 2.)

Annual bluegrass *(Poa annua)*   **Creeping bent grass** *(Agrostis stolonifera)*

Bermuda grass *(Cynodon dactylon)*   **Tall fescue** *(Festuca elatior* or *F. arundinacea)*

QUACK-UP SLUG COOKIES

Are slugs chomping the daylights out of your groundcovers? Don't despair! A powerful weapon could be waiting right in your own backyard—that is, if you have a patch or two of quackgrass. It kills slugs fast, and what's more, the slimers love the stuff! So invite 'em over for a party, and serve 'em these deadly treats.

1 part dried quackgrass blades, finely chopped
1 part wheat bran*
1 can of beer

Mix the quackgrass and bran in a bowl, then slowly add the beer, stirring until the mixture has the consistency of cookie dough. Run the dough through a meat grinder, or chop it into small bits (roughly ⅛ to ¼ inch thick). Let the "cookies" air-dry overnight, sprinkle them on the ground among your plants, and let the good times roll! (To be on the safe side, put these treats where children and pets can't get to them. Quackgrass is often infected with a fungus that is harmful if ingested by humans or animals.)

*Available in supermarkets and health-food stores.

★ WEED ★

WILD VIOLET *(Viola papilionacea)*

Distinguishing features: Broad, heart-shaped leaves and (of course) those beautiful, delicate flowers that are usually violet blue, but sometimes white or pink.

Modus operandi: Cool-season broadleaf perennial. Brings a welcome breath of spring to any lawn. Unfortunately, in its favorite conditions—a cool, shady site with moist, fertile soil—it wears out its welcome by reproducing faster than the speed of light.

★ WEED ★

WITCHGRASS *(Panicum capillare)*

Distinguishing features: A crabgrass look-alike (see page 245), but with wider, hairier leaves branching out from the base. The fingerlike "flowers" resemble those of crabgrass, too, but instead of containing a multitude of seeds, each witchgrass spikelet has only one seed at the very tip.

Modus operandi: Warm-season narrowleaf annual. Seeds germinate in spring and grow like crazy in newly sown turf.

★ WEED ★

YELLOW NUT SEDGE   *(Cyperus esculentus)*

Distinguishing features: Upright, triangular stems with smooth, grassy leaves, in shades of pale green to greenish yellow, with sheaths that overlap at the node (the point where the leaf attaches to the stem). Clusters of brushlike, yellow flowers grow out from the top of the main stem, turning chestnut or golden brown as they mature.

Modus operandi: Warm-season narrowleaf perennial. Can show up just about anywhere, but has a strong preference for closely cropped lawns growing in damp soil. Spreads both by seed and by tiny, football-shaped tubers, called *chufas*, produced near the ends of each plant's fibrous roots.

★ WEED ★

YELLOW WOOD SORREL   *(Oxalis stricta)*

Distinguishing features: Erect stems, about 6 inches high, with bright green, cloverlike leaves that are usually folded up, rather than opened flat. Five-petaled, yellow flowers give way to long, skinny seedpods that start out green, but turn brown as they age.

Modus operandi: Warm-season broadleaf annual. Blooms from spring through fall in any sunny spot, and multiplies by seeds that burst from each mature seedpod.

Star-Spangled *Lawn* Lore

The nutlike tubers that give yellow nut sedge its name are edible. In fact, they're downright yummy, either raw (when they taste like coconut), or roasted (when they have a mild almond flavor). Native Americans considered them a great delicacy, and I have friends who actually cultivate the plant so they can have a steady supply of chufas. I hasten to add that these folks grow their supply in wildflower meadows—not in neatly manicured lawns!

CHAPTER 12

When Mother Nature Frowns

By now, you've read 11 chapters filled with my best advice on lawn care, including dozens of terrific tips, tricks, and tonics. If you put all of that grow-how into practice, you're guaranteed to have a lifetime of positively gorgeous, trouble-free turf, right? WRONG! How come? Because Mother Nature is always warming up in the bull pen, getting ready to throw you a lightning-fast curveball in the form of a drought, flood, heat wave, ice storm—you name it, she's got it tucked up her sleeve. After all, *somebody* has to keep you from getting bored, right?

 ## When in Drought

Back in Chapter 6, I gave you the general scoop on satisfying your lawn's thirst in ways that will keep it—and your bank account—in the green. In this section, I'll clue you in on my strategies for coping with prolonged dry spells—which seem to be hitting more of the country every year, and lasting longer than they used to.

BEFORE THE CLOUDS ROLL BY

The time to start protecting your grass from drought is long before you pick up the newspaper and read that dreaded proclamation from City Hall saying, "No lawn watering until further notice." Here are some simple ways to strengthen your turf's defenses:

Give it super soil. Strong, healthy soil makes for strong, healthy grass that's better able to cope with whatever trouble comes its way, drought included. (You'll find the whole lowdown on soil in Chapter 3.)

Air it out. Dethatch and aerate your soil in the spring, so that water—whether it comes from the sky or your sprinklers—can penetrate down to the tips of the grass roots.

Water wisely and well. By that, I mean soak your lawn slowly until the water has penetrated to a depth of 6 to 8 inches. Then don't water again until the soil has dried out. That way, you'll encourage your grass to grow deep roots. And when the clouds dry up, those underground, parts will turn into superheroes, snagging moisture from deep in the ground long after you get that "No watering" notice.

Sprinkle right. Buy the best-quality sprinklers you can afford, make sure

DROUGHT BUSTER BREW

Your lawn should sail right through hot, dry weather with flying colors if you give it a weekly drink of this timely tonic.

1 can of beer
1 cup of Thatch Buster™
½ cup of liquid lawn food
½ cup of baby shampoo

Mix these ingredients in a 20 gallon hose-end sprayer, and apply to the point of run-off in the early morning. This timing will minimize evaporation and give the grass plants ample time to digest the brew before nightfall.

they're appropriate for the size and shape of your lawn, and keep them in A1 condition. That way, you won't be delivering too little water to some spots and too much to others. (You can read all about sprinklers in Chapter 6.)

Mow high, mow sharp. Tall grass shades the ground, helping keep moisture in the soil. But grass that's too tall encourages weeds. And leaves that are whacked off with a razor-edged blade have clean, even ends that hold water inside the plant. On the other hand, the jagged tears that are delivered by dull blades let much-needed H_2O evaporate into thin air. (For everything you need to know about mowing, see Chapter 7.)

Spread the wealth. In spring and fall, top your lawn with a ½- to 1-inch layer of good old "black gold," a.k.a. compost. That security blanket will conserve precious moisture—besides feeding your grass, killing disease germs, and discouraging weeds from sprouting!

SOW SMART

Anytime you start a new lawn, renovate an old one, or simply overseed bare spots, look for the most drought-tolerant grasses that will thrive in your region and the growing conditions in your yard. But for best results, don't settle for just one type. Instead, use a blend of several varieties, because diversity will help your lawn weather drought—and any other setback in its growing conditions. New, improved grasses are coming out all the time, so before you head off to the garden center or the sod farm, confer with the folks at your Cooperative Extension Service about the best varieties for your area.

DO SOME DOWNSIZING

As obvious as it may seem, one of the best ways to ease the effects of drought stress—on you as well as your grass—is simply to reduce the size of your lawn.

If dry weather is a fact of life where you live, maybe it's time to step back and think about how much turf grass you really want to fuss with. In Chapter 1, you'll find all sorts of inspiration to launch your planning session. Then, for tons of terrific tips on lawn alternatives, including decks, patios, and water-thrifty groundcovers, see Chapter 15.

HIGH AND DRY

If you've followed the general lawn-care tips earlier in this book, as well as my drought-preparedness measures on the previous pages, your grass should be in good shape to handle a prolonged dry spell. Still, as long as the tough times last, your lawn will still need special treatment. Here's your plan of action (or in some cases, nonaction):

Spread the wealth (again). If you're fortunate enough to have some warning that a hot, dry period is looming in the

Super ★ Secret

These Are the Champions

When it comes to holding firm against drought, these five grasses are the hands-down winners:

- ★ Bermuda grass
- ★ Buffalo grass
- ★ Fine fescue
- ★ Tall fescue
- ★ Zoysia grass

not-too-distant future, give your lawn extra protection by applying another ½-inch layer of compost to it. (This should be in addition to the layer you spread earlier in the spring.)

Hold the chow. Feeding your lawn a meal of fertilizer during drought will only add to its stress load. And, as we've seen in earlier chapters, stressed-out grass is a sitting duck for pests, diseases, and weeds.

Declare a truce. Speaking of pests, diseases, and weeds, if they do show up, just ignore them until cooler, wetter weather arrives. Believe it or not, engaging in battle now won't help matters any. In fact, it'll only make things worse!

Keep watering. Continue your normal watering routine as long as your municipality allows. And be sure to perform this chore early in the morning, so as little H$_2$O is lost to evaporation as possible. Whatever you do, don't water in the evening, because grass that stays wet

after dark—especially on a hot night—is fair prey for foul fungi.

Serve cool drinks. Once a week, overspray your turf with my Drought Buster Brew (see page 262). This bracing beverage will give your grass the strength it needs to bounce back like a champ once the dry days have passed.

DROUGHT RECOVERY TONIC

No matter how well you look after your lawn during a drought, hot, dry weather can take its toll. So, plan to give your turf some extra TLC to help it recover. Once the crisis ends, apply a dry, organic fertilizer at half of the recommended rate, adding 1 pound of sugar and 1 pound of Epsom salts per bag (enough for 2,500 sq. ft.). Then overspray the turf with this timely tonic.

> **1 can of regular cola (not diet)**
> **1 cup of baby shampoo**
> **1 cup of ammonia**

Mix these ingredients in a 20 gallon hose-end sprayer, and saturate the turf to the point of run-off every two weeks until the grass returns to normal. And remember, you need to deliver this life-giving moisture slowly so it reaches a good 6 to 8 inches below the surface. This deep watering will encourage deep grass roots that will be able to stand up and say "Bring it on!" to the next drought that rolls around.

Super ★ Secret

Don't Walk, Don't Run

Stay off of the lawn as much as possible during periods of drought—regardless of whether you're still able to water, or you've had to let the grass go dormant. Otherwise, the added trauma of foot traffic just may put that turf over the edge, and it'll never come back to life.

THAT'S ALL, FOLKS!

It's gone and happened: The drought has lasted so long that the Powers That Be have put a ban on all nonessential water use—which, of course, includes irrigating your lawn. *Now* what do you do? Well, unless you want to risk a hefty fine (not to mention your town's Bad Citizen of the Year Award), just ride it out and pray for rain. And try not to fret too much. Remember, summer dormancy is business as usual for northern grasses that don't get a steady supply of moisture. Of course, no grass can make it through an *entire* summer without *some* H$_2$O (see "Is There Any Drought?" on page 138). But as long as you've delivered the kind of TLC I've recommended throughout this book, and the hard times don't last for more than a month or so, your turf should green up just fine once the rains return. To give it a healthy kick-start, apply my Drought Recovery Tonic (at left).

HIGHER PRIORITIES

It's important to keep foot traffic to a minimum. But, if you have young children, grandchildren, or dogs on the scene, you can't expect them to sacrifice their outdoor playtime just for the sake of keeping some grass from getting traumatized. (A pristine, green lawn may be *your* idea of heaven on earth, but it couldn't be further from *their* minds!) So give a little: If you don't want to risk ruining your whole yard, at least set aside an out-of-the-way corner where kids and pets can romp in the fresh air and sunshine. After all, isn't that what the good old summertime is really all about?

THE WORST-CASE SCENARIO

So what happens if your lawn goes without water for so long that it up and dies? Well, first, try to keep things in perspective: After all, in the course of world events, you could encounter far worse disasters than dried-up grass. Then, as soon as the weather and City Hall permit, overseed your lawn with either annual bluegrass or annual ryegrass. This will get the ground covered quickly, thereby keeping the soil from eroding and weeds from moving in. The following spring, reseed or resod, following my guidelines in Chapter 3.

AND NEXT SPRING...

Before summer sails in with a vengeance, spray your lawn with an anti-desiccant spray, such as my WeatherProof™. It gives the grass blades a protective coating that locks moisture in the plants, while locking out the hot sun, drying winds, and even air pollution.

★ Declare Your Independence

The way some folks talk, you'd think that there are only two possible responses to a drought: Either you grin and bear it, or you let off steam by cursing Mother Nature, the TV weathercaster, and the entire staff of your local water department. Unfortunately, neither of those approaches will help your lawn one iota. But these nuggets of Yankee ingenuity surely will.

Super ★ Secret

Everything But (Maybe) the Kitchen Sink

Some of the most valuable water of all flows out of your kitchen faucets. That's because the H_2O that you use to wash dishes contains plenty of organic matter—and by now you know how important that is for your lawn! Unfortunately, the residue in dishwater causes problems in some types of graywater hardware (see "Going Gray" below). For that reason, some communities prohibit including kitchen sinks in your system. If it is legal where you live, and you want to take advantage of this free treasure, make sure you mention that to the salesclerk when you're shopping for your equipment. That way, you won't have clogs to deal with later.

GOING GRAY

In water conservation circles, "graywater" is the term for the slightly used H_2O that comes out of sinks, showers, bathtubs, and washing machines (not toilets!). Believe it or not, on average, every single day in our country, a family of four sends 160 gallons of this valuable liquid right down the drain and into the sewer system. That's enough to provide a 2,250-square-foot lawn with 1 inch of life-giving moisture each week. So how can you put this liquid gold to work in the service of your lovely landscape? Start with a call to the helpful folks at your Cooperative Extension Service. They can clue you in on the regulations governing graywater usage, which vary from state to state and often from town to town. Most likely, they can also steer you to someone who can install a system that diverts water from your household drains and sends it straight to those thirsty grass roots.

YOU SHOULD ALSO KNOW...

Although, as I said above, communities regulate graywater usage in different ways, just about all of them agree on two points:

1 Although graywater is fine to irrigate lawns, trees, shrubs, and ornamental flowers, it should never ever be used on edible plants.

2 Water that contains certain substances must go off to a septic system or a sewage-treatment plant—not into your landscape. These no-nos include:

• Residue from washing diapers or similar articles (for instance, rags that you've used to clean up a puppy's deposits on your rug)

• Solvents or other chemicals used in projects like painting or furniture refinishing

• Grease, oil, or other petroleum products (say, from cleaning your car or lawn mower)

SAVE FOR A RAINY DAY

I should say, for a lot of *non*rainy days! Back when I was a lad, everybody had a bunch of rain barrels around the place. That way, they could collect those drops as they fell from the sky, then dish 'em out to their plants when the clouds closed up shop. Like a lot of other old-time ideas, this one is staging a big-time comeback. The bad news is that, unless you have either an enormous number of barrels or a teeny-tiny yard, you won't accumulate enough rain to get all of your turf grass through a dry spell. But the good news is that, most likely, your liquid savings account will help you save at least part of your lawn.

Star-Spangled Lawn Lore

According to the latest estimates, there are 31 million acres of lawns growing across this great country of ours. If you put 'em all together, they'd cover an area the size of New England. How'd ya like to have to water that baby?

⭐ Enough, Already!

Sometimes, a lawn keeper's biggest weather woe isn't rain that doesn't come—it's rain that just won't quit! Well, you can't make the clouds dry up, no matter how much time you spend looking out the window and chanting, "Rain, rain, go away. Come again some other day." But there's plenty you can do to help your lawn rebound once the blue skies return.

HELP, I CAN'T BREATHE!

If you're new to the business of lawn tending, you may be wondering why a torrential downpour could be so perilous. Well, the answer is simple: Once the soil becomes saturated, most of the air gets pushed out of it, and the grass roots can't get the oxygen they need to survive. Fortunately, most turf grasses (and other plants, too) can endure waterlogged conditions for a short time without serious damage—but you do need to be Johnny-on-the-spot with your recovery effort.

I'VE SAID IT BEFORE...

And I'll say it again. The best thing you can do to help your grass weather a seemingly endless storm, or any other trouble, is to feed it plenty of organic matter—especially compost—*before* trouble strikes. So, no matter what other lawn-care chores you let slip by the wayside, make sure you find the time to spread at least ½ inch of "black gold" over your turf in the spring and again in the fall.

I'LL DRINK TO THAT!

Organic matter doesn't just come in solid form. You'd be amazed at how many of the liquids that you pour down the drain every day are chock-full of the stuff. Even if you don't opt for a graywater system (see "Going Gray" on page 266)—or if your town prohibits hooking the lines to your kitchen sink—you can still serve up life-giving libations to your lawn and the rest of your landscape. (Just remember to pour slowly, so the moisture sinks down deep.)

Super ★ Secret

Dig In

To help restore your lawn to health after heavy rains subside, strap on a pair of aerating lawn sandals or golf shoes, and walk all around your lawn. The small holes you produce with the shoes' spikes will help water percolate into the soil. Just be sure to do this after all standing water has dried up or been diverted elsewhere.

Here are some of my favorite forms of liquid compost:

• Used water from fish tanks and over-the-hill floral arrangements

• Water that's been used to cook eggs, vegetables, rice, or pasta

• Over-the-hill juices (like the half-empty bottles you forgot to toss before you went on vacation)

• Water that you've used to rinse out glasses or bottles that held beverages, such as beer, coffee, juice, milk, soda, tea, whiskey, or wine

• Water that's been sitting in your cat's or dog's dish.

KEEP OFF!

For a lot of kids I know, there's no better fun than splashing around on a puddle-filled lawn. Unfortunately, though, romping on sopping-wet grass will put your soil on the road to compaction—in the fast lane. So, while the raindrops are falling, and until the ground dries out later, declare your turf off-limits to nonessential foot traffic.

ALL ABOARD!

Of course, there are some chores you need to do as soon as the deluge stops, even though the soil will still be wet— for example, providing aid to your flowering plants, or maybe gathering

from the **MAIL BAG**

Dear Jerry,

My yard is so full of clay I could open a pottery factory! I read somewhere that adding a truckload of sand might help improve the drainage. Should I give it a try?

A. *Not unless you want to mix up a yard full of concrete! The best way to improve clay soil is to work in as much organic matter as you can—and the chunkier the better, because along with the other benefits of organic matter, the big pieces will help aerate the soil. Straw, chopped-up yard waste, coarse vegetable scraps, peanut shells, and pine needles are all good choices. Then, to help curb compaction (a constant menace in clay soil), apply my Aeration Tonic (see page 95) once a month.*

herbs or vegetables from your garden. At those times, it's still possible to go out into the yard—just lay old boards over the ground and use them as a temporary walkway. It'll distribute your weight and limit the amount of soil compaction caused by your footsteps. It'll also help your shoes stay clean and dry!

HOW DRY IT'S NOT

As soon as the heavy rains stop, get rid of any standing water on your lawn. In most cases, digging simple trenches should do the trick. Make each one about 8 inches deep and 4 inches wide. And, of course, dig them so they slope downward from the mini-lake to a storm drain, roadside ditch, or other place where the water will do no dam-

age. If you're not blessed with such a handy receptacle, simply dig a hole downhill from the puddle, and end your trench there. How deep it needs to be depends on how well drained the soil is in that spot, and how much standing water you've got. Start with a hole that goes down about a foot, then dig deeper if you have to. And, for safety's sake, cover the opening with a board propped up with stones. That way, the water can run in, but nobody will accidentally stumble into the abyss.

THE RECOVERY PROCESS

Once you've sent all the surface water on its way, follow this four-step plan to put your soil (and therefore, your grass) on the road to recovery:

STEP 1. Shove the tines of a garden fork into the soil, and move it back and forth a few times to enlarge the holes. This will help the H_2O that's lingering under the soil surface to percolate downward.

STEP 2. Apply gypsum at a rate of 50 pounds per 2,500 square feet of lawn area. This will loosen the soil to encourage better drainage. It works almost like an

Save Those Worms!

Although earthworms live underground, they can't live underwater. That's why, when the soil gets really wet, they make a bee-line for the surface. It's a sound strategy, but more often than not, instead of drowning down below, these soil-building heroes get eaten by birds, flattened by car tires and human feet, or fried by the sun. So do yourself a favor: After a rain, go out and scoop up all the worms you can find, and give them a safe haven in a groundcover bed, under a low-growing shrub, or on the edges of your compost pile. (Don't throw them into the middle—the heat could bake them!)

army of little rototillers—but without the damage rototilling can do to the soil structure. (You can read all about that on page 51.)

STEP 3. One week after you apply the gypsum, follow up with a premium, natural, organic fertilizer at the recommended rate.

STEP 4. In the fall, feed your lawn according to my directions in Chapter 5 (see "Gettin' on Toward Bedtime" on page 119).

STOP PREMATURE BALDING

When your soggy lawn starts to thin out, your best bet is to reseed the bare spots with a grass that performs well in wet soil. Be quick about it, so you can get that ground covered before wily weeds move in! And to make sure those seeds take off like an Apollo rocket, soak them for 24 hours in my Seed Starter Tonic (see page 187). Your best choices for wet sites: Kentucky bluegrass or perennial ryegrass for open, sunny areas. For sites that are on the shady side, go with Sabre bluegrass (*Poa trivialis* 'Sabre'). You'll find my easy lawn reseeding guidelines in Chapter 4.

Super★Secret
Look Sharp

Many lawn pests and diseases target turf that's under stress from extended periods of heat, drought, or excessive moisture. Often the demons strike while the unpleasant conditions are still in full sway, but generally, you won't see any symptoms until life has returned to normal. So, after the weather has taken a turn for the better, keep an eagle eye out for signs of trouble. For the complete scoop on identification and control measures, see Chapters 9 and 10.

ROLL OUT THE GREEN CARPET

Do you live in one of our country's hot, damp regions, like the Gulf Coast, where the soil never seems to dry out? Then consider replacing your current turf with carpet grass (*Axonopus affinis*). It can't handle cold at all, but it positively thrives in poor, acidic, wet soil, and it will do well in any kind of light—from full sun to moderate shade.

DRAIN FOR GAIN

If water puddles up on your lawn after even moderate rain showers, or if it hangs around for days after a heavy one, you have drainage problems. If they're minor, the simple, do-it-yourself methods described in Chapter 3 should save the day. But if you even *suspect* that the situation might be serious, ask a landscape architect to have a look at your property, and advise you on your best options. This service won't come cheap, but the price for a few hours of consultation time will be money well spent. Trust me on this—it could save you big bucks and horrendous headaches down the road!

WHERE'S NOAH WHEN YOU NEED HIM?

A lawn that's in good health can usually survive a short dunking, but serious flooding is another matter. To tell the extent of the damage, after the rain stops, stepoutside and take a deep breath. If you smell what you'd swear was raw sewage, it means just one thing: Your lawn has become a drowning victim, and you'll be lucky to find even a few live grass plants. But if you don't detect that, um, distinctive odor, there's still hope. Just examine the grass. Living plants will have firm leaves, stems, roots, and (depending on the grass type) aboveground runners in healthy shades of green and white. On the other hand, brown or soft, milky white stems and roots indicate that those plants are goners.

YOUR GOOSE IS COOKED

Rather, your grass could be cooked—or "scalded," as they call it in professional lawn circles. It's a condition that occurs when a few hot, sunny days come along while the turf is covered with 2 to 4 inches of water. Then, Ol' Sol's rays can heat up that liquid so much that the grass plants are literally cooked. As you might expect, it's primarily a problem in the ovenlike South and Southwest. Your coping options—as you also might expect—are limited: You drain the water, rake off the dead grass and other debris, and reseed, resod, or replug your lawn. And if lawn submersion is fairly common in your neck of the woods, go with Bermuda or Bahia grass. They're the most flood-tolerant types of all.

☆ It's Too Darn Hot

Even when a good, steady supply of moisture is falling from the sky, hot weather can take its toll on your turf. Unfortunately, you can't send your lawn off to a cool, mountain lake to chill out for a few weeks. But you can lend it a helping hand in other ways.

BEAT THE HEAT

When the mercury skyrockets, a few simple measures can spell the difference between a lawn that goes down, gasping and panting, and one that eases on through the steamy weather. Here's your list of dos and don'ts:

Do serve refreshments. Every three weeks throughout the summer, give your lawn a dose of my All-Season Green-Up Tonic (see page 85). It'll provide all the nutrients your grass needs to stay strong and healthy, without bogging it down.

Do water regularly. You'll have to deliver H_2O more often than you do in cool weather, but the precise timing will depend on many factors, including the kind of grass in your lawn, the level of light, and the type and condition of your soil. For everything you need to know about watering—in good times or bad—see Chapter 6.

Do send it to the showers. Every now and then, instead of letting your sprinklers do the watering, haul out the hose and give your lawn a long, cool soak with my Summer Soother Tonic (see page 143). It's the perfect de-stresser on a sweltering summer day!

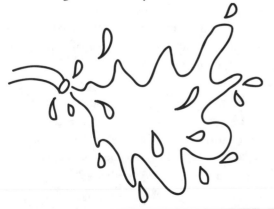

Don't feed it. Extreme heat puts grass plants under big-time stress (just as it does most of us humans). And one of the worst things you can do to a stressed-out lawn is serve it a big, heavy meal. There's also another reason for holding the chow, especially if you use a synthetic, chemical fertilizer: During hot, sunny weather, your grass is much more likely to be damaged by a spill or an accidental overdose.

Don't give it a crew cut. When a heat wave strikes, you may feel better with an ultra-short haircut, but for your lawn, it's a different story. The higher the temperature rises, the more important it is to keep your grass growing at its maximum recommended height (see "How High I Am" on page 156). That way, those tall blades can shade the soil, and keep the roots cooler.

Don't fuss with it. For the duration of the hot spell, put a hold on routine weed, pest, and disease control chores. Just like feeding, these maneuvers increase your lawn's stress level, and make it more vulnerable to trouble.

LIFE ON THE EDGE

When a heat wave hits, some parts of your lawn are more vulnerable to damage than others. The prime victims fall into three categories:

• Strips of grass adjacent to paved areas, such as driveways, patios, and sidewalks

Yankee Doodle Data

Hot Shots and Cool Customers

It only stands to reason that, generally speaking, warm-season grasses handle the heat better than their cool-season counterparts, and cool-season kinds are the champs at winter survival. But within each seasonal category, some types perform better than others. Here's a breakdown.

WARM-SEASON GRASSES	COOL-SEASON GRASSES
HEAT TOLERANCE (FROM HIGHEST TO LOWEST)	
Zoysia grass	Tall fescues
New Bermuda grass hybrids	Kentucky bluegrass
Common Bermuda grass	Colonial bent grass
Centipede grass	Red fescue
St. Augustine grass	Perennial ryegrass
Bahia grass	Creeping bent grass
COLD TOLERANCE (FROM HIGHEST TO LOWEST)	
Zoysia grass	Kentucky bluegrass
Common Bermuda grass	Creeping bent grass
New Bermuda grass hybrids	Colonial bent grass
Centipede grass	Perennial ryegrass
St. Augustine grass	Red fescue
Bahia grass	Tall fescue

• Areas next to fences or walls

• Spots just outside of glass doors or big, ground-level windows

The reason is a matter of physics: Glass and white or pale-colored surfaces reflect and intensify sunlight, while dark-colored surfaces capture and radiate heat. And either action can burn your blue-grass, fry your fescue, or zap your zoysia to kingdom come. So what can you do about it? There are a couple of simple ways to solve this problem:

Baby the grass. Give those high-risk areas extra doses of compost, and water them more often than you do the rest of your lawn. The easiest way to do that is to install soaker hoses and just turn them on whenever the grass needs a drink. (For my guidelines on telling for sure when your turf is thirsty, see Chapter 6.)

Guard the grass. Plant buffer gardens of dry-heat-lovers between the grass and the heat reflectors. Use low-growing annuals or perennials below windows and along walkways and other paved surfaces. In front of walls or fences, go with taller, bushier perennials, ornamental grasses, and shrubs. But don't forget: Although these plants can take the heat better than turf grass can, they'll still need more water than they would if they were growing in a cooler setting.

Brrrr!

If you live in our country's snowbelt, you know what a mess Old Man Winter can make of your lawn. Here are some pointers for helping your turf button up its overcoat when it's cold outside.

START SMART

Anytime you start a new lawn or renovate an old one, use the most cold-hardy grass that's suitable for the growing conditions in your yard. All types of cool-season grasses can survive northern winters, but some handle frigid weather better than others.

For the lineup, see "Hot Shots and Cool Customers" at left. And, as always, before you buy your seed or sod, call your Cooperative Extension Service and ask which varieties are recommended for your home, sweet home.

PLAN AHEAD

With just a little preparation in the fall, you can head off a whole lot of springtime headaches. Here's your five-item to-do list:

1 Keep mowing. Throughout the fall, cut the grass to its maximum recommended height until it stops growing or goes dormant. Then drop the blade a notch, and mow one last time.

2 Give it a good supper. Feed your lawn according my directions in Chapter 5 (see "Gettin' on Toward Bedtime" on page 119). And don't forget to apply my Last Supper Tonic (see page 108) as a finishing touch to the goodnight ritual.

3 Give it a bedtime bath. Before the temperature falls to 50°F, give your lawn a final wash-down with my Fall Clean-Up Tonic (see page 276). How come? Because a lawn that goes to bed clean is more likely to wake up healthy in the spring!

FALL CLEAN-UP TONIC

Fend off snow mold, foul fungi, and other wintertime nasties with this excellent elixir.

1 cup of baby shampoo
1 cup of antiseptic mouthwash
1 cup of tobacco tea*
1 cup of chamomile tea
Warm water

Mix the shampoo, mouthwash, tobacco tea, and chamomile tea in a bucket, then add 2 cups of the mixture to a 20 gallon hose-end sprayer, filling the balance of the jar with warm water. Overspray your turf when the temperature is above 50°F. Follow up with your regular fall lawn feeding and a dose of my Last Supper Tonic (see page 108) to put your lawn to bed.

* To make tobacco tea, place half a handful of chewing tobacco in an old nylon stocking and soak it in a gallon of hot water until the mixture is dark brown. Pour the liquid into a glass container with a tight lid for storage.

4 **Give it a blanket.** Also before winter hits, apply a thick coat of my WeatherProof™ to your lawn and all of your evergreen trees and shrubs to guard against drying winds. It will reduce moisture loss by up to 50 percent.

5 **Pray for snow.** And count your lucky stars if the ground stays covered with at least 6 inches of the white stuff. Even when the winds howl and air temperatures dip well below zero, that thick layer of snow should keep the soil temperatures at a root-pleasing 20° to 25°F.

TWINKLE, TWINKLE

To my way of thinking, a lawn never looks prettier than it does on those first cold fall mornings, when it's all frosty and glistening with ice crystals. It's mighty tempting to run out onto the turf for a closer look. But don't do it! In early fall, grass is still in growth mode, and so are foul fungi and pesky pests. If you walk on the frozen blades, you'll break them, and the resulting wounds will leave them wide open to attack from all directions. Instead, wait until the frost melts before you head out to do any yard work. Later, after several hard frosts have hit, and the grass has gone dormant, it's safe to walk around all you want!

HEAVE-HO!

As we all learned in high school physics class (or should have, if we were paying attention!), water expands as it freezes, and contracts as it thaws. So when soil freezes and thaws over and over again, it often heaves up, breaking the roots of any plant that's growing there—including grass. The damage will appear in the spring as a rough and uneven-looking lawn. As soon as you spot this type of trouble, reseed, following my directions in Chapter 4. And be sure to use a good wet-soil

The Wayward Wind

Super ★ Secret

A nice, gentle breeze is a wonderful thing for your lawn, because it helps chase away fungal diseases that thrive where there's poor air circulation. But heavy wind is a whole different kettle of fish. It dries out your grass and all the other plants in your yard, giving them a thirst that won't quit. What's more, steady winds or strong gusts put your whole landscape under constant stress—making it a sitting duck for every pest and disease under the sun. Fortunately, there's a simple solution to this problem: Plant a windbreak. If you're not sure what direction your prevailing winds come from, pound a few stakes in the ground and tie a ribbon or a strip of cloth to each one. Then watch to see which way the wind is blowing the cloth strips. Plant a row of stocky evergreen trees or shrubs to block the gales. For extra protection, plant two alternating, overlapping rows.

When you're planning your windbreak, remember that the larger your yard is, the taller your plants will have to be. Just make sure you buy trees or shrubs that will be the height and width you need when they reach maturity—not when you see them in their nursery pots. Then, plant them so their branches will just touch when they're fully grown. Your Cooperative Extension Service can clue you in on winners for your area, but here's a starter list of champion wind blockers:

Arborvitae (*Thuja occidentalis*); 6 to 25 feet, USDA Zones 3 to 7

Canada hemlock (*Tsuga canadensis*); 40 to 70 feet, Zones 4 to 8

Foster holly (*Ilex* x *attenuata* 'Foster'); 25 to 40 feet, Zones 6 to 9

Fraser photinia (*Photinia* x *fraseri*); to 15 feet, Zones 6 to 9

Japanese privet (*Ligustrum japonicum*); 12 to 18 feet, Zones 7 to 10

Leyland cypress (*Cupressocyparis leylandii*); to 60 feet, Zones 6 to 8

Norway spruce (*Picea abies*); 40 to 60 feet, Zones 2 to 7

Red cedar (*Juniperus virginiana*); to 40 feet, Zones 2 to 9

Swiss stone pine (*Pinus cembra*); to 35 feet, Zones 4 to 8

Wax myrtle (*Myrica cerifera*); 10 to 20 feet, Zones 7 to 9

performer like Kentucky bluegrass, perennial ryegrass, or (for shadier sites) Sabre bluegrass (*Poa trivialis 'Sabre'*).

KEEP 'EM SNUG

Although you can't keep winter's ups and downs from doing a number on your turf grass, you *can* protect your shrubs, perennials, and ornamental grasses. Just lay a loose mulch over their beds *after* the soil freezes in early winter. Then, later on, after you're through with your Christmas tree, cut off the branches and add them to the bed. The idea is to keep the soil frozen, so it'll stay calmly in place all winter long.

DEAD AS A DOORNAIL

If dead patches appear on your lawn in the spring, don't be too quick to blame pests or diseases. The problem may be winterkill, which can happen for several reasons:

Dehydration. This can occur in very early spring if, for several days in a row, the ground is frozen but there's no snow cover, and the weather is brilliantly sunny and very windy. As a result, the soil thaws down to a few inches, and the wind quickly dries it out. The roots can't go deeper for moisture, because the soil at lower levels is still frozen. So the grass dies.

Starvation. Grass that's received inadequate TLC throughout the growing season is the prime victim of this nastiness. Because the plants don't have adequate food reserves in their roots to get them through the winter, they simply up and die.

Suffocation. Suspect this as a cause of your dead spots if you've had a brief warm spell in late winter, when the snow melted a little, then froze again, leaving your lawn covered with a layer of ice. When this happens, the grass plants can

---

Super ★ Secret

Up and Out!

It's always a bummer to find that heaving soil has done a number on your lawn and your favorite landscape plants. But if you've been battling woody weeds, like wild blackberries or other brambles, here's one consolation: Thanks to the earth's upward thrusts, you can send those tough customers packin' once and for all. The time to strike is after the ground has been frozen for a week or more, then first begins to thaw. The roots will have so little grip on the soil that you can just grab on to the main stem, and pull out the whole kit and caboodle. Just be sure to wear good, thick gloves because, although the roots may be weak, the thorns will still be killer-dillers!

suffocate. As with most forms of trouble, though, the most likely targets are lawns that are already suffering from disease, or are stressed out because of poor care or other environmental woes.

TINY TRICKSTERS

Sometimes, what appears to be winterkill is actually the dirty work of winter grain mites. These minute marauders target northern lawns planted with bent grass, fine fescue, Kentucky bluegrass, and red fescue. They lay their eggs in the fall, and do most of their damage in the winter and early spring—the same time Old Man Winter is leaving his almost-identical calling card. The good news: Unlike most of their little cousins, adult winter grain mites can be spotted with the naked eye. Look for olive green, spiderlike critters with red legs. And to send 'em on their way, follow my anti-mite measures in Chapter 9.

WHAT A DRAIN

When standing water remains on a lawn going into winter, it can lead to a condition called winter scald: The water freezes, and the sun shining through the ice warms up the soil so much that the grass breaks dormancy and starts growing. But, because no air can get through the ice, the plants can't survive for long. Even if the ice melts and the grass blades can breathe, the saturated soil below will cause the roots to die.

SINGIN' THE BROWN GRASS BLUES

You folks in warmer regions may not have the life-and-death struggles that northern lawn keepers face, but there's still one nagging nuisance: While cool-season grasses stay nice and green right up until the snow falls, warm-season types get one taste of frost and turn brown. Fortunately,

HOMEMADE BIRD TREATS

Songbirds are gung-ho gobblers of grain mites, and a whole slew of other lawn and garden bad guys. When you serve up these gourmet goodies, your feathered friends will flock to your feeder—and hang around to put a big dent in the pest population.

   1 part cornmeal
   1 part wild birdseed
   Bacon grease (room-temperature)
   2 pinches of sand or crushed
      eggshells

Mix the cornmeal and birdseed with enough bacon grease to get a bread-dough consistency. Add the sand or eggshells. Shape the dough into a ball, put it in a mesh onion bag, and hang it from a sturdy tree branch or bird-feeder post. Then, get out your binoculars and have fun watching the action!

there's a simple way to keep your lawn looking great all winter long: Just overseed in October with annual rye-grass. It'll establish itself in a flash, stay green all through the cooler months, then fade away just as your warm-season turf is gearing up for a new season in the sun.

A SHADE OF DIFFERENCE

Shade is not normally considered a natural calamity, but if your grass starts growing poorly for no apparent reason, take a look around. It just could be that your yard is a lot shadier than it was in your lawn's younger days, and the cause could be as far beyond your control as any of nature's shenanigans. How so? Well, trees outside your property line may have grown bigger and broader (as trees are wont to do), or maybe a tall fence or a new house has gone up nearby, blocking the sun's path to your yard. Your best plan of action depends on how dense the shade is, and how much time and energy you want to devote to your lawn. Here are your options:

• If the light is only a little dimmer than it used to be, replace your current turf with a more shade-tolerant type (see "A Few Shady Customers" on page 45). But bear in mind that although these grasses can tolerate more shade than

> ### Super★Secret
> ### It May Seem Efficient, But...
> Never apply fertilizer and lime to your lawn at the same time. The two substances react in a way that causes nitrogen to turn to gas and fly off into the atmosphere. If you need to lower your soil's acidity, feed the grass first, then wait several weeks to a month before you spread your lime. Or, instead of lime, use one or more of the natural anti-acids I recommended in Chapter 3 (see "For the Long Haul" on page 64).

most, they'd really prefer to grow in full sun. And that means to keep them thriving, you'll have to give them extra TLC at every step of the way.

• In really shady spots, or if you have better things to do than coddle a lot of grass, plant shade-loving groundcovers, or install a nonliving surface-like a deck or patio. Whichever route you choose (maybe a combination of both), you'll find some terrific options in Chapter 15.

CHAPTER 13

Oops, I Did It Again!

When bad things happen to good lawns, you can't always blame Mother Nature. Sometimes, the unwitting culprit is you. (Remember all those Saturday mornings when your *body* was working in your yard, but your *mind* was someplace else entirely?) Or sometimes, your turf grass is the victim of a well-intentioned, but careless third party, like the local public works crew, your next-door neighbor, or even the youngster who delivers your paper. In this chapter, I'll tell you how to tackle mini-disasters ranging from oil spills to tire ruts—and get your grass growin' great and green again fast!

★ Spills and Splatters

Gasoline, oil, and other powerful chemicals can do serious damage to your lawn. But there's no need to panic when one of these mini-disasters strike. Just grab a trick from this bagful, and leap into action.

GAS OVERBOARD!

We've all been there: You're filling up the old mower, someone calls to you from the house, and you turn around to answer. The next thing you know, there's gasoline running onto your lawn. The good news is that if you act fast, and the spill is small, you can probably head off any damage to the turf. Here's your action plan:

Saturate the soil with soapy water. Use ½ cup of dishwashing liquid per gallon of water. Better yet, use pure liquid soap if you have some close at hand. (Liquid Castile soap is perfect; you can find it in the health and beauty section of your supermarket.) Whatever you do, don't use detergent, or any soap product that contains degreasers or antibacterial agents. Those chemicals will kill your grass as dead as the gas will!

Let the soapsuds soak in. Wait 3 or 4 minutes, then grab the hose and give the accident scene a thorough dousing. Let the water run for a good 10 to 15 minutes.

IT DIDN'T WORK

If brown spots develop in spite of your fast response to a gas spill, or if someone else spilled the gas and you learned about it later, follow this four-step routine:

Step 1. Remove the damaged grass, and toss it in the trash can. Don't put it on the compost pile!

Star-Spangled *Lawn* Lore

Speaking of gasoline, here's a pretty amazing statistic: Every year, Americans use 580,000,000 gallons of the stuff in their lawn mowers. On that much fuel, you could see a lot of the U.S.A. in your Chevrolet!

Step 2. Dig out the soil to a depth of at least 8 inches, and throw it away, too.

Step 3. Fill the hole with a mixture of 2 parts topsoil, 1 part compost, and 1 part peat moss. The peat moss is your magic ingredient: It supports a kind of bacteria that actually eats petroleum!

Step 4. Reseed the area following my directions in Chapter 4 (see "10-Step Repair Plan: Reseeding Made Easy" on page 101).

YOU STRUCK OIL!

Or, rather, oil struck your lawn. In this case, don't reach for the soapy water. Instead, as soon as you notice the damage, haul out your trusty 20 gallon hose-end sprayer, and fill the jar with regular cola. (Don't even think of using the diet version!) Spray the oily area with mild pressure until the sprayer jar is empty. Then, fill 'er up and go at it again. Repeat the process until you've doused that petro-puddle with a full gallon of Coke® or Pepsi®.

After that, remove the sprayer, and saturate the site with clear water. You may still see some damage to your lawn, but if you give it normal TLC, it should make a comeback like a champ. (For a comparison of the bounce-back capabilities of major grass types, see "Standing Up to Trouble" on page 284.)

I know: It seems impossible that a simple soft drink—even one of these all-American superstars—could actually clean up an oil spill. The secret to its success is that an ingredient in the cola helps to break down the oil, and the sugar activates microbes that kick the soil and grass roots into recovery mode. (That's why it's crucial to avoid the artificially sweetened stuff.)

BUT ON THE OTHER HAND...

If the oil spill happened when you weren't around to rush to the aid of your turf, dig out and discard (don't compost!) the affected grass and soil as described in "It Didn't Work" (at left). Then reseed according to my guidelines in Chapter 4. And don't forget to work in that petroleum-defeating peat moss!

IT'S ON MY DRIVEWAY!

When it was time to put oil in your mower, your young lawn-care helper parked the machine on your nice, flat concrete driveway, just as you'd told him to do. Unfortunately, either he didn't use a funnel when he filled the tank, or his aim was rotten—or maybe both. You know that, because when you came home from your vacation, you found the evidence: a big, ugly, black stain on the concrete. Well, don't fret. Here's my surefire formula for getting oil off of a driveway, garage floor, or any other concrete surface:

Step 1. Pour paint thinner onto the concrete, saturating the spots, and the area 8 to 12 inches around them.

Step 2. Spread a good, thick layer of cat litter over the whole area—thick enough that you can't see the concrete

Yankee Doodle Data

Standing Up to Trouble

When it comes to taking punches—or bouncing back from a knockout—all grasses are not created equal. Whether you're reseeding dead spots, or installing a whole new lawn, this comparison chart will help you choose the right grass for your situation. Bear in mind, though, that turf grass breeders are constantly developing new and better varieties, so before you buy seed or sod, call your Cooperative Extension Service and ask what they'd recommend for your situation.

WARM-SEASON GRASSES	COOL-SEASON GRASSES
ESTABLISHMENT RATE FROM SEED, SPRIGS, OR PLUGS (FROM FASTEST TO SLOWEST)	
Common Bermuda grass	Perennial ryegrass
New Bermuda grass hybrids	Tall fescue
St. Augustine grass	Fine fescue
Bahia grass	Colonial bent grass
Zoysia grass	Creeping bent grass
Buffalo grass	Kentucky bluegrass
RECUPERATIVE POWER AFTER DAMAGE (FROM STRONGEST TO WEAKEST)	
New Bermuda grass hybrids	Kentucky bluegrass
Common Bermuda grass	Creeping bent grass
St. Augustine grass	Tall fescue
Bahia grass	Perennial ryegrass
Zoysia grass	Fine fescue
TOLERANCE TO SALTY SOIL (FROM HIGHEST TO LOWEST)	
New Bermuda grass hybrids	Creeping bent grass
Zoysia grass	Tall fescue
St. Augustine grass	Perennial ryegrass
Common Bermuda grass	Kentucky bluegrass
Buffalo grass	Fine fescue
Bahia grass	Colonial bent grass

Standing Up to Trouble	
WARM-SEASON GRASSES	**COOL-SEASON GRASSES**
WEAR AND TEAR RESISTANCE (FROM HIGHEST TO LOWEST)	
Zoysia grass	Tall fescue
New Bermuda grass hybrids	Perennial ryegrass
Common Bermuda grass	Kentucky bluegrass
Bahia grass	Fine fescue
Buffalo grass	Colonial bent grass
St. Augustine grass	Creeping bent grass

underneath. I prefer clumping litter for this purpose, because it absorbs better than the clay kind.

Step 3. Let it sit for an hour or two. Then sweep it up with a broom.

If the stain has been around for a while, you may need to repeat the procedure once or twice. One note of caution: Good ventilation is a must for this job, so if you're working inside the garage, be sure to keep the door open!

WHO SPILLED THE BEANS?

Or rather, the fertilizer? You set the bag on the ground for just a minute, while you went to fetch the spreader. When you came back, the sack was on its side, and there was a thick patch of lawn food on the grass. What do you do now? Act fast, that's what! Grab your wet/dry vac

from the garage, or run to the house for your hand-held vacuum cleaner. If you can't get to either machine quickly, use a brush or broom and dustpan, or even a piece of cardboard. Sweep up as much of the potent powder as you can. Then, get the hose and drench the spill site thoroughly. This should head off any damage to the grass—so breathe a sigh of relief, and give yourself a big pat on the back for a job well done!

DINNER WAS SERVED EARLIER

If a fertilizer spill occurred when you weren't around (and maybe the exact timing is anybody's guess), follow this rescue routine:

Step 1. Sweep up the fertilizer, as described in "Who Spilled the Beans?" at left.

Step 2. Saturate the area with soapy water (½ cup of mild dishwashing liquid or liquid soap—*not* detergent, and *not* antibacterial soap—per gallon of water).

Step 3. Wait a few minutes to let the solution seep in, then give the soil a good soaking with the hose.

Step 4. Water deeply every day for three or four days, then apply gypsum at the rate of 50 pounds per 2,500 square feet of lawn area.

In a month or two, that grass should be back to its old green self again.

IT'S NOT EVEN, STEVEN

If your lawn is sporting streaks or irregular patterns—some too thin, some overly lush, maybe some a deeper green color—most likely the problem lies in your fertilizer application. (You'll know for *sure* that's the case if the streaks follow the path you normally take with your spreader.) Either you've used a food with too much concentrated nitrogen, or the stuff has been spread unevenly

Super ★ Secret

No Hot Meals

One of the surest, and fastest, ways to burn your grass is to feed it during hot weather. This is sure to happen if you're using a quick-release form of nitrogen. So, when the temperatures rise—no matter how hungry you may think your lawn is—just cool it! Take it from me: You'll be glad you did. (But it *is* okay to serve light snacks, in particular, my All-Season Green-Up Tonic. You'll find the recipe on page 85.)

across the turf. To start the recovery process, first leach the area with water, and apply gypsum at the rate of 50 pounds per 2,500 square feet of lawn area. Then, to avoid future problems:

• Feed your lawn only as much chow as it needs for good health, and not one crumb more! (For my complete dietary guidelines, see Chapter 5.)

• Go easy on the nitrogen, especially in the spring.

• Always use slow-release, preferably natural/organic forms of nitrogen (see "The Best of the Big N" at right).

• Be sure to calibrate your spreader, so you'll know the contents will be deposited as uniformly as possible across your lawn (see "Drop It Right There!" and "The Big Broadcast" both on page 288).

THE BEST OF THE BIG N

Back in Chapter 5, I talked a whole lot about the importance of slow-release nitrogen, but it bears repeating here, because an overdose of N, especially in powerful, chemical form, is one of the most common causes of turf grass injury. So, anytime your lawn needs an extra jolt of nitrogen—or if you want to mix up your own ultra-safe organic fertilizer—reach for one or more of these gentle sources:

★ Alfalfa meal

★ Bird guano

★ Bloodmeal

★ Coffee grounds

★ Cottonseed meal

★ Fish emulsion

★ Fish meal

★ Manure (all kinds)

★ Soybean meal

TWO, FOUR, SIX, EIGHT...

Why do we have to calibrate? When you buy a spreader—either a drop or a broadcast type—it's already preset to apply various fertilizers at specific rates,

Star-Spangled *Lawn* Lore

Want to wager a guess as to how many pounds of grass clippings the average half-acre American lawn produces in a single season? The answer: 5,500. That's a whale of a lot of free nitrogen— and it's guaranteed not to burn your lawn!

according to the amount of nitrogen needed per 1,000 square feet of lawn area. So you might think that going through this exercise yourself is a waste of time. Well, it's not, and for two very good reasons:

1 As time goes by, the settings can get out of kilter, which means that either too much or too little food will come out of the spreader. So it's a good idea to calibrate your trusty helper every year or two.

2 There's a good chance that the spreader you bought doesn't have a specific setting for the fertilizer you've chosen. And if you're using one of my down-home lawn food recipes, I'll bet you francs to fish meal that you won't find a setting for it. (For help, see "Drop It Right There!" on page 288.)

DROP IT RIGHT THERE!

Here's the simple routine for calibrating a drop spreader:

Step 1. Make a trough out of plastic or heavy cardboard, or cut one side off a piece of aluminum gutter. Your device can be either box- or V-shaped, but it needs to cover the entire length of your spreader's output area.

Step 2. Fasten the trough to the under-side of your spreader with baling wire or heavy picture wire.

Step 3. Set the spreader at the manufac-turer's specified number for the fertilizer you're using. If your lawn food isn't mentioned in the guidelines, use the lowest setting.

Step 4. Carefully pour your fertilizer into the hopper.

Step 5. Push your spreader over a 100-square-foot section of your lawn (see "Be There and Be Square" below).

Step 6. Remove the trough, pour the contents into a paper or plastic container, and weigh it. (Weigh the empty con-tainer first, then subtract that number from the total.) Then multiply by 10, and bingo—you've got the amount of fertilizer you would apply for 1,000 square feet.

THE BIG BROADCAST

It's all but impossible to catch fertilizer as it's flying out of a broadcast spreader, so calibrating one of these babies is a lit-tle trickier. It's certainly doable, though. Here's the process:

• Choose a size for your test site, and weigh enough fertilizer to cover it. I

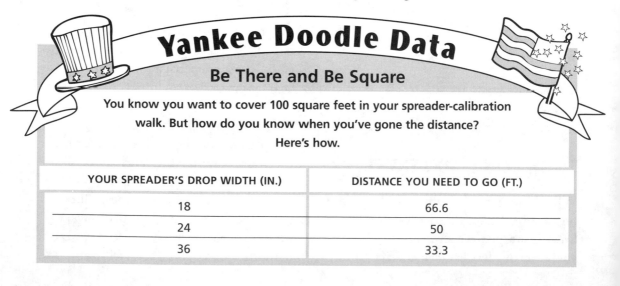

Yankee Doodle Data

Be There and Be Square

You know you want to cover 100 square feet in your spreader-calibration walk. But how do you know when you've gone the distance? Here's how.

YOUR SPREADER'S DROP WIDTH (IN.)	DISTANCE YOU NEED TO GO (FT.)
18	66.6
24	50
36	33.3

• Eyeball the hopper. If you reached the finish line just as the last food was flying out, write down the setting number, and use it every time. But if you ran out of fertilizer early, or you've got leftovers, repeat the test in another area, using either a lower or higher setting, respectively.

LOCATION, LOCATION, LOCATION

generally use an area that's 200 square feet, or one-fifth of 1,000 square feet. That makes for easy calculatin' because, as we saw in Chapter 5, you want to serve up no more than 1 pound of nitrogen per 1,000 square feet at any one time. So, for example, if you're using a lawn food that contains 25 percent nitrogen, you need 4 pounds for 1,000 square feet. Divide those 4 pounds by 5, and you get 0.8 pound—the amount needed for 200 square feet.

• Mark off a starting point, push your spreader a few feet, and measure the width of its spread path.

• Calculate and mark off the test area. Let's say your spreader broadcasts across a 5-foot-wide path. In that case, you'd measure a distance of 40 feet (5 x 40 = 200), and lay a stick on the ground to show the end point. Then spread your fertilizer.

Some folks like to calibrate their spreaders right on the lawn. Others prefer to do the job on a paved surface, like a street or driveway. Each site has its pros and cons. When you do the test on your lawn, you know that your fertilizer won't go to waste. Nor will it be washed into storm drains, streams, or other waterways. On the downside, you risk the very situation you're trying to avoid: damage to your turf from uneven application.

Spreading the test material over pavement eliminates the chance of winding up with burned or overly lush grass. Furthermore, it lets you see exactly what the drop or broadcast pattern is. If you opt for this locale, just be sure to sweep up every last bit of the fertilizer, and dispose of it properly. Don't use it to feed your lawn, because it's bound to contain dirt and other debris that will throw off your food portions and could clog your spreader.

Yankee Doodle Data

Accident Management at a Glance

When you're at the scene of a lawn mishap, you know immediately what went haywire. Then, it's easy to spring into action and set things right again. After the deed's been done, it's a whole other story. That's when you want to reach for this handy chart. It'll help you pinpoint the problem, patch up the damage—and see that it doesn't happen again.

SYMPTOM	LIKELY CAUSE	YOUR ACTION PLAN
In early spring, dead or yellowed grass along driveways, sidewalks, or roadsides	Damage from deicing salt	**Repair** As soon as nighttime temperatures are above 35°F, rake away the dead grass, water the site heavily to get rid of the salt, and reseed with a salt-tolerant grass variety (see "Standing Up to Trouble" on page 284). **Prevention** In areas within your control, use substances other than salt to melt ice and provide traction (see "Hold the Salt" on page 294). To protect areas along the road, where your town's snow-removal crew spreads salt or other harsh chemicals, apply my Winter Walkway Protection Tonic (see page 294).
Streaks, bands, or irregular patches of dead or yellowed grass	Fertilizer burn— in particular, an overdose of concentrated nitrogen	**Repair** If the crown tissue has been damaged, dig out the dead grass and reseed following my directions in Chapter 4. If only the blades have been affected, saturate the area to leach out the excess nitrogen. **Prevention** Use a fertilizer that contains slow-release nitrogen, preferably in natural/organic form. Avoid applying too much nitrogen in any form, especially in the spring (see Chapter 5 for the nitrogen needs of various turf grass types). Calibrate your spreader to ensure uniform application.

Accident Management at a Glance

SYMPTOM	LIKELY CAUSE	YOUR ACTION PLAN
Black or dark brown spots or patches	Oil or gasoline spills	**Repair** Dig out the affected grass and soil to a depth of at least 8 inches, and fill the hole with a mixture of 2 parts topsoil, 1 part compost, and 1 part peat moss. Then reseed with a fast-recovering grass variety (see "Standing Up to Trouble" on page 284). **Prevention** Fill your mower's gas and oil tanks on a level, nonliving surface—never on your lawn. And don't park cars or other gasoline-powered vehicles in places where their plant-killing fluids could leak onto your lawn.
Large, yellow patches near your swimming pool	Chlorine damage	**Repair** Saturate the soil with water, so the chlorine can leach out. Then reseed the damaged area, following my guidelines in Chapter 4. **Prevention** Install a broad, paved surface around your pool so that the chlorinated water can't splash onto the grass.
Dead grass in a new lawn, with no sign of trouble; brown, dead patches in a mature lawn, with no trace of pests or disease	Herbicide damage	**Repair** Dig up the dead grass, and reseed or resod, following my guidelines in Chapter 4. **Prevention** Never use any kind of herbicide (even my Wild Weed Wipeout Tonic) on a lawn that contains grass that's less than 4 months old. And always follow the tonic recipe or label instructions *to the letter*. Remember: More is not better! (see "Involuntary Herbicide" on page 296).

IN A BROADER CONTEXT

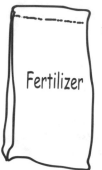

Fertilizer

Fertilizer that's spilled, over-used, or mishandled can do a number on your lawn, all right. But, more important from a long-term perspective, it can also pollute the groundwater under your lawn, as well as our lakes, rivers, streams, and shining seas. So do your grandchildren—and their grandchildren--a favor, and use this potent stuff with care. In particular, follow these guidelines:

Test your soil. That way, you'll know exactly what nutrients your lawn needs. (For the lowdown on soil tests and essential nutrients, see Chapters 3 and 5.)

Heed the results. Don't apply any nutrients that your soil doesn't need. For instance, if the test shows that your home ground contains plenty of phosphorus, don't give it any more!

Feed right. By that, I mean give your lawn its meals at the right times and in the right portions. For my complete feeding guidelines, see Chapter 5.

Go deep. A lawn with a deep, healthy root system generally cleans its plate—so little, if any, fertilizer runs off to places where it doesn't belong. (In Chapter 6, you'll find terrific tips for helping your grass's roots take the plunge.)

Go slow. Always use slow-release forms of nitrogen—preferably natural/organic sources. In addition to helping your grass grow stronger and healthier, they're less likely to leach through the soil and into the groundwater. If you want to be even more cautious, choose a grass type with a small nitrogen appetite (see "Nitrogen Appetite Levels" at right).

Leave the clippings. They're one of the best slow-release N sources of all! By not removing them when you mow, you can supply 25 percent or more of the nitrogen your grass needs for good growth.

Drop, don't broadcast. When you use a drop spreader, all of the fertilizer goes right where you want it to. On the other hand, a broadcast model can send the stuff flying onto sidewalks and streets, almost ensuring that those chemicals will wind up in some body of water.

Don't "feed" the hardscape. Not that you'd do it on purpose, of course! But when you're in a rush, it's easy to forget to shut off the spreader when you cross a walk or driveway. So do what I do: Tie a string around your finger—or a ribbon around the handlebars!

Rinse your spreader on the lawn. When you're through serving your lawn its dinner, park the spreader on the grass to hose it off. That way, the fertilizer can't be washed down the drain and into the sewer line.

The Salt o' the Earth

Salt kills grass, plain and simple. Whether it floats in on coastal breezes or gets dumped out of a truck by your local snow-removal crew, the results are the same. Regardless of where that old NaCl came from, here's your plan for damage control—and prevention.

SPRING IS IN THE AIR

And the salt is in your soil—and you've got dead grass all along your roadside to prove it. So what do you do? Well, don't do anything until you're sure the nighttime temperatures will stay above 35°F. As soon as you've passed that milestone,

remove the dead grass and water thoroughly to wash away the salt. Then, reseed with the most salt-tolerant grass that will perform well in your growing conditions. (For a list of stellar candidates, see "Standing Up to Trouble" on page 284.)

A SALTY DEFENSE

Before the first snow flies, take these two simple steps to help your grass survive its next run-in with road salt:

Step 1. Apply my Winter Walkway Protection Tonic (on page 294) to lawn areas that border a road, sidewalk, or any other surface that may be the recipient of deicing salt.

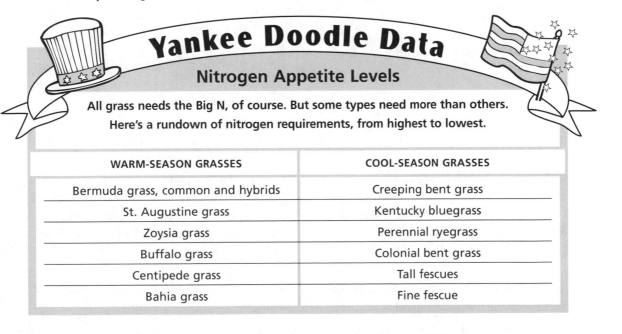

Yankee Doodle Data

Nitrogen Appetite Levels

All grass needs the Big N, of course. But some types need more than others. Here's a rundown of nitrogen requirements, from highest to lowest.

WARM-SEASON GRASSES	COOL-SEASON GRASSES
Bermuda grass, common and hybrids	Creeping bent grass
St. Augustine grass	Kentucky bluegrass
Zoysia grass	Perennial ryegrass
Buffalo grass	Colonial bent grass
Centipede grass	Tall fescues
Bahia grass	Fine fescue

Step 2. One week later, follow up with a dose of my WeatherProof™. It works like an overcoat to block damage to your lawn from salt and other winter woes, like sunscald, windburn, and pollution.

HOLD THE SALT

Where your roadside grass is concerned, you have to take whatever the highway department dishes out (unless you've got a *lot* of clout at City Hall). But in the rest of your yard, you don't have to put up with one iota of salt damage. The next time you wake up to an ice-covered patio, walkway, or driveway, reach for something that'll cover the ice and keep you standing upright, without harming your grass or any other plants in your landscape. Any of these will do the trick:

• Cinders

• Clay cat litter (not the clumping kind)

• Sand

• Wood ashes

ICE BE GONE!

When you need to melt ice, rather than simply cover it up, use one of these chemical-free remedies:

Alfalfa meal. This is a natural, nitrogen-rich fertilizer that does quadruple duty:

WINTER WALKWAY PROTECTION TONIC

This "suit of armor" will guard your grass from winter's onslaught of ice-melting salt. First, in late fall, liberally spread gypsum over the turf in a 5-foot band along roadsides, walkways, or any other surface that will be on the deicing list. Then overspray the gypsum with this protective potion.

> **1 cup of dishwashing liquid**
> **½ cup of ammonia**
> **½ cup of beer**

Mix these ingredients in a 20 gallon hose-end sprayer, and apply over the gypsum to the point of run-off. Then your soil and grass will sail through the winter in fine shape.

Its gritty texture provides traction, the nitrogen it contains promotes ice melting, and the resulting run-off is harmless to masonry and good for your grass and any other plants it encounters.

Fire power. When you need to clear a walkway or driveway on the double, fire up a propane weed torch, and take aim. But first, make sure that you have a place for the melted ice to drain; otherwise, you'll just be moving your problem from one spot to another!

Pet-safe commercial deicers. No, you don't need to own a pet to use these

products! They're usually labeled that way because they are safe to use around dogs and cats, unlike salt, which irritates their paws and upsets their stomachs when they lick the residue off their feet. But these kinder, gentler ice melters are also harmless to grass and landscape plants. Furthermore, they won't damage concrete, brick, or wooden surfaces like salt will. Granted, most brands cost a lot more than salt—but they'll set you back by a whole lot *less* than replacing your grass or repairing your deck.

DOWN BY THE SEASIDE

For most of us folks, there's nothing more refreshing than a dose of tingly ocean air. But for most grasses, those salty breezes are a menace. So, if you're one of the lucky ducks whose yard runs right down to the shore, how do you protect your lawn? Just take these two simple steps:

Step 1. Plant the most salt-tolerant grass that will thrive in your area. You'll find a starter list in "Standing Up to Trouble" on page 284. But before you make a decision, check with your Cooperative Extension Service, because new varieties are hitting the garden center shelves

from the MAIL BAG

Dear Jerry,

My brother-in-law rode his motorcycle over to my place, and parked on my lawn. The next day, as I was mowing that area, I found burned patches on the grass. Is it possible that his bike actually caused them?

A. *It sure is! From what my biker friends tell me, motorcycle mufflers burn hot, and they're notorious for scorching lawns. But it's unlikely that major damage was done. Just scrape away the dead grass, and water well. Before you know it, that turf'll be its old self again. But to head off future trouble, gently suggest to your brother-in-law that he hightail it down to his 'cycle dealer and order a heat shield for that muffler!*

every season, and many of them are bred for superstar performance in very specific geographic regions.

Step 2. Between your lawn and the shoreline, install a buffer zone of coastal plants that are native to your area. These naturally nautical types can take all the salt spray and even the waves that ol' Neptune can toss their way. What's more, unlike their garden-variety cousins—and your turf grass—these wild and woolly wonders don't have to be fed, watered, or otherwise coddled. Your best plant options depend on where you live, and the microclimates we're talking about are so tiny that I won't even attempt to give you suggestions here. (That would take a whole book!) It's easy to learn more, though: Just get in touch with your local native plant society, or the closest Audubon Society or Nature Conservancy office. The folks there will be happy to clue you in on the best candidates for your defensive line.

A SOUTHERN SUPERSTAR

If you live in one of our country's warmest coastal regions, you should know about seashore paspalum (*Paspalum vaginatum*). It's been around for thousands of years, growing wild in tropical and subtropical regions all over the world. But it's only now finding its true calling as an American turf grass with real star power. Paspalum doesn't just *tolerate* salt water—it actually thrives right on a beach or even in a salt marsh. What's more, it can hold its own in a drought, needs little nitrogen, will grow in any soil pH from 4 to 9, and thumbs its nose (so to speak) at pests, diseases, and weeds. And, oh yes, the leaves have a fine texture like Bermuda grass, so this stuff makes one good-looking lawn. To learn more, call your Cooperative Extension Service, or crank up your favorite Internet search engine and type in "seashore paspalum."

Involuntary Herbicide

Herbicides were invented to wipe out plants that people don't want to live with (i.e., weeds), and they generally do a pretty thorough job of it. But these chemical weapons often kill or injure turf grass and valuable landscape plants, too. Whether the unintentional evildoer was you, a neighbor, or your town's weed-control squad, you'll find your best coping strategies right here.

SAME OLD BROWN SPOTS

In a mature lawn, herbicide damage generally appears as dead, brown spots, with no sign of pests or diseases. The unsightly patches resemble those caused by a zillion and one other factors (for some of the most common, see "What Happened to My Lawn?" on page 98). Fortunately, you don't really need a positive diagnosis, because regardless of what killed your grass, you have only one treatment option: Dig up the affected turf, and reseed or resod, following my guidelines in Chapter 4.

As for heading off trouble in the future, it couldn't be simpler: Just follow these commonsense guidelines:

★ Don't use chemical herbicides! Instead, reach for one of my trusty weed-busting tactics in Chapter 11.

★ Even when you use nonchemical means, like corn gluten meal, my Wild Weed Wipeout Tonic (see page 243), or even plain old vinegar, be careful. Aim your spray bottle carefully, and always follow the tonic recipe or label instructions to the letter. Remember, as I've said time and again, more is not better!

BRING IT BACK ALIVE

If you've inherited a lawn that's been repeatedly treated with herbicides, or if you've decided to go organic after rou-

ALL-PURPOSE PERENNIAL FERTILIZER

Herbicides sprayed on lawns or along roadsides often drift onto perennial flower beds—with ugly results. But this health-giving snack will put your blooms on the fast track to a full recovery.

3 parts bonemeal

3 parts greensand or wood ashes

1 part bloodmeal

Mix these ingredients in a bucket or wheelbarrow. Then, after you've clipped off the affected foliage, scatter 2 tablespoons of the mix around each clump of perennials, and scratch it lightly into the soil with a garden fork.

tinely using chemical weed killers in the past, here's an unpleasant fact you need to know: The residue can hang around in the soil for as long as five years, upsetting the balance of life underground. Fortunately, there are ways you can speed up its exit and return your soil to the land of the living:

• Start by adding heaping amounts of organic matter to the soil (for my easy method, see "Holey Moley!" on page 96).

• Always water thoroughly and deeply to help wash away the toxins.

• If the contamination is causing severe problems with your grass—or you want to turn part of your yard into an ornamental food garden—mix activated charcoal with the soil, at a rate of 17 pounds per 2,500 square feet of lawn area. (For more on ornamental edible gardens as turf grass alternatives, see Chapter 15.)

COLLATERAL DAMAGE

The flowering plants in your yard can suffer from herbicide damage even if you don't use a drop of the stuff on your grass. It happens most often in spring and summer, when folks (and public works crews) are spraying weed killers on lawns and along roadsides. Here are some of the symptoms you might see on annuals or perennials:

• Cup-shaped leaves, often with the veins close together

• Stems twisted into spirals

• Scorched, brown spots on leaves and stems

• Normal side shoots absent and replaced by stunted rosettes of short shoots and malformed, straplike leaves

So what do you do? Well, first cut off the damaged areas and destroy them. Don't toss 'em on the compost pile— those chemicals have done enough damage already! Then, to promote healthy new growth, water well, and give

BLUE PLATE SPECIAL

ANNUAL FLOWER FEEDER TONIC

When your annuals have a run-in with drifting herbicide, remove the affected plant parts and water well. Then, to get them back in shape fast, serve this powerful potion.

> **1 can of beer**
> **2 tbsp. of fish emulsion**
> **2 tbsp. of dishwashing liquid**
> **2 tbsp. of ammonia**
> **2 tbsp. of hydrogen peroxide**
> **2 tbsp. of whiskey**
> **1 tbsp. of clear corn syrup**
> **1 tbsp. of unflavored gelatin**
> **4 tsp. of instant tea granules**
> **2 gal. of warm water**

Mix these ingredients together in a large bucket, then pour the solution into a watering can. Feed your stricken annuals with this mix after you've removed the damaged foliage, and then every two weeks throughout the growing season.

your plants a snack of my All-Purpose Perennial Fertilizer (see page 297) or Annual Flower Feeder Tonic (see above). If you know where the herbicides came from, you can probably defend your garden against future attacks. Just call the folks who did the spraying, and ask them (politely) to let you know in advance of their next assault: That way, you can cover up your plants with sheets, paper sacks, or plastic garbage bags until the foul stuff has blown away.

CHAPTER 14

Games People Play

You might say that athletes are folks who don't let the grass grow under their feet. In fact, if your yard plays host to regular games of soccer, volleyball, and other outdoor activities, you probably know just how hard it can be for grass to grow in spots where sports are played. What's a lawn lover to do? Give sports-scuffed turf lots of TLC, and try out my tips for tending a home field that's an advantage in every game you play.

☆ Great Grasses for Good Sports

From horseshoes and croquet to badminton and bocci, games on grass are all-American good fun. These not-so-leisurely pursuits help us unwind, get us out in the fresh air, and give us a chance to burn off that extra hot dog we ate at the cookout. Whether your idea of at-home athletics involves leaping above the net to spike a volleyball or gently rolling a bocci ball across the grass, creating a lawn that suits your family's favorite activities makes games more fun and helps protect your turf—and you—from sports-related injuries.

TURF THAT CAN TAKE IT

Having a lawn that can take the treatment that backyard athletes dish out really boils down to having healthy, well-tended grass (like I've been telling you about for the past couple-hundred pages or so). Here's what I mean:

Start with superior soil. You wouldn't build your house on a shoddy foundation (at least I sure hope you wouldn't!), and you shouldn't base your lawn on less-than-well-prepared soil. Back in Chapter 3, I went into great detail on the hows, whens, and whys of starting a new lawn, including how to get the soil ready before you sow. Chapter 4 is packed with tips for renovating an old lawn. Turn to those chapters if you need to learn how to perk up the soil below the grass you've already got!

Sow (or sod) the right stuff. See what local golf courses and high schools grow on fairways and football fields in your area. Any grass that can stand up to a steady parade of weekend golfers or the cleated feet of dozens of high school ball players is likely to tolerate even the most vigorous croquet match. In general, if you live north of the "bluegrass line" (the imaginary boundary between good growing conditions for cool-season turf and climates that favor warm-season grasses), your best choice for a sports-tolerant lawn will be a combination of turf-type tall fescue and Kentucky blue-

grass. Southern sports usually are played on fields of Bermuda grass that may be overseeded with perennial ryegrass to keep them greener longer.

North or South, look for improved varieties that have been specially selected for playing-field perfection.

LEVEL THE FIELD

Ups and downs on a playing area are turned ankles waiting to happen. Long before you get out the chalk marker to line the court or mark play area boundaries, smooth out any uneven spots by taking action:

Star-Spangled Lawn Lore

In 2003, American consumers spent more than $21 billion on sports equipment. That's a lot of baseball mitts and soccer balls!

• Slice off bumpy places. Use a sharp, square-bladed shovel to lift healthy sod covering the area, and stow that sod in a shady spot until you're ready to replace it. Keep it moist, too. Then shovel away as much soil as needed to even things out, and work about an inch of compost into the soil. Water lightly, then replace the sod and soak it with my Kick-in-the-Grass Tonic (see page 100).

• Fill in dips and holes. Mix compost and topsoil in a 1 to 1 ratio and shovel it right over the grass in the littlest low spots—healthy turf will grow up through it in no time. To lift deeper depressions, you'll want to take up the sod first, then fill in the low spots with a compost/topsoil combo. Follow up with a gentle watering; put the sod back, and give it a good drink of my Kick-in-the-Grass Tonic.

• Give the playing area a slight slope for good drainage (about ¼ inch of slope per foot is all you need).

KEEP OFF THE GRASS!

It's tough, but keep avid athletes off of newly seeded or sodded areas until the grass is well established (meaning it's had at least two mowings). Waiting is worth

Super ★ Secret

Get Even

An 8-foot length of two-by-four lumber and a carpenter's level both come in real handy when you're handling highs and lows in the lawn. After you've filled in a dip or brought down a bump, lay the two-by-four over the spot and set the level on top of it. You'll be able to see straightaway if it's smoothed to your satisfaction.

it if you avoid trampling too-tender turf and don't have to start all over again.

"AIR" ON THE SIDE OF CAUTION

Compacted soil and bare spots are two of the biggest threats to grass on a playing field. Baselines, volleyball service boxes, even horseshoe pitching foul lines—anyplace where folks stand or run over and over is in danger. Here's what you need to know:

★ Pay particular attention to any at-risk areas when you're aerating your lawn (see "Aerating 101" on page 94).

★ Be sure to treat play areas to monthly applications of my Aeration Tonic (see page 95).

★ Sure, things like horseshoe pits may be pretty permanent, but moving anything that can be moved will give trampled turf a chance to recover.

★ Set up the badminton net perpendicular to where it was last time, and shift the croquet course to the right or left.

★ If you notice an area that looks like it's really taking a beating, give it a little TLC after the game with a dose of my Kick-in-the-Grass Tonic (see page 100), and then mark it off with stakes and strings for a few days to give it a rest.

MOW IN THE KNOW

Mowing with know-how helps build a thick, healthy lawn that's a pleasure to play on. (See Chapter 7 for tons of tips on how and when to mow.) Here's a short guide to mowing for sports activities:

• Keep the grass on your court mowed to the height it prefers.

Star-Spangled *Lawn* Lore

Back in the 1930s and 1940s, badminton was popular with the Hollywood set. Among those known to take a swing at the shuttlecock were well-known celebrities like James Cagney, Bette Davis, Boris Karloff, and Ginger Rogers.

• Mow with a sharp blade, and don't cut off more than one-third of the grass's height at one time.

• When possible, leave the clippings on the lawn and douse them with a dose of Grass Clipping Dissolving Tonic (see page 171), to help them break down more quickly into a tasty meal for your turf.

• If highly competitive contests require you to remove those nourishing clippings from your gaming grass, it's extra important to keep up with regular servings of my All-Season Green-Up Tonic (see page 85), so your grass doesn't grow hungry.

PUT STRESS TO REST

Treat your home "court" just as you would any other lawn area that you want to keep looking good and growing well.

Here's how:

★ Give it water when it's dry.

★ Stay off of it when it's wet.

★ Supply the nutrients it needs.

★ Nip problems like compacted soil or pests in the bud.

Be a good sport about giving your grass the care it needs, and it will give you season after season of backyard fun.

Super ★ Secret

Get Reel!

To give your backyard sports areas a professional look, you may need a new mower. Most rotary mowers (the kind where the blade spins parallel to the ground under a rounded housing) aren't good for cutting heights of 1 inch or lower. That means they go low enough for casual play and for most types of cool-season grass, but it's on the high side for things like putting greens and "serious" croquet courts. It's also taller than is desirable for Bermuda grass or creeping bent grass (the preferred turf of putting greens). For a spiffy look and for certain grasses, you'll need a reel mower (typically a "push" mower with blades that travel perpendicular to the grass) to give your turf the kind of tidy trim it needs.

OVERLOOK CLOVER

Clover may be welcome in many laid-back lawn situations, but it's not the best choice for spaces where backyard athletes compete. Why not? Clover's round leaves create a more slippery surface than grasses' narrow blades, and they deliver darker "grass" stains, too. Bees find clover blossoms mighty inviting, as well, and those buzzin' buddies don't always appreciate being disturbed by a vigorous game of volleyball.

☆ Let the Games Begin!

For an old lawn lover like me, games on the grass are the perfect excuse for getting out there and enjoying the turf I've tended so well. The simple pleasures of backyard contests such as badminton or croquet are reason enough to lure anyone outdoors, where they can fully appreciate the sight, smell, and texture of all that great, green, growing goodness.

BIRDIES IN YOUR BACKYARD

When it's played in official competition, badminton is the second fastest racket sport in the world, bearing little resemblance to the lazy summer afternoon contests held in backyards across North America. I've always found that a short session of batting the birdie, or shuttlecock, back and forth over the 5-foot-high net is a good excuse to then enjoy a long session of sitting in the shade with a tall glass of iced tea!

Occasional, casual badminton competitions rarely do much harm to a healthy lawn. If wear and tear on the court is a concern, adjust the arrangement of the net between matches to give tired turf a rest. Another plus: Driving the net poles and anchoring stakes into the ground gives your lawn a little extra aeration each time you set up the net.

BOWLING WITHOUT AN ALLEY

The Italian neighbor who introduced me, years ago, to the game of bocci would scoff at the casual way it is played in most backyards. *His* bocci was played on a tidy packed-earth court that had sidewalls and a backboard, and the heavy bocci balls were rolled—never tossed—toward the pallino. Of course, my old friend would also be skeptical about claims that this traditional Italian pastime has origins in countries other than Italy!

Regardless of where it got its start, when played on an open lawn, bocci is a game that backyard athletes of all ages

Star-Spangled *Lawn* Lore

It's estimated that more than one million Americans try their rackets at a recreational game of badminton each year.

and skill levels can enjoy. And the varied terrain of a home landscape can add a bit of a challenge to the task of rolling balls closest to the target ball (known as a pallino, or jack).

CHECKMATE!

For lawn games that take more brains than brawn, how about a backyard chess or checkers board? I don't mean nailing a regular board to the top of a stump and pulling up a couple of lawn chairs—think big and get creative! You can have as much fun assembling this game as you'll have playing it. An easy way to start is by using 32 square

pavers and alternating them with 32 equal-size squares of grass in eight rows of eight to create the classic look of a checkerboard. Here's how:

Yankee Doodle Data

Courts for Sports

Looking to install a regulation-size space for your favorite lawn game?
Here are the dimensions used for official playing areas of some of the
more popular backyard sports.

GAME	COURT DIMENSIONS	EQUIPMENT
Badminton	44 ft. × 17 ft. (singles) or 44 ft. × 20 ft. (doubles)	Rackets, shuttlecocks/birdies, 5-ft.-high net
Bocci/Bowls/ Lawn bowling	Varies: roughly 12–15 ft. × 60–95 ft.	8 balls about 4½ in. in diameter and weighing about 3 lbs. each; one smaller target ball, called the pallino, or jack
Croquet	100 ft. × 50 ft.	9 wickets, 2 end stakes, 6 balls and mallets
Horseshoes	40 ft. × 3 ft.	4 "shoes" weighing 2½ lbs. each with openings no greater than 3½ in.; 2 metal stakes 1-in. in diameter; foul lines at 27 and 37 ft. from each stake
Lawn tennis	78 ft. × 27 ft. (singles) or 78 ft. × 36 ft. (doubles)	Rackets, felt-covered balls, 3-ft.-high net
Volleyball	59 ft. × 29½ ft.	Net height: 7 ft. 11⅝ in. (men), 7 ft. 4⅛ in. (women); 6½ ft. free zone around court recommended

1 Choose a level lawn area for your "board" of 64 squares.

2 Mow the grass in the board area to the lowest height recommended for your turf type.

3 With stakes and string, mark off a square that's eight times the width of your pavers. For example, if your

pavers are 1 square foot each, your playing board will be 8 feet by 8 feet. Use additional stakes and string as straight lines for setting each row of pavers.

4 Put the pavers in place, leaving a paver's width of uncovered grass after each one, so that each row has four pavers and four grassy squares.

5 When you're finished, take down the stakes and string and admire your handiwork. Then get busy coming up with super-size playing pieces to match your large-scale board (see "King Me!" below).

KING ME!

Laying out a lawn-scale board is only half the fun of backyard chess or checkers. Next you need to don the ol' thinking cap and come up with 24 checkers (12 of each color) and/or 32 chess pieces (16 of each color and identified as pawns, rooks, knights, bishops, kings, or queens). Don't get hung up on traditional shapes—checkers might be made of 1-gallon plastic milk jugs painted red or black and filled with enough sand (or water) to keep them from blowing off the board on breezy days. By marking those same jugs with letters to designate the different chess pieces, you can use them for either game.

Here are some ideas to get you started. Just remember that you'll want to paint or otherwise color your pieces, and be sure to plan for "weights" to keep them from leaving the board.

sand

Super ★ Secret

Make Way for Mowing

To tend the turf inside a backyard chess or checkers board, use a string trimmer to give each grassy square a quick cut. If you'd like to be able to run your mower over the board, dig up paver-size pieces of sod in a checkerboard pattern and set the pavers even with the soil surface instead of laying them on top of the lawn. Use the sod you take out of play to patch bare spots elsewhere in the yard, or stack the pieces root-side up for composting. Don't forget to water and feed the squares of gaming grass just like the rest of your lawn, so your board will stay fresh and green and ready for action.

CHECKERS

- 1-gallon plastic milk or juice containers
- 1-liter plastic soda bottles
- Beanbags
- Clay flowerpots
- Frisbees™
- Heavy-duty plastic plates

CHESS PIECES

- Coffee cans
- Oatmeal canisters
- Old trophies (check yard sales to gather a supply of these)
- Powdered drink mix canisters
- "Shaped" plastic bottles, such as the Mrs. Butterworth's® syrup bottles

HAVE A WICKET
GOOD TIME

I think youngsters are attracted to croquet because it's one of the rare times
when adults actually give them a big
mallet to play with. And more mature
players (you know who you are) can
appreciate the subtle aspects of this old-
time lawn game: the finesse it takes to
send your ball smoothly through the
double-diamond arrangement of wickets, or the thrill of knocking your
opponent's ball out of bounds.

Croquet is just plain old fun, and
it's a great way to show off your first-
rate lawn, too. A regulation croquet
court covers a level 100- by 50-foot
rectangle of close-cropped grass, with
nine wickets in a double-diamond
pattern. But a casual game can bear a
resemblance to miniature golf (without
the windmills), particularly in yards
where uneven terrain leads to more creative wicket setups.

THE GREATEST
GAME ON GRASS

Even though it's nothing like a backyard
sport—unless you have one heck of a
backyard!—I can't ignore golf in a dis-
cussion of games on the grass. After all, I
think a little of golf's allure lies in the
pleasant fantasy that all the land you're
playing on *is* your yard. And other people
are mowing it for you!

If you're a serious golfer, or if putting
is the part of the game you prefer, a
backyard green might be just the ticket
for hours of at-home pleasure. Installing
one is easier than you might expect, and
you can help to dispel the myth that
greens keeping requires dozens of harsh
chemicals by having the greenest green
in town using only my safe and sensible
tonics. Here's how to go about it:

STEP 1. Select a site that gets full sun
and has good air movement. Avoid any
low-lying areas.

STEP 2. Plan the size and shape of your
green, and prepare the soil for planting.
Contour the green for good drainage and
improve the soil with plenty of compost.

STEP 3. Choose a variety of creeping
bent grass that's adapted for your
region—ask at a few local golf clubs for
recommendations. Sow at the rate of ½

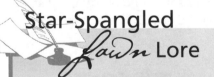

Star-Spangled
Lawn Lore

*In Annapolis, Maryland, croquet
teams from St. John's College and
the nearby U.S. Naval Academy
meet each spring to compete for
the Annapolis Cup. As of their
2004 meeting, the Johnnies had
bested the midshipmen in 18 out
of 22 contests.*

pound of seed per 1,000 square feet, and follow up with the care I recommend for newly planted lawns in Chapter 3.

STEP 4. Use a reel mower to cut the grass to about ¼ inch high two or three times per week. Water in the early morning and only when the grass shows signs of drought stress. Feed according to my easy-to-use program, described in Chapter 5. Top-dress with a thin layer of fine, screened compost in early May and late September, using a push broom to work the topdressing down into the turf.

STEP 5. Putt away! One advantage your natural green will have over a home putting green covered with artificial turf is that you can move the hole around to create all kinds of different situations. And that's a "hole" lot more fun!

BAREFOOT HORSES OPTIONAL

There's no need to worry about robbing ponies of their footwear when you want to include a friendly game of horseshoes in your picnic plans. Standardized "shoes," each weighing about 2½ pounds, are readily available for pitching at your favorite post. Many public parks offer horseshoe courts, but it's fun to be able to go into your own backyard after dinner to pitch horseshoes with the family on long summer evenings.

This is a game that pretty much everyone can play and enjoy, but it takes a bit of skill to be able to reliably pitch a "ringer." When I was a kid, I used to get a kick out of pitching horseshoes with my uncles and cousins at our Putt family reunions. It seemed like it was always the old guys who landed the most ringers, even when the younger generations appeared to have stronger arms. I guess that means I should be pretty good at horseshoes by now!

ORDER IN THE COURT

Having your own horseshoe "court" can be as simple as driving a couple of sturdy iron stakes into the ground 40 feet apart, leaving 15 inches sticking up above the surface to catch your shoes. But it won't take too many ringers to loosen those stakes, even if the belowground part extends 20 inches or so into the soil.

If you plan to pitch horseshoes on a regular basis, you'll save yourself some work and simplify lawn care around the stakes by setting up a more permanent playing area. Here's how:

STEP 1. Start with two 36-inch-long, 1-inch-diameter iron or steel stakes. Sink the end of each stake into a bucket of

concrete that will help to anchor it into the soil. Keep in mind that the smaller the bucket, the less digging you'll have to do to bury it!

STEP 2. Measure 40 feet between the spots where you want your horseshoe pits. One stake will go at each end of that 40-foot line in the center of a pit.

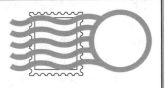

Dear Jerry,

I've heard that golfing and bird-watching are incompatible activities because all the chemicals used on golf courses are harmful to birds and other wildlife. I really enjoy golf; should I give it up to protest the damage it's causing to the environment?

A. *Absolutely not! In the past 10 or so years, golf courses around the globe have made dramatic strides toward good environmental stewardship—and golfers are enjoying spectacular wildlife sightings along with their 18 holes. While only a few courses can say their grounds are 100 percent organic, many course superintendents are working to wean their greens and fairways off of the most toxic chemicals, and to replace synthetic fertilizers with natural soil-building products. These aren't second-rate courses with patchy greens, by the way. Pebble Beach, the host course for the U.S. Open in 2000 and 2010 and the 2005 AT&T Pebble Beach National Pro-Am, is certified by Audubon International's Cooperative Sanctuary Program, as is New York's Bethpage State Park, site of the 2002 U.S. Open. Courses in Audubon International's program focus on environmental planning, wildlife and habitat management, integrated pest management, water conservation, and other good stuff. I wonder if any of them include "Tiger" on the list of wildlife you might see while playing a round?*

STEP 3. Remove the sod from an area roughly 3 feet by 4 feet around the point where the stake will stand. (Don't you dare let that sod go to waste! Use it to patch bare spots elsewhere in the yard or pile it root-side up in your compost bin.) Loosen the soil enough to let you dig down to bury the anchored end of the stake.

STEP 4. Set the concrete-enrobed stakes into the ground so they're 40 feet apart and leaning slightly toward each other (12 degrees from vertical, says the National Horseshoe Pitchers Association). Firm the soil in the pit so that 15 inches of each stake are aboveground. This is one place where compaction is a good thing—you want those stakes to stand firm for plenty of pitches.

STEP 5. If desired, add sand or clay (moist blue clay is what the pros use) around the stake. You can also frame the pit area with a border of rot-resistant timbers to keep sand, clay, or soil in place around the stake. And a wooden backboard behind each pit will save you from chasing errant horseshoes that go past the stake.

STEP 6. You can use pavers, chalk lines, or temporary markers to indicate the points to pitch from. According to official horseshoe rules, men should pitch from 37 feet away from the stake; women and kids from 27 feet. If these pitching points start to show wear and tear from

Star-Spangled Lawn Lore

In 1909, the first (albeit self-proclaimed) World Horseshoe Tournament took place in Bronson, Kansas, with 34 men tossing for top honors. Several decades and thousands of shoes later, 1,201 competitors, ranging in age from 6 to 86, pitched in the 80th Annual World Horseshoe Pitching Championships, held in 2004 in Pocatello, Idaho.

too many tosses, consider using pavers (or pouring concrete pads) to create a pitching platform behind each foul line.

Now fire up the grill, and get ready for your first neighborhood horseshoe tournament!

GET A REAL HOME-COURT ADVANTAGE

I always liked those "10SNE1" license plates favored by tennis devotees. But I have to tell you that, apart from the grass courts of The All England Lawn Tennis and Croquet Club where Wimbledon is played, lawn tennis is a bit of a myth. And, unless you have a full-time staff to tend the grounds like they do at the All England Club, it's unlikely that you'll have a grass court in your own yard. It's just not that practical (and tennis balls don't bounce nearly as well on grass as they do on other surfaces).

What is practical, however, is this: *If* you are one of those tennis devotees with the clever license plate and a hankering to play the sport any chance you get, and *if* you would rather play tennis than tend your tennis-court-size lawn, you should give serious consideration to paving your yard and installing a tennis court. Even if the initial installation of a tennis court is on the pricey side, maintenance is virtually nil once it's in. Plus, it can save you a bundle in club fees and in time and fuel spent traveling to places to play. If one of your kids or grandkids grows up to be the next big thing in competitive tennis because he or she had a handy court to play on, you'll recover your investment many times over. Don't get me wrong—I'm a lawn lover. But you might just like tennis more.

from the MAIL BAG

Dear Jerry,

My family loves all sorts of lawn games, but I'm tired of being a good sport about the grass stains they wear in from the backyard. Is there an easy way to get rid of this unwanted evidence of their athletic activities?

A. *When you're batting cleanup in the household laundry, grass stains can have anyone hollering "Foul!" Here's a sweet trick my Grandma Putt taught me for dealing with this turf, I mean, tough problem: Rub molasses into grass stains, and let the garments sit overnight. Wash with mild laundry soap (not detergent), and you'll find that the stains are as gone as a Barry Bonds homer.*

THE ORIGINAL KICK IN THE GRASS

I know soccer's not a true grass-court sport—the game that the rest of the world calls football is played on fields that may be as large as 130 yards by 100 yards. Even the smaller fields used for youth soccer range from 50 yards by 30 yards up to the minimum official field size of 100 yards by 50 yards. What I mean to say here is that unless your yard measures a lot more yards than average, you're probably not going to set up a regulation soccer field in it!

But the great thing about soccer is that a casual game takes nothing more than a ball and some open lawn to kick it around in. With a few everyday objects—empty cans, Dad's shoes, plastic nursery pots—to mark the goals, kids (as few as two, as many as two dozen) can have a first-class good time right there in the backyard. All that's required of your yard is turf that can stand up to the pitter-patter of running, kicking feet—most soccer fields only show wear around the goals, a condition you can combat by urging the soccer stars in your yard to move their goals from one game to the next. If you "fancy" things up by providing actual goals with nets, simply keep them portable and anchor them with sandbags during play.

Star-Spangled Lawn Lore

Of the 32 teams in the National Football League, only 11 play their home games on artificial turf (there are only 10 fields with artificial turf, however, because the New York Giants and Jets share a stadium). To keep the remaining 21 grass-clad fields in peak playing condition throughout the football season, stadium groundskeepers and designers go to all sorts of lengths. For example, a new stadium being built for the Arizona Cardinals will feature both a retractable roof and a movable field to make sure the turf gets the light it needs to grow.

VOLLEY AWAY!

Leaping. Spiking. Diving. Digging. Yep, it's been a few years since ol' Jerry has had the kind of vim and vigor it takes to play a lively game of volleyball. But I still think it's a top-notch sport for backyard athletes. From a groundskeeper's point of view, though, there are a few key points to preparing a lawn for volleyball:

• **Smooth it out.** Be rigorous about leveling the ground to get rid of high or low spots. Players who are looking up to see the ball coming toward them are at risk of tripping over uneven turf.

• **Give 'em room.** The leaping and diving that take place on the volleyball court often wind up off the court, so make sure there are no solid obstacles (like trees) for players to crash into immediately around the court.

• **Keep the lawn on the low side.** Turf experts at Michigan State University recommend mowing lower (1½ to 2½ inches) and more often (at least twice a week) to keep grass on playing fields dense and healthy. Researchers at Ohio

State University report that lower mowing heights prevent bunch grasses, such as tall fescue, from forming clumps that can trip players in any game that's played on grass.

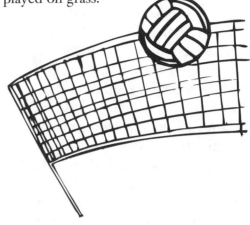

A Snappy Setup

If hitting a volleyball over the net sounds like more fun than hitting a stake for net setup, try this nifty trick:

STEP 1. Get two pieces of pipe, each about 1 foot long and just big enough around for the poles of your volleyball net to fit inside.

STEP 2. Plug up one end of each pipe. At the spots where you want the supporting poles for your net, drive the closed-up ends of the pipes into the ground so their tops are flush with—or slightly below—the soil surface.

STEP 3. When it's time for a game, setup's a breeze—just stretch out the net and slip the poles into the waiting pipes. If the net poles are a little loose within the pipes, stick in a few wooden shims around the poles to steady the net.

STEP 4. Takedown's easy, too, leaving your yard free for other activities when volleyball's not in session. Between games you can mow your volleyball court without a hitch—the pipes that hold the net rest snug in the soil, below the path of whirling mower blades.

⭐ Children at Play

Kids and yards seem like one of nature's perfect combinations. There's nothing like hearing the sound of children playing outdoors on a summer afternoon—especially if you're the parent who's just sent them out of the house! One of the primary purposes of our all-American lawns is to give our kids a safe place to play—close enough for Mom or Dad to keep an eye (or ear) on them, but far enough away to allow for games and adventures. It's undoubtedly the finest reason I can think of for having a well-planned play area in your backyard.

TERRIFIC TAKEOFFS

Backyards have launched literally millions of young imaginations. Your child can be a major league baseball player or the captain of a rocket ship without leaving the yard. As parents and grandparents, we should give those flights of fancy a place to soar while keeping their pilots suitably safe. Here are a few things to think about when you're planning a play site in your landscape:

• Make supervision easy, but unobtrusive. Locate play areas where you can see them through a window from inside the house, ideally from a room you're likely to watch from, such as the kitchen.

• Don't use herbicides and pesticides. Kids are the best reason to be organic in every way you can—their smaller bodies and faster metabolisms make them much more susceptible than adults to suffering ill effects from exposure to harmful chemicals.

• Skip the splinters. If you're thinking about a play structure with swings, slides, ladders, and more, take a look at the new setups made from recycled plastic. They're easy to clean, they don't need painting or staining, they don't become dangerous through decay, and they don't give kids splinters.

• Let 'em play. Give kids equipment for a few games and maybe a swing set to clamber over. But be careful of providing too much stuff to guide their activities, and leave plenty of space for their imaginations to run wild.

SOFT LANDINGS

For games on the ground, it's hard to beat grass as a playing surface. But when play moves even a few feet above terra firma, grass becomes less ideal. Sure, grass is better than paving around your backyard jungle gym, but even the cushiest turf feels pretty firm if you land on it from a few feet up. And mowing around kids' play structures is fiddly work that prolongs your lawn-care chores and puts your mower in close proximity to children at play—a risky recipe for injuries from blade-thrown sticks or rocks.

Instead of grass or concrete, pad the surfaces below and around swings, slides, and climbing structures with a thick, shock-absorbing layer of mulch. Wood chips, rubber chips made from recycled tires, and sawdust are a few favorites for topping the ground around the jungle gym. In addition to protecting your kids from harm, these mulches spare you from trying to tend turf in the tight spots under swings and slides. Whichever mulch you choose, put down a layer of heavy plastic or landscape fabric on the bare soil before you spread the mulch, to keep weeds from growing up between the chips.

Yankee Doodle Data

Mulch for Play Areas

Pad the ground beneath play structures with one of these marvelous mulch materials. Be sure to extend the mulched area around play equipment as well as under it.

MULCH MATERIAL	RECOMMENDED DEPTH (IN.)	ADDITIONAL INFO
Recycled tires	4–6	Springy surface for bouncy kids; comes in different colors; less depth needed than for other mulches for same amount of protection against falling injuries; pricier than other materials, but long-lasting
Wood chips	6–8	Fine- to medium-size chips are best for this use; can be a splinter source where kids play barefoot; relatively inexpensive and widely available; need to be replenished regularly
Sand	6–10	Can become compacted and hard; durable, inexpensive, and widely available
Pea gravel	6–12	Safer than solid paving or packed soil, but not the best cushioning material in a fall

★ Backyard Fun for Fido

Dogs benefit from fresh air and exercise just as we two-legged critters do, and they appreciate a regular chance to romp on the grass, too. If your family includes a four-legged friend of the canine type, you may want to set aside some yard space for Rover's enjoyment while protecting your lawn from doggone damage. Here's a whole litter of ideas to help you create a place that's darned near pooch perfect.

DELETE DOGGY DANGERS

If protecting your health and your family's is the No. 1 reason to avoid using toxic pesticides and herbicides on your lawn, then safeguarding your dog's health must run a very close second. Think about how much time your beloved pet spends in close contact with the grass, rolling in it, sleeping on it, even eating a few bites now and then. Treat your turf

Star-Spangled *Lawn* Lore

Dogs are part of the family in nearly 4 out of every 10 American households. That adds up to about 68 million canines across the country!

with my dog-safe tonics, and rest easy the next time you find Fifi enjoying a grass snack. Here are a few other things to leave out of a pooch play area:

Flower bulbs. Plant them elsewhere. Some bulbs (daffodils, autumn crocus) are poisonous, but that won't stop your dog from digging up these treasures and perhaps sampling them.

Old favorites. Toss out tired toys before they begin to fall apart and become a choking hazard.

Sticks and stones. Sharp sticks can poke a dog's mouth or eyes, and stones may damage her teeth. Use balls, Frisbees®, and other suitable toys for playing fetch.

Utilities. Keep garbage cans, compost bins, and recycling containers out of Skippy's reach. Dogs are curious and will work hard to get into anything that smells "yummy," even if it's really bad for them. Avoid temptingly chewy electrical wires and power cords, too.

FENCE 'EM IN

Even the most well-behaved dog will get the urge to run now and then, and it's all too easy for him to wind up in trouble: in the street, in a fight, or in your neighbor's prize-winning begonia patch. Whether you enclose your whole yard or just a section for Buster is up to you and your budget, but a nice-size enclosed area will give your pup room to stretch his legs even when you're not available for a walk.

CREATURE COMFORTS

Make sure your dog's outdoor area includes shelter, shade, and clean water, as well as room to roam. Well-fed pets can suffer from weight problems if they don't get enough exercise (just like their owners). Here's how to make the most of your pet zone:

• Daily walks and play sessions can help keep your pup (and you) in the pink, but household schedules sometimes cut into pet playtimes, so be sure your pet's area is well stocked with safe doggy toys for entertainment when you're not around.

• Create an area of soft, bare soil where your dog can exercise his urge to dig without disturbing your flowers.

• You can also make a doggy "workout" zone with low barriers and ramps for jumping and climbing, but check with your vet before you go whole dog...I mean, hog. Young dogs

Super★Secret

Plan for Your Pet's Potty

Looking at some dog owners' lawns, you can see why folks often name their pets "Spot". When your dog does her business on your grass, she's just doing what comes naturally. The resulting dead spots in the yard are not her fault. If you're planning a part of your yard specifically for dog habitation, plant urine-resistant fescue or perennial ryegrass and avoid urine-sensitive Bermuda grass or Kentucky bluegrass. Even then, you'll want to train your pet to use a "go-dog-go zone" that's as out of the way as possible, and follow my recommendations on page 212 for reviving grass that's suffering from too many doggy deposits.

can hurt themselves falling or jumping from even moderate heights.

• Install a pet-size pool. A kiddie pool filled with water is a perfect place for your dog to cool off on a hot summer's day. Toss in a few balls for a wet-and-wild game of fetch. Be sure to "lifeguard" small or short-legged dogs while they're in the water, and make sure they can safely jump out of the pool.

Way to Go, Scoopy Doo!

Super★Secret

Owning a dog means cleaning up after a dog, a responsibility that—thank heavens!—most pet owners take seriously. Still, solid-waste management rarely tops the list of pleasures people get from their canine companions. To make this task a less intrusive part of your daily dog-care routine, take a look at a nifty item called the Doggie Dooley™. This simple unit works like a mini–septic system, using a combination of enzymes and bacteria to break down dog deposits into liquid that's absorbed into the soil. Now that's a real scoop!

BEWARE OF BONES

Don't be a bonehead! (That means don't get hit in the head with a flying bone!) Before you mow any lawn areas where your dog hangs out, do a thorough reconnaissance to locate any balls, chew toys, and forgotten bones that could turn into dangerous projectiles when they meet up with a spinning mower blade.

KNICKKNACK, PADDYWHACK...

Mail your dog a bone! To be sure that you have doggy toys, brushes, and other pet-owner interaction items on hand when you take Sparky out for a romp on the lawn, turn a mailbox into on-the-scene storage. Simply mount the box in a spot near your usual puppy play site, and stock it with toys and tidbits for your faithful friend. Paint the mailbox brown or green if you'd like it to blend in with its surroundings. Or go to the other extreme and decorate it in bright colors. For fun, paint your dog's name on the side—and don't forget to deliver him a bone every now and then!

CHAPTER 15

A Lawn?
Who Needs It?!

Lawns—and lawn care—aren't for everyone. Even folks who enjoy grassy yards—and that means you—may have good reasons for reducing the total amount of turf in their landscapes. Whether you're looking to have a little less lawn, or no lawn at all, I've packed this chapter with acres of terrific turf alternatives, from ornamental grasses and groundcovers to meadows, water features, and paving.

☆ Limit Your Lawn

Here's a little secret I've saved clear until the last chapter: The key to having a great-looking yard is to have only as much lawn as you can take care of. If you frequently feel frustrated by the amount of time you're spending mowing, feeding, watering, and otherwise tending your turf, then you probably have too much of it. It's time to cut your grass down to size—and I don't mean with a mower!

TERRIFIC TURF TRADE-INS

Relax. Reducing the size of your lawn—or even eliminating it—doesn't mean you have to grin and "bare" it. Sure, paving your whole landscape can be an easy-care option, but there are plenty of absolutely fantastic alternatives to turf that don't involve a concrete mixer. For starters:

Consider an ornamental option.
There's a whole slew of spectacular ornamental grasses that are meant to be grown unmown. With lots of sizes, foliage colors, and species to choose from, it's easy to find one or more types of ornamental grass to suit your site. To get you started, see "Ornamental Grasses on the Job" on page 322.

Put in a problem-solver. Every landscape seems to have at least one or two places where lawn growing and mowing are downright difficult. Instead of tangling with turf in these tough places, fill them up with easy-growing groundcovers. Explore "Groundcovers Galore" (see page 325) to get a taste of the smorgasbord of available choices.

Grow natural. Meadow and prairie plantings offer a less-care kind of lawn that mixes native grasses and flowers into a casual combo that's great for informal landscapes. Meadow mowing is usually a once-a-year activity; the rest of the time you can enjoy watching the birds and butterflies visit your little patch of nature.

Get into bed(s). If you'd rather pamper peppers or cultivate carrots than spend your time playing the Lawn Ranger, why not swap some of that great big grass garden for a few (or several) raised beds?

Star-Spangled *Lawn* Lore

Way back when the buffalo roamed, North America featured one of the biggest "lawns" around—some 1.4 million square miles of native grasses and wildflowers that stretched from central Canada down to southern Texas and Mexico, and from Indiana to the Rocky Mountains. The rich soil that built up around the roots of all those prairie plants became the fertile farmland that feeds our country. Today, only 1 to 2 percent of the original prairie remains.

Don't worry if digging's not your thing—follow my instructions for building super soil sandwiches (see page 335) and you can make as many soft, fluffy garden beds as you need. No sod stripping or serious shovel work required!

Make a splash. Turn wet spots in your yard into bog gardens and save yourself the trouble of tugging your mower out of the mud. Or go whole hog and replace part of your lawn with a garden pond. There's quite a variety of aquatic plants and critters that'll turn your little water hole into your favorite garden spot. Or, for the ultimate water feature, replace the healthy exercise of mowing the yard with the healthy exercise of swimming—a swimming pool takes up a lot of space that you'll never have to mow again.

Just pave it. I don't mean your whole yard! But there are places where it just doesn't make sense to work hard at getting grass to grow. Use patios and other kinds of paving to create useful outdoor spaces where you and your family can relax, play, and picnic.

SHAPE UP YOUR SPACES

Start your lawn-reduction effort by getting rid of tight corners and hard-to-mow spaces. (Have another look at Chapter 7 if you need a refresher course on ways to make mowing easier.) Taking a few simple steps to decrease the time you spend mowing and trimming your turf might be just the ticket to increasing your satisfaction with the grassy areas you have left. Here's where to start:

★ Dig up individual plants in your yard and place them into mulched beds to eliminate elaborate mowing patterns and cut back on fussy trimmer work.

★ Shape borders and beds with gentle curves that make mowing a breeze.

★ If you have a substantial yard, divide it into "use" areas—patio, play space, vegetable gardens, and so forth. Leave broad, grassy (easy to mow) "pathways" in between to link the different parts of your landscape.

Grasses, Not Grass

I'm not talking about more green turf here, but rather grasses of the *ornamental* kind. Ornamental grasses make sense for spots in your yard where you're looking to replace lawn with something that requires less care. For example, instead of weekly mowings throughout the growing season, most of turf's taller kin are satisfied with an annual cutting. These plants can pack quite a punch in the looks department, too—use 'em in places where you want to increase the "wow" factor in your landscape. Stretch out your definition of grass to include the best nonturf types, and discover just how good your yard can look (and how easy it can be to care for)!

ORNAMENTAL GRASS CHOW

Give ornamental grasses a super start: Plant them in early spring in well-prepared planting holes along with a good helping of this hearty chow recipe. It's just what they need to really get growing!

2 lb. of dry oatmeal
2 lb. of crushed dry dog food
1 handful of human hair

Mix these ingredients in a bucket. Toss a handful of this mixture into each planting hole and work it into the soil. Set in the plants, backfill with soil, then scatter any leftover chow on top of the soil.

Yankee Doodle Data

Ornamental Grasses on the Job

Trade in your turf, and solve some of the tricky spots in
your yard, with these hard-working, good-looking ornamental grasses.

WHAT IT IS	HOW IT GROWS	WHERE IT GROWS BEST
Bowles' golden sedge (*Carex elata 'Aurea'*)	Clump-forming with narrow green-edged, golden leaves; grows in constantly wet sites; grows to 2 ft. tall	Shade, sun, moist soil; Zones 5–9*
Indian grass (*Sorghastrum nutans*)	Clump-forming with light green-to-blue foliage that turns orange in fall; long, feathery, reddish flower clusters in late summer; grows to 3 ft. tall with 6-ft. flower stalks	Sun, dry soil; warm season; Zones 4–9
Japanese silver grass (*Miscanthus sinensis*)	Clump-forming with silvery leaves that turn shades of red and yellow in fall; silver-to-purple flower plumes from midsummer into fall; grows to 3–5 ft. with flower stalks of 6–10 ft.	Sun, moist soil; warm season; Zones 5–9
Little bluestem (*Schizachyrium scoparium*)	Clump-forming with fine-textured leaves that turn bright, coppery orange in fall; spiky midsummer flowers; spreads readily by seeds; grows to 1 ft. tall with flower spikes up to 3 ft. tall	Sun, dry soil; warm season; Zones 3–10
Northern sea oats (*Chasmanthium latifolium*)	Clump-forming with light green foliage and oatlike seedheads; salt-tolerant; grows 2–3 ft. tall	Shade, sun; warm season; Zones 5–9
Quaking grass (*Briza media*)	Clump-forming with delicate flowers that shake in the breeze throughout the growing season; grows 1–2 ft. with 2–3 ft.-tall flower stalks	Shade, sun, moist soil; cool season; Zones 4–10
Ravenna grass (*Erianthus ravennae*)	Clump-forming with gray-green foliage that turns orange and purple in fall; early fall purple-tinted silvery flower spikes; 3–5 feet tall with 8–12 ft.-tall flower stalks	Sun, dry soil; warm season; Zones 5–10
Sideoats grama grass (*Bouteloua curtipendula*)	Clump-forming with narrow gray-green foliage and red-to-purple early summer flowers that hang on one side of the flower stems; grows to 2 ft. with flowers to 15 inches tall	Sun, dry soil; warm season; Zones 4–9

Ornamental Grasses on the Job

WHAT IT IS	HOW IT GROWS	WHERE IT GROWS BEST
Switch grass (*Panicum virgatum*)	Clump-forming with narrow, dark green foliage that turns buff in fall; pinkish midsummer flower clusters have brown fall color; grows to 3 ft. tall with flower stems 4–8 ft. tall	Sun, dry soil, moist soil; warm season; Zones 5–9
Tufted hair grass (*Deschampsia cespitosa*)	Airy flower clusters age from green to gold to bronze above narrow, dark green leaves; grows to 2 ft. tall with flowers to 3 ft. tall	Shade; cool season; Zones 4–9
Variegated hakone grass (*Hakonechloa macra 'Aureola'*)	Spreading with green-striped yellow leaves that resemble bamboo; grows 1½ to 2 ft. tall	Shade, moist soil; warm season; Zones 6–9
Woodrush (*Luzula sylvatica*)	Tufted spreader with fuzzy, grayish green foliage; often evergreen; creamy spring flower clusters; grows to 1 ft. tall with flower stalks to 2 ft. tall	Shade, dry soil, moist soil; Zones 4–9*

Sedges and rushes look a lot like grasses, but their growth patterns don't necessarily follow the cool-season/warm-season schedule.

MAKE THE MOST OF ORNAMENTALS

Perk up a plain part of your yard by replacing tired turf with showy ornamental grasses. Try these tips to put maximum pizzazz into your landscape:

★ Grow 'em in groups. Avoid the tufted look of one grass plant here, another over there—that makes more work, not less! Ornamental grasses are at their best in swaths of three or five (or more), so you can really appreciate their color and texture through the seasons.

★ Tuck perennials and flowering shrubs in around them. These grasses are stars in their own right, but they're also great backdrops for bright flowers.

★ Dress up difficult sites. These plants can be picture-pretty, but that doesn't mean they're too dainty to tackle tough conditions; see "Ornamental Grasses on the Job" (above and at left) for species to use where the growing gets tough.

★ Let the wind blow. Plant ornamental grasses in a spot where you can see—and hear—the wind rustling through their leaves. You might like their natural "music" better than your neighbor's 99-cent wind chimes!

★ Skip fall cleanup. Some ornamental grasses have seedheads that birds will dine on during the winter months; others just look pretty when glazed with ice or dusted with snow.

★ Make hay while the (spring) sun shines. In early spring, just as new growth is starting to appear, cut back last year's growth. It makes nice "hay" that you can chop up and use for mulch or add to your compost bin.

GIVE 'EM THE GROW-AHEAD

Launch your nonlawn grasses with some good ol' TLC, and they'll repay you with years of (almost) carefree good looks. Here's the step-by-step:

STEP 1. Prepare the soil, loosening it to about 6 inches deep and working in an ample inch of compost. Clear out any weeds that might compete unfairly with your grasses while they're just getting going.

STEP 2. Space according to height. For example, give a grass that'll grow 2 feet tall a similar leeway around it. If coverage is a real concern, you can tighten up the spacing a bit, but don't pack 'em too close or you'll wind up having to dig and divide to relieve overcrowding.

STEP 3. Set plants in the ground at the same depth as they grew in their pots or in the nursery. Aim to put the crown—where the leaves and roots meet—right at the soil surface. Add a handful of my Ornamental

RUST BLOCKER TONIC

Although they're mostly trouble-free, ornamental grasses can come under attack from rust, a disease that causes streaks of rusty orange on leaves and stems. Use this super solution to fend off the fungus and keep rust-prone plants green all summer long.

6 tbsp. of vegetable oil
2 tbsp. of baking powder
2 tbsp. of liquid kelp
1 gal. of water

Mix these ingredients in a bucket, and pour the solution into a hand-held sprayer. Shower your grasses with it one morning per week throughout the growing season.

Grass Chow (see page 321) to the soil in each planting hole.

STEP 4. Water the young plants thoroughly and tuck them in with an inch or two of mulch to keep moisture in and weeds out.

STEP 5. Water regularly during the first growing season, but hold off on further feedings that can make your grasses prey for problems.

WARM OR COOL?

Like their turf-type cousins, ornamental grasses can be split into cool-season and warm-season groups. That tells you when they do their best growing—and when they'll do less for your landscape during their dormant periods. Here's the scoop:

Cool customers, such as blue fescue (*Festuca glauca*), are often evergreen or semi-evergreen, and grow year-round in mild-winter climates. They tend to get growing early in the spring and usually flower before summer arrives. They may go dormant in the hot part of summer, then perk up and start growing again when cool weather returns in the fall.

Warm-weather winners, like Japanese silver grass (*Miscanthus sinensis*), start growing a little later in the spring, bloom in summer, and enter dormancy in the fall—often with a change in foliage color that mimics the changing leaves of deciduous trees.

★ Groundcovers Galore

Giving up on grass can be ever so easy when you discover just how many other fantastic plants you could be growing instead. The lawn alternatives are almost limitless, even for those trouble spots where the growing gets tough. Stop fretting over sparse turf, and get growing with plants that are perfectly suited to your specific site.

PUT GROUNDCOVERS TO WORK

I think it's clear that I'm mighty fond of lawns. But I'm not too stubborn to see the advantages of covering the ground—particularly in turf trouble spots—with low-growing, spreading perennials, vines, and shrubs, instead of good ol' grass. Gussy up your yard with groundcovers, and let them do more, while you do less. Here's the rundown:

Less trimming. Replace the turf under trees with shade-tolerant spreaders and put an end to tedious trimming around your tree trunks.

Less mowing. Grass needs mowing, but most other groundcovers don't. Blanket slopes and other hard-to-mow places with plants that you can let grow without a weekly "haircut."

Less weeding. A struggling lawn leaves plenty of room for weeds to move in—and leaves you to referee the resulting battle for root space. Give up on unhappy grass and let a more suitable groundcover crowd weeds right out of the picture.

Less raking. Groundcovers under trees will "absorb" a lot of leaves—they'll simply sift down to ground level where they'll feed the groundcover. No raking needed!

SPEED THEM TO SUCCESS

Give groundcovers what they need to succeed, and they'll take off like Seabiscuit out of the starting gate. Follow these steps to make sure that your plants get off to a strong start and grow quickly to fill in bare areas:

STEP 1. Do the math. Most groundcovers should be planted 6 to 10 inches apart. Measure the space you want to fill, and calculate how many plants you'll need per square foot. Don't skimp on plants, unless you're willing to wait longer for complete coverage.

STEP 2. Straight rows are a no-go. A diamond planting pattern will fill the space more efficiently.

STEP 3. Don't skip breakfast. Send plants off to the races with a hearty helping of my Groundcover Starter Chow (at right).

STEP 4. Set up the sprinkler. Even drought-tolerant plants need watering when they're getting started. Keep a close eye on newly installed plantings and make sure they get about an inch of water each week, whether from rain or your faucet.

STEP 5. Manage with mulch. Some spreaders may take up to three years to fill their new homes. In the meantime, cover bare ground between 'em with weed-blocking, soil-protecting mulch.

STEP 6. Yank weeds while they're young. Don't let pest plants get a roothold among your groundcovers. Pull out invaders before they have a chance to spread.

HOPE FOR SLOPES

There's no need to wrestle your mower uphill and down when you plant steep sites with soil-securing groundcovers. Leave grass on the (mostly) level areas,

Super ★ Secret

Divide and Conquer

Filling a sizable space with groundcovers can get pricey if you set out in the spring to buy enough plants to fill that area. So instead, do your shopping when temperatures are rising and plant prices are falling—you may find that you can cover a lot more ground for a lot less money. Look for bargains in mid- to late summer when garden centers are eager to reduce their stock and plants in pots are crowded and in need of division. You'll often find that you can afford twice as many containers and that you can then get two or three plants from each pot.

and let these no-mow spreaders handle the hills:

FOR SHADY SLOPES

Ajuga (*Ajuga reptans*)

Common periwinkle (*Vinca minor*)

English ivy (*Hedera helix*)

Japanese pachysandra
(*Pachysandra terminalis*)

Virginia creeper
(*Parthenocissus quinquefolia*)

Wintercreeper (*Euonymus fortunei*)

Yellow archangel (*Lamium galeobdolon*)

FOR SUNNY SLOPES

Creeping juniper (*Juniperus horizontalis*)

Goldmoss stonecrop (*Sedum acre*)

Moss phlox (*Phlox subulata*)

Mother of thyme (*Thymus serpyllum*)

St. John's wort (*Hypericum calycinum*)

Tawny daylily (*Hemerocallis fulva*)

Wintercreeper (*Euonymus fortunei*)

Woolly yarrow (*Achillea tomentosa*)

GOOD SCENTS

There's more to outdoor "aromatherapy" than flowers and fresh-cut grass! Herbal groundcovers make sense (and scents) in spots where you'll brush them or crush

BLUE PLATE SPECIAL

GROUNDCOVER STARTER CHOW

When you plant them in well-prepared soil, you can expect groundcovers to form a solid carpet in two to three years. Give them a smart start with a serving of my starter chow at planting time!

3 parts bonemeal

1 part Epsom salts

1 part gypsum

Mix these ingredients in a bucket. Place ½ cup in each planting hole, and spread another ½ cup on the soil surface to encourage groundcover expansion.

them, releasing their fragrance, as you walk through your yard. Here are four of my favorites—they're something to sniff at!

Bigroot cranesbill (*Geranium macrorrhizum*)

Mints (*Mentha*)

Roman chamomile (*Chamaemelum nobile*)

Thymes (*Thymus*)

WATCH OUT FOR GREEDY GROUND GRABBERS!

A word of caution about groundcovers: The very qualities that make them perfect for populating tough spots can turn them into real land hogs when the growing gets good. Now, almost any plant

Super★Secret

Slope Security

Even vigorous spreaders need a year or two to fill in before you can count on them to hold a hill against running water or strong winds. Before you put in the plants that will gradually grow into the job, cover a bare slope with an erosion mat, a layer of burlap, or heavy paper. Pin it down with stakes or "staples" made from wire clothes hangers, and cut holes through it for installing your groundcovers. The mat will protect the soil in between the young plants, slowly breaking down while the groundcover fills in and takes over the task of securing the slope.

that spreads as it grows has a tendency to creep into places where it's not wanted. Of course, there are plenty of sites where vigorous spreaders are welcome. Plants such as bishop's weed (*Aegopodium podagraria* 'Variegatum'), creeping Jenny (*Lysimachia nummularia*), crown vetch (*Coronilla varia*), mints, running bamboos, and 'Chameleon' houttuynia (*Houttuynia cordata* 'Chameleon') can prove very useful in difficult growing conditions, but can quickly grow from problem-solvers to plain old problems. If you use one in your yard, be prepared to pull out errant shoots or seedlings, and be warned—once a greedy ground grabber gets a grip, it can be devilishly difficult to get rid of.

Use these clues to help you sniff out aggressive spreaders before they set root in your yard:

★ Be wary of plants that have a reputation for growing "almost any-where." That's a sure sign that they're capable of growing *everywhere*, too.

★ Watch out for "weeds." If something is widely known as a weed, chances are that it is one.

★ Look gift plants in the roots. The creeping crawlers most likely to scramble out of control in your landscape are plants that spread by rhizomes and stolons. Watch out for friends and neighbors who have "plenty to share" of a particular groundcover—that's often code for a plant that's growing out of control in their yard.

Keep in mind that the list of plants that are considered to be invasive varies widely across North America. All sorts of growing conditions—such as high and low temperatures, rainfall and humidity, soil texture and pH—help determine whether a plant is a rampant rambler or a well-behaved soil saver. What's welcome in the landscapes of one region may be banned from the backyards of another. Check with your state Department of Natural Resources or the U.S. Department of Agriculture's regional office for your area to find out which plants are considered big no-nos where you live.

Star-Spangled Lawn Lore

Kudzu, "the vine that ate the South," might be described as a birthday present gone bad. It arrived in the United States back in 1876 as part of a garden exhibit by the Japanese government at the Centennial Exposition in Philadelphia. Later, it was grown as forage for livestock and was planted widely in the 1930s and 1940s for erosion control. In 1972, the USDA declared kudzu to be a weed, and for good reason—in ideal growing conditions, the vines can grow as much as 60 feet per year!

GROUNDCOVERS WITH FLOWER POWER

You can use flowering annuals, bulbs, or perennials to add sparkle to plain green groundcovers like English ivy or creeping juniper. Or you can choose groundcover plants that are beautiful bloomers in their own right. These flowers will brighten shady spots or spread blankets of color over sun-drenched slopes, while the leaves and roots will protect the soil from wind and rain:

- **Basket of gold** (*Aurinia saxatilis*): full sun, well-drained soil; Zones 4 to 8

- **Dalmatian bellflower** (*Campanula portenschlagiana*): full sun to light shade, well-drained soil; Zones 4 to 7

- **Dwarf Chinese astilbe** (*Astilbe chinensis* var. *pumila*): partial shade, moist soil; Zones 4 to 8

- **Evergreen candytuft** (*Iberis sempervirens*): full sun, well-drained soil; Zones 5 to 9

- **Goldenstar** (*Chrysogonum virginianum*): sun to partial shade, moist soil; Zones 5 to 8

- **Heather** (*Calluna vulgaris*): full sun, well-drained soil; Zones 5 to 7

- **Leadwort** (*Ceratostigma plumbaginoides*): full sun to light shade, well-drained soil; Zones 6 to 9

- **Lily-of-the-valley** (*Convallaria majalis*): full sun to deep shade, moist soil; Zones 2 to 7

- **Moss phlox** (*Phlox subulata*): full sun to partial shade, well-drained soil; Zones 3 to 8

- **Prostrate speedwell** (*Veronica prostrata*): full sun to light shade, well-drained soil; Zones 5 to 8

- **Showy sundrops** (*Oenothera speciosa*): full sun, well-drained soil; Zones 5 to 8

- **Shrubby cinquefoil** (*Potentilla fruticosa*): full sun, well-drained soil; Zones 3 to 7

JUST DESSERTS TONIC

Perk up groundcovers with a midsummer serving of this tonic. It will keep their flowers and foliage looking fine right on into fall.

4 tbsp. of hydrogen peroxide

1 tbsp. of Epsom salts

1 tbsp. of baking powder

1 tbsp. of ammonia

½ tsp. of unflavored gelatin

½ tsp. of dishwashing liquid

4 multivitamin tablets with iron, dissolved in 1 cup of hot water

1 gal. of rainwater or filtered water

Mix the peroxide, Epsom salts, baking powder, ammonia, gelatin, dishwashing liquid, and dissolved vitamins in a bucket. Mix 1 cup of this liquid with the rainwater or filtered water, and treat your plants liberally with the mixture.

- **Spotted deadnettle** (*Lamium maculatum*): Partial to deep shade, moist to dry soil; Zones 4 to 8

- **Spring heath** (*Erica carnea*): full sun to light shade, well-drained soil; Zones 5 to 7

THEY'RE THE BERRIES

Flowers aren't the only way to get more color out of your groundcovers. Try one—or more—of these low-growing berry bearers and enjoy the bright fruits that follow the flowers. Some are attractive to birds and other wildlife; others are just plain attractive. And a few produce berries that you and your family can eat—if you get to them before the critters do!

Bearberry (*Arctostaphylos uva-ursi*)

Cranberry (*Vaccinium macrocarpon*)

Lingonberry (*Vaccinium vitis-idaea* var. *minus*)

Lowbush blueberry (*Vaccinium angustifolium*)

Partridgeberry (*Mitchella repens*)

Rockspray cotoneaster (*Cotoneaster horizontalis*)

Strawberries (*Fragaria*)

Wintergreen (*Gaultheria procumbens*)

TWELVE FOR UNDER TREES

The combination of shade and dry soil beneath trees is a double whammy that spells serious trouble for lawn grasses and many other landscape plants. Instead of struggling along with patchy turf and puny perennials, try out one or more of this durable dozen—groundcovers that can survive and thrive in low light amid thirsty tree roots:

Ajuga (*Ajuga*)

Common periwinkle (*Vinca minor*)

Epimedium (*Epimedium*)

Hostas (*Hosta*)

Japanese pachysandra (*Pachysandra terminalis*)

Lilyturf (*Liriope spicata*)

Spotted deadnettle (*Lamium maculatum*)

Sweet violet (*Viola odorata*)

Sweet woodruff (*Galium odoratum*)

Variegated hakone grass (*Hakonechloa macra* 'Aureola')

Wild gingers (*Asarum*)

Wintercreeper (*Euonymus fortunei*)

Star-Spangled *Lawn* Lore

Lucky New Englanders don't have to plant lowbush blueberries in their yards to enjoy the flavor of these tasty natives—the pretty shrubs grow wild across much of the northeastern United States. Still, lowbush blueberries make a handsome groundcover in almost any landscape, producing white spring flowers, sweet fruits, and glossy green foliage that turns rich red in the fall.

FRONDS YOU CAN RELY ON

Don't be fooled by the delicate appearance of most ferns. Hiding behind those lacy looks are some surprisingly sturdy plants. Looking to fill in a shady site where grass can't get a grip? Shade-loving ferns may be just what you need. (Some of them will fill a sunny, damp location, too.) Here are five ferns to consider for light-challenged spaces in your landscape. Perhaps one of them will become your new best frond!

★ **Christmas fern** (*Polystichum acrostichoides*): prefers shade and moist soil; dark green evergreen fronds reach 10 to 20 inches tall; Zones 3 to 9

★ **Hay-scented fern** (*Dennstaedtia punctiloba*): tolerates dry soil in sun or shade; invasive in good growing conditions; 15 inches tall; Zones 3 to 8

★ **Japanese painted fern** (*Athyrium niponicum* 'Pictum'): gray-green leaves with deep red stems in shade and moist soil; 14 inches tall; Zones 3 to 8

★ **Ostrich fern** (*Matteuccia struthiopteris*): sun or shade in moist, rich soil; to 6 feet tall; Zones 2 to 8

★ **Royal fern** (*Osmunda regalis*): good for wet soil in sun or light shade; will grow in shallow water; 2 to 6 feet tall; Zones 3 to 9

TIPTOE UNDER THE TREES

Take it easy on your trees when you start planting in the ground beneath their branches. Use a small spade to locate "pockets" of soil and tuck your plants into those, instead of slicing through your tree's support system. If you run into a real riot of roots, consider brightening that area with shade-tolerant potted annuals like begonias, coleus, and impatiens.

MAKE SOME MOSS MAGIC

Some folks think moss is a nuisance—and if you're in that camp, you'll want to take a look at my Moss Buster Brew back in Chapter 11 (see page 255). But moss has its place in some landscapes, particularly where grass won't take hold in damp, shady sites with acidic soil. That's just what moss loves best, and it grows in those spots when almost nothing else will (except some ferns, which offer an excellent upright contrast to moss's low mounds).

Growing moss really boils down to having the right conditions, like those I've described here, and having a bit of moss to start with. Mix up a blenderful of my Moss-Grow Tonic (above) and dab your way to mossy magic. While your moss is getting started, cover it with a lightweight plastic mesh net to keep birds and squirrels from digging it up. Keep that netting handy in the fall and use it to catch leaves before they

MOSS-GROW TONIC

Nothing gives a lawn that relaxed, old-time feeling like a little moss. Here's an easy recipe for making that green cushion grow along a stone wall, between the roots of a big ol' tree, or between stones in a pathway.

½ qt. of buttermilk
1 cup of moss
1 tsp. of corn syrup

Mix these ingredients in an old blender, then dab the mixture onto the ground where you want to encourage moss. Once it's growing, keep it in good health by "watering" it with plain buttermilk every few weeks.

mat down over the moss—lifting trapped leaves off is much easier on the moss than raking.

WHERE IT'S WET

There's no sense trying to mow through a mud bog every week— or more often, since grasses tend to grow lush and lanky in soggy spots. There are plenty of fine plants to fill low-lying damp locations that will save you the trouble of putting pontoons on your mower. Here are my picks:

GROUNDCOVERS

Creeping Jenny (*Lysimachia nummularia* 'Aurea')

Dwarf Chinese astilbe (*Astilbe chinensis* var. *pumila*)

Japanese primrose (*Primula japonica*)

Lady's mantle (*Alchemilla mollis*)

Rushes (*Juncus*)

Sedges (*Carex*)

PERENNIALS

Blue flag (*Iris versicolor*)

Butterbur (*Petasites japonicus*)

Cardinal flower (*Lobelia cardinalis*)

Goatsbeard (*Aruncus dioicus*)

Goldenstar (*Chrysogonum virginianum*)

Hostas (*Hosta*)

Marsh marigold (*Caltha palustris*)

Meadow rue (*Thalictrum rochebruneanum*)

Siberian iris (*Iris sibirica*)

Turtlehead (*Chelone lyonii*)

SHRUBS AND TREES

Red maple (*Acer rubrum*)

Red-osier dogwood (*Cornus stolonifera*)

River birch (*Betula nigra*)

Willows (*Salix* spp.)

Winterberry (*Ilex verticillata*)

ON THE DRY SIDE

Lawn tending is a bit easier in dry soil than in wet, since it's generally easier to add water than to remove it. But turf suffers in sites that are consistently sunny and dry, and applying water to keep it growing takes time and costs money. Look for replacement plants, with water-conserving features like these that make them masters of minimal moisture management:

★ Fuzzy foliage

★ Narrow leaves

★ Thick, fleshy leaves and stems

★ White or silvery leaves

Here are some sturdy spreaders that can help solve sunny, thirsty sites in your yard:

Beach wormwood (*Artemisia stelleriana*)

Lamb's ears (*Stachys byzantina*)

Lavender cotton (*Santolina chamaecyparissus*)

Prickly pear (*Opuntia compressa*)

Rock rose (*Helianthemum nummularium*)

Sedums and stonecrops (*Sedum*)

Snow-in-summer (*Cerastium tomentosum*)

☆ Magnificent Meadows and Beds

Replacing lawn grass with a combination of native grasses and bright wildflowers is a top-notch way to cut back on mowing, watering, and fertilizing, but it won't eliminate those tasks. New gardens, even natural-looking ones, are like new babies—they need lots of care at the start, and they gradually become more self-sufficient as they grow. Fortunately, meadows grow up quicker than children do—and you won't have to send your meadow to college! In addition to meadows, you can swap turf for beds filled with your favorite vegetables, fruits, and herbs to further decrease those mowing and grass-tending chores.

STEP INTO YOUR MEADOW

The best meadows look like they were planted by Mother Nature herself. But a landscape version takes a fair amount of planning and preparation to turn it into a pretty-as-a-picture planting while keeping it from becoming a weedy vacant-lot mess along the way. Follow these steps to beautiful meadow-making:

STEP 1. Check local zoning laws regarding landscape maintenance. Many towns have what they call "weed ordinances" that require property owners to keep their lawns mowed. If your meadow is considered a violation of such laws, you could be fined and/or charged for having a city crew come to mow your meadow. Talk to your neighbors, too, to make sure they're not unpleasantly surprised by your "relaxed" landscape look.

STEP 2. Know what to grow. Seek local information on grasses and wildflowers that are native to your neck of the woods. Your local Cooperative Extension office is a good place to start.

STEP 3. Prepare the soil. Remove weeds and smother existing sod or strip it away. Add 1 to 2 inches of compost and mix it into the top inch of soil. This is where you'll realize that it's helpful to start small—you can always expand later if you like how it looks.

STEP 4. Plant in late summer to late fall. Give perennial plants time to settle in before cold weather arrives; sow seeds of grasses later for spring sprouting. Mulch in early winter to prevent heaving.

STEP 5. Provide ongoing care. Keep the planting weeded and watered while your plants get established. Learn to tell the difference between your wildflowers and meadow grasses, and weeds. Get a scythe and learn how to use it—your meadow will need occasional cutbacks and most rotary mowers are well below the desired height of about 6 inches for those first cuttings.

Beware the Meadow Mix!

Don't be tempted by those pre-mixed seed combos in a can that you see on sale now and then. You might get something that looks like the colorful picture on the label—for the first year. After that, most of the annual flowers that make up the bulk of such mixtures will be gone, and weeds will begin to colonize the bare space that's left behind. Grandma Putt always told me that if a thing looks too good to be true, it probably is. To which I'll add, "If you really could buy a meadow in a can, a lot more folks would have one!"

START BUILDING SANDWICHES

I'm usually in favor of anything that starts with making a sandwich. But this one's for your garden, so you can eventually have slices of tomatoes, cucumbers, peppers, radishes, and whatever else you love on your own sandwiches. For best results, start a whole season ahead of when you want to plant your garden. Here's what you do (remember—no digging!):

1 Mark out the space where your garden will be. For prime vegetable growing, choose a spot that gets at least six hours of sun each day. If you have big plans for plenty of produce, lay out several small beds—5 feet by 10 to 20 feet is a nice size—instead of one large garden. Your soil will stay softer and weeds will be less of a problem if you don't walk on your beds, and a 5-foot width will let you work from either side without setting foot on the soil.

2 Use a garden fork—or a long metal rod and a hammer—to poke holes into the soil where your bed will be. This is only necessary if the ground's really hard, but it's a big help to the earthworms if that's the case.

3 Cover the bed with 1 to 2 inches of newspapers, overlapping their edges and tamping down any tall weeds in the way. Give the papers a thorough soaking with water.

4 Top the newspaper layer with 1 to 2 inches of compost, then cover that with about 6 inches of any organic matter you have on hand: leaves, grass clippings, shredded paper, sawdust, and so on.

5 Now add more layers, alternating between compost and other organic materials until your "sandwich" is 1 to 2 feet high.

6 Soak the whole heap with my Super Soil Sandwich Dressing (see page 53), and leave it to "cook" until the

following spring, when you'll find a rich, loose planting bed that's about 6 to 8 inches deep and ready for action. If you can't wait until next spring to get started, make your top layer a 50-50 mixture of topsoil and compost, douse it with Super Soil Sandwich Dressing as before, and let it rest for two weeks before planting.

7 Add transplants and/or seeds, and mulch with screened compost or other fine organic matter.

Maybe I was hungry when I started to tell you about building "soil sandwiches," but I want to make it clear that they're not just for growing edibles. You can build beautiful perennial borders, plant tall trees for future generations to enjoy, or mix up a colorful collection of flowering shrubs—just about any kind of plant you want to grow will gladly sink its roots into this garden-growing goodness.

GIVE YOUR BEDS A RAISE

One advantage of my super soil sandwiches is the good drainage they provide to keep your gardens healthy. Their height, even after they've "cooked down" to 6 or 8 inches, makes them just right for raised beds. You can enjoy them "as is," or add frames to keep all that rich garden goodness in place and to give your gardens a more orderly look.

If your vegetable garden holds a highly visible spot in your yard, framing your beds can help to make it pretty and productive. Be sure to leave wide pathways between the beds so you can get your cart or wheelbarrow where it's needed. Topping the paths with wood chips or other mulch material saves you from mowing them, and lets you walk into the garden even on wet days to pick a ripe tomato for the salad.

Super ★ Secret

On-the-Spot Compost

Framing your soil sandwiches makes it extra-easy to add fresh layers from year to year. In the fall, I like to use a piece of garden fencing to make a temporary compost pen on top of my raised garden bed. I fill it with fall leaves and other tasty tidbits, then top it with an inch of compost and a healthy helping of Super Soil Sandwich Dressing (see page 53) before the snow flies. By spring, it's all decomposed into rich soil for my garden, and it's right where I need it!

PLANT SOME PRETTY PRODUCE

I hope by now you've figured out that your vegetable garden doesn't have to look like a smaller version of a farmer's field, with long, straight (ho-hum) rows and bare soil in between. On the contrary, attractive kitchen gardens are all the rage these days, packed with veggies, herbs, and flowers to create

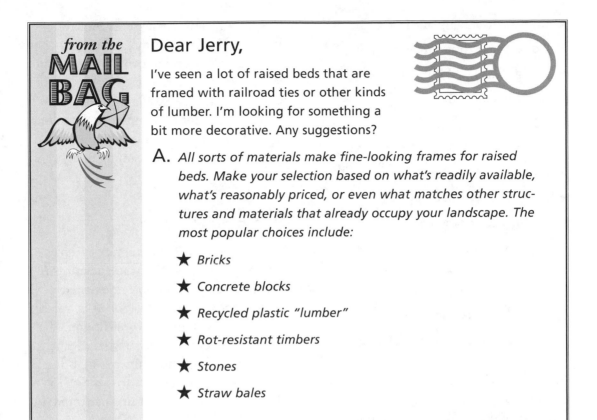

from the
MAIL BAG

Dear Jerry,

I've seen a lot of raised beds that are framed with railroad ties or other kinds of lumber. I'm looking for something a bit more decorative. Any suggestions?

A. *All sorts of materials make fine-looking frames for raised beds. Make your selection based on what's readily available, what's reasonably priced, or even what matches other structures and materials that already occupy your landscape. The most popular choices include:*

★ *Bricks*

★ *Concrete blocks*

★ *Recycled plastic "lumber"*

★ *Rot-resistant timbers*

★ *Stones*

★ *Straw bales*

plantings that please the eye and the stomach. Instead of tucking them off in a corner of the backyard, out of sight (and, too often, out of mind), these good-enough-to-eat gardens usually grow front-and-center, near the house where folks can see 'em and get to 'em quickly to gather fresh ingredients for every meal.

The key to creating a kitchen garden that looks as good as its harvest tastes is mixing up a pretty collection of herbs and vegetables, tucking in some bright (and maybe edible) flowers, and keeping the whole thing healthy. To make the beds even brighter, you can fill them with vegetables that are known for their ornamental qualities. Don't worry, they taste good, too! Here are just a few to get your mouth watering:

- 'Gold Mine' beans
- 'Purple King' beans
- Scarlet runner beans
- 'Bull's Blood' beets
- 'Bright Lights' chard
- 'Ruby' chard
- 'SuperSweet 100' cherry tomatoes
- 'Little Fingers' eggplant

- ★ 'Rosa Bianca' eggplant
- ★ 'Copacabana' hot peppers
- ★ 'Hungarian Wax' hot peppers
- ★ 'Red Russian' kale
- ★ 'Red Salad Bowl' lettuce
- ★ 'Red Velvet' okra
- ★ 'Jingle Bells' peppers
- ★ 'Orangetti' spaghetti squash
- ★ 'Yellow Pear' tomatoes
- ★ 'Goldrush' zucchini

How About a Liquid Lawn?

Solving a soggy place in your yard can mean giving up on the lawn and making the most of the moisture. From bog gardens to ponds, water features can add sparkle and splash to any landscape. Wildlife and birds will come to visit—and often to stay—where there's fresh water, particularly if your garden includes a fountain or other moving water. People like the sounds, too—they're very relaxing at the end of a busy summer day.

WATER SAFETY

Birds and four-legged creatures aren't the only ones who find water features of all sizes attractive. People, particularly youngsters, will want to look at it, splash in it, maybe even wade or swim in it. If kids are a likely part of your landscape, consider adding water in ways that don't put anyone in danger of drowning. To play it safe, keep a few things in mind:

Think shallow. It takes only a few inches of water to create a drowning hazard for a toddler. But a thin film of water, pumped over stone or masonry and circulated from a hidden reservoir, creates a delightful water feature that's safe and beautiful.

Think of ways to keep kids out. Make a small garden pond safe by laying sturdy wire mesh—strong enough to support a child's weight—just beneath the

Super ★ Secret

Stop the Skeeters!

Avoiding itchy bites seems like enough reason to wage war on pesky mosquitoes, but it's also important to reduce the risk of the diseases they can deliver. These pests prefer to lay their eggs in still water, so a pump or fountain is a good way to block the bite. For nonflowing water gardens, use mosquito "dunks"—compressed cakes that contain a people-, plant-, and pet-safe biological control, *Bacillus thuringiensis* var. *israelensis* (also called Bti), that spells doom specifically for mosquito larvae.

surface of the water. You won't be able to see it, and kids won't be able to fall through it.

Think fencing. Large garden ponds and swimming pools require extra steps to keep them secure. Even if someone enters your pond or pool without your permission, you may be held responsible if they're injured. A sturdy fence with a locking gate is almost a necessity for a swimming pool; you can further protect yourself and others with a floating alarm device that sounds whenever an object (or person) falls into the water. Likewise, a big water garden might make a back-yard fence necessary to protect uninvited visitors from themselves—and you from unwelcome lawsuits.

PRACTICAL POOLSIDE PLANTING

A swimming pool is undoubt-edly a great way to eliminate a large amount of lawn. And splashing (or floating peace-fully) in a pool on a summer afternoon is much more appealing than pushing a mower! The nicest pools fit into the landscape, instead of looking like they were plopped in with no connec-tion to their surroundings. Although you'll want to include a fence for security

purposes, adding plants makes a dandy distraction from drab fencing and dresses up the pool area. Here are a few hints for choosing and using poolside plants:

- Use tall plants around the pool area to provide privacy and to reduce breezes that chill swimmers and increase evaporation of the pool water. Evergreens and tall ornamental grasses make super screens.

- Choose plants that can tolerate the reflected heat and light from the water and paved surface around it. Seaside natives are good choices, and they are also more tolerant of the chemical treatments common in pool water (in case they get splashed).

- Plant flowering vines like morning glories or trumpet creeper *(Campsis radicans)* where they can clamber over the outside of the fence, brightening it with their blooms.

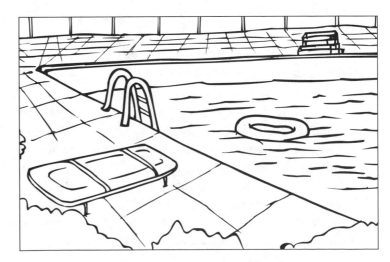

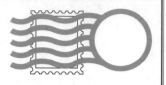

Dear Jerry,

Every fall, my garden pond collects loads of leaves that clog up the pump, gunk up the water, and generally create a lot of extra work. I don't want to get rid of the trees or the pond, but I'm tired of wading in cold water each autumn to clean up this mess. What should I do?

A. *Put away your chainsaw! There's a much simpler solution to your fall frustrations: black plastic netting. Just before the leaves begin to drop, stretch a layer of mesh over the top of your pond, securing it so it doesn't sink down into the water. From a distance, the net will be completely invisible—it won't even show much when you're up close. When the mesh gets covered with leaves, lift it off and empty the leaves into your compost bin, then put the mesh back in place to collect more falling foliage.*

• Stick with man-made shade. Deciduous trees near swimming pools—or any other water gardens—spell work. Skimming fallen leaves out of the pool is not nearly as much fun as swimming in it. Keep leaf-shedding plants away from the pool and use tall screening plants to trap leaves that might blow in from other parts of the yard.

• Make it a fruit-free zone, too. Keep fruiting plants at a distance from the pool to avoid attracting yellow jackets and other stinging insects to your pool party.

No Mo' Mowing

If, at the end of the day, there are places in your landscape that you don't want to mow, water, weed, fertilize, or cultivate in any way, then you might as well pave them. Grass, of course, has its uses in the yard—it filters the water that flows through it and cleans the air, while paving does neither of those things. A whole yard of nothing but hardscape is not what most folks are thinking of when they consider a lawn-reduction plan, but paved surfaces certainly have their place in a less-grass (not grassless) lawn.

WHERE TO PAVE

By paving, I mean a whole slew of surface treatments from gravel and bricks to wooden decking and concrete, plus everything in between. Chosen with care and properly installed, paving materials enhance and complement your landscape while reducing your lawn-care chores. I don't recommend paving the whole thing—hey, I told you I'm a lawn lover. But there are places where paving makes more sense than grass:

Where you walk the walk. High-traffic areas are the first places to look at when you're thinking about trading in grass for something sturdier. Compacted soil and constant crushing take a heavy toll on even the sturdiest turf.

Select surfaces and sizes that match the type of traffic each walkway handles (see "Plan the Span" below).

Where you talk the talk. Outdoor entertaining spaces are the next logical location for paved surfaces in your yard. A smooth concrete patio or a sturdy deck eliminates everything from uneven lawn chairs and picnic tables to spilled salads and dropped drinks. Use container plants around the deck or patio to soften hard edges and connect it to your landscape.

Where you trim. Replace grass that's growing snug against the edges of beds and borders with mowing strips, rims of paving that let you mow around a planting instead of treating it with your trimmer.

Yankee Doodle Data

Plan the Span

When you're thinking about pathways, it pays to think about who'll use them, how they'll use them, and where they lead to. Each factor matters in determining the best material for making the path, as well as its width.

PATH PURPOSE	BEST SURFACE	WIDTH (FT.)
Strolling in landscape	Bark mulch, gravel, pebbles, stepping stones	1½ to 2
Passage for carts or mowers	Bricks, interlocking pavers, wooden decking	At least 3
Walkway to front entrance	Bricks, concrete, mortared stone	At least 4

Grab the Right Gloves

Sturdy gloves are essential to protect your hands from the abrasive surfaces of bricks, preformed pavers, or flagstones. A short session of putting down paving can leave you with sore fingers and scraped knuckles if you decide to work bare-handed. And not just any gloves will do the job, either! I learned this lesson the hard way when I destroyed a pair of good leather gardening gloves while installing a flagstone path. They seemed durable enough to me, but I didn't work very long before the sharp edges of the stones had worn holes in some of the fingertips of both gloves. So take it from me, be sure you have two pairs of gloves: one pair for gardening, and a heavy pair of work gloves with reinforced fingertips for projects like paving and other hardworking hand tasks.

Where things get hot. A pad of interlocking pavers or poured concrete keeps a hot grill on an even keel and reduces the fire hazard posed by hot sparks on dry grass.

Wherever smooth moves matter. Whether it's the path you take with your bags full of groceries or the route you usually follow with an armload of firewood, paving makes sense anyplace where secure footing is important.

PERFECT PAVING PUT-DOWNS

Because walkways and patios are meant to be permanent parts of your landscape, it pays to do the job of installation right. Before you lift a single brick or move the first flagstone, mark off and measure the area you plan to pave. Make sure you have enough bricks, pavers, or flagstones to fill your space. Then follow these steps:

STEP 1. Remove the sod. Use it to patch bare places in your yard, or stack it root-side up for composting.

STEP 2. Excavate the area to a depth of at least 4 inches, depending on the thickness of your paving material and how well your soil drains. (You'll need to go deeper if you have thick pavers and/or heavy soil.) Good drainage is essential to keep your paving from becoming icy in winter and to protect it from heaving caused by freezing and thawing. Use the soil you've removed to serve as layers in your compost pile, to build up raised garden beds, or to fill in low spots in your lawn.

STEP 3. Add a 2-inch layer of crushed stone and tamp it down firmly. Make this layer deeper if poor drainage is a concern.

STEP 4. Lay landscape fabric over the crushed stone to prevent weeds from growing up through the paving.

STEP 5. Add a 1-inch layer of rock dust or coarse sand.

STEP 6. Install your pavers, maintaining a slight slope ($\frac{1}{4}$ inch per 2 feet of width) to let water drain off the surface. Use a carpenter's level and a two-by-four to check the slope as you work and to make sure none of your pavers sticks up above the others.

STEP 7. Sweep coarse sand (also called sharp or builder's sand) into the joints after you're finished.

BABY YOUR BRICKS

While a brick walkway or a flagstone patio needs a whole lot less attention than a similar amount of turf, these surfaces aren't completely care-free. The good news is that a little maintenance goes a long way toward keeping paved places smooth, safe, and looking their best. Here's what you need to know:

★ Water is paving's biggest enemy. You can dip bricks into a waterproofing solution before you place them, or apply a coating of sealant over mortared bricks, stones, or pavers.

★ Did you ever think about mulching your paver paths? It's not as crazy as it sounds! If heaving bricks are a problem because of winter freezes and thaws, top walkways with a 6-inch mulch of hay or straw after the ground freezes. You can walk on the mulch over the winter months, then rake it up in the spring to add to your compost pile.

★ Watch for weeds. Don't let plant pests get their roots in between your pavers. As soon as you spot an unwelcome sprout, use a garden knife or similar tool to scrape it right out of there, before it begins pushing up paving or crowding out the desirable plants you're growing in the path.

Jerry's Blue Plate Specials

By now, you've heard me say over and over again that my Blue Plate Specials can make you a true-blue, All-American lawn-care hero. In this section, I've collected all those recipes in one handy place. So whether you want to whip up a hearty meal for your lawn, march into battle against pesky pests and dastardly diseases, or hold the line against Mother Nature's shenanigans, you'll find all the ammunition you need right here!

AERATION TONIC

This fabulous formula will help prevent soil compaction, so water, nutrients, and oxygen can penetrate deep into the turf.

> **1 cup of dishwashing liquid**
> **1 cup of beer**

Combine these ingredients in a 20 gallon hose-end sprayer, and fill the balance of the sprayer jar with warm water. Just before you aerate, spray your lawn to the point of run-off. From then on, spray once a month throughout the growing season to help keep the soil loose and fluffy. (For related text, see page 95.)

ALL-PURPOSE PERENNIAL FERTILIZER

Herbicides sprayed on lawns or along roadsides often drift onto perennial flower beds—with ugly results. But this health-giving snack will put your blooms on the fast track to a full recovery.

> **3 parts bonemeal**
> **3 parts greensand or wood ashes**
> **1 part bloodmeal**

Mix these ingredients in a bucket or wheelbarrow. Then, after you've clipped off the affected foliage, scatter 2 tablespoons of the mix around each clump of perennials, and scratch it lightly into the soil with a garden fork. (For related text, see page 297.)

ALL-PURPOSE PEST PREVENTION POTION

Skunks and just about any other critters I can think of will run away when they get a whiff of this strong tonic.

> **1 cup of ammonia**
> **½ cup of urine**
> **½ cup of dishwashing liquid**
> **¼ cup of castor oil**

Mix all of these ingredients in a 20 gallon hose-end sprayer. Then, thoroughly saturate the places where you don't want the little varmints venturing. (For related text, see page 217.)

ALL-SEASON CLEAN-UP TONIC

This is the one tonic that you absolutely need to use religiously throughout the growing season. The shampoo cleans the plants and helps the other ingredients stick better; the mouthwash kills bad bacteria and discourages insects; and the tobacco tea contains nicotine, which does a double whammy on those pesky pests.

> **1 cup of baby shampoo**
> **1 cup of antiseptic mouthwash**
> **1 cup of tobacco tea***

Mix these ingredients in a 20 gallon hose-end sprayer, and give everything in your yard a good shower every two weeks in the early evening throughout the growing season. You'll have the healthiest yard in town—guaranteed! (For related text, see page 218.)

*To make tobacco tea, place half a handful of chewing tobacco in an old nylon stocking and soak it in a gallon of hot water until the mixture is dark brown. Pour the liquid into a glass container with a tight lid for storage.

ALL-SEASON GREEN-UP TONIC

This tonic will get your newly sodded lawn off to a sensational start—and supercharge the rest of your green scene.

> **1 can of beer**
> **1 cup of ammonia**
> **½ cup of dishwashing liquid**
> **½ cup of liquid lawn food**
> **½ cup of molasses or corn syrup**

Mix all of these ingredients together in a large bucket, and pour the mixture into a 20 gallon hose-end sprayer. Then spray your lawn (and every other green, growing thing in your yard) to the point of run-off every three weeks throughout the growing season. (For related text, see page 85.)

ANNUAL FLOWER FEEDER TONIC

When your annuals have a run-in with drifting herbicides, remove the affected plant parts and water well. Then, to get them back in shape fast, serve this powerful potion.

> **1 can of beer**
> **2 tbsp. of fish emulsion**
> **2 tbsp. of dishwashing liquid**
> **2 tbsp. of ammonia**
> **2 tbsp. of hydrogen peroxide**
> **2 tbsp. of whiskey**
> **1 tbsp. of clear corn syrup**
> **1 tbsp. of unflavored gelatin**
> **4 tsp. of instant tea granules**
> **2 gal. of warm water**

Mix these ingredients together in a large bucket, then pour the solution into a watering can. Feed your stricken annuals with this mix after you've removed the damaged foliage, and then every two weeks throughout the growing season. (For related text, see page 298.)

BRUSSELS SPROUTS WEED BRUSH-OFF

This marvelous mix delivers a knock-out punch to weeds. Serve it up in early spring, before the weed seeds germinate.

1 cup of Brussels sprouts*
½ tsp. of dishwashing liquid
Water

Blend the Brussels sprouts with just enough water to make a thick mush. Then add the dishwashing liquid, and pour the mixture into cracks in your sidewalk or driveway, or anyplace you want to stop weeds before they pop up. Just don't use it in places where you want flower, herb, or veggie seeds to grow. (For related text, see page 248.)

* Or substitute cabbage leaves.

BUZZ BUSTER LEMONADE

If mosquitoes are making your lawn watering chores a nightmare, send 'em packin' with this citrusy beverage. There's nothing skeeters hate more than the scent of lemon! (For more on conquering these vile vampires, see Chapter 9.)

1 cup of lemon-scented ammonia
1 cup of lemon-scented dishwashing liquid

Put these ingredients into a 20 gallon hose-end sprayer, and hose down everything in your yard three times a week, preferably early in the morning. (For related text, see page 152.)

CATERPILLAR KILLER TONIC

This potent brew means death on contact to armyworms and any other cantankerous caterpillars.

½ lb. of wormwood leaves
2 tbsp. of Murphy's Oil Soap®
4 cups of water

Simmer the wormwood leaves in 2 cups of the water for 30 minutes. Strain, then add the Murphy's Oil Soap and the remaining 2 cups of water. Pour the solution into a 6 gallon hose-end sprayer jar, and saturate your lawn in the early evening, when armyworms (and other grass-munching caterpillars) come out to dine. Repeat this treatment until the varmints are history. (For related text, see page 194.)

CHILLIN' OUT BREW

Mowing the lawn can be mighty hot work. So before you start, mix up a batch of this cooling spray, and tuck the bottle into your pocket. Then, every once in a while, as you're goin' about your yard chores, give yourself a few spritzes. You'll stay as cool as a cucumber!

2 tsp. of witch hazel tincture
12 drops of lavender essential oil
10 drops of peppermint essential oil

Mix these ingredients with enough water to fill an 8-ounce spray bottle, and use it to keep cool. (For related text, see page 157.)

CHINCH BUG TONIC

If chinch bugs are running rampant all over your lawn, make up a batch of this brew.

> **1 cup of Murphy's Oil Soap®**
> **3 cups of warm water**
> **Gypsum**

Combine the soap and water in a 20 gallon hose-end sprayer, and saturate your lawn. After it dries, apply gypsum to the bug-infested areas at the recommended rate. (For related text, see page 196.)

COMPOST BOOSTER

To give your compost a boost, spray it once a month with this bracing beverage.

> **1 can of beer**
> **1 can of regular cola (not diet)**
> **1 cup of ammonia**
> **½ cup of weak tea water***
> **2 tbsp. of baby shampoo**

Mix all of these ingredients together in a bucket and pour the solution into a 20 gallon hose-end sprayer. Saturate your compost to really keep things cookin'! (For related text, see page 67.)

To make weak tea water, soak a used tea bag in a solution of 1 gal. of warm water and 1 tsp. of dishwashing liquid until the mix is light brown. Store leftover liquid in a tightly capped jug or bottle for later use.

COOL-SEASON PREMIUM MIX

This is my favorite grass seed combo for lawns on the north side of the "bluegrass line," the imaginary border between cool-season and warm-season regions.

> **40 percent Kentucky bluegrass**
> **40 percent perennial ryegrass**
> **20 percent creeping red fescue**

(For related text, see page 48.)

DOG-BE-GONE TONIC

Whether it's a beagle bashing your bluegrass, a poodle peeing on your pachysandra, or a St. Bernard making an unsightly mess of your St. Augustine, the pitter-patter of pet paws can mean real trouble for your lawn. The simple solution: Lay out the unwelcome mat with this untantalizing tonic.

> **2 cloves of garlic**
> **2 small onions**
> **1 jalapeño pepper**
> **1 tbsp. of hot sauce**
> **1 tbsp. of chili powder**
> **1 tbsp. of dishwashing liquid**
> **1 qt. of warm water**

Chop the garlic, onions, and jalapeño pepper finely, and combine them with the rest of the ingredients. Let the mixture sit and marinate for 24 hours, strain it through cheesecloth or old pantyhose, then sprinkle the resulting liquid on any areas where dogs are a problem. This spicy potion will keep man's best friend from becoming your lawn's worst enemy! (For related text, see page 213.)

DROUGHT BUSTER BREW

Your lawn should sail right through hot, dry weather with flying colors if you give it a weekly drink of this timely tonic.

> **1 can of beer**
> **1 cup of Thatch Buster™**
> **½ cup of liquid lawn food**
> **½ cup of baby shampoo**

Mix these ingredients in a 20 gallon hose-end sprayer, and apply to the point of run-off in the early morning. This timing will minimize evaporation and give the grass plants ample time to digest the brew before nightfall. (For related text, see page 262.)

DROUGHT RECOVERY TONIC

No matter how well you look after your lawn during a drought, hot, dry weather can take its toll. So, plan to give your turf some extra TLC to help it recover. Once the crisis ends, apply a dry, organic fertilizer at half of the recommended rate, adding 1 pound of sugar and 1 pound of Epsom salts per bag (enough for 2,500 sq. ft.). Then overspray the turf with a dose of this mix.

> **1 can of regular cola (not diet)**
> **1 cup of baby shampoo**
> **1 cup of ammonia**

Mix these ingredients in a 20 gallon hose-end sprayer, and saturate the turf to the point of run-off every two weeks until the grass returns to normal. And remember, you need to deliver this life-giving moisture slowly so it reaches a good 6 to 8 inches below the surface. This deep watering will encourage deep grass roots that will be able to stand up and say "Bring it on!" to the next drought that rolls around. (For related text, see page 264.)

ENERGIZING ELIXIR

There's no doubt about it, installing a lawn is mighty thirsty business—and it always has been. Before fancy sports drinks came on the market, folks took a break from their outdoor chores by sitting under a shady tree and sipping this restorative drink.

> **2½ cups of sugar**
> **1 cup of dark molasses**
> **½ cup of vinegar (either white or cider)**
> **1 gal. of water**

Mix all of the ingredients together in a big jug. Then get your lawn crew out of the sun, and pour everyone a nice, tall, refreshing glass. (For related text, see page 58.)

FAIRY RING FIGHTER TONIC

When circles of mushrooms sprout in your lawn, leap into action with this timely tonic.

> **Dry, mild laundry soap* (1 cup for every 2,500 sq. ft. of affected lawn area)**
> **1 cup of baby shampoo**
> **1 cup of antiseptic mouthwash**
> **1 cup of ammonia**

First, pour the dry laundry soap into a hand-held spreader, and spread it over the affected area. Then mix the remaining ingredients in a 20 gallon hose-end sprayer and apply to the point of run-off. Those 'shrooms will be history! (For related text, see page 224.)

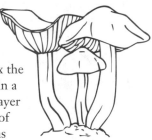

* *Such as Ivory Snow®*

FALL CLEAN-UP TONIC

Fend off snow mold, foul fungi, and other wintertime nasties with this excellent elixir.

> **1 cup of baby shampoo**
> **1 cup of antiseptic mouthwash**
> **1 cup of tobacco tea***
> **1 cup of chamomile tea**
> **Warm water**

Mix the shampoo, mouthwash, tobacco tea, and chamomile tea in a bucket, then add 2 cups of the mixture to a 20 gallon hose-end sprayer, filling the balance of the jar with warm water. Overspray your turf when the temperature is above 50°F. Follow up with your regular fall lawn feeding and a dose of my Last Supper Tonic (see page 108) to put your lawn to bed. (For related text, see page 276.)

*To make tobacco tea, place half a handful of chewing tobacco in an old nylon stocking and soak it in a

gallon of hot water until the mixture is dark brown. Pour the liquid into a glass container with a tight lid for storage.

FUNGUS-FIGHTER SOIL DRENCH

When foul fungi are fussin' around in your soil, makin' a mess of your lawn, polish 'em off with this potent potion.

4 garlic bulbs, crushed
½ cup of baking soda
1 gal. of water

Mix these ingredients in a big pot and bring them to a boil. Then turn off the heat, and let the mixture cool to room temperature. Strain the liquid into a watering can, and soak the ground in the problem areas (remove any dead grass first). Go VERY slowly, so the elixir penetrates deep into the soil. Then dump the strained-out garlic bits onto the soil, and work them in gently. (For related text, see page 222.)

GET-UP-AND-GROW TONIC

After applying my Spring Wake-Up Tonic (see page 123) to your lawn, overspray it with this tonic to kick it into high gear.

1 cup of baby shampoo
1 cup of ammonia
1 cup of regular cola (not diet)
4 tbsp. of instant tea granules

Mix these ingredients in a 20 gallon hose-end sprayer, and apply to the point of run-off. This tonic will get all that good stuff working to help your grass off to a super start—so get ready for the most terrific turf in town! (For related text, see page 124.)

GOD-SINK-THE-QUEEN DRENCH

When fire ants are driving you up a wall, serve their boss-lady this fatal cocktail.

4 cups of citrus peels
3 gal. of water
1 willing helper
1 long, sharp stick

Toss the peels into a pot with the water, bring the mixture to a boil, and let it simmer for about 10 minutes. Grab the pot, and with your partner, tiptoe as softly as you can up to the mound—fire ants are ultra-sensitive to ground vibrations. Have your cohort poke the entrance with the stick. *Immediately* pour the boiling solution into the hole. Then turn around and run like the dickens! The boiling water will polish off any ants it reaches, and the citrus-oil fumes will send more to the gas chamber. Repeat the procedure every two or three days, until there's no sign of life in the mound. (For related text, see page 206.)

GOPHER-GO TONIC

When your lawn has more tunnels than the New York subway system, it's time to reach for this remarkable recipe.

4 tbsp. of castor oil
4 tbsp. of dishwashing liquid
4 tbsp. of urine
½ cup of warm water
2 gal. of warm water

Combine the oil, dishwashing liquid, and urine in ½ cup of warm water, then stir the solution into 2 gallons of warm water. Pour the mixture over any problem areas, and the greedy gluttons will gallop away! (For related text, see page 214.)

GRANDMA PUTT'S ORGANIC FERTILIZER

Back in the good old days, folks couldn't just drop by the garden center for a sack of lawn fertilizer. They had to mix up their own brand of comfort food. This is the recipe Grandma Putt came up with to keep her lawn in tip-top shape—and it still works wonders today!

> **5 parts seaweed meal**
> **3 parts granite dust**
> **1 part dehydrated manure**
> **1 part bonemeal**

Thoroughly mix these ingredients in a large wheelbarrow. Apply the mixture evenly over your turf with a broadcast spreader, then stand back and watch that grass go to town! (For related text, see page 113.)

GRANDMA PUTT'S SOOTHING SUNBURN TONIC

If lawn care in the sunny South leaves you in the painful pink, cool your overheated hide with this aromatic "tea."

> **2 fresh garlic cloves, chopped**
> **2 cups of water**

Combine the garlic and water in a pan, and simmer for 5 minutes. Turn off the heat, cover the pan, and let the mixture steep for 45 minutes. Cool, strain, and store covered in the refrigerator. To soothe sunburned spots, soak a washcloth or hand towel in the cool garlic tea, wring out the excess liquid, and put the damp cloth on the painful area. Leave it on for about 20 minutes. Replace it with a freshly moistened cloth until you feel relief from the discomfort. (For related text, see page 27.)

GRASS CLIPPING COMPOST STARTER

Every time you add a new batch of grass clippings to your compost pile or bin, speed up the decomposition process with this magical potion.

> **1 can of regular cola (not diet)**
> **½ cup of ammonia**
> **½ cup of liquid lawn food**
> **½ cup of dishwashing liquid**

Mix these ingredients in a 20 gallon hose-end sprayer and soak each new layer of grass clippings and other yard fodder. (For related text, see page 169.)

GRASS CLIPPING DISSOLVING TONIC

If you leave your grass clippings in place (whether your mower mulches them or not), spray your lawn twice a year with this timely tonic. It'll help the clippings break down more quickly and give your lawn a chance to breathe better, too.

> **1 can of beer**
> **1 can of regular cola (not diet)**
> **1 cup of ammonia**
> **1 cup of dishwashing liquid**

Mix these ingredients in a bucket and pour the solution into a 20 gallon hose-end sprayer. Apply to the point of run-off. Those clippings will decompose almost before your very eyes! (For related text, see page 171.)

GROUNDCOVER STARTER CHOW

When you plant them in well-prepared soil, you can expect groundcovers to form a solid carpet in two to three years. Give them a smart start with a serving of my starter chow at planting time!

3 parts bonemeal

1 part Epsom salts

1 part gypsum

Mix these ingredients in a bucket. Place ½ cup in each planting hole, and spread another ½ cup on the soil surface to encourage groundcover expansion. (For related text, see page 327.)

HIT THE TRAIL MIX

When cats are cuttin' capers in your lawn, or gunnin' for your feathered friends, put up a Keep Out! sign in the form of this zesty potion.

4 tbsp. of dry mustard

3 tbsp. of cayenne pepper

2 tbsp. of chili powder

2 tbsp. of cloves

1 tbsp. of hot sauce

2 qt. of warm water

Mix all of the ingredients, and sprinkle the solution around the perimeter of your yard, or any place where Fluffy isn't welcome. She'll get her kicks elsewhere! (For related text, see page 211.)

HOMEMADE BIRD TREATS

Songbirds are gung-ho gobblers of grain mites, and a whole slew of other lawn and garden bad guys. When you serve up these gourmet  goodies, your feathered friends will flock to your feeder—and hang around to put a big dent in the pest population.

1 part cornmeal

1 part wild birdseed

Bacon grease (room-temperature)

2 pinches of sand or crushed eggshells

Mix the cornmeal and birdseed with enough bacon grease to get a bread-dough consistency. Add the sand or eggshells. Shape the dough into a ball, put it in a mesh onion bag, and hang it from a sturdy tree branch or bird-feeder post. Then, get out your binoculars and have fun watching the action! (For related text, see page 279.)

HOT BITE SPRAY

When armadillos or other ornery critters wander out of your lawn and into your flower beds, whip up a batch of this timely tonic.

3 tbsp. of cayenne pepper

1 tbsp. of hot sauce

1 tbsp. of ammonia

1 tbsp. of baby shampoo

2 cups of hot water

Mix the cayenne pepper with the hot water in a bottle, and shake well. Let the mixture sit overnight, then pour off the liquid without disturbing the sediment. Mix the liquid with the other ingredients in a hand-held sprayer. Keep a batch on hand, especially when tender shoots and new buds are forming, and spritz the plants as often as you can to keep them hot, hot, hot! No critter who tastes the stuff will come back for a second bite. (For related text, see page 210.)

HOT BUG BREW

This potent beverage will deal a death blow to mole crickets or any other bug that's buggin' your lawn.

> 3 hot green peppers
>   (canned or fresh)
> 3 medium cloves of garlic
> 1 small onion
> 1 tbsp. of dishwashing liquid
> 3 cups of water

Purée the peppers, garlic, and onion in a blender. Then pour the mixture into a jar, and add the dishwashing liquid and water. Let stand for 24 hours. Strain out the solids, pour the liquid into a spray bottle, and blast the mole crickets to kingdom come. **Note:** You probably won't get all the varmints on the first try, so you may need to repeat the process a few times. (For related text, see page 200.)

JERRY'S ANTI-SUMMER-PATCH TONIC

Summer patch is caused by a fungus that aggressively attacks grass during periods of wet, warm weather from late spring to late summer. This remarkable recipe will help send it packin'!

> 1 cup of dishwashing liquid
> 1 cup of tobacco tea*
> 1 cup of antiseptic mouthwash
> 1 cup of ammonia
> 3 tbsp. of saltpeter

Combine all the ingredients in a large bucket and pour the solution into a 20 gallon hose-end sprayer. Apply it to your lawn to the point of run-off every three weeks during the growing season. (For related text, see page 233.)

* To make tobacco tea, place half a handful of chewing tobacco in an old nylon stocking and soak it in a gallon of hot water until the mixture is dark brown. Pour the liquid into a glass container with a tight lid for storage.

JUST DESSERTS TONIC

Perk up groundcovers with a midsummer serving of this tonic. It will keep their flowers and foliage looking fine right on into fall.

> 4 tbsp. of hydrogen peroxide
> 1 tbsp. of Epsom salts
> 1 tbsp. of baking powder
> 1 tbsp. of ammonia
> ½ tsp. of unflavored gelatin
> ½ tsp. of dishwashing liquid
> 4 multivitamin tablets with iron,
>   dissolved in 1 cup of hot water
> 1 gal. of rainwater or filtered water

Mix the peroxide, Epsom salts, baking powder, ammonia, gelatin, dishwashing liquid, and dissolved vitamins in a bucket. Mix 1 cup of this liquid with the rainwater or filtered water, and treat your plants liberally with the mixture. (For related text, see page 330.)

KICK-IN-THE-GRASS TONIC

After you've given your lawn a sod "bandage," apply this timely tonic to get it off to a rip-roarin' start.

> 1 can of beer
> 1 cup of antiseptic mouthwash
> 1 cup of dishwashing liquid
> 1 cup of ammonia
> ½ cup of Epsom salts

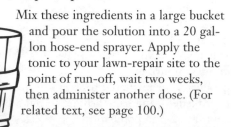

Mix these ingredients in a large bucket and pour the solution into a 20 gallon hose-end sprayer. Apply the tonic to your lawn-repair site to the point of run-off, wait two weeks, then administer another dose. (For related text, see page 100.)

LAST SUPPER TONIC

This soothing beverage is the equivalent of a bedtime cup of cocoa for your lawn.

½ **can of beer**

½ **cup of apple juice**

½ **cup of Gatorade®**

½ **cup of urine**

½ **cup of fish emulsion**

½ **cup of ammonia**

½ **cup of regular cola (not diet)**

½ **cup of baby shampoo**

 Mix these ingredients in a large bucket, and pour the solution into a 20 gallon hose-end sprayer. Apply it to your lawn to the point of run-off, immediately after the last fall feeding. It'll soften up the ingredients in the dry fertilizer, so your grass's roots can absorb the nutrients all winter long. (For related text, see page 108.)

LAWN FRESHENER TONIC

When your lawn tells you it needs a drink, serve it this refreshing, restorative cocktail.

1 **can of beer**

1 **cup of baby shampoo**

½ **cup of ammonia**

½ **cup of weak tea water***

Mix these ingredients in a 20 gallon hose-end sprayer, and apply the elixir to the point of run-off. Then watch your tired-looking lawn spring back to life! (For related text, see page 144.)

*To make weak tea water, soak a used tea bag in a solution of 1 gal. of warm water and 1 tsp. of dishwashing liquid until the mix is light brown. Store leftover liquid in a tightly capped jug or bottle for later use.

LAWN FUNGUS-FIGHTER TONIC

At the first sign of foul fungi, fight back *fast* with this fabulous formula.

1 **tbsp. of baking soda**

1 **tbsp. of instant tea granules**

1 **tbsp. of horticultural oil or vegetable oil**

1 **gal. of warm water**

Mix all of the ingredients in a large bucket. Then pour the solution into a hand-held sprayer, and lightly spray the affected turf. Do *not* apply to the point of run-off! Repeat in two to three weeks if necessary. (For related text, see page 225.)

LAWN MILDEW-RELIEF TONIC

When your grass shows the first signs of powdery mildew, whip up this remarkable recipe, and let 'er rip.

1 **cup of baby shampoo**

1 **cup of hydrogen peroxide**

4 **tbsp. of instant tea granules**

Water

Mix the shampoo, peroxide, and tea granules in a 20 gallon hose-end sprayer, filling the balance of the jar with water. Spray the affected area every week to 10 days, and your lawn will soon be spotless once more. (For related text, see page 228.)

LAWN SAVER TONIC

When bad things happen to good grass (courtesy of a pooch who didn't know better), reach for this liquid safety net.

½ **can of beer**

½ **can of regular cola (not diet)**

½ **cup of ammonia**

Combine these ingredients in a 20 gallon hose-end sprayer. Then saturate your grass to the point of run-off. (For related text, see page 212.)

LAWN SNACK TONIC

Served as a chaser to your lawn's spring and fall feedings, this tasty tonic will give you better-looking turf than you've ever imagined.

1 can of beer
1 cup of dishwashing liquid
Ammonia

Mix the beer and dishwashing liquid in a 20 gallon hose-end sprayer, filling the balance of the jar with ammonia. Overspray your lawn to the point of run-off. Apply this tonic in the morning, within two days of putting down your lawn's main meal of dry fertilizer and Epsom salts. (For related text, see page 125.)

MILDEW CHASER

Damp foliage—whether it's leaves of grass or of other landscape plants—is an invitation to the pesky fungi that cause powdery mildew. If your lawn develops a powdery white coating, take aim with this tonic to set things right.

4 chamomile tea bags
2 tbsp. Murphy's Oil Soap®
1 qt. of boiling water

Put the tea bags in a pot, pour the boiling water over them, and let the tea steep for an hour or so until the brew is good and strong. Let it cool, then mix in the Murphy's Oil Soap. Pour the tea into a 6 gallon hose-end sprayer, and treat the affected area with this tonic every week to 10 days until the mildew is history. (For related text, see page 47.)

MITE NOT TONIC

When mites are making a mighty mess of your lawn, reach for this simple, but fabulous formula. It's a powerful mite killer and mild fertilizer all in one.

1 cup of ammonia
½ cup of dishwashing liquid

Mix these ingredients in a 20 gallon hose-end sprayer. Then spray your beleaguered lawn every five days for three weeks, and you'll moan over mites no more! (For related text, see page 198.)

MOLE-CHASER TONIC

Moles will pack up and head outta town (or at least out of your yard) when they get a taste of this potent potion.

1½ tbsp. of hot sauce
1 tbsp. of dishwashing liquid
1 tsp. of chili powder
1 qt. of water

Mix these ingredients in a bucket, and pour a small amount of the solution into each mole hole. The little guys will get a taste they won't soon forget! (For related text, see page 219.)

MOSS BUSTER BREW

Does moss keep cropping up, no matter how many times you rake it away and sow grass seed in its place? Moss thrives in shady, often poorly drained sites with acidic soil, while grass prefers neutral to slightly alkaline soil, excellent drainage, and a lot of sunshine. This brew is the perfect temporary remedy, but for long-term results, you need to doctor up your soil (see Chapters 3 and 4) and add more light to the scene.

1 cup of antiseptic mouthwash
1 cup of chamomile tea
1 cup of Murphy's Oil Soap®

Mix these ingredients in a 20 gallon hose-end sprayer, and apply to your lawn to the point of run-off every two weeks until the moss is history. (For related text, see page 255.)

MOSS-GROW TONIC

Nothing gives a lawn that relaxed, old-time feeling like a little moss. Here's an easy recipe for making that green cushion grow along a stone wall, between the roots of a big ol' tree, or between stones in a pathway.

> ½ qt. of buttermilk
> 1 cup of moss
> 1 tsp. of corn syrup

Mix these ingredients in an old blender, then dab the mixture onto the ground where you want to encourage moss. Once it's growing, keep it in good health by "watering" it with plain buttermilk every few weeks. (For related text, see page 332.)

ORNAMENTAL GRASS CHOW

Give ornamental grasses a super start: Plant them in early spring in well-prepared planting holes along with a good helping of this hearty chow recipe. It's just what they need to really get growing!

> 2 lb. of dry oatmeal
> 2 lb. of crushed dry dog food
> 1 handful of human hair

Mix these ingredients in a bucket. Toss a handful of this mixture into each planting hole and work it into the soil. Set in the plants, backfill with soil, then scatter any leftover chow on top of the soil. (For related text, see page 321.)

POLLUTION SOLUTION TONIC

Over the winter, a lawn tends to accumulate a load of dust, dirt, and other crud, and that can add up to trouble in the spring. So give your turf some relief by applying this mighty mixture as soon as the snow melts.

> 50 lb. of pelletized lime
> 50 lb. of pelletized gypsum
> 5 lb. of Epsom salts

Mix these ingredients together in a big tub, and spread the mixture over your lawn, using either a drop or broadcast spreader. Then wait at least two weeks before giving your lawn its first spring feeding (see "Spring Startup" on page 117). This recipe makes enough for 2,500 sq. ft. of lawn area. (For related text, see page 130.)

QUACK-UP SLUG COOKIES

Are slugs chomping the daylights out of your groundcovers? Don't despair! A powerful weapon could be waiting right in your own backyard—that is, if you have a patch or two of quackgrass. It kills slugs fast, and what's more, the slimers love the stuff! So invite 'em over for a party, and serve 'em these deadly treats.

> 1 part dried quackgrass blades, finely chopped
> 1 part wheat bran*
> 1 can of beer

Mix the quackgrass and bran in a bowl, then slowly add the beer, stirring until the mixture has the consistency of cookie dough. Run the dough through a meat grinder, or chop it into small bits (roughly ⅛ to ¼ inch thick). Let the "cookies" air-dry overnight, sprinkle them on the ground among your plants, and let the good times roll! (To be on the safe side, put these treats where children and pets can't get to them. Quackgrass is often infected with a fungus that is harmful if ingested by humans or animals.) (For related text, see page 255.)

*Available in supermarkets and health-food stores.

RISE 'N' SHINE CLEAN-UP TONIC

First thing in the spring, spray down your lawn, and everything else in your yard, with this powerful potion. Besides getting your whole green scene off to a squeaky-clean start, it'll stop bad bugs in their tracks.

> 1 cup of Murphy's Oil Soap®
> 1 cup of tobacco tea*
> 1 cup of antiseptic mouthwash
> ¼ cup of hot sauce
> Warm water

Mix the Murphy's Oil Soap, tobacco tea, mouthwash, and hot sauce in a 20 gallon hose-end sprayer, filling the balance of the jar with warm water. Apply to everything in your yard to the point of run-off. (For related text, see page 122.)

To make tobacco tea, place half a handful of chewing tobacco in an old nylon stocking and soak it in a gallon of hot water until the mixture is dark brown. Pour the liquid into a glass container with a tight lid for storage.

RUST BLOCKER TONIC

Although they're mostly trouble-free, ornamental grasses can come under attack from rust, a disease that causes streaks of rusty orange

on leaves and stems. Use this super solution to fend off the fungus and keep rust-prone plants green all summer long.

> 6 tbsp. of vegetable oil
> 2 tbsp. of baking powder
> 2 tbsp. of liquid kelp
> 1 gal. of water

Mix these ingredients in a bucket, and pour the solution into a hand-held sprayer. Shower your grasses with it one morning per week throughout the growing season. (For related text, see page 324.)

SEED STARTER TONIC

This powerful potion will have your grass seed popping out of its jacket in no time flat!

> ¼ cup of baby shampoo
> 1 tbsp. of Epsom salts
> 1 gal. of weak tea water*

Mix these ingredients in a large container. Drop in your grass seed and put the mixture into the refrigerator for 24 hours. Then strain out the seed, spread it on paper towels to dry, and sow as usual. (For related text, see page 187.)

To make weak tea water, soak a used tea bag in a solution of 1 gal. of warm water and 1 tsp. of dishwashing liquid until the mix is light brown. Store leftover liquid in a tightly capped jug or bottle for later use.

SKUNK-AWAY PET BATH

There's almost nothing worse than getting up close and personal with a skunk. Fortunately, you can rely on this super de-skunking solution to save the day—whether the victim is Rover, Fluffy, or you.

> 2 cups of hydrogen peroxide
> ¼–½ cup of baking soda
> 1 tbsp. of mild dishwashing liquid

Mix these ingredients in a bowl, and apply the solution to your pet's coat (but don't get it on his

head or near his eyes or ears). Rub the mixture in, then wash it out. Presto: Your best pal will smell fresh and clean again. If a human being was the recipient of the skunk's offerings, follow the same procedure. (For related text, see page 217.)

SOIL PREP TONIC

Two to three days before you sow grass seed, treat your soil to this terrific tonic. It'll get the seed off and growing in no time flat.

1 cup of fish emulsion
½ cup of ammonia
¼ cup of baby shampoo
¼ cup of corn syrup

After you've applied your starter fertilizer (see page 75) to the area, mix these ingredients in a 20 gallon hose-end sprayer and saturate the soil. (For related text, see page 76.)

SPOT SEED TONIC

Make your lawn-repair job a super success with this sensational solution.

1 cup of beer
1 cup of baby shampoo
4 tbsp. of instant tea granules

Combine these ingredients in a 20 gallon hose-end sprayer, and lightly apply the mixture to the mulch covering your newly seeded areas. (For related text, see page 103.)

SPRING WAKE-UP TONIC

As soon as possible in the spring, issue a wake-up call to your lawn with this marvelous mixture.

50 lb. of pelletized gypsum
50 lb. of pelletized lime
5 lb. of bonemeal
2 lb. of Epsom salts

Mix these ingredients in a wheelbarrow, and apply to your lawn with a broadcast spreader no more than two weeks before fertilizing. This will help aerate the lawn, while giving it something to munch on until you start your regular feeding program. (For related text, see page 123.)

SQUEAKY CLEAN TONIC

This powerful tonic deals a mighty blow to cutworms and other bad guys who are buggin' your lawn.

1 cup of antiseptic mouthwash
1 cup of tobacco tea*
1 cup of chamomile tea
1 cup of urine
½ cup of Murphy's Oil Soap®
½ cup of lemon-scented dishwashing liquid

Mix all of these ingredients in a large bucket. Then pour the solution into a 20 gallon hose-end sprayer, and apply it to your lawn to the point of run-off. (For related text, see page 197.)

* To make tobacco tea, place half a handful of chewing tobacco in an old nylon stocking and soak it in a gallon of hot water until the mixture is dark brown. Pour the liquid into a glass container with a tight lid for storage.

STRESS RELIEVER TONIC

For those of you who live in the Sun Belt states, winter is feeding time for your lawn. First, apply any premium dry lawn food at half of the recommended rate, adding 1 pound of Epsom salts to each 25 pounds of lawn food. (If you're using a synthetic fertilizer, rather than a natural/organic type, spread the lawn food and the salts separately.) Then follow up with this tonic to keep your lawn relaxed through the winter months.

> 1 cup of baby shampoo
> 1 cup of antiseptic
>   mouthwash
> 1 cup of tobacco tea*
> ¾ cup of weak tea water**
> ¼ cup of ammonia

Mix these ingredients in a 20 gallon hose-end sprayer, and apply once a month to the point of run-off. (For related text, see page 190.)

To make tobacco tea, place half a handful of chewing tobacco in an old nylon stocking and soak it in a gallon of hot water until the mixture is dark brown. Pour the liquid into a glass container with a tight lid for storage.

**To make a weak tea water, soak a used tea bag in a solution of 1 gal. of warm water and 1 tsp. of dishwashing liquid until the mix is light brown. Store leftover liquid in a tightly capped jug or bottle for later use.*

SUMMER SOOTHER TONIC

Automatic sprinklers provide a simple, efficient way to water your lawn. But every now and then, I like to take hose in hand and do the job the old-fashioned way. When I do that, I soothe my whole yard with this nice, relaxing shower.

> 2 cups of weak tea water*
> 1 cup of baby shampoo
> 1 cup of hydrogen peroxide

Mix these ingredients in a 20 gallon hose-end sprayer, and give everything in sight a good soaking. Your yard will thank you for it! (For related text, see page 143.)

To make weak tea water, soak a used tea bag in a solution of 1 gal. of warm water and 1 tsp. of dishwashing liquid until the mix is light brown. Store leftover liquid in a tightly capped jug or bottle for later use.

SUPER SCALE SCRUB

This double-barreled potion works in two ways: The soap kills the unprotected scale babies, a.k.a. crawlers, and the alcohol cuts right through the grownups' waxy shells.

> 1 cup of 70% isopropyl (rubbing)
>   alcohol
> 1 tbsp. of dishwashing liquid
> 1 qt. of water

Mix these ingredients in a hand-held sprayer, and treat your scale-stricken grass every three days for two weeks. The scale will sail off into the sunset. (For related text, see page 200.)

SUPER SOIL SANDWICH DRESSING

When you've got your "ingredients" stacked up, top off your super soil sandwich with this zesty condiment. It'll kick-start the cooking process and get your new lawn off and running.

1 can of beer

1 can of regular cola (not diet)

½ cup of ammonia

¼ cup of instant tea granules

Mix all of these ingredients in a bucket and pour the solution into a 20 gallon hose-end sprayer. Then spray your "sandwich" until all the layers are saturated. Let it cook for at least two weeks (longer if you can), then get sowin'! (For related text, see page 53.)

TERRIFIC TURF TONIC

No matter what mower you use, or how carefully you mow, having that little bit taken off the top is a shock to your grass. To help it recover, apply this gentle, but effective elixir once a month.

1 cup of baby shampoo

1 cup of ammonia

1 cup of weak tea water*

Warm water

Mix the shampoo, ammonia, and tea water in a 20 gallon hose-end sprayer, filling the balance of the jar with warm water. Then, just after you mow your lawn, apply the solution to the point of run-off. (For related text, see page 173.)

* To make a weak tea water, soak a used tea bag in a solution of 1 gal. of warm water and 1 tsp. of dishwashing liquid until the mix is light brown. Store leftover liquid in a tightly capped jug or bottle for later use.

THATCH BLASTER TONIC

This excellent elixir will help keep your lawn free of nasty thatch all season long.

1 cup of beer or regular cola (not diet)

½ cup of dishwashing liquid

¼ cup of ammonia

Mix all of these ingredients in a 20 gallon hose-end sprayer. Fill the balance of the sprayer jar with water, and saturate the entire turf area. Repeat once a month during the summer, when the grass is actively growing. (For related text, see page 92.)

TIRE-TRACK REMOVER TONIC

When your lawn is damp, anything on wheels can leave its mark in the turf—delivery trucks, cars, bicycles, wheelbarrows, and even your lawnmower. The good news is that, regardless of what caused them, getting rid of those ruts is simple. Just wait for the soil to dry out a little, and then stroll across the area with your aerating sandals, or punch holes in the ground with a garden fork. Spread gypsum over the damaged area at the recommended rate, and overspray it with this timely tonic.

1 cup of ammonia

1 cup of beer

½ cup of baby shampoo

¼ cup of weak tea water*

Warm water

Mix the ammonia, beer, shampoo, and weak tea water in a 20 gallon hose-end sprayer, filling the balance of the jar with warm water. Apply to the point of run-off. Repeat this treatment every three weeks to get your lawn on the road to recovery! (For related text, see page 184.)

* To make a weak tea water, soak a used tea bag in a solution of 1 gal. of warm water and 1 tsp. of dishwashing liquid until the mix is light brown. Store leftover liquid in a tightly capped jug or bottle for later use.

TREE-PLANTING BOOSTER MIX

Serve up a hearty helping of this potent powder at planting time to give trees a surefire start. This mix helps the soil drain well *and* hold moisture—just what a newly planted tree needs.

> 4 lb. of compost
> 2 lb. of gypsum
> 1 lb. of Epsom salts
> 1 lb. of dry dog food
> 1 lb. of dry oatmeal

Mix the ingredients together in a bucket. Then work a handful or two into the bottom of the planting hole, and sprinkle another handful over the soil after planting. (For related text, see page 20.)

'TWEENER PREMIUM MIX

For lawns in that tricky ol' transition zone, I like to mix up some warm- and cool-season seeds for a yardful of green almost all year long.

> 25 percent Bermuda grass
> 25 percent buffalo grass
> 25 percent Kentucky bluegrass
> 25 percent perennial ryegrass

(For related text, see page 48.)

WARM-SEASON PREMIUM MIX

Whipping up a seed mix for the sunny South can be a bit tricky—these warm-season grasses tend to be real ground-grabbers that don't always earn top marks for sharing. But this combo of Bermuda, carpet, and Bahia grass gets along pretty well, especially since they're all starting out together, and it grows into a durable, drought-tolerant lawn.

> 40 percent Bermuda grass
> 30 percent carpet grass
> 30 percent Bahia grass

(For related text, see page 48.)

WILD WEED WIPEOUT TONIC

When you've got weeds that won't take no for an answer, knock 'em flat on their backs with this potent potion.

> 1 tbsp. of gin
> 1 tbsp. of white vinegar
> 1 tbsp. of baby shampoo
> 1 qt. of very warm water

Mix these ingredients together, and pour the solution into a hand-held sprayer. Then, drench the weeds to the point of run-off, taking care not to spray any plants that you want to keep. (For related text, see page 243.)

WINTER WALKWAY PROTECTION TONIC

This "suit of armor" will guard your grass from winter's onslaught of ice-melting salt. First, in late fall, liberally spread gypsum over the turf in a 5-foot band along roadsides, walkways, or any other surface that will be on the deicing list. Then overspray the gypsum with this protective potion.

> 1 cup of dishwashing liquid
> ½ cup of ammonia
> ½ cup of beer

Mix these ingredients in a 20 gallon hose-end sprayer, and apply over the gypsum to the point of run-off. Then your soil and grass will sail through the winter in fine shape. (For related text, see page 294.)

Index